Name Your Baby's Destiny:
Assisting Parents, Personnel Managers and Playwrights

By Guy Gifford

 *3Fire* Publishing

Copyright © 2000

Acknowledgements

To Irina and our children, Julia and Alex, I affectionately dedicate the pages of this book and the remaining years of my life. Georgia, thank you for your willingness to volunteer when I'd come to my end.

ISBN 0-615-11488-1 (3FIRE)

Published by 3Fire Publishing, 4141 Palm Ave #648, Sacramento, CA 95842

Printed in the United States of America
Layout and editing: Guy Gifford, Georgia Shoemaker
Cover design: Guy Gifford, Georgia Shoemaker

Contents

CHAPTER ONE:
BASIC GUIDANCE FOR NAMING YOUR BABY:

"That which we call a rose, by any other name would smell just as sweet"—William Shakespeare. Or would it?

UNIQUENESS:

We Americans like unique names. It seems to reflect our culture which honors individuality. Three humorous parents during 1994 in Los Angeles county were not so successful in having a unique daughter, when they each named their daughters "Eunique". But even more revealing of American's desire to be individuals is the parents who named their daughter "Imunique". Even then, there were two girls given the name "Imunique" in the same county in just one year. And parents keep trying very hard to have a unique daughter or name. I wonder of the success of the parents whose girl was ercently named "Imyunique". And I also wonder why the parents named their daughters Nemesis. But I do like the seldom used names of: America, Treasure, Princess, Cherish, Trinity, and Malaysia, although there is not enough data to say what type of personalities they would have.

There seems to exist what I call the Disney explosion. That is, in the recent years after the release of a new Disney feature cartoon, the name of its heroine gets a large jump in popularity. An example of this event is the release of Disney's Aladdin and the jump in popularity of the name Jasmine to number fourteen in California. The heroine's name may be unique when the movie is released, but don't expect it to stay so unique in the years following.

The recent choice of Harley for a girls name seems to be related to the near fanatic popularity of the Harley-Davison motor cycle. Be aware that any trends and fashions will likely cause a name's popularity to surge as is true with names like Channel, Armani and fashion brands.

Many people have heard Johnny Cash's hit song, 'A Boy Named Sue'. The song told of the great trouble and struggles of a boy having a girl's name. In the song, the boy was often fighting for respect. He hated the name, and he hated his father for giving it to him, so much that he set out to find him and kill him. Your life is in your hands.

Yes, there are names which are too unique. In addition to the obvious mistake of naming your child with a name popular for use in naming the opposite gender, those names which may be too unique often fit certain categories: 1) names which are difficult to pronounce properly by native English speakers, leaving the person with a name which is constantly butchered and often replaced with a nick-name, such as Sam; 2) names which have sounds which are so uncommon in an English name that it just sounds strange, like Varvara;3) names which sound too much like something repulsive in English, like

Nastia which doesn't click in the brain with anything but nasty.

I have also heard from a man whose father was, at the time of his son's birth, a hockey fanatic. The father named his son, Puck. Until the boy reached 18 years old and had his name changed to Jim, he complained that he was constantly having to explain to people that his name was not a nick-name.

Many have also heard of rocker Frank Zappa naming his children Moon Unit, Dweezil, Ahmet and Diva. Why would any LOVING parent give any such names, except out of the parent's SELFISHNESS. My first name, Guy, was difficult enough to bear in childhood. I heard the question, "Is Guy a nick-name?" more times than I wished. Parents, please, have sensitivity in picking a name, and don't label your child with a name that would be considered STRANGE to others and cause your child to be ridiculed. But feel free, if you wish, to give a fairly unique name, like Sierra or Guy, only after you have asked the opinion of adults from previous generations. If you're looking for a unique name for your daughter, consider the nearly unknown name Svetlana, which also has good personality characteristics.

The letter "Z" is used in some cultures instead of the letter "S". Parents desiring a name which starts with the letter "S" may give the name a unique twist while retaining personality characteristics by substituting the letter "Z".

SPELLINGS AND PRONUNCIATION:

Additionally, it is wise to avoid unusual spellings, like "Syndee". Just as we dislike having people ask, "What's does your nick-name stand for?" and "What's your real name?", we equally dislike having to correct people's miss-spelling of our names. The easiest way to avoid your child having to regularly correct the spelling of his or her own name is to GIVE THE SIMPLEST AND MOST COMMON SPELLING of the name. If you want the name to sound "Cindy", name her "Cindy", the most common spelling of this name. Avoid the spelling "Keyhannah" in favor of the spelling "Kiana". Additionally, the shorter spelling of the name sound should generally be favored over long spellings. If you have a long name, you'll easily understand what I'm saying. When filling out your name on form, after form, after form, which we inevitably are required to do, it just takes longer if you have a longer name. When I recall all the applications for employment and government forms I've had to fill, I'm grateful that I didn't have to write Ferdinand Canning Scott Schiller each time. And what do you do when the form only gives you 15 blocks for your name when your name requires 32 blocks? People with long spellings have this hassle to deal with regularly. The possible answers for names that don't fit in a form include using initials in substitution for names or omitting names. When picking a name spelling, use the KISS principle: " Keep It Simple, Stupid!"

GEOGRAPHICAL:

Geographical names have come and gone and come again. Names like Montana, Phoenix, Savanna, Catalina, Marina, Dallas and Salt Lake City have become more popular names for girls; well, maybe not Salt Lake City. Pittsburgh is not a popular name for children either, but Sierra sounds pretty nice. Obviously, some geographical names are nicer than others. If you want to name your child with a geographical name, go for it! But keep in mind that these names have both meanings and subtle implications. For example, the name Canyon might work well for your son, but would be inappropriate for your daughter.

STEREOTYPES:

Besides negative and positive, name stereotypes come in two categories: accurate and inaccurate. An accurate name stereotype would reflect the general reality and would be true a certain, less than random, percentage of the time. Whereas an inaccurate stereotype does not reflect anything more than random occurrence and may actually be opposite of the truth. One of the objects of this book is to collect the accurate stereotypes.

In the study of comedy, we've found that one of the elements in successful humor is the exaggeration of a commonly experienced truth. Likewise, stereotyping in society usually reflects some shared experience, based in truth. In my research, I've found that at least in certain positive stereotypes, there is also usually some basis in truth.

But there are some names which have received such strong negative associations, like Judas and Adolph, which may always retain this negative association in our society, in spite of whatever positive personality qualities are linked to the names. Similarly, the names Bertha and Bruno are associated with obesity and bully behavior respectively. Since negative name associations often transfer to their bearer, if you don't want people to have negative association with your child before they even meet, consult others to avoid picking such names.

INITIALS:

Some claim that a person will be successful in life if their initials spell a word. It is doubly cute if the initials spell the first name or a nick-name, like K.A.T. - Katerina Alisha Thompson, where Kat is also the nickname for Katerina. But more pragmatic advise is "Beware of the initials spelling something negative like BUM, PIG, HAG, ODD or COW." If the initials do spell a word, you can bet that it will be your child's nickname at least by some.

RELIGION:

Some people feel it is important to use names which are culturally traditional to the religion. Some Christians choose names from the Bible. Some Muslim converts choose an Arabic name. Jews have traditionally chosen the name of a deceased relative. Protestants sometimes choose a name from either the Old or New Testaments. Until the Second Vatican Counsel (Vatican II) in the early 1960s, Roman Catholics were taught to choose names from among the names of Catholic Saints. Even adult converts would change their names to reflect their new ideology and lifestyle, reflecting complete rejection of their pagan past. This teaching caused the parents of one of my Catholic friends to name their daughter after Saint Kathleen, but her parents had wanted to name her Kelly and so she was always called Kelly. You may wish to choose a name which reflects your religion, although, I am not aware of any religion which requires this today. This book includes a list of Catholic saints, if you are so inclined (see appendix).

NATIONALITY:

It was fairly traditional in America for parents to choose names which are from their previous national heritage. Scandinavians would choose a Scandinavian name, Italians would choose an Italian name, etc. But this is not the case so much today with mass media and mobility defining our culture. Today, it is much more the case that only new immigrants to America exclusively name after one's previous heritage. This is sometimes distressing to the child who feels labeled as a foreigner by his or her uniquely foreign name, while the child is desperately trying to fit in to this great melting pot called America. It appears to be easier for a child, whose parents are native born Americas, to feel comfortable with an uncommon name. Likewise, girls seem to enjoy having a unique name more than do boys. If you want a unique name, you shouldn't avoid using ethnic names. But if you speak English poorly or as a second language, it may be wisest to choose a name which is commonly used throughout America. Additionally, if you choose a foreign-sounding name, be sure that it is not a burden to your child by being difficult to pronounce or spell. Also see the section about unique names.

SOUNDS, RYTHMS & RHYMES:

The combinations of names can produce aesthetic sounds or disharmonic sounds. Harry Herbert Holt the 3rd sounds very stilted, because there is no aesthetically pleasing rhythm; although the repeated initial H or any repeated initial letter is aesthetically pleasing. The combination Mike Fredericnicklebaum Smith will make people chuckle. A one syllable surname, like Smith, simply doesn't fit the rhythm created by the longest name chosen here, Fredericnicklebaum. Moreover the one syllable first name, Mike, aggravates the rhythm established by the long, multi-syllable second name. Furthermore, a one syllable first name combined with a one syllable surname, like Mike Smith, is also a bit difficult to say. If you have a one syllable surname, like Smith, try a multi-syllable first name like Michael, instead of Mike. The rythm of a second name with this combination, will sound just fine if it is any length from one to about four syllables. There is an exception to this rule, as there are exceptions to most rules. If the surname is one syllable and long sounding, combining it with a single syllable first name can be quite powerful as is shown with Mark Twain, Charles Rath, James Bond and Sam Spade. If your surname is more than one syllable, a single or multiple syllable first name will match. If you choose a one syllable first name, avoid a one syllable middle name for example Rick John Adams. Better John Richard Adams. You can always call your child by the child's middle name if that is the name you prefer.

Rhyming names are not recommended. Priscilla Aquilla and Ray Spay just get the wise-crackers and bullies started. Puns, irony or any humor in a name is just as bad. What child could live down a name like Harry Caray, Imunique, Aileen Dover or I.P. Freely. They may be fun to invent and laugh over, but leave them behind in favor of a name with which your child will feel comfortable. Alliterations like Guy Gifford and Jessica Jackson are fine and possibly even recommendable. One study indicated that people with name alliterations are more likely to be successful.

Word pairs which paint a picture are also not recommended. Rose Bush, Harry Cary, Dark Knight and Running Bear are equally tempting targets for jokes.

NUMBER OF NAMES:

Start with your surname, the only predetermined part of the naming responsibility. But even then, some states don't require that the child bear either parent's surname. Some parents have just given a letter in substitution for one or more names. The S in former U.S. president Harry S Truman's name was just an S and was not an initial letter of a middle name. It is typical for American parents to give their children both a first and a second name in addition to the family name. This convention helps differentiate the numerous people with the same first and last names. This is an important purpose as can be seen by my own uncommon name, Guy Gifford. There are currently at least seven Guy Giffords in the United States today. Imagine how many John Smiths there are. In this highly mobile and communicative world, it is useful to have at least a second name in addition to the family name. In the future, I suspect a great many more parents will give their children three names in addition to their family name, simply to help differentiate them from the other David John Smiths in the world. The British monarchy follows this technique. Queen Elizabeth II of England's four children were each given four names. Prince Charles' full name is Prince Charles Philip Arthur George. The closest thing he has to a surname is "the House of Winsor". More over, he was given the second name Philip after his father.

SON-SEN-BEN-ABDUL-VICH-MAC-etc.:

Before family names, it was traditional in a number of cultures that a child was known by the father's given name in addition to the child's given first name, often with an the attachment meaning "son of". Examples are: Jack Johnson, Sven Jansen, David Benjamin, Boris Ivonavich, Jamal Abdul Ahmed, Darby MacDonald. In fact, this is still true in some cultures today. In many cases, these surnames remained. Today, it is not uncommon to find cases where parents are giving these conjunctives alone as first names, such as Abdul and Mack.

SMITH-TANNER-FOWLER-etc.:

In the days of yore, it was normal for a father to train his son in his occupation. So the metal smith and the tanner would each train their sons their craft from generation to generation. This being the case, it was quite natural for the craft name to be associated with all the family members and eventually become permanently attached as the family name, as with Smith and Tanner.

NAMESAKES:

Often parents wish to name their child in honor or in memory of a relative or famous person. Great grand mother Gertrude may be remembered through the naming of little Gertrude. But who in their right mind would name her daughter with a name which is so out-dated that everyone tags it to the days of out-door plumbing? Or the father strokes his ego by naming his son Junior. And as a consequence, people are forever getting confused between father, son and even grandson. Famous black U.S. heavyweight boxing champion George Foreman took this vanity to the extreme by naming each of his several sons, George. And among black Americans the name George has been used often in honor of George Washington Carver, a famous black American scientist, who was obviously named in honor of the first U.S. president George Washington, who may have been named after the Kings of England.

Generally, it is wiser to be sure that a namesake name is chosen on its own merits, above any warm feelings you have for the predecessor. Additionally, if you wish to name your child in honor of its father or other relative, it is recommend that the middle name be given in honor of the relative.

PROGRESSIVE NAMES:

If you really love the idea of having a "Junior", instead, consider a progressive name. This naming system, which could also be called Series, Sequential or Daisy Chained names, is accomplished by adding a new first name to the front of the father's name in each successive generation. Imagine having a great grandson named Jonathan Michael David Charles Smith where Charles Smith is the great grandfather's name, David Charles Smith is the grandfather's name, Michael David Charles Smith is the father's name, and Jonathan is a new given first name added to the root. This would be an honoring and continuous reminder of the contributions of each of these ancestors. Thus, the name could get longer and more unique with each generation, or the oldest ancestor's first name could be dropped to keep the name from growing too large. Of course, if the name becomes too long, names can be omitted or initials substituted during daily use, as we already do when we say Mister Jones instead of Mr. Michael Jones or Nick instead of Nicholes. Of course, this can also be done for females in the family by using the female ancestor's first names as a root.

NICKNAMES:

In our culture, as is true in many cultures, we commonly use nicknames in substitution for names. Some names already have a tradition of nicknames associated with them and some do not. Michael becomes Mike or Mick, William becomes Bill or Will, and Robert becomes Bob or Rob. Typically, the likelihood of being called a nickname based on the name increases with increased syllables in the name. The name Guy, for example, is quite barren of nickname associations. But you can bet that your daughter named Anastasia will be called by a nickname. When picking a name, be aware of its likely nickname, because you may not like it. If your child has a longer name, you as a parent may not be able to keep your daughter's friends from calling her by a nickname, but you can control what nickname she will be called, if you are preemptive. By calling your daughter named Josephine by the nickname Josie from her birth, you can minimize the chance of her being nicknamed Jo or Fifi, if you don't wish to leave it to chance.

Some parents choose a typical nickname for the child's given name simply because they like it best or wish to ensure that the child will be called this name instead of one of the other nicknames associated with the traditional name. This is not necessary, nor advisable, since your child may wish to be known by a more sophisticated "adult" name throughout adulthood, which is the vast majority of years for most people. Many people would think it is strange to call a person who is in authority, such as a boss or senior citizen, Chrissy or Davy. So, if you want to call your little munchkin by a name of affection or child's name, go ahead and call him or her by a nickname for the few years of childhood, but it is probably best to legally name your child with a more formal or sophisticated name which is less likely to become outdated.

MEANINGS OF NAMES:

Most names have meanings. Often the meaning of the name seems to be one of the characteristics which the person bears. This may be observed when looking at the names in this book. But more Americans are inventing names for their children from sounds they like. Unfortunately when parents do this, they don't realize that most every name which you could possibly create likely has a meaning in one of the many languages of the world and may carry that meaning to the name's bearer or may have an embarrassing meaning to the local people in the culture your child may visit. The word "guy" has the meaning of "male" and "person" in America, but has long been used as a name in England with meanings of "guide" and "warrior" in French and Old German. However, in Russian it means "police". The name Marsha with its Latin origin additionally has the slang meaning in Russian for female genitalia. If a name's personality is included in this book, the origin's meaning has already been examined for a link with the personality. But if the name's personality is not included in this edition, a link to the name's meaning has not generally been witnessed.

Here are more examples of language translation problems taken from advertising: An Electrolux Vacuum advertisement translated from Scandinavian became "Nothing Sucks Like an Electrolux". Clairol "Mist-Stick" when translated into German became "Manure-Stick". Gerber baby food packaging has long had a picture of a baby on it, but when marketed to Africa it wouldn't sell because the Africans thought it had baby inside the jar. Colgate successfully introduced a toothpaste in France called "Q", which is also the name of a French pornography magazine. Pepsi's "Come Alive with the Pepsi Generation" translated directly into Chinese is "Pepsi Brings Your Ancestors back from the Grave". Frank Purdue Chicken's "It Takes a Strong Man to Make a Tender Chicken" translated into Spanish becomes "It Takes an Aroused Man to Make a Chicken Affectionate". Coca-Cola phonetically translated into Chinese means "bite the wax tadpole" and into a Chinese dialect "Female horse stuffed with wax". Parker Pen's "It won't leak in your pocket and embarrass you" got translated for the Mexican market to "It won't leak in Your Pocket and Make You Pregnant". A beer advertisement, "Turn It Loose", became "Suffers from Diarrhea".

POPULARITY:

Names may be popular in two ways. The obvious way to judge the popularity of a name is by how many people bear the name at any given time or by how many babies are given the name in any given year. These can be determined by census or birth record data. Name popularity is cyclical. The most popular names to be given to children each year tend to be faddish, rising and ebbing within a few years. These names tend to be greatly influenced by popular culture, often reflecting the names of current celebrities, such as Ashley. However, there are other names which have historical longevity, whose cycle of popularity runs through centuries, such as Mary. The most common names in America such as Mary, Patricia, Linda and Barbara, may not be among the most common names chosen in any given year. The second type of popularity is the positive or negative feelings and attributes which we associate with a name, such as Oprah and Rush. Some of these names or their name bearers are so unique that the name is nearly never used again, some examples of this might be Voltaire and Jesus. However, if a man has the name Jesus in America, it is a solid bet that he is Hispanic, since the name is considered sacred to most North Americans and Northern Europeans, but is a popular name in Mexico. Which brings me to the point that even in "the great melting pot" called America, there are names which are strongly associated with one ethnic group like Jose, Boris, Muhammad and Sven. If you have a strong attachment to one ethnicity and you wish to help your child fit into America, you may desire to choose a common English name for your child.

MASCULINE AND FEMININE:

Masculine names, like masculine fashions, tend to change gradually over generations. Whereas, feminine names, like feminine fashions, tend to change more frequently than masculine. In America, there is a greater expectation for female names to be unique. This search for unique names for daughters has caused the modern feminization of seldomly used male names. Unlike the traditional feminization of male names which involved adding a feminine suffix to a male name, like Fredricka, parents are taking some less common male names to name their daughters without adding a femininizing suffix. Jordan, Ashley, Tyler, Casey, Tayler, Sidney, Ryan, Dylan, Peyton, Cody and Daniel all have gained popularity among female usage. It is a shame that these names are being turned into unisex, since there are so many female names available for choosing between. Generally, a boy named Jordan or Tyler doesn't appreciate having a girl in his class with the same name, nor is the girl too pleased, knowing her name is traditionally a masculine name. More over, most cultures separate masculine names from feminine names at least by suffix, if not by exclusive usage. In fact, some feel that a masculine name given to a girl will masculinize her.

It is recommended that parents picking a name for a daughter use a traditionally feminine name or they end the name with a traditional suffix at minimum. The most common female name suffix is "a" or "ah", as in Karla and Sarah, which is also the last sound in several other female name endings. Others are "an", "ane", "ann", "ana" and "anna" which means "graceful" is used in forms of Diana; "lin", "linn", "lyn", "lynne", "lina", "line", "leen", "lene", "lena", "lenna" and "lynn" which means "pool" is used in forms of Madeline; "ita", "et", "ett", "ette", "eta" and "etta" which means "little" is in forms of Lynette; "al", "alle", "el", "ele", "ella", "ela" and "elle" which means "her, she" is in Michelle; "ee", "y", "ey", "i", "ia", "ya", "ea", "e", "ye", "ie" as in "Nellie"; "ique" as in Dominique; "ine", "inne", "ina", "inna" as in Irine; "otte", "otta" as in Charlotte; "is", "es", "ez", "ess", "esa", "essa", "ice", "yssa", "ysa", "ise", "isa", "issa" as in Clarissa; "ca", "ka" as in Bianca. Masculine names typically end with a consonate sound, whereas feminine names typically end with a vowel sound. However, this is not always the case. To be sure that your daughter's name is feminine, end it with the short "a" vowel sound.

Although we seem to be leaving the feminist era which attempted to tell us that all behavioral differences between boys and girls was caused by how they are nurtured and that behavioral differences in the sexes are bad; science shows us, now, that the brain development in males and females is profoundly different from within the first weeks after conception. The fear of type casting children into gender narrow roles because of the gender laden names they were given had caused "experts" to give the screwy advise that parents should choose unisex names. The seventies utopia (which means: "no-place"), where gender role differences don't exist and everyone lives in some great communist brotherhood has been shown to be impossible at every level, except within the Godless minds of socialist and communists. Unisex names are out, in favor of powerfully masculine boys names and powerfully feminine girls names. No more do children have to suffer the humiliation of boys being mistaken for girls or girls being mistaken for boys because of their unisex name. Moreover, boys feel more threatened or insulted when they are presumed to be girls, than do girls when presumed to be boys. Finally, don't needlessly trouble your child by attaching a name which is typically used for the opposite gender. We have no need for a confused or angry "Boy Named Sue".

UNDERSTANDING THE DATA:

Within the individual name data of this book: 1) Writers include poets, playwrights, novelists, journalists, essayists, short-stories writers, children's book writers and all those who write; 2) Commanders include generals, admirals, ships captains, and soldier leaders. Although not listed within this book as such, commanders are also a form of political leader and many famous commanders have gone on to become elected politicians. 3) Artists include painters, sculptors, engravers, lithographers, and sometimes architects and photographers; 4) Clergy includes religious ministers, priests, missionaries and religious reformers. The word "prudence" is a good word which describes a person who prefers caution to recklessness, but may still include calculated daring.

SOME NAMES OF INTEREST:

In doing the research for this book, I discovered that some names have unusually high numbers of famous bearers with certain characteristics. There is Bob the athlete. David who is an actor, but generally a supporting actor and not usually a leading man. Donald the astronaut. Irving is a deep thinker and strategist. José, the freedom fighter. George represents a high percentage of generals. Frances have been famous children's writers, educators, librarians, activists, freethinkers and non-traditionalists. Virginias are novelist and children's writer. Theodores and Teds in the press, have recently represented seemingly high numbers of mentally unbalanced or skew thinkers. Famous Timothys and Tims tend toward a bit timid and non-dominating. Gabriel is honest, fair and a poor name for a villain. Giovanni is the artistic type with over 60 percent of famous Giovannis being artists.

CHAPTER 2:
NAME HER BEAUTY, NAME HIS STRENGTH — A DETAILED DISCUSSION

"Michael Michael Bo BichaelBanana Fanna Fo FichaelFe Fi Mo IchaelMichael!" - Shirley Ellis

When you hear the name Bruno, what type of person do you expect? How about Jessica? Thin or Fat, active or inactive, artistic or mathematical, cute or ugly? While watching a movie, TV show, or play, the actors talk about a character which you have not yet seen. Do you ever anticipate what that person is like either in behavior or looks? When this character came on stage, were you ever so surprised at what the character was like that you found the character unbelievable for the role? Whould you believe Brunno to be a skinny, nerdy, pencel-necked geek? Nearly all of us have some expectation of a person which we have never met, simply from a name.

It has often been observed that a name suits the person who bears it. The implication is that the name seems to be a reflection of the personality. To modern scientific man, any real connection seems preposterous, since a name is generally bestowed long before any personality develops. Arthur Custance responded to this common skepticism:

> While we look upon such mystical connections between a name and the personality or a name and an object with some cynicism, the same cynicism is not felt by a large number of societies who do not share our particularly materialistic bias. This mystical connection has been rediscovered in recent times by some of the best modern students of language. So bound together are the names which things bear and the very existence of those things, that namelessness tends to be synonymous with nonexistence. It is merely an extension of the idea that until an individual has a personal name he does not have a personality, he is a nonentity, soulless, merely an "it" or a thing...

> ...Every man's soul is so closely identified with the name he bears that to declare his name publicly is tantamount to making a public confession of what he is really like, and since such knowledge gives a potential enemy power over him, names are secret possessions known only to those in whose hands it is safe to trust himself entirely.

In a remarkable way, the Bible makes use of this deeply rooted feeling of attachment to and identity with one's name to bring out many things related to God's dealings with the individual. An understanding of this background supplies a commentary on some important aspects of Christian experience which otherwise may appear as interesting enough but of little real consequence. In truth, it appears that somewhat more attention should have been paid by commentators generally in dealing with a whole class of passages in Scripture which involve the giving of names, the use of names, and finally and more importantly, the changing of names.

...It is only in comparatively recent years that we in our culture have begun to rediscover what people in other cultures less sophisticated than our own have always recognized: that in some way a person's name is more than just a device by which to identify him in a crowd.

...The persuasive feeling that there is an agreement between name and personality is very ancient and widespread.[1]

Many people feel uncomfortable in the company of people who's names they do not know. Upon learning a persons name, we often have a new confidence. With a name, we feel we know them, though often we know virtually nothing else about them. Usually, the first and often only response to the broad question "who is that?" is the person's name. Moreover, once the name is given, no further revelation is often requested.

BIBLICAL VIEW OF NAMES.

After millennium of scrutiny in the Western world, we have long held to the mystical power of the truths about human nature revealed in the Bible. The Bible also supports the belief that names and characteristics are mystically linked:

The Bible begins with a chapter describing creation in which the naming of things plays a preeminent part. The light and dark are named as day and night, so the land and the sea, earth and heaven, and even the stars in the sky are named. When we are told in Psalm 147:4, "He calleth all the stars by their names," we are really being told that in spite of their apparently infinite number, each one was nevertheless brought into being by the Word of God - by whom God the Father created all things.

The process of naming is then turned over to Adam himself. The simple story describing how Adam named the animals - a story which reads as though it were written for children and has on that account by pseudo-intellectuals been viewed with some condescension - is in fact a profound statement. Part of the inspired character of Scripture is the universality of its message in terms of the ages of its readers. The simplest child may be reading this story in one room of the house while in another room his father, a mature and deeply thoughtful man, may also be studying the very same words - each being stirred by the same record in appropriate yet quite different ways. The words are for children, but the thoughts are for men. And the man who reads it and smiles condescendingly at the childlikeness of the story is merely confessing in fact that he himself is still a child.[2]

We have in Scripture not a few instances of people who acquired a *new* name. ... When Saul was converted (Acts 9) ... he did not immediately receive a new name, for he was still being referred to as Saul after that (Acts 13:2). He continued to be called Saul until there came the significant words, "then Saul who was also called Paul, being filled with the Holy Spirit . . ." (Acts 13:9). Such was his character thereafter that he never looked back, never returned to his old way of life, and never longed to be anything but this new man: and thereafter he is never again referred to as Saul.[3]

Jacob also was renamed after meeting up with God, however, he was not always called Israel thereafter. Nor were his descendants always referred to as Israel. The use of the name Jacob in the Bible instead of the name Israel seems to be based on which characteristics are being exhibited by the man or nation: "Jacob" the natural man or "Israel" the man of God.

RESEARCH SAYS...

More serious scholars agree that name [characteristic associations] definitely exist. For example, studies show that qualities (such as good or bad, strong or weak, or active or passive) are associated with particular names. According to Bruning & Husa (1972), [name suppositions] seemed to start as early as kindergarten and became more rigid in the later grades. College men and women also showed name [preferences]. For example, they rated the name *Dave* "strong and active" (Lawson, 1973, 1974) and judged names like *Alfreda, Percival*, and *Isidore to be* "bad, weak, and passive" (Buchanan and Bruning, 1971).[4]

More recently, Lansky & Sinrod surveyed over 75,000 people to determine name images and stereotypes broadly across the general population.[5] This researcher doesn't endorse this method as it gives as much weight to the average person's lack of discernment as it would to a discerning Albert Einstein type. The results of Lansky & Sinrod's undiscriminating survey speaks for itself. Conflicting results abound. Throughout the book there are numerous dichotomies and trichotomies, such as "an old spinster who is plain, quiet, lackluster, and secretive ... (or) ... sophisticated and sexy." Their survey addition-ally adds caricatures like Elmer Fudd the cartoon, story characters like Sherlock Holmes and celebrities like Kareem Abdul

Jabbar all of whom are widely known by the respondents and may be the only character whom they know with this name. Another example from their survey is "Elvira (a) tramp who is weird, spooky, and sexy". Although it was a nice try, only a personality expert could extract the gold from the gravel in their results. But none the less, the underlying belief in the name - characteristics link is broad.

Moreover, the belief that names are connected with characteristics appears to be universal. There are books linking names and characteristics in many different languages and cultures. But the belief is also deeply seated.

> ... This is the case of the woman whose basic personality seems to have been expressed when she responded to the name of Eve but who, when assuming either of two other names, became an entirely different personality.[6] The "experts" are satisfied that this woman is only one person really. But to read the account of the numerous interviews that she had with a number of psychiatrists and others - who all agree upon the fact that the three "individuals" who seem to be indwelling her were as different in character as it is possible to conceive, with different voices, different handwriting, different encephalograms, different tastes in clothing, different mannerisms, and different facial expressions - one has a strong feeling that we do really have three residents taking turns with one another to have possession by some kind of mutual agreement. A popular but informative account appeared in the Canadian *MacLean's* magazine under the title "Three Women: One Body." [7] Some years later this same individual became yet another person, and her story was published by McGraw-Hill in 1958 in a book written by Evelyn Lancaster and James Poling entitled *The Final Face of Eve.* A useful popular review of this book appeared in *Life* magazine under the caption "The Fourth Face of Eve."[8,9]

To answer the question, "Is the name - characteristics link simply a popular fiction or folk tale?" I say this: It may be a coincidence that males named William or Bill seem so obsessed with an interest that they often achieve great things with it. But with research over time, I have come to accept it to be true and chose names for my children in agreement with it. This approach seems more practical than to fight the apparent connection of personalities with names. It seems silly for parents to choose names for thier children which are counter to the parents hopes and dreams for their children's success.

Although this book reflects the belief that names can play a part in determining personality characteristics, it is only a part in this very complicated matter. The complication of name-personality is compounded by one's other names (i.e. First , middle, etc.), which also contribute to personality. However, there is a question in this author's mind as to how much a surname (family name) contributes to personality. But in the argument over nurture and nature, there is no question that although name personality comes under the category of nature, nurture also plays a very significant part in determining the extent of success of each person. For example, a prolonged traumatic situation, such as divorce, loss of relationship or abuse, in the life of a child can have a dramatic effect on the personality, changing an otherwise outgoing and optimistic personality type into a reserved or reclusive personality. Children of drug or alcohol abusers often become skilled reconcilers or diplomats. Additionally, abandonment or neglect to nurture and guide a child can allow the child to grow wild and in this wildness, some characteristics would not develop and the display of other characteristics would be develop differently than un-neglected children.

NAMING SIGNIFICANCE IN HISTORY:

My wife, reacting to her name's personality characteristics, asked, "Why doesn't it say beautiful, pretty, intelligent, sexy and humble?" (Husband-wife diplomacy is always a sensitive matter.) Well, that's a good question. So taking to mind those famous words of Ricky Ricardo, "Lucy, You've got some esplainin' to do!" I will try to answer it and other questions, which may come to mind.

If names are just labels and have no significance, it would seem strange that wherever mankind exists, there are name preferences. Additionally, the name preference seems to be mysteriously linked with honor, achievement, leadership, beauty, and intelligence as well as their opposites. Parents have chosen names for their children based on aesthetics or for kings, poets, theologians, conquerors, presidents, actresses, models, friends and relatives. Sometimes names have been chosen hoping the child will reflect certain characteristics of their name-sake. Other times, simply to honor a loved one.

WHAT CAUSES THE LINK BETWEEN NAME AND PERSONALITY?

"Give me a child until he is five and I will give you a man" - *Unknown.*

Besides the obvious meta-physical explanation of the link between a person's name and one's characteristics, there are at least two science based arguments which might explain the phenomena. They could be understood as the two sides of the common sociological argument of Nature verses Nurture, but with possibly interesting twists.

THE MOST OBVIOUS CONNECTION - NURTURE:

Of course, there are some completely logical connections between names and personalities. The most obvious fall under the category of names having a "known meaning." What does it mean that a name has "known meaning"? Names having "known meanings" would include names with common non-name usage such as "Faith" and "Patience" as well as names without generally known meanings, but still known to the bearers of them. An example of the latter would be when the mother tells the child that his name was chosen because it means "strong," thus instilling in the child his parent's goal that he will be strong. Other "known meaning" examples include: being named after an honored person known by the bearer; and the named child knowing someone holding the same name. In either case, the child may assume to have similar characteristics to another person with the same name. Thereby "living up to" or "living down to" the name. This link is a completely natural assumption for a child, since it follows the same rule we use with naming everywhere. That rule being: all things categorized with names share certain characteristics, just as all chairs are made for sitting and all tables have a flat top. The "scientific" skeptic, who does not see such an obvious link, may deny any link at all, fearing that he may fall into an abyss of the meta-physical. Some such pseudo-scientists prefer to condemn without looking any further for possible scientific answers or new knowledge.

SECOND NURTURE EXPLANATION:

The second scientific argument fits under the category of Nurture. Simply, the care givers' subconscious expectations of a child with a certain name causes the child to develop characteristics in line with society's expectations. This idea is in line with a similar study which showed that if a child is repeatedly told he is dumb, he will under perform others, but if he is repeatedly told he is smart, he will out perform others. This is a reasonable explanation, but it doesn't explain why society expects a girl named Nicole to be attractive. Of course, society's expectations of innate physical attributes, such as beauty or height, associated with a name might be purely fantasy.

FIRST GENETIC-CHEMICAL EXPLANATION:

A third scientific argument fits best under the category of Nurture with shades of Nature. In line with mankind's nature-based "agreement" to enjoy sweet foods and "support" the Golden Rule, humans also generally agree as to which sounds are harsh or gentle. So also, parents' personal taste in sounds will determine what sound they choose for naming their child. The link between sounds and personal attitudes in humans is easy to establish. Mankind as a whole generally agree on the meanings of sounds. In the situation of a German man speaking loving romantic words in German to a Spanish lady who doesn't understand German and an English man who also doesn't understand German overhears, it is likely that both of the hearers understand this as wooing, even without visually seeing it. From crying and cooing of a baby's first sounds of through to the grunts and yells of dominance of a man through to the gentle attentive whispers of love by mothers and lovers, human sounds are universally and undeniably linked to attitude. Therefore, every sound relates attitudinal information and every time a name is spoken aloud or pronounced within the mind's ear, a subconscious primal attitude is reinforced about the characteristics of a person, which universally become accepted by the person. Additionally, these name based attitudes, which determine personality, are agreed to and again reinforced by the person each time he or she declares his or her name. Therefore, sounds in a name could convey attitudes and characteristics which subconsciously have meaning to the hearer. A name, therefore could transmit many expectations, shaping a person subconsciously, similar to the more conscious study of "the power of expectations" mentioned above. Thus, a name could be subconscious programming of a primal order.

SECOND GENETIC-CHEMICAL EXPLANATION:

A few years ago, it was discovered that each person's primary attitudes become established as his of her norm early in life. These are attitudes such as: joy of living, trust of others, depression or fear and other such mentally "up" or "down" attitudes. These primary attitudes become established through a chemical balance in the brain, reportedly based on early life situations which stimulate chemicals in the brain, thereby altering its structure and establishing a chemical norm for each brain, which in turn the brain then tries to maintain, thereby reinforcing those attitude on the brain. It's a "catch 22" and very similar to a chemical addiction to drugs. For example: A boy scared for his safety because of regularly running from danger or regularly being yelled at and physically abused by someone may establish his normal adrenaline level higher, thereby establishing the boy's chemical balance needing to regularly feel that adrenaline rush as a thrill seeker or trouble maker.

Therefore, it can be argued that the link between personality and name, when being given by the parents, may be a direct result of the genetic and chemical composition of the parents. That is to say, since science has shown that the character of a person is undeniably and mutually linked with his or her brain's chemical-stimuli balance in a mutually supportive manner, the character of the parents and their genetics may strongly influence their "taste" preference in names. Thus, the parents have a predisposition for certain name sounds and therefore they end up choosing from names with associated characteristics which are similar. This link is then further reinforced by the parents during the child's character development. The parent reinforces the name characteristics in the child by creating and sustaining an atmosphere through nurture which supports the child in developing those subconsciously desired traits and hinders the development of the undesired traits. In the same way, the parents have also received their names by this same ancestrally linked cause, and the grandparents before them. Thus the personality/name link might be understood as an unending ancestral chain of genetic and chemical cause and effect.

Explained further, the genetic and chemical characteristics (which cause and support the parents' own characteristics of likes, dislikes, skills and weaknesses) cause them to name their child based on those conscious and subconscious genetic/chemical/situation stimuli. Since the name they choose fits both the genetic characteristics passed on by the parents to the child and the brain's chemical balance (or disposition) of the parents who raise the child, the parents consciously and subconsciously pick a name which fits the child genetically and the way the child will be raised by them. For example: the characteristics of Robert and Diane's second born is highly determined by the parents genetics and their brain's chemical balance. Therefore, if the child is a girl, she will have the genetic/chemical characteristics of an Alicia passed down from her parents, so the parents will choose the name Alicia or a name which reflects those similar characteristics. Summarizing, these parents named their child Alicia, because it fits their situation. If that is what causes the link, then the mystery is a near scientific impossibility to prove. How could one prove a link between name characteristics and how the parents subconsciously know which name fits their situation, both in genetics and atmosphere?

Of course, that choice could be explained in the natural (but none the less genetic) likes and dislikes which are common to all humans. Here are two examples of human agreement based in nature: 1) all humans enjoy eating more refined sugars, like candies, cookies, etc., for a biological reason and; 2) humans universally agree in morality with the "Golden-Rule," we should treat others the way we want to be treated. Of course, both of those examples break-down: some people hate sweet cake frosting and we don't always live by the Golden Rule. Frankly, the great latitude of human choice seems to argue soundly against the robotics idea that precise name choice is entirely predetermined and excludes free will. Nobody did anything because he must, but rather, he felt it was his best choice.

This explanation is further supported by general naming history and its incidence of the phenomena called onomatopoeia. Onomatopoeia is the formation or use of words such as *buzz* or *murmur* that imitate the sounds associated with the objects or actions they refer to. The support is that by this phenomena we know that our brains have developed a table of meanings associated with sounds which do not necessarily make up words. Further support that this phenomena is present in the name/characteristics link may be witnessed by the occurrence of people's characteristics which strangely match the meaning of their name.

WHAT DOES A NAME INFLUENCE?

We are well aware of the unique individuality of each person, and therefore, if the total personality was completely expressed by the name, this individuality would be much less obvious and we could turn out Einsteins and Edisons like Ford Motor Company turns out Mustangs. Since this is not the case, "What area of the person does a name influence?"

The name primarily seems to influence a person's central personality, one's attitude about life or reason for being. Is life a game, a competition, a major social event, an art show, an opportunity to create, etc. or some mix of these attitudes? This mixture establishes one's general likes and dislikes and therefore one's areas of strength or weakness. Consequently, it influences his abilities, competitiveness, work choice, type of person he marries, how he gets along with others; virtually every attitude of life. Secondly, it seems to influence physical characteristics such as beauty, weight and body shape. However, it does not appear that each different name influences each of these areas to the same degree. That is to say, Danielles tend to be strikingly attractive, but Beverlys don't seem to have any consistency toward or against loveliness. Not to say that one couldn't be a goddess; simply that Beverly's beauty is not a characteristic noticeably influenced by the name, either positively or negatively.

Likewise, the absence of a characteristic (such as beautiful or athletic) in the description is not an indication that a person with that name will not possess that characteristic; it simply means that this characteristic is either too common in that gender to include or not noticed as an outstanding characteristic in persons with that name as compared to the population in general.

Being that the assessing of personal characteristics is an art and not a science, at this point, omissions of some characteristics which are generally reflected in persons with that name or inclusions of other characteristics which are not generally reflected in persons with that name may occur in this volume. We request that you submit any corrections or additions for our consideration in updating of future additions.

THAT DOESN'T DISCRIBE ME!

In writing this book, I'm aware that certain readers will disagree with the analysis of certain characteristics associated with their name. You may be right. However, this reminds me of two people: the man who argued vehemently that he was not argumentative; and the man who rejected the idea that he was proud, to a friend who had noticed that he never would admit to being wrong. There is also the fact that everyone believes that their "goodness" is generally better than average or even in the case of vile criminals, who believe that they are not really any worse than most people, they just got caught.

MEANINGS AND DERIVATIVES:

Often, one of a name's characteristic is reflected in the original meaning of the name, such as in the case of Joy, but this is not necessarily the case; for example Angelas are not "angels", although she may be generally well behaved. (In the specific case of Angelas, they often rebel against the impossible to reach label of Angel, which was given.) Within chapter seven and eight, if a name's associated characteristic is reflected by the meaning of the name, this characteristic will often be included within the listing.

Many names have several derived forms, both in the same gender and in the other gender. For example: the common derivatives and root of Charles are Charles, Carl, Chuck, Carol and Carla. In similarly related names, expect to see these names carry similar, non-gender specific, characteristics to one another. But since, there appear to be personality differences, even within related names such as Carla and Carol, these names are listed separately often with additional unique characteristics or differentiating characteristics.

Comparing derivatives and the root name is often enlightening, since the differences in characteristics between related names are not to the order of magnitude of black verses white. Rather, there is often great similarity and overlap. Remember, the names are related, so looking at the characteristics of another related name may further reveal the name as well as the shades of differences. These shades of differences between related names will typically be either a softening or intensifying of characteristics, not the difference between night and day.

The differences in spelling of a name between derivatives with the same sound does not seem to be reflected in personality (i.e. Kathy/Cathy and Carlee/Karly), supporting the "Sound/Personality Link" theory. Although, this might be "splitting hairs" on the matter. However, differences in personality between these and other similar names are probably reflections, rather, in the differences in personality between the birth names Kathleen and Catherin, which contain uniquely different sounds to one another (see section on what causes the link between name and personality).

DOES IT MATTER WHICH NAME IS USED?

It appears that personality characteristics are linked with the usage of a name in preference to the person's legal name. So, if a person's legal name is Katherine, but she is usually called Kelly and seldom Katherine, expect her to have dominant characteristics of Kelly and the subordinate characteristics of Katherine and any other names which may be used to address her.

This author can not adequately explain why names are linked to characteristics or why the name commonly used for a person would carry more personality weight than a legal name, although suggestions have been made in the Chemical-Genetic cause sections of this book. It is enough for this book to recognize this relationship, offer possible explanations and match names with characteristics. It is my hope, that someone would further study this link of names and characteristics, scientifically, for I believe there is a whole world of scientific knowledge available by delving these depths.

SOME THINGS DO CHANGE:

There may be changes in the attributes associated with a name over the years. I don't believe it has to do with true changes in the attributes as it does with the relative perspective of the persons judging this. Certainly, relative changes occur as the name mixture and societal characteristic preferences change. Some names are considered old fashioned, the name of a geriatric patient or pioneering settler, having had its usage abandoned years ago. Other names are forever with us, being rooted in history or more especially religion. A person may be considered a leader among weaker personalities, but a follower among strong leaders. Likewise, Beverly might be the Homecoming Queen in a village, but the least attractive in a room filled with names such a Lori and Danielle. Certainly, our opinion of what constitutes desirable attributes changes through culture and history. A common example of this is what constitutes beauty as recorded by artists. The relatively plump women adored and recorded by 17th century painters would be unacceptable bikini models today. Our attitude about other social attributes have similarly changed.

SOME RECOMMENDATIONS:

In recommending possible names for your child, I suggest generally avoiding plant names, unless of course, you desire your child to look like a plant. It amazes me to see such high percentages of funny or peculiar looking girls with flower names. In contrast, girls with the name Holly seem to define the word pretty. Maybe, tree names are OK? Or maybe generalizing about plant names as a group should be avoided, rather looking at each specific name as an individual.

If your desire is for a beautiful girl, parents who have chosen uncommon names have faired quite well. I think of Farrah, Vanna, and Vendela for example. But be aware of easy bias because of a few high profile public figures. Names which start with the letter V seem to have a better percentage chance of being very attractive girls. But although this might be true, it still seems name specific. If a beautiful daughter is your desire, you'll have better odds with Vanessa than with Valentina.

It seems that name personalities that end with the letters INE are more serious, calculating and less bouncy than related names which end with the lighter sounding letters Y or I (e.g., Katherine, Kari and Karry).

The name's personality associated with a more serious sounding name is more serious. Likewise a less weighty name is associated with a less serious personality. It's hard to imagine anyone with the name Cici as being too serious, punitive or calculating. Often a person changes the name they use from that his or her mother used to a more formal, serious, beautiful, or weightier name during adulthood.

The seriousness or weightiness of a name seems somewhat related to its length, but may be more likely associated with the sounds of which it is made (see section on what causes the link between name and personality). Generally, names which start with the sounds TH or W and end with the sounds M or R, like William and Theodore, seem to be weightier than names which start with soft A or S and end in the soft A or long E sounds, like Alissa and Sarah. Likewise, the personality of a name seems to go with its weight. One may generally agree with this observation, but argue that this is simply because of a global convention to generally end females names with the soft A or long E sounds. Yes, that is true, but among men's names, the personalities associated with these lighter sounds seem to be linked with a more sensitive personality (e.g. Audie Murphy, Andrae).

Combination names are those names which are made by combining names or parts of two or more names to form the name, such as Marianne, which is made up of root names Mary and Anne. When these occur, it is typical that the characteristics linked to the name are, as you probably suspected, a combination of the root names' characteristics, so it would be good to look at the root names.

A listing for a name often includes related names, which often have similar characteristics to the first listed name. The listed characteristics are, however, for the first listed name and may not be reflected in one of the related names to the same degree.

D in a male's name seems to be associated with a high degree of "goal orientation" and apparent "courage" such as is reflected in Dave, Dan, Don and Derrick. This may also be true for female names (i.e. Debby, Diane).

When considering characteristics associated with names, keep in mind that many of the historically famous people became famous for activities which we no longer celebrate to the same extent in modern times. For example, many were famous for their poetry. Poetry does not have the same following and interest today that it did before the movie, television, and computer age. A person who is gifted in poetry may find his/her niche in another area of writing or art or may have a skill which for which he/she is more desired in modern times, such as writing computer games.

AM I DOOMED!?!

Every person is likely to have multiple talents and no person is doomed or destined for greatness simply because of the characteristics which are associated with the name. There are many people in occupations today who are not using their greatest abilities to reach their greatest potential. A person named Emil is not forced to be a social scientist simply because he has talent in this area. He may become a millionaire janitor or he may work in a widget assembly-line. Which brings us to another point. People do not generally become famous and their name added to history books through their work as janitors and other blue collar jobs, even after becoming a wealthy business owner or CEO. Non-celebrity does not equal poverty or failure.

Not all occupations are treated equally or represented equally by this research. The opportunity of a person to be included in history books is increased by doing activities which uniquely affect society. People with occupations such as scientist, artists, politician, writers, actors, journalists, inventors, clergy and heroes are more likely to be included in the history books used to research part of this book than are other occupations. Simply being included in a history book because of accomplishments does not indicate the success of that person in other areas such as finances or family. So keep in mind that occupations of individuals should be used as a guide to assess the talents associated with each name, not as any guarantee that a child so named will have that occupation.

WHAT ABOUT EDUCATION, TRAINING AND FATE?

There is some amount of fate involved in everyone's success. Additionally, successful people are disciplined people. A child may have great natural talents in any number of areas, but without self-discipline and training, the child may never have the opportunity in later life to pursue occupations which might give the greatest successes and contributions to humanity.

Some name personalities are more focused than others; for example some names are very strongly associated with success in one or few occupations and other names seem more multi-talented, having success in many different occupations. Some name bearers seem to have less public success than others, with a few that are not associated with public success at all. Totals are summaries of the historically most famous people, determined from Encyclopedic sources. They do not reflect the whole population, but do reflect a subset of the population, consisting of persons whose activities have made them famous. Therefore, although totals are not scientific, they do give some indication of abilities, skills, characteristics and interests of those bearing the name and might be used to roughly compare to other names. This is more useful than an exhaustive summary, including all persons bearing a name. Such an exhaustive summary, if it were possible to produce, would include the masses of people, wandering aimlessly through life, who never find their heart's work, their passion, or show how their strongest abilities can make a lasting impact in the world. This book is intended to help show the activities to which a person's characteristics may help him excel. Again, these are activities these famous people have done and not necessarily their livelihood.

[1]Custance, Arthur C.; The Flood: Local or Global?; The Doorway Papers, Volume IX, Zondervan, Grand Rapids, 1978.
[2]Custance, Arthur C.; The Flood: Local or Global?; The Doorway Papers, Volume IX, Zondervan, Grand Rapids, 1978.
[3]Custance, Arthur C.; The Flood: Local or Global?; The Doorway Papers, Volume IX, Zondervan, Grand Rapids, 1978.
[4]Cameron, Catherine; The Name Givers, Prentice-Hall, Englewood Cliffs, NJ, 1983.
[5] Lansky, Bruce and Sinrod, Barry, The Baby Name Personality Survey, Meadowbrook Press, 1990.

[6]Thigpen, Corbett H., and Cleckley, Hervey, <u>The Three Faces of Eve</u>, Regnery, 1954.

[7]<u>MacLean's</u>, 15 September 1954, pp. 12-15, 67-75.

[8]<u>Life</u>, 19 May 1958, pp. 101-14.

[9]Custance, Arthur C.; <u>The Flood: Local or Global?</u>; The Doorway Papers, Volume IX, Zondervan, Grand Rapids, 1978.

CHRISTIAN SAINTS

Technically, this is a list of saints recognized by the Roman Catholic church. There are several other sources for Christian saints. If you are interested, you might try the Orthodox Christian saints list, listings of famous missionaries or Fox's Book of Martyrs. Vatican II resulted in some "folk-saints" being removed from the list, such as the popular Saint Christopher, but since there was a second Saint named Christopher, we are not without a Saint Christopher on the list. "Bl" indicates the title "Blessed." It is not clear whether someone designated as "Blessed" is a Catholic saint. For more information on each of these saints refer to www.catholic.org on the Internet.

A

St. Aaron
St. Acacius
St. Acacius
St. Acacius
St. Achatius
St. Achilleus
St. Adalbert of Prague
St. Adamnan
St. Adelaide
St. Adelard
Bl. Adeline
St. Adeodatus I
Adeodatus II
St. Adrian
Adrian II
St. Adrian III
Adrian IV
Adrian V
St. Adrian, Abbot

St. Adrian III
St. Aelred of Rievaulx
St. Agape
St. Agatha
St. Agatho
St. Agilbert
Bl. Agnello of Pisa
St. Agnes
St. Agnes of Rome
St. Aidan of Lindisfarne
St. Ajuture
Bl. Alan de la Roche
St. Alban
St. Alban of Britain
St. Albert the Great
St. Aldo
St. Alexander
St. Alexander I
Alexander II

Alexander III
Alexander IV
St. Alexander Nevski
St. Alexis
St. Aleydis
St. Alice
Bl. Alix Le Clercq
St. Alphonsus
St. Aloysius Gonzaga
St. Alvarez
St. Amand
St. Ambrose
St. Anacletus
St. Anastasia
Anastasius I
Anastasius II
Anastasius III
Anastasius IV
Bl. Andre Bessette

St. Andrew
St. Andrew of Crete
St. Andrew Kim Taegon *et al*
St. Angela of Foligno
St. Angela Merici
Beato Angelico
St. Angelo
St. Angelus of Acri
St. Angus MacNisse
St. Anicetus
St. Anne
Bl. Anne Mary Taigi
St. Ansegisus
St. Anselm
St. Ansgar
St. Anskar
St. Anterus
St. Anthony the Abbot
St. Anthony the Hermit
St. Anthony of Padua
St. Apollinaris
St. Apollonia
The Apostles
St. Aquilina
St. Aquilinus
St. Arcadius
St. Artaldus
St. Artemius
St. Ashley
St. Athanasius
St. Aubin
St. Audrey (Ethelreda)

St. Augustine of Canterbury
St. Augustine of Hippo
St. Augustus Schoffler
St. Aurea
St. Aurelius
St. Ava

B

St. Bacchus
St. Barbara
St. Barnabas
St. Bartholomew
Bl. Bartholomew Laurel
St. Basil the Great
St. Basilissa
St. Bavo
St. Bean
St. Beatrice da Silva Meneses
St. Begga
St. Benedict
Benedict I
St. Benedict II
Benedict III
Benedict IV
Benedict V
Benedict VI
Benedict VII
Benedict VIII
Benedict IX
Benedict X

Bl. Benedict XI
Benedict XII
St. Benedict of Aniane
St. Benedict Biscop
St. Benedict the Black
St. Benedict the Moor
St. Benedict of Nursia
St. Benilde
St. Benjamin
St. Benno
Bl. Berka Zdislava
St. Bernard of Clairvaux
St. Bernard of Montjoux
St. Bernadette
St. Bernardine of Siena
St. Bernardino Realino
St. Bernward
St. Bertha
St. Bertin
St. Bessarion
St. Beuno
St. Bibiana
St. Bichier
St. Blaise
St. Blandina
St. Blane
St. Bonaventure
St. Boniface I
Boniface II
Boniface III
St. Boniface IV
Boniface V

Boniface VI
Boniface VII
Boniface VIII
Boniface IX
St. Boniface of Mainz
St. Bonitus
St. Botulph
St. Braulio
St. Brendan
Bl. Brian
St. Brice
St. Bridget
St. Bridget of Sweden
St. Brigid of Ireland
St. Brogan
St. Bruno
St. Buonfiglio Monaldo
St. Burkard

C

St. Caedmon
St. Caesaria
St. Cajetan
St. Calixtus
Pope St. Callistus I
Callistus II
Callistus III
St. Camillus de Lellis
St. Candida
St. Canice

St. Carmen
St. Casimir
St. Caspar del Bufalo
St. Castorius
St. Castulus
St. Catherine of Alexandria
St. Catherine of Bologna
St. Catherine Laboure
St. Catherine de Ricci
St. Catherine of Siena
St. Catherine of Sweden
St. Cecilia
St. Cedd
St. Celestine I
Celestine II
Celestine III
Celestine IV
St. Celestine V
St. Celine
St. Celsus
St. Ceratius
St. Cerbonius
St. Cerneuf
Bl. Ceslaus
St. Charbel
St. Charity
St. Charles Borromeo
Ven. Charles de Foucauld
St. Charles Garnier
Bl. Charles the Good
St. Charles Joseph Eugene de Mazenod
St. Charles Lwanga *et al*

St. Charles of Sezze
St. Chastan
Bl. Christian
St. Christina
St. Christopher
St. Chrysanthus
St. Chrysogonus
St. Cianan
St. Clare
St. Clare of Montefalco
Bl. Clare of Rimini
St. Clarus
St. Clarus
St. Claud
St. Claudia
Pope St. Clement I
Clement II
Clement III
Clement IV
Clement V
Clement VI
St. Clement of Rome
St. Cletus
St. Clotilde
St. Cloud
St. Colette
St. Colman of Cloyne
St.Colman of Dromore
St. Columba
St. Columban
St. Columbanus
Conan

St. Condedus
St. Conrad
St. Constantine
St. Constantine
Bl. Constantius
St. Corentin
St. Cornelius
St. Cosmos
St. Crescentia
St. Crispin
St. Crispinian
St. Croix
St. Culen
St. Cunegundes
St. Cuthbert
St. Cuthburga
St. Cyril of Alexandria
St. Cyril Jerusalem
St. Cyrus

D

St. Dallan
St. Damasus
Damasus II
St. Damian
Pope St. Damasus I
St. Daniel
St. Daniel the Stylite
St. Dativus
St. David

St. Declan
Bl. Delphina
St. Denis
St. Desideratus
Bl. Diana
St. Didacus
St. Didier
St. Didier
Bl. Diego De Avezedo
St. Dionysia
St. Dionysius
St. Dismas
St. Dominic
St. Dominic Savio
St. Donald
St. Donan
St. Donus
St. Dorothy
St. Dunstan
St. Dymphna

E

St. Eata
St. Ebba
St. Ebba
St. Edith of Polesworth
Bl. Edith Stein
St. Edith of Wilton
St. Edmund Arrowsmith
St. Edmund Campion

St. Edward the Confessor
Bl. Edward Jones
St. Edward the Martyr
St. Edwin
St. Egbert
St. Eleutherius
St. Eleutherius
St. Elian
St. Elias
St. Eligius
St. Elizabeth
St. Elizabeth Ann Seton
St. Elizabeth of Hungary
St. Elizabeth of Portugal
St. Elzear
St. Emiliana
Bl. Emily Bicchieri
St. Emily de Rodat
St. Emily de Vialar
St. Emma
St. Enda
St. Ephrem
St. Erasmus (St. Elmo)
Eric
St. Ernest
St. Ethelreda (Audrey)
St. Eugene
Eugene II
Eugene III
Eugene IV
St. Eugene de Mazenod
St. Eugenia

St. Eulalia of Merida
St. Euphrasia Pelletier
St. Euplius
St. Eusebius of Rome
St. Eusebius of Vercelli
St. Eustace
St. Eustachius
Bl. Eustochium
St. Eustorgius II
St. Euthymius
St. Eutychian
Bl. Eva of Liege
St. Evaristus
St. Expeditus

F

St. Fabian
St. Fabiola
St. Fachanan
St. Faith
St. Fara
Bl. Faustina
St. Faustinus
St. Febronia
St. Fechin
St. Felicity
St. Felix I
St. Felix III
St. Felix IV
St. Felix of Cantalice

St. Felix of Nola
St. Ferdinand III of Castile
St. Fiacre
St. Fidelis
St. Fillan
St. Finan of Lindisfarne
St. Finbar
St. Fina "Seraphina"
St. Flannan
St. Flavia
St. Flavia Domitilla
St. Flora
St. Florian
Formosus
St. Frances Rome
St. Francis Borgia
St. Francis Nagasaki
St. Francis of Paola
St. Francis Solano
St. Francis Xavier
St. Frances Xavier Cabrini
St. Francis Assisi
St. Francis de Sales
St. Frederick
St. Fronto
St. Frumentius

G

St. Gabriel, the Archangel
St. Gabriella
St. Gaius
St. Gall
St. Gaspar
St. Gelasius
St. Gelasius I
Gelasius II
St. Gemma Galgani
St. Genesius
St. Genevieve
St. George
St. Gerald
St. Gerard Majella
St. Germaine Cousin
St. Gertrude
St. Gertrude the Great
St. Gervase
St. Getulius
St. Ghislain
St. Gilbert of Sempringham
St. Giles of Abbot
St. Giles of Assisi
Bl. Giuseppe Maria Tommasi
St. Godfrey
Bl. Gonzalo de Amarante
St. Gottschalk
St. Gratia
St. Gregory II

Pope St. Gregory III
Gregory IV
Gregory V
Gregory VI
Gregory VII
Gregory VIII
Gregory IX
Gregory XI
Gregory XII
St. Gregory Barbarigo
St. Gregory the Enlightener
Pope St. Gregory the Great
St. Gregory of Nazianzus
St. Gregory of Nyssa
St. Gregory Palamas
St. Gregory the Sinaite
St. Gregory Thaumaturgus
St. Grimonia
Our Lady of Guadalupe
St. Gummarus
Bl. Gunther
St. Guthlac
St. Guy of Anderlecht
St. Guy of Pomposa
Bl. Guy Vignotelli

H

St. Hallvard
St. Harvey
St. Hedwig

St. Helen of Skovde
St. Helena
St. Henry
St. Henry of Sweden
St. Henry of Uppsala
St. Herbert
Bl. Herman the Cripple
Bl. Herman Joseph
St. Hermes
St. Herve
St. Hilarion
St. Hilarius
St. Hilary
St. Hilary of Poitiers
St. Hilda
St. Hildegarde
St. Hippolytus
St. Homobonus
St. Honoratus
Honorius I
Honorius II
Honorius III
Honorius IV
St. Hope
St. Hormisdas
St. Hubert
St. Hugh
St. Hugh of Lincoln
Bl. Humbert
Bl. Humbert
St. Hyacinth
St. Hyginius

I

St. Ignatius of Antioch
St. Ignatius of Loyola
St. Ildephonsus
St. Imelda
Bl. Inez
St. Ingrid of Sweden
St. Inigo
St. Innocent I
Innocent II
Innocent III
Innocent IV
Innocent V
Innocent VI
Innocent VII
Innocent VIII
St. Irenaeus
St. Irene
St. Irmina
St. Isaac the Great
St. Isaac Jogues
St. Isabel of France
St. Isadore the Farmer
St. Isadore of Seville
St. Isidore
St. Ita
St. Ivo

J

St. Jacques Fremin
St. James the Greater
St. James Intercisus
St. James the Lesser
St. James of the Marches
St. Jane Frances de Chantal
St. Januarius
St. Jarlath
St. Jason
St. Jean de Brebeuf
St. Jeremy
St. Jerome
St. Jerome Emiliani
St. Jessica
St. Joachim
St. Joan of Arc
St. Joan de Lestonnac
St. Joan of Valois
St. Joanna
St. Jodoc
John I
John II
John III
John IV
John V
John VI
John VII
John VIII
John IX

John X
John XI
John XII
John XIII
John XIV
John XV
John XVII
John XVIII
John XIX
John XXI
John XXII
St. John the Almsgiver
St. John the Apostle
St. John the Baptist
St. John Baptist de la Salle
St. John Baptiste de Rossi
St. John Berchmans
St. John of Beverly
St. John Bosco
St. John of Capistrano
St. John Chrysostom
St. John Joseph of the Cross
St. John of the Cross
St. John of Damascus
St. John the Dwarf
St. John the Evangelist
St. John Eudes
St. John Fisher
St. John Francis Regis
St. John Gaulbert, Abbot
St. John of God
St. John Kanty

St. John Leonardi
St. John Lloyd
St. John of Martha
St. John Nepomucene
St. John Neumann
St. John Ogilvie
St. John of Rila
Bl. John Roche
St. John of Ruysbroeck
St. John of Sahagun
St. John Serapion
St. John Vianney
Bl. Jordan
St. Josaphat Polotsk
St. Joseph
St. Joseph Cafassa
St. Joseph Cottolengo
Venerable Joseph de Veuster
St. Joseph of Cupertino
St. Joshua
Bl. Juan Diego
St. Jucundus
St. Judas Cyriacus
St. Jude of Thaddaeus
St. Judith
St. Julia
St. Julian
St. Juliana Falconieri
St. Julie Billiart
St. Julius
Bl. Junipero Serra
St. Justa

St. Justin
St. Justin de Jacobis
St. Justina of Antioch
St. Justina of Padua
St. Justus of Beauvais

K

Bl. Kateri Tekakwitha
Bl. Katharine Drexel
St. Kenneth
St. Kevin
St. Keyne
St. Kieran
St. Kilian
St. Kundegunda

L

St. Ladislaus
St. Landericus
St. Laura
St. Laurentinus
St. Lawrence
St. Lawrence of Brindisi
St. Lawrence martyr
St. Lazarus
St. Lea
St. Leander of Seville
St. Leger

St. Lelia
St. Leo II
Leo III
St. Leo IV
Leo V
Leo VI
Leo VII
Leo VIII
Leo IX
St. Leo the Great
St. Leonard
St. Leopold
Liberius
St. Linus
St. Longinus
St. Lorenzo Ruiz
St. Louis IX
St. Louis Bertrand
St. Louis Mary Grignion
St. Louise de Marillac
St. Louis King of France
St. Luchesio
St. Lucius I
Lucius II
Lucius III
St. Lucy
St. Ludmilla
St. Luke
St. Lupus
St. Lutgardis
St. Lydia Purpuraria
St. Lydwine

M

St. Macrina
St. Macrina the Younger
St. Madeleine Sophie Barat
St. Malchus
St. Marcarius of Jerusalem
St. Marcella
St. Marcellina
St. Marcellinus
St. Marcellus
St. Marculf
St. Margaret of Antioch
Bl. Margaret of Castello
Bl. Margaret of Citta-di-Castello
St. Magaret of Clitherow
St. Margaret of Cortona
St. Margaret of Hungary
St. Margaret Mary Alacoque
St. Margaret of Scotland
Bl. Margaret Ward
St. Marguerite Bourgeoys
St. Marguerite D'Youville
St. Maria Croifissa Di Rosa
St. Maria Goretti
St. Maria Michaela Desmaisieres
St. Maria Soledad
St. Marian
St. Mariana
Bl. Marie Rose Dorocher
St. Marina

St. Marius
St. Mark
St. Mark
St. Maro
St. Martha
St. Martial
Pope St. Martin I
Martin IV
St. Martin de Porres
St. Martin of Tours
St. Martina
St. Martinian
St. Mary Di Rosa
St. Mary of Egypt
St. Mary Magdalene de Pazzi
St. Mary Magdalene Postel
St. Mary Magdelene
St. Mathilda
St. Matilda
St. Matrona
Ven. Matt Talbot
St. Matthew
St. Matthias
St. Maura
St. Maura Troyes
St. Maurice
St. Maurus
St. Maxima
St. Maximaian
St. Maximilian Kolbe
St. Medard
St. Medericus

St. Meinrad
St. Mel
St. Melania
St. Melanie
St. Merryn
St. Methodius
St. Michael, the Archangel
St. Michael de Sanctis
St. Michael Garicoits
St. Melito of Sardis
Bl. Miguel Pro
St. Mildred
St. Miltiades
St. Modwenna
St. Monan
St. Monica
St. Moses the Ethopian

N

St. Narcissus
St. Natalie
St. Nathanael
St. Nathy
St. Nereus
St. Nicetas
St. Nicholas
St. Nicholas I
Nicholas II
Nicholas III
Nicholas IV

Nicholas V
St. Nicholas Owen
St. Nicholas of Tolentino
St. Nina
St. Ninian
St. Noel
St. Noel Chabanel
St. Norbert

O

St. Odilia
St. Odilo
St. Odo
St. Olaf
St. Olga
St. Oliver Plunkett
Bl. Olivia
St. Olympias
St. Onouphrius
St. Oswald
St. Othmar
St. Ouen

P

St. Pachomius
St. Pancras
St. Paphnutius
St. Pammachius

St. Pantaenus
St. Pantaleon
St. Paschal
Paschal I
Paschal II
St. Patricia
St. Patrick
St. Paul
St. Paul I
Paul II
St. Paul of the Cross
St. Paul Miki
St. Paula
St. Pega
St. Pelagia
Pelagius I
Pelagius II
St. Peregrine Laziosi
St. Perpetua
St. Peter
St. Peter Canisius
St. Peter in Chains
St. Peter Chanel
St. Peter Chrysologus
St. Peter Claver
St. Peter Damian
St. Peter Julian Eymard
St. Peter Gonzales
Bl. Peter Rene Roque
St. Peter of Sebaste
St. Peter of Verona
St. Petroc

St. Petronilla
St. Philip
St. Philip the Deacon
St. Philip Evans
St. Philip Neri
St. Philomena
St. Piran
St. Phocas
St. Phoebe
Padre Pio
Pope St. Pius X
St. Polycarp
St. Pontian
St. Pontianus
St. Pope John I
St. Praxedes
St. Priscilla
St. Prosper of Aquitaine
Pius I
Pius II

Q

St. Quentin
St. Quiteria

R

St. Radegunde
St. Raphael

St. Raymond Nonnatus
St. Raymond of Pennafort
St. Regina
St. Remigius
St. Rene Goupil
St. Richard
St. Richard of Wyche
St. Rigoberto
St. Rita
St. Robert Bellarmine
St. Robert of Newminster
St. Roch
St. Roderic
St. Roger
St. Romaric
St. Romuald
St. Roque Gonzalea de Santa Cruz
St. Rosalia
Bl. Rose
St. Rose of Lima
St. Rose Phillipine Duchesne
St. Rufina
St. Rufus
St. Rupert of Salzberg
St. Rusticus

S

St. Sabas
St. Sabas of Serbia
St. Sabina

Sabinian
St. Salome
St. Salvatore
St. Samuel
St. Saturninus
St. Saturninus
St. Sava
St. Scholastica
St. Sebastian
St. Secundinus
St. Senan
St. Seraphina
St. Sergius
St. Sergius I
Sergius II
Sergius III
Sergius IV
St. Sergius of Radonezh
St. Servelus
St. Severinus
Bl. Sidney
St. Sigfrid
St. Silas
St. Silverius
St. Simeon Metaphrastes
St. Simon
St. Simon Stock
St. Simon of Zealot
St. Simplicius
St. Siricius
Sisinius
St. Sixtus I

Sixtus II
Sixtus IV
St. Socrates
St. Sofia
St. Solange
Bl. Solanus
St. Sophronius of Jerusalem
St. Soter
St. Spyridon of Tremithius
St. Stanislaus
St. Stephen
St. Stephen I
Stephen II/III
Stephen III/IV
Stephen IV/V
Stephen V/VI
Stephen VI/VII
Stephen VII/VIII
St. Stephen the Great
St. Swithun (Swithin)
St. Sulpicius
St. Susanna
St. Sylvester
Sylvester II
Sylvester III
St. Sylvia
St. Syncletica

T

St. Tarasius
St. Tarsicius
St. Tatiana
St. Telemachus
St. Telesphorus
St. Teresa of Avila
St. Teresa of Portugal
St. Thea
St. Thecla
St. Theodora
St. Theodore
Theodore I
Theodore II
St. Theodore of Pavia
St. Theophanes
St. Theophilus of Alexandria
St. Therese of Lisieux
St. Thomas
St. Thomas Aquinas
St. Thomas Becket
St. Thomas More
St. Thorfinn
St. Thorlac Thorhallsson
St. Tigernach
St. Timothy

U

St. Ubald Baldassini
St. Ulric
St. Ulrich
St. Urban
St. Urban I
Urban II
Urban III
Urban IV
Urban V
Urban VI
St. Ursula
St. Usthazanes

V

St. Valentina
St. Valentine
Valentine
St. Valerian
St. Valerie
St. Vedast
St. Venantius
St. Venerius
St. Vergil of Salzburg
St. Veronica
St. Viator
St. Victor
Victor

St. Victor
St. Victor in Paris
St. Victoria
St. Victor Maurus
Bl. Victoria Strata
Vigilius
St. Vincent Ferrer
St. Vincent de Paul
St. Vincent Pallotti
St. Vincent Pallottiano
St. Vincent Saragossa
St. Vincent Strambi
St. Vincentia Maria Lopez Y Vicuna
St. Virgil of Arles
St. Vitalian
St. Vitalis
St. Vitus
St. Vladimir

W

St. Walburga
St. Waldebert, Abbot
St. Walfrid
St. Walter of Pontoise
St. Wenceslaus
St. Wilfrid
St. Wilgefortis
St. William, Abbot
St. William of Bourges
St. William of Dijon

St. William of Rochester
St. William of Vercelli
St. William of York
St. Winifred
St. Wiro
St. Wisdom

Y

Bl. Yvette

Z

St. Zachary
St. Zachary
St. Zeno
St. Zenobius
Ven. Zepherin Namuncura
St. Zephyrinus
St. Zita
St. Zoe
St. Zosimus

Beauty Contestant Winners

This table is a list of the occurances of the first names of Beauty Contestant Winners who made it to the Miss America contest.

Name	Count	Name	Count	Name	Count	Name	Count
Mary	76	Betty	17	Shirley	11	Angela	7
Susan	48	Debra	17	Elaine	10	Carole	7
Barbara	43	Jean	17	Ellen	10	Christine	7
Patricia	43	Jeanne	17	Laurie	10	Connie	7
Linda	42	Pamela	17	Michelle	10	Dawn	7
Karen	36	Suzanne	17	Paula	10	Doris	7
Lisa	35	Ann	16	Robin	10	Jo	7
Carol	33	Beverly	16	Sally	10	June	7
Nancy	32	Janet	16	Alice	9	Katherine	7
Jennifer	29	Julie	16	Anne	9	Marion	7
Sandra	29	Kimberly	16	Charlotte	9	Melissa	7
Carolyn	26	Janice	15	Dana	9	Peggy	7
Kathleen	26	Lori	15	Debbie	9	Sheila	7
Donna	22	Cynthia	13	Frances	9	Sherry	7
Jane	22	Gloria	13	Joyce	9	Terry	7
Margaret	22	Stephanie	13	Judy	9	Amanda	6
Deborah	21	Amy	12	Marcia	9	Anna	6
Sharon	21	Lynn	12	Sarah	9	Bonnie	6
Virginia	21	Phyllis	12	Anita	8	Cathy	6
Diane	20	Ruth	12	Diana	8	Claire	6
Dorothy	20	Brenda	11	Gail	8	Darlene	6
Elizabeth	19	Catherine	11	Heather	8	Eileen	6
Judith	19	Helen	11	Kathryn	8	Esther	6
Marilyn	19	Jill	11	Kathy	8	Georgia	6
Cheryl	18	Laura	11	Pam	8	Holly	6
Joan	18	Lois	11	Tamara	8	Joanne	6
Rebecca	18	Martha	11	Teresa	8	Kelly	6

Kim 6	Rhonda 5	Claudia 3	Rachel 3
Kristi 6	Roberta 5	Deanna 3	Robbie 3
Lee 6	Sue 5	Dianne 3	Sandy 3
Marie 6	Tiffany 5	Dolores 3	Tami 3
Marjorie 6	Toni 5	Edna 3	Teri 3
Michele 6	Victoria 5	Emily 3	Theresa 3
Rosemary 6	Andrea 4	Florence 3	Tina 3
Sara 6	Delores 4	Gina 3	Trisha 3
Tammy 6	Denise 4	Glenda 3	Trudy 3
Terri 6	Irene 4	Grace 3	Vanessa 3
Valerie 6	Kari 4	Gwen 3	Violet 3
Vicki 6	Kay 4	Heidi 3	Wanda 3
Wendy 6	Kristine 4	Jana 3	Annie 2
Annette 5	Leah 4	Janie 3	April 2
Audrey 5	Leslie 4	Joy 3	Arlene 2
Becky 5	Louise 4	Julia 3	Avis 2
Beth 5	Lynne 4	Kristen 3	Bernice 2
Charlene 5	Mildred 4	Kristin 3	Bette 2
Cindy 5	Miriam 4	Libby 3	Bettye 2
Colleen 5	Nicole 4	Lillian 3	Blanche 2
Evelyn 5	Norma 4	Lorene 3	Brooke 2
Jacqueline 5	Shannon 4	Lucia 3	Candy 2
Jacquelyn 5	Sheri 4	Lucille 3	Carla 2
Maria 5	Sherri 4	Lynda 3	Carlene 2
Marlene 5	Stacey 4	Margo 3	Carmen 2
Marsha 5	Stacy 4	Marguerite . . . 3	Caroline 2
Melanie 5	Vicky 4	Marian 3	Carrie 2
Monica 5	Alison 3	Molly 3	Cecelia 2
Patti 5	Amber 3	Muriel 3	Cherie 2
Penny 5	Betsy 3	Nanette 3	Christi 2
Polly 5	Bobbie 3	Patsy 3	Constance 2
Renee 5	Bobby 3	Priscilla 3	Crystal 2

Cyndi 2	Jodi 2	Robyn 2	Alisa 1
Daphne 2	Joleen 2	Rosalie 2	Allyn 1
Darla 2	Joni 2	Rowena 2	Anabel 1
Debby 2	Juanita 2	Sandi 2	Andra 1
Debbye 2	Juli 2	Shari 2	Angelina . . . 1
Desiree 2	Juliana 2	Shelly 2	Angi 1
Eleanor 2	Karissa 2	Sonja 2	Annabelle . . . 1
Elisa 2	Karol 2	Sonya 2	Annalee 1
Erica 2	Keri 2	Stacie 2	Annalou 1
Erin 2	Kitty 2	Suzan 2	Annice 1
Felicia 2	Kristie 2	Sylvia 2	Araminta . . . 1
Flora 2	Kristina 2	Tania 2	Ardyce 1
Frieda 2	Lauren 2	Tanya 2	Arian 1
Gale 2	Lila 2	Tara 2	Atlanta 1
Gayle 2	Lorna 2	Therese 2	Aubrey 1
Geraldine 2	Lorraine 2	Tia 2	Aura 1
Gerry 2	Lorrie 2	Tillie 2	Aurora 1
Gladys 2	Lynette 2	Tracy 2	Barrie 1
Gretchen 2	Lynnette 2	Tricia 2	BaShara 1
Gwendolyn . . . 2	Madeline 2	Vera 2	Bea 1
Hilda 2	Mae 2	Veronica 2	Beatrice 1
Ingrid 2	Maryalice . . . 2	Vivian 2	Bee 1
Jackie 2	Maureen 2	Yolanda 2	Bekki 1
Jamie 2	Maxine 2	Yvonne 2	Belinda 1
Jan 2	Megan 2	Ada 1	Berta 1
Jeanette 2	Myra 2	Adelyn 1	Betha 1
Jeanine 2	Natalie 2	Adria 1	Bethany 1
Jeannette 2	Natasha 2	Aimee 1	Bianca 1
Jeannie 2	Paige 2	Alansa 1	Billi 1
Jeannine 2	Penelope 2	Alberta 1	Billie 1
Jenny 2	Regina 2	Alecia 1	Billy 1
Joanna 2	Rita 2	Aline 1	Blythe 1

Bobbye 1	Chuti 1	Dixie 1	Francine 1
Brantlee 1	Cindi 1	Dolly 1	Freita 1
Britta 1	Clara 1	Dona 1	Gabriella 1
Brittny 1	Clare 1	Donese 1	Gayla 1
Bunnie 1	Claudette 1	Donna- 1	Gene 1
Burma 1	Cleo 1	Dora 1	Geneva 1
Callie 1	Cody 1	Dorcas 1	Genevieve 1
Camille 1	Coline 1	Dorie 1	Georganne ...1
Candace 1	Coni 1	Dottye 1	Georgiana ...1
Candice 1	Corinne 1	Drina 1	Georgietta ...1
Cara 1	Cornelia 1	Dulcie 1	Georgina 1
Carene 1	Courtney 1	Dusene 1	Georgine 1
Carin 1	Crystale 1	DuSharme 1	Geraldina 1
Carly 1	Cullen 1	E. 1	Gertrude 1
Carolee 1	Dakeita 1	Echo 1	GiGi 1
Carolie 1	Dalia 1	Edith 1	Gina-Lynne ...1
Ceil 1	Daly 1	Edye 1	Ginger 1
Celeste 1	D'Ann 1	Elana 1	Glenna 1
Celia 1	Darby 1	Eleanore 1	Glynnelle 1
Chardelle 1	Darcie 1	Elisabeth 1	Gordean 1
Charlavan 1	Darsi 1	Elise 1	Greta 1
Charlean 1	Daureen 1	Ella 1	Gunnel 1
Charlet 1	Dawne 1	Emilie 1	Gussie 1
Charmaine ...1	Dayna 1	Emma 1	Guylyn 1
Charmayne ...1	Debi 1	Erika 1	Gwenn 1
Cheri 1	Dell-Fin 1	Ethel 1	Harriet 1
Cherry 1	Dellynne 1	Eula 1	Haunani 1
Cheryl- 1	Delta 1	Fairfax 1	Hela 1
Cherylann 1	Dena 1	Ferol 1	Herma 1
Cheryle 1	Deneen 1	Florine 1	Honey 1
Chris 1	Dianna 1	Fran 1	Honora 1
Christina 1	Dione 1	Francesca 1	Idell 1

Ilona 1	Jonna 1	Keungsuk 1	Lenore 1
Ina 1	Josette 1	Kimberlee 1	Lesley 1
Ivy 1	Joylynn 1	Kimilee 1	Lesly 1
Jacque 1	Julianne 1	Kippy 1	Leslyn 1
Jacquie 1	Juliet 1	Kirsten 1	Letitia 1
Jaime 1	Kalyn 1	Kirstin 1	Lex 1
Jaleigh 1	Kamala 1	Krista 1	Lezlie 1
Jami 1	Kamara 1	Kristan 1	Ligaya 1
Janelle 1	Kandace 1	Kristl 1	Lilly 1
Janene 1	Kanoe 1	Kristy 1	Linette 1
Janette 1	Kara 1	Kylene 1	Linnea 1
Janis 1	Karin 1	Kym 1	Lita 1
Jayna 1	Karla 1	Lacy 1	Loi 1
Jayne 1	Karlyn 1	LaDonna 1	Lola 1
Jeana 1	Karlyne 1	Lael 1	Loni 1
Jeanie 1	Karmyn 1	LaFrance 1	Lora 1
Jenelle 1	Karri 1	Lana 1	Loretta 1
Jeni 1	Karrie 1	Laronda 1	Lorine 1
Jenna 1	Karyn 1	LaTanya 1	Louisa 1
Jennie 1	Katerina 1	Launa 1	Luana 1
Jere 1	Kathlyn 1	Laverda 1	Luanna 1
Jerri 1	Kathryne 1	Lavinia 1	Lucianne 1
Jessie 1	Katrina 1	LaVonne 1	LuLong 1
Jewel 1	Kayanne 1	Lea 1	Lyda 1
Jinx 1	Kaye 1	Leann 1	Lyndra 1
Joann 1	Kelli 1	LeAnna 1	Lyndsay 1
Jo-Anne 1	Kellye 1	Leanza 1	Lynnae 1
Jo-Carroll 1	Kelsey 1	Leesa 1	Mabel 1
Jody 1	Kendi 1	Leinaala 1	Maggie 1
Joey 1	Kendra 1	Lencola 1	Mai 1
Jone 1	Keone 1	Lenena 1	Majorie 1
Jonelle 1	Kerri 1	Lennie 1	Malia 1

Mara 1	Merrilee 1	Norine 1	Ruthellen 1
Marci 1	Meta 1	Northrup 1	Samantha 1
Mardi 1	Mia 1	Onalee 1	Saundra 1
Maree 1	Michaline 1	Pat 1	Scarlet 1
Margaretta . . .1	Mifaunwy 1	Pati 1	Seva 1
Margie 1	Mikka 1	Patience 1	Shan 1
Marianne 1	Mindee 1	Patrice 1	Shani 1
Marisol 1	Mineola 1	Pattie 1	Sharen 1
Marissa 1	Mirian 1	Patty 1	Sharlene 1
Marjean 1	Miss 1	Patty-Jo 1	Sharron 1
Marla 1	Misty 1	Pennisue 1	Shawna 1
Marlena 1	Mitzi 1	Phoebe 1	Shawntel 1
Marlesa 1	Mitzie 1	Ra 1	Shea 1
Marlinda 1	Moira 1	Rachael 1	Shelby 1
Marlise 1	Mollie 1	Rae 1	Sheliah 1
Marlyse 1	Mona 1	Raye 1	Shellene 1
Marquessa 1	Monnie 1	Reba 1	Shelley 1
Marti 1	Monta 1	ReJean 1	Sher 1
Marvene 1	Myrna 1	Rena 1	Sheron 1
MaryAnn 1	Myrrah 1	Rickee 1	Sheryl 1
Mary-Ann 1	Myrtice 1	Robbin 1	Shireen 1
MaryGrace . . .1	Najla 1	Rochelle 1	Simone 1
Maryline 1	Nancee 1	Ronda 1	Soncee 1
Matilda 1	Nanci 1	Ronnee 1	Sophia 1
Maurine 1	Naylene 1	Ronnetta 1	SoYoung 1
May 1	Nell 1	Rosa 1	Stephany 1
Maya 1	Nelle 1	Rosanna 1	Stuart 1
Melanne 1	Nettie 1	Rose 1	Suellen 1
Melinda 1	Nicci 1	Roseann 1	Susanne 1
Melody 1	Nickey 1	RoseAnna 1	Susie 1
Melonie 1	Nona 1	Roselyn 1	Suzette 1
Meredith 1	Noralyn 1	Ruby 1	Sydney 1

Talia 1	Tori-Lynn 1	Van 1	Wando 1
Tamra 1	Tosca 1	Vanadora 1	Wayring 1
Tana 1	Traci 1	Vanita 1	Wendi 1
Tawny 1	Trelynda 1	Vannessa 1	Wilda 1
Terrilynn 1	Trina 1	Velva 1	Willock 1
Timmy 1	Trish 1	Verona 1	Wren 1
Titilayo 1	Trudi 1	Viola 1	Ysleta 1
Tommy 1	Trudie 1	Vivienne 1	Yun 1
Tommye 1	Valorie 1	Vonda 1	Zoe 1
Tonya 1			

Richest In America

Some of these names are spouses and children of a founder or president and may not have been the primary wealth builder, but possibly were involved or a supporting factor in wealth building. Wealth building, although it needs a point person of great ability, also requires great team support. There are 24 "Juniors" and two "3rds". The first column is the total number of the those reported in the Forbes 400 Richest people in America who did not inherit their wealth record by first name. The third column is a value adjusted for the relative frequency of the first name within America. An adjusted value of "X" indicates that this name is so uncommon that there was no frequency number with which to adjust, thereby causing "X" to approach infinity, which is meaningless. The number of names included in the Forbes 400 list may be such a relatively small number compared to the general population that any comparison may be meaningless.

Total	First Name	Adjusted	Total	First Name	Adjusted
22	John Jon Jean	6.4	3	Alfred	18.5
15	Robert Roberto	4.6	3	Bruce	11.4
13	William	5.3	3	Carl	8.7
12	Michael Michel Micky Mitchell	4.4	3	Ernest	14.0
11	Richard	6.5	3	Frank Franklin	4.6
9	James Jim	2.6	3	Gary	4.6
8	Charles	5.3	3	Lawrence Laurence	3.2
7	George	7.6	3	Leonard	16.1
7	Steven Stephen	4.4	3	Leslie(m)	37.0
6	Donald	6.4	3	Ronald Ronnie	3.6
5	David	2.1	3	Walter	7.5
5	Edward	6.4	2	Alan	9.8
5	Harold Harry	8.0	2	Arthur	3.0
5	Henry	13.7	2	Craig	9.7
5	Samuel	3.3	2	Edmund	66.6
4	Frederick Fred	9.9	2	Forrest	285.7
4	Kenneth Kenny	42.5	2	Jack	6.3
4	Thomas	2.9	2	Jay	16.9

Total	First Name	Adjusted	Total	First Name	Adjusted
2	Joseph	1.4	1	Bradley	6.3
2	Keith	6.5	1	Christopher	1.0
2	Leon	17.9	1	Clayton	16.7
2	Lewis Louis	5.8	1	Clemmie	100.0
2	Mark Marc	2.0	1	Curtis	5.6
2	Marvin	11.7	1	Daniel	1.0
2	Mary	0.8	1	Dean	9.6
2	Monroe	250.0	1	Dennis	2.4
2	Norman	11.3	1	Dirk	125.0
2	Patrick Patrizio	5.1	1	Doris	3.0
2	Paul	2.1	1	Dwight	17.2
2	Peter Pierce	7.8	1	Edgar	12.5
2	Philip	4.6	1	Eli	62.5
2	Ray Raymond	3.1	1	Fayez	X
2	Sidney Sid	17.9	1	Floyd	9.3
2	Stanley	5.4	1	Glen	10.6
2	Stewart Stuart	30.3	1	Gordon	9.6
2	Theodore	16.3	1	Grover	62.5
1	Abigail	18.9	1	Guilford	X
1	Albert	3.2	1	Harris	111.1
1	Alexander	7.6	1	Helen	2.4
1	Amar	X	1	Herbert	6.5
1	Amos	50.0	1	Jackson	83.3
1	Andrew	1.9	1	Jerome	9.3
1	Anne	0.8	1	Jesse	4.8
1	Archie	30.3	1	Joyce	3.7
1	Aubrey	52.6	1	Julian	19.2
1	Bernard	7.9	1	Kathryn	2.9
1	Billy	4.0	1	Kirk	20.4
1	Blase	X	1	Lee	6.2

Total	First Name	Adjusted	Total	First Name	Adjusted
1	Leona	12.3	1	Preston	29.4
1	Lester	11.0	1	Ralph	3.5
1	Lowell	236.1	1	Rex	27.0
1	Lowry	X	1	Riley	100.0
1	Margaret	1.2	1	Roger	3.1
1	Marshall	20.4	1	Roy	3.7
1	Maurice	10.3	1	Rupert	200.0
1	Max	16.9	1	Sanford	111.1
1	Melvin	6.2	1	Sanjiv	X
1	Nancy	1.5	1	Sheldon	43.5
1	Nelson	16.4	1	Summerfield	X
1	Oakleigh	X	1	Sumner	X
1	Ollen	91.0	1	Sydell	X
1	Oprah	X	1	Virginia	2.3
1	Pauline	2.3	1	Warren	9.1
1	Perry	20.4	1	Wendell	23.8
1	Pincus	X			

Most Popular Names In America

The One Hundred Most Common Female Names In America

1	MARY	26	JESSICA	51	ALICE	76	IRENE
2	PATRICIA	27	SHIRLEY	52	JULIE	77	JANE
3	LINDA	28	CYNTHIA	53	HEATHER	78	LORI
4	BARBARA	29	ANGELA	54	TERESA	79	RACHEL
5	ELIZABETH	30	MELISSA	55	DORIS	80	MARILYN
6	JENNIFER	31	BRENDA	56	GLORIA	81	ANDREA
7	MARIA	32	AMY	57	EVELYN	82	KATHRYN
8	SUSAN	33	ANNA	58	JEAN	83	LOUISE
9	MARGARET	34	REBECCA	59	CHERYL	84	SARA
10	DOROTHY	35	VIRGINIA	60	MILDRED	85	ANNE
11	LISA	36	KATHLEEN	61	KATHERINE	86	JACQUELINE
12	NANCY	37	PAMELA	62	JOAN	87	WANDA
13	KAREN	38	MARTHA	63	ASHLEY	88	BONNIE
14	BETTY	39	DEBRA	64	JUDITH	89	JULIA
15	HELEN	40	AMANDA	65	ROSE	90	RUBY
16	SANDRA	41	STEPHANIE	66	JANICE	91	LOIS
17	DONNA	42	CAROLYN	67	KELLY	92	TINA
18	CAROL	43	CHRISTINE	68	NICOLE	93	PHYLLIS
19	RUTH	44	MARIE	69	JUDY	94	NORMA
20	SHARON	45	JANET	70	CHRISTINA	95	PAULA
21	MICHELLE	46	CATHERINE	71	KATHY	96	DIANA
22	LAURA	47	FRANCES	72	THERESA	97	ANNIE
23	SARAH	48	ANN	73	BEVERLY	98	LILLIAN
24	KIMBERLY	49	JOYCE	74	DENISE	99	EMILY
25	DEBORAH	50	DIANE	75	TAMMY	100	ROBIN

The 100 Most Common Male Names In America

1	JAMES	26	GARY	51	JOE	76	JEREMY
2	JOHN	27	TIMOTHY	52	JUAN	77	AARON
3	ROBERT	28	JOSE	53	JACK	78	RANDY
4	MICHAEL	29	LARRY	54	ALBERT	79	HOWARD
5	WILLIAM	30	JEFFREY	55	JONATHAN	80	EUGENE
6	DAVID	31	FRANK	56	JUSTIN	81	CARLOS
7	RICHARD	32	SCOTT	57	TERRY	82	RUSSELL
8	CHARLES	33	ERIC	58	GERALD	83	BOBBY
9	JOSEPH	34	STEPHEN	59	KEITH	84	VICTOR
10	THOMAS	35	ANDREW	60	SAMUEL	85	MARTIN
11	CHRISTOPHER	36	RAYMOND	61	WILLIE	86	ERNEST
12	DANIEL	37	GREGORY	62	RALPH	87	PHILLIP
13	PAUL	38	JOSHUA	63	LAWRENCE	88	TODD
14	MARK	39	JERRY	64	NICHOLAS	89	JESSE
15	DONALD	40	DENNIS	65	ROY	90	CRAIG
16	GEORGE	41	WALTER	66	BENJAMIN	91	ALAN
17	KENNETH	42	PATRICK	67	BRUCE	92	SHAWN
18	STEVEN	43	PETER	68	BRANDON	93	CLARENCE
19	EDWARD	44	HAROLD	69	ADAM	94	SEAN
20	BRIAN	45	DOUGLAS	70	HARRY	95	PHILIP
21	RONALD	46	HENRY	71	FRED	96	CHRIS
22	ANTHONY	47	CARL	72	WAYNE	97	JOHNNY
23	KEVIN	48	ARTHUR	73	BILLY	98	EARL
24	JASON	49	RYAN	74	STEVE	99	JIMMY
25	MATTHEW	50	ROGER	75	LOUIS	100	ANTONIO

The Most Frequently Used Given Names For Births In 1999

Rank	Male	Female	Rank	Male	Female
1	Michael	Emily	26	Robert	Anna
2	Jacob	Samantha	27	Jose	Morgan
3	Matthew	Madison	28	Kyle	Stephanie
4	Christopher	Ashley	29	Kevin	Julia
5	Joshua	Sarah	30	Samuel	Rebecca
6	Austin	Hannah	31	Christian	Brittany
7	Nicholas	Jessica	32	Benjamin	Grace
8	Tyler	Alyssa	33	Thomas	Haley
9	Joseph	Alexis	34	Hunter	Danielle
10	Andrew	Kayla	35	Ethan	Destiny
11	Daniel	Abigail	36	Cameron	Natalie
12	Ryan	Taylor	37	Nathan	Jennifer
13	Brandon	Elizabeth	38	Aaron	Alexandra
14	Anthony	Olivia	39	Caleb	Amber
15	David	Brianna	40	Cody	Hailey
16	William	Victoria	41	Steven	Katherine
17	John	Emma	42	Eric	Kaitlyn
18	Zachary	Megan	43	Luis	Maria
19	Dylan	Rachel	44	Timothy	Katelyn
20	James	Amanda	45	Jason	Mary
21	Alexander	Courtney	46	Adam	Shelby
22	Justin	Nicole	47	Charles	Andrea
23	Jonathan	Lauren	48	Isaac	Sierra
24	Jordan	Jasmine	49	Brian	Vanessa
25	Noah	Sydney	50	Jesus	Savannah

Rank	Male	Female	Rank	Male	Female
51	Richard	Allison	77	Ian	Alexa
52	Sean	Erin	78	Jake	Jacqueline
53	Gabriel	Gabrielle	79	Nathaniel	Jade
54	Bryan	Kimberly	80	Garrett	Bailey
55	Jack	Sara	81	Lucas	Briana
56	Jared	Chloe	82	Victor	Caroline
57	Juan	Michelle	83	Stephen	Katie
58	Alex	Sophia	84	Trevor	Kylie
59	Connor	Breanna	85	Bradley	Mariah
60	Devin	Brooke	86	Brett	Riley
61	Isaiah	Kathryn	87	Bryce	Angela
62	Antonio	Makayla	88	Jackson	Kiara
63	Carlos	Jordan	89	Adrian	Mikayla
64	Elijah	Kaylee	90	Brendan	Cassidy
65	Logan	Mackenzie	91	Evan	Erica
66	Patrick	Madeline	92	Gavin	Veronica
67	Mark	Melissa	93	Paul	Autumn
68	Jesse	Christina	94	Tanner	Cassandra
69	Chase	Marissa	95	Tristan	Diana
70	Cole	Paige	96	Dalton	Gabriella
71	Luke	Sabrina	97	Devon	Jenna
72	Seth	Alexandria	98	Kenneth	Michaela
73	Angel	Kelsey	99	Spencer	Alicia
74	Dakota	Laura	100	Xavier	Faith
75	Jeremy	Miranda	101	Colton	Kelly
76	Alejandro	Molly			

Female Names

WARNING: It is very important to read the first chapters of this book. Failure to heed the first chapters may cause serious detrimental consequences in your hopes and dreams for the person who's name you intend to choose!

Aaliyah.

Abbey // Abby. *Familiar forms of* Abigail.

Abigail // Abagail, Abbey, Abby, Abigael, Abigale, Gail, Gale. *Hebrew:* "source of joy". Capable, able, caring. *Abigail Van Buren*, famous etiquette writer. ***Abigail Adams***, (1744-1818), U.S. writer, wife of President John Adams, and mother of President John Quincy Adams, strong proponent of women's rights, well-educated without formal schooling, she wrote many letters that created a vivid portrait of the times, strongly supported American independence, vehemently antislavery.

Adah // Ada, Adan, Adda, Addi, Addia, Addie, Addy, Adey, Adi, Aida, Aide, Aidee, Eada. *Hebrew:* "pretty, ornament"; *Old English:* "prosperous, happy". *Short form of* Adelaide. Biblical: first wife of Lemech. Implusive, stubborn, fearless, achieves her goals through her hard work, popular with guys, usually poor relationship with mother, marriage often unsuccessful, lawyers, musicians, hair-dressers, coaches, accountants. *Adah Menken*, (1835-68), U.S. actress, began career as ballet dancer. *Ada*

Rehan, (1860-1916), U.S. actress, leading lady, also high comedy and farce.

Adela // Adele. *Germanic:* "noble".

Adelaide // Addi, Addie, Addy, Adel, Adela, Adelaida, Adele, Adelheid, Adeline, Adelle, Adilene, Aline, Del, Della, Delly, Edeline, Heidi. *Germanic:* "nobility, kind". *Adelaide Crapsey*, (1878-1914), U.S. poet, poems have delicacy and subtle charm. *Adelaide Procter*, (1825-64), British poet, early advocate of women's rights. *Adelaide Ristori*, (1822-1906), Italian tragic actress, greatest of her generation. *Adele Astaire*, (1898-1981), U.S. dancer and actress, sister of Fred Astaire, his co-star in musical comedies.

Adilene. *Form of* Adelaide.

Adora // Adoree, Dora, Dori, Dorie, Dory. *Latin:* "beloved".

Adriana // Adrianna. *Form of* Adrienne. Adrienne, Adrea, Adrian, Adriana, Adriane, Adrianna, Adriena. *Latin:* "dark, rich". *Feminine form of* Adrian. Adrienne Lecouvreur, (1692-1730), popular French actress whose extraordinary beauty and charm became legendary.

Agatha // Ag, Agace, Agata, Agathe, Aggi, Aggie, Aggy. *Greek:* "good, kind". *Agatha Christie*, (1890-1976), famous mystery writer, volunteer nurse during WW I, created characters Hercule Poirot and Miss Jane Marple.

Agnes // Ag, Aggi, Aggie, Agna, Agnella, Agnese, Agnessa, Agnesse, Agneta, Agnola, Aigneis, Ina, Ines, Inessa, Inez, Nessa, Nessi, Nessie, Nessy; Nesta. *Greek:* "pure". possibly a writer or social activist. Not shy, like to perform before others, good student, like sports but little achievment, leader among pears, honest, principled, just, argumentative to prove point. Pragmatic, careful chooser, thinks before acts, often exemplory pupal, looks like mother, home body, likes symphony, likes reading. *Agnes de Mille*, (born 1905), ballerina, dancer-choreographer, played gauche cowgirl. *Agnes Royden*, (1876-1956), British social worker and preacher, author, part founder of Fellowship Services, first woman in United Kingdom to occupy pulpit of regular place of worship. *Agnes Sorel*, (1422?-50), remembered chiefly for beauty and charm. *Agnes Baden-Powell*, (1858-1945), British founder of Girl Guides. *Agnes Christina Laut*, (1871-1936), Canadian author, authoritative historical books on early explorers and pioneer life in the Northwest. *Agnes Macphail*, (1890-1954), first woman member of Canadian Parliament, influential worker for disarmament and world peace. *Agnes Strickland*, (1796-1874), English historical writer. *Agnes Hewes*, U.S. author of children's books with historical setting.

Aida // Aide, Aidee. *Forms of* Adah.

Aileen // Aila, Ailea, Ailee, Ailene, Ailey, Alene, Ailey, Aili, Eileen, Eleen, Elene, Ileana, Ileane, Ilene, Lena, Lina. *Gaelic:* "lightbearer". *Irish form of Helen.* possibly a writer or social activist; *Aileen Fisher*, (born 1906),

U.S. poet and author of children's books.

Aimee // Aime, Aimi, Aimme, Aimmy, Aimy. *French form* of Amy.

Aisha // Aesha, Aisa, Aisah, Aisel, Aishah, Aishia, Aishwarya, Aisiah, Aisleem, Aiszellyn, Ayesha, Iesha. Aishwarya Rai - Actress.

Aja // Ajae, Ajaee, Ajaleek, Ajane, Ajanee, Ajarae, Ajee, Ajeekaloni, Ajeenea, Ajeeta, Ajia, Ajone, Ajouraye, Ajunye.

Akiko.

Akira.

Alanna // Alahnah, Alaila, Alain, Alaina, Alaine, Alana, Alanah, Alane, Alani, Alanis, Alanna, Alannah, Alanni, Alanya, Alayda, Alayna, Alaysia, Alsayzia, Alazia, Alayne, Alleen, Allene, Allina, Allyn, Lana, Lanna. *Gaelic:* "fair, beautiful". *Feminine form of* Alan. Also see Helen. *Alanis Morissette* - Actress.

Alba // Albina, Alby. Latin: "white". *Feminine form of* Albine. Principled, stubborn, bit arrogent, usually good marriage, follows the interests of husband if he is attentive to her, good hostess, good cook, jealous of women around her husband, chooses her occupation first by her interest, prestiege and pay secondary, resembles father.

Alberta // Albertina, Albertine, Ali, Alli, Allie, Ally, Alverta, Auberta, Aubine, Bert, Berta, Berte, Berti, Bertie, Berty, Elberta, Elbertina, Elbertine. *Old English:* "noble, brilliant". *Feminine form of* Albert. *Alberta Watson* - Actress.

Alexandra // Alec, Aleck, Alecxa, Alecxia, Alecxis, Alejandra, Alejandrina, Alessandra, Alex, Alexa, Alexandrea, Alexandria, Alexandrina, Alexi, Alexia, Alexie, Alexina, Alexine, Alexis, Alexsandra, Alexsis, Alexus, Ali, Alix, Alla, Alli, Allie, Allix, Ally, Cesya, Lexi, Lexie, Lexine, Lexy, Sande, Sandi, Sandie, Sandra, Sandy, Sandye, Sondra, Zandra. *Greek:* "helper and defender of mankind". *Feminine form of* Alexander. Likes sports, camping, traveling, likes to watch sports such as soccer, hockey and football, strict mother, pretty, often quite lovely, reserved, nice, competent, social, one or two close friends, thin, decisive. *Queen Alexandra of England*. *Alexandra Feodorovna*, empress of Russia, wife of Czar Nicholas II. *Alexandra Danilova*, (born 1904), U.S. ballerina.

Alexis // Alexi, Alexia. *Forms of* Alexandra.

Alfreda // Alfi, Alfie, Alfy, Elfie, Elfreda, Elva, Freda, Freddie, Freddy, Frieda. *Old English:* "wise and diplomatic counselor". *Feminine form of* Alfred. *Frieda Hempel*, (1885-1955), U.S. coloratura soprano. *Alfre Woodard* - Actress.

Ali. *Short form of* Alexandra, Alice or Alyssa. Actresses: Ali Sheedy, Ally Walker.

Alice // Alecia, Aleece, Ali, Alica, Alicea, Alicia, Alisa, Alisha, Alison, Alissa, Alla, Alli, Allie, Allison, Allyce, Alyce, Alysia, Alyss, Alyssa, Elissa, Iesha, Ilysa, Ilyssa, Lissa, Lyssa. *Greek:* "truth"; *Old German:* "noble". Also see Alyssa. Helpful, honest, conscientious, diligent student, not pushy, a bit reserved, somewhat sporty. *Alice Cary*, (1820-71), U.S. poem writer. *Alice Munro*, (born 1931), multi-award winning Canadian author, known for her intense narrative style and imagery. *Alice Marble*, (1913-90), U.S. tennis champion, aggressive serve-and-volley style. *Alice B. Toklas*, (1877-1967), secretary, author and companion to Gertrude Stein. *Alice Walker*, (born 1944), U.S. writer and feminist, 'The Color Purple'. *Alice Birney*, (1858-1907), U.S. cofounder of National Congress of Mothers. *Alice Rice*, (1870-1942), U.S. novelist. *Alice Hamilton*, (1869-1970), U.S. physician, author, medical teacher, research and warnings on industrial diseases led to workmen's compensation laws. *Alice Meynell*, (1847-1922), British poet and essayist. *Alice Paul*, (1885-1977), U.S. woman suffragist, imprisoned six times for activities. *Alice Dalgliesh*, (1893-1979), U.S. author and editor of children's books. *Alice Palmer*, (1855-1902), U.S. educator, president Wellesley College. *Alice Barrett* - Actress.

Alicia // Alisa, Alise, Alisha, Alissa, Aliza, Alize, Iesha. *Forms of* Alice and Alyssa. *Alicia Markova*, (born 1910), (born Lilian Alicia Marks) ballerina and dance teacher noted for the lightness and delicacy of her dancing. *Alicia Silverstone*, *Alicia Witt* - Actresses.

Alina // Aleen, Alena, Alene, Aline, Allene, Lina. *Latin:* "foreign, different"; *Slavic:* "bright, beautiful". Good learner, likes historical, stuborn, not patient, going from one extream to another, opinionated, moody, sharp retorts, dresses nice, good taste, follows fashions, general talents, teaching as an occupation contradicts her character, brags, self confident.

Allison // Ali, Alie, Alisen, Alisha, Alison, Alissa, Alli, Allie, Allyson, Alyson, Alyssa, Lissi, Lissie, Lissy. *Gaelic:* "little, truthful"; *Old German:* "famous among the gods".

Form of Alice. Truthful, forthright, good learner, may be near the top of her class or group or may not try very hard, prefers to share leadership/group effort, pretty good at the things she does such as sports, music and school, writer. *Alison Elliott* - Actress.

Alma. *Arabic:* "learned"; *Latin:* "nourishing, cherishing". *Alma Gluck*, (1884-1938), U.S. dramatic soprano.

Alondra // Alora.

Alyssa // Alicia, Alisa, Alise, Alisha, Alissa, Aliyah, Aliza, Alize, Allissa, Alliyah, Alycia, Alysa, Alyse, Alysha, Alyshia, Alysia, Ilyssa, Lyssa. Accommodating, pragmatic, very neat, frugal, takes care of her possessions, squeamish, puts a lot of effort into her marriage, doctors, architects, artists, journalists. *Alyssa Milano* - Actresses.

Amairani // Amairany.

Amanda // Amandi, Amandie, Amandy, Manda, Mandi, Mandie, Mandy. *Latin:* "worthy of love". co-leader, follower, athletic, capable. *Amanda Plummer* - Actress.

Amaris // Amara, Ameera, Ameerah, Amereah, Amerra, Amira, Amirah, Ammarah. *Greek:* "of eternal beauty". Peaceful.

Amber // Ambar, Ambur, Ambyr. *Old French:* "amber". Sporty, cute, short to medium build, energetic, self-confident, accepting of others, seldom fat, intelligent, logical, good dresser. *Amber Smith* - Supermodel.

Amelia // Amalea, Amalia. *Old German:* "hardworking". *Feminine form of* Amal. Also form of Emily. America. *Latin:* "rich eternal beauty". Currently used to honor or refer to America or the United States of America.

Amina // Aminah, Aminata, Aminta.

Amy // Aimee, Ame, Amee, Ami, Amie, Amii. *Lain:* "beloved". Physically attractive, cute, semi-energetic, generally calm, occasionally excitable, likes everyone, everyone naturally likes her, easy to talk to, very capable leader, organizer, worker, good nature, tries to please others and usually succeeds, however, when unable to please the one she's set to please (i.e. Teacher or boss) she's depressed, nice to have around. *Amy Lowell*, poet and critic. *Amy Sherwin*, singer. *Amy Alcott*, golfer. *Amy Jo Johnson*, *Amy Pietz*, *Amy Weber*, *Amy Yasbeck* - Actresses.

Ana. *Form of* Ann. Popular name to combine with other names, eg. Anamaria, Anakarina.

Anahi // Anahe, Anahid, Anahis, Anahit, Anahiz, Anahy, Anai. Anais, Anai.

Anastasia // Ana, Anastasie, Anastassia, Anestassia, Anstice, Asia, Stace, Stacey, Stacie, Stacy, Tasia. *Greek:* "the Resurrection, springtime". *Feminine form of* Anastas. Trustable, tender personality, can be good actress, kindergarten teacher, gets married early, prefers strong-masculine often military man, compassionate, swayed by others opinions, faithful and caring wife, loyal non-flirting personality, good mother, good relationship with in-laws, works to make friend of enemies, likes to give unique gifts, anticipates every day as joyous, likes life.

Andrea // Andee, Andi, Andie, Andreina, Andria, Andy, Aundrea, Ondrea. *Latin:* "womanly". *Feminine form of*

Andrew. Average student, good person, likes to show excitement in anticipation, bouncy personality, hopeful,

Andie McDowell - actress.

Angela // Ange, Angel, Angelica, Angelika, Angelina, Angeline, Angelique, Angelita, Angella, Angelle, Angie, Angil, Anjelica. *Greek:* "angel, messenger". No "angel", but tries to do her best, hard physical worker, but often a so-so student earlier in life (often from lack of interested), irritable, stubborn, strong, knows how to reach her goals, likes to give orders to her peers, ignores suggestions, follows her own leanings, doesn't rely on others, doesn't rely on her beauty, more concerned with her intellegence and professionalism, likes to hostess more than guest, distant with guys except for her ideal. *Angela Davis*, (born 1944), U.S. black-militant philosophy professor, Black Panther, and Communist. *Angelica Kauffmann*, (1741-1807), Swiss portrait painter, graceful but poorly drawn pictures. *Angela Bassett*, *Angela Lansberry*, *Angelina Jolie* - Actresses.

Angelica. *Familiar form of* Angela.

Angie. *Familiar form of* Angela. *Angie Dickinson* - Actress. *Angie Everhart* - Supermodel.

Anita. *Spainish form of* Ann. Shrewd, capable, leader by nature and expects people to follow her leadership, looses her temper on poor followers, independent, can handle difficult situations, far from shy, participates in sports but not a star athlete, some are musically talented, chooses calm agreeable husband. *Anita Mui*, *Anita Yuen* - Actresses.

Ann // Ana, Anette, Anita, Anna, Annetta, Annette, Annie, Anny, Anya, Hanna, Hannah, Nancy. *English form of* Hannah. *Hebrew:* "graceful, blessing". Popular in combination names, eg. Annalisa. More energetic, gentle, kind, fairly serious; inquisitive; strong, wise; self-secure; ask good questions; analytical; friendly nice; judge through logic; good decision maker; diplomatic, excellent personnel manager or business leader; leader; honest and forthright with feelings; not particularly-athletic, artistic, likes everything beautiful, seemingly unending kindness, giving, no enemies, does not live a selfish life but also cares for other's needs, others sometimes take advantage of her but she is not offended, takes care of her appearance, not obsessed with fashion, dresses fairly nicely, styles her hair, good worker, money is not her motivation for good work, faithful-patient spouse, may choose disfunctional man and willingly stay attached baring her cross, infidelity of her spouse is very tramatic. *Anne Boleyn*, (also called Anne of the Thousand Days) (1507-36), 2nd queen of Henry VIII of England. *Anne Frank* - famous for her diary. *Queen Anne of England*. *Ann Reinking*, *Anna Magnani*, *Anna Nicole Smith*, *Anne Bancroft*, *Anne Baxter*, *Anne Heche*, *Anne Parillaud*, *Ann-Margret* - Actresses.

Annette. *Familiar form of* Ann. *Annette Strauss*, (born 1924), public relations consultant and fund-raiser, elected mayor of Dallas.

Antoinette // Antonette. Antonia, Netta, Netty, Toni, Tonia. *Latin:* "priceless". *Feminine form of* Anthony. Kind as a wise way to recieve kindness, acts mature as child often with strong emulation of her teacher and mother, may supervise her peers as kindergartener, mother's little

Chapter 7 — Female Names

helper, responsicble child, good worker, bit despotic boss, in marriage - all her efforts directed toward well being and happiness of her family, good money-manager, kind, helpful, she has lots of friends. A*ntoinette Blackwell*, (1825-1921), U.S. minister, first woman Unitarian minister, lectured on abolition, temperance, and women's rights. *Antonia Novello*, (born 1944), Puerto Rican physician, in 1990 became first woman named surgeon general of U.S., taught pediatrics.

April // Avril. *Latin:* "opening". Kind, nice, pretty; mellow to perky, lacking self-confidence, greatly looks for approval of others (can cause obvious problem when courting), follower, not interested in sports (i.e. weak at hand-eye games); low drive for business success, hoping for rescuer/male/husband, easily dominated, very submissive, loyal, imprudent, compulsive in relation-ships.

Araceli // Aracely, Araseli, Arcelia, Areli, Arely.

Aretha // Retha, Rita. *Greek:* "best". *Aretha Franklin*, (born 1942), famous U.S. pop singer, career as pop, soul, and gospel singer.

Arianna // Arianne. *Italian.*

Ariel // Ariela, Ariella, Arielle. *Hebrew:* "lioness of God". Disney's Little Mermaid was named Ariel.

Arlene // Arlana, Arleen, Arleene, Arlen, Arlena, Arlenne, Arlette, Arlin, Arlyn, Lena, Lina. *Gaelic:* "pledge". *Feminine form of* Arlen.

Asah // Asa, Asha, Aza. Impulsive, stubborn, sassy disobedience to parents and teachers, prefer to make

friends with guys over girls, bold, daring, won't subjugate herself, personality of mother but poor relationship, resemble father, usually marry twice, usually have daughters, good hostess, leader in the family, doctor, accountant, coach, engineer, hair-dresser, guide, wait-ress.

Ashley // Ashely, Ashlee, Ashleigh, Ashlie, Ashly, Ashlyn, Ashlynn, Ashton, Ashtyn. *Old English:* "ash tree meadow". *Laura Ashley*, (1925-85), Successful English fashion designer. Supermodel: *Ashley Richardson*. *Ashley Olsen* and *Ashley Peldon* - Actresses

Asia. *English:* "Asian". *Form of* Anastasia.

Astrid // Astra, Astrie. *Scandinavian:* "as beautiful as a god".

Athena // Athene. *Greek:* "wisdom". Mythological war goddess of wisdom and crafts.

Audrey, Audi, Audie, Audrie, Audry. *Old English:* "noble strength". Noble strength. *Audrey Hepburn* , popular US actress. *Audrey McLaughlin*, (born 1936), first woman in Canada to lead a major political party.

Aubrey // Aubree, Aubrie, Aubry. *Old French:* "blond ruler, elf ruler".

Audrey // Audra, Audre, Audree, Audrie, Audrina, Audrine, Audry, Audrye. *Old English:* "noble strength". *Audrey McLaughlin*, (born 1936), first woman in Canada to lead a major political party, elected 1989 as leader of the socialist New Democratic Party. *Audrey May Wurdemann*, (1911-60), U.S. poet, poems marked by skilled craftsmanship. *Audrey Hepburn*, (born 1929), celebrated

62   *Name Your Baby's Destiny*

U.S. actress, U.S. motion pictures 'Roman Holiday', 'Breakfast at Tiffany's', 'My Fair Lady'.

Aurora // Aura, Aurea, Aureal, Aurel, Aurelia, Aurore, Aury, Ora, Oralee, Oralia, Oralie, Orel, Orelee, Orelia, Orelie. *Latin:* "golden". *Latin:* "dawn". Mythological goddess of the dawn. *English:* "display of colored light in the night sky of high latitudes". Princess in Disney's Sleeping Beauty. Perceviering, stubborn, resemble father with character of mother, finish what they start, not ordinary thinker or dresser.

Auxanna // Ocsanna, Ocxanna, Oczanna, Oxanna, Oxzanna. *Ukrainian form of* Ksenia. Possibly from *Greek:* Kasenia, "hospitality" or Ksenos, "foreign". Beautiful, frugal, aware shopper, determined, set in her ways, jealous, faithful, withdraws when jealous; not easy but interesting lives, often seem gloomy and stubborn as child, independent, persistent in fulfilling her wishes, if you block her goal, she can become hysterical; loud games don't attract her, she prefers games requiring more concentration; usually good student, but without enthusiasm; prefers friendships with other females, doesn't share her secrets even with her best friend; not a sober judge of herself, often blames others or bad luck for her failures; calculating, economizing, patient, stays unpredictable, impulsive and stubborn about it, loyal love, tries to change her husband's behavior, but stops when rebuffed, tries to live independent from in-laws.

Ava // Avalon. *Latin:* "birdlike". *Ave Gardner.* - Actress

Ayana // Aya, Ayanna, Ayla. Supermodel: *Aya Thorgren.*

Azalea // Azalia, Azalie. *English:* fragrant deciduous flower shrub.

Azucena // Azusena, Azuzena.

Bailey // Bailee, Baylee, Bayley, Baylie, Bayla. *Old English:* "meadow by the bay".

Barbara // Barb, Barbi, Barbie, Barbra. *Greek:* "foreign". Beautiful, intelligent, creative, energetic, scholarly, if she pursues college, she'll go far academically, may become doctor or lawyer or office manager, often ignores college to marry and have children while young but likely pursues some education later, not athletic. *Barbara Eden*, B*arbara Stanwyck*, *Barbara Streisand*, *Barbi Benton* - Actresses.

Bathsheba // Bathsheva. *Hebrew:* "daughter of the oath, seventh daughter". Biblical: one of the wives of the wives of King David.

Beatrice // Bea, Beata, Beatris, Beatrisa, Beatrix, Beatriz, Bebe, Bee, Beitris, Trix, Trixi, Trixie, Trixy. *Latin:* "she that makes happy, one who blesses, bringer of joy". Contradictory nature, creative but infantile, very attractive, success with men, knows how to entice men, soft as a kitten -beware of the claws, jealous, may divorce and be flirtative. *Beatrice Webb*, (1858-1943), half of a husband-and-wife team of socialist economists who profoundly influenced English radical thought. *Beatrice Harraden*, (1864-1936), British novelist. *Beatrice Lillie*, (Lady Peel) (1898-1989), actress, best known as a comedienne, autobiography 'Every Other Inch a Lady'. *Beata Pozniak*, *Bebe Neuwirth* - Actresses.

Becky // Becca. Form and type of Rebecca but a bit more athletic. See Rebecca.

Belinda // Bel, Belle, Linda, Lindie, Lindy. *Spanish:* "beautiful".

Belle // Bella. *Latin*: "beautiful". Belle, the heroine of Disney's Beauty and the Beast. Principled and logical, but still can be impusive, talkative and easy-going, easily gets aquanted with people, not much of a home-maker, likes to sleep late, cooks only when neccisary, sensitive and emotional, slow to pick husband, first marriage doesn't last long, not patient, business-woman, can be very succesful. *Belle Boyd*, (1844-1900), U.S. Confederate spy.

Bernadine // Bernadette, Berna, Berni, Bernie, Berny. *French*: "brave as a bear". *Feminine form of* Bernard. Cheerful, friendly, helpful, somewhat reserved. *Bernadette Peters* - Actress.

Bernice // Berenice, Berenis, Berenise, Bereniz, Berni, Bernie, Berny. *Greek:* "bringer of victory". Bertha. *Germanic:* "bright". Often over-weight, tends to be quiet. *Baroness Bertha von Suttner*, (1843-1914), Austrian author and peace advocate. *Bertha Wilson*, (born 1923), Canadian Supreme Court jurist. *Bertha Dunham*, (1881-1957), award winning Canadian children's author and librarian. *Bertha Miller*, (1882-1969), award winning U.S.

editor and publisher.

Beth. *Hebrew:* "house". *Short form of names containing* "beth". Also see Elizabeth. Tend to be socially active whether in church, politics, or human wealfare. Beth and Betsy tend to have a little stronger mothering tendencies.

Bethany // Beth, Bethanee, Bethania, Bethanie. *Aramaic:* "house of poverty". Geographical: a village near Jerusalem.

Betsy // Bette, Betty. *Familiar form of* Elizabeth. Possibly writer, activist, politician. *Betty Friedan*, (born 1921), U.S. author and feminist, cofounder president National Organization for Women 1966-70. *Betty Boothroyd*, (born 1929), British politician, first woman elected speaker of House of Commons (1992). *Betsy Ross*, (originally Elizabeth Griscom) (1752-1836), traditionally maker of first U.S. flag. *Betsy King*, (born 1955), U.S. top ladies' professional golfer. *Bette Davis*, *Bette Midler*, *Betty Grable* - Actresses.

Beverly // Bev, Beverley. *Old English:* "beaver-meadow". Goal orientated, competent achiever, mentally strong, manager. *Beverly Johnson*, (born 1951), U.S. statuesque black model. *Beverly Cleary*, (born 1916), award winning U.S. children's author. *Beverly D'Angelo* - Actress.

Bianca // Biancha, Bianka, Blanca. *Italian form* of Blanche: "white". The heroine mouse in Disney's Rescuers.

Billie // Billi. *Old English:* "Strong willed". *Feminine form of* Bill and William. Strong willed, somewhat imprudent, energetic, stuborn or determined, often (raised?) a tomboy, athletic. *Billie Holiday*, (1915-59), Lady Day, as she was usually called, was the finest jazz singer of her generation. _Billie Jean King_, (born 1943), the greatest woman doubles player in tennis history, she was also an activist for women's rights.

Blair // Blaire. _Gaelic:_ "dweller on the plain". _Blair Lent_, (born 1930), award winning U.S. illustrator and children's author.

Bobbi // Bobbie, Bobby. _Familiar form of_ Roberta. Cute, pretty, energetic, determined, often athlete, fairly competitive, reserved, mothering, loves children.

Bonita // Bonnee, Bonni, Bonnie, Bonny. _Spanish:_ "pretty"; _Scottish:_ "beautiful, pretty". Gentle heart, strong mother. _Bonnie Hunt_ - Actress.

Brandy // Brandee, Brandi, Brandie. _Dutch:_ "brandy, a liquor distilled from wine or fermented fruit juice". Cute, pretty, liked, sometimes socially imprudent/wild before married, possibly bar dancer.

Brenda. _Old English:_ "firebrand". A _feminine form of_ Brendan. Cute, capable, helps with leadership, intelligent, good at sports maybe even excels, opinionated, not boy crazy or marriage hungry but ready. Singer: _Brenda K. Starr_.

Brenna // Bren, Brenn. _Gaelic:_ "raven (haired)". _Feminine form of_ Brendan.

Brianna // Brana, Breana, Breanne, Breena, Breonna, Bria, Briana, Brianda, Briann, Brianna, Brianne, Brina, Briney, Brinn, Brinna, Brionna, Brionne, Briny, Bryana, Bryn, Bryna, Brynn, Brynne. _Gaelic:_ "strong". A _feminine form of_ Brian.

Bridget // Bridgett, Bridgette, Brigette, Brigitte. _Gaelic:_ "resolute strength". Cute, friendly, so-so at academics, weak at mathematics, flighty, marriage hungry. _Saint Bridget of Sweden_. _Bridgette Fonda_, _Bridgette Wilson_, _Brigitte Bardot_, _Brigitte Nielsen_ - Actresses.

Brittany // Brit, Britney, Britni, Britt, Britta, Brittan, Brittaney, Brittani, Brittanie, Britteny, Brittnee, Brittney, Brittni, Brittnie, Brittny. _Latin:_ "England".

Brooke // Brook. _English:_ "brook". A _feminine form of_ Brook. _Brooke Shields_ - Actress.

Caitlin // Caitlyn, Catlee, Catlin, Kaitlin, Kaitlyn, Kaitlynn. _Irish form_ of Catherine.

Cameron // Cam, Cambria, Camey Cammy. _Gaelic:_ "crooked nose". More commonly a male or family name. _Cameron Diaz_ - Actress.

Camille // Cam, Camala, Camel, Cami, Camila, Camile, Camilla, Cammi, Cammie, Cammy, Milli, Millie, Milly. _Latin:_ "freeborn girl ceremonial attendant". Cute, steady, loyal, supportive, not the leader, shy, weak hearted, good follower, passionate, dreams of marriage and motherhood.

Candace // Candi, Candie, Candice, Candis, Candy, Kandace, Kandy. _Greek:_ "glittering, flowing white". Able leader, noble, intelligent, friendly, logical, not given to runaway emotions. *Candace Bergen, Candace Cameron* - Actresses.

Candy. *Familiar form of* Candace. Very cute, feminine, friendly, very social, a bit imprudent.

Cara // Caralie, Cari, Carina, Carine, Carrie, Kara. *Gaelic:* "friend"; *Latin:* "dear". Also see Carrie and Karen. Dear friend, gentle, capable, able follower, a bit reluctant to lead, stable, a little shy or reserved.

Carina // Carena, Carin, Caryn, Karena, Karina, Karine. *Latin:* "keel". Also see Karen.

Carissa // Caresa, Caressa, Carrissa, Charissa, Karisa, Karissa. *Greek:* "loving".

Carla // Karla. *Short form of* Carol and Caroline. *Feminine form of* Carl and Charles. Fun, quite intelligent, very able leader, positive or optimistic attitude, leads without degrading others, energetic, great team person, often own small business, marries: sensitive relational leader. *Carla A. Hills*, (born 1934), U.S. government official, lawyer.

Carly // Carlee, Carley, Carli, Carlie, Carlye, Karlee, Karli, Karlie, Karly. *Familiar forms of* Caroline and Charlotte. *Carly Simon*, (born 1945), U.S. singer and songwriter, 'That's the Way I Always Heard It Should Be'.

Carmel // Carma, Carmela, Carmelina, Carmelita. *Hebrew:* "garden". Cute, steady, loyal, supportive, not the leader, shy, weak hearted?, good follower, passionate, dreams of marriage and motherhood.

Carmen // Carma, Carmelina, Carmelita, Carmencita, Carmina, Carmine, Carmita, Charmaine, Karmen. *Latin:* "song". *Carmen Lawrence*, (born 1948), first woman to head an Australian state. *Carmen Electra* - Actress.

Carol // Carey, Cari, Carla, Carleen, Carlen, Carlene, Carley, Carlin, Carlina, Carline, Carlita, Carlota, Carlotta, Carly, Carlyn, Carlynn, Carlynne, Caro, Carola, Carole, Carolin, Carolina, Caroline, Carolyn, Carolynn, Carolynne, Carri, Carrie, Carroll, Carry, Cary, Caryl, Charla, Charleen, Charlena, Charlene, Charlotta, Charmain, Charmion, Charyl, Cheryl, Cherlyn, Karel, Kari, Karla, Karleen, Karlen, Karlene, Karlotta, Karlotte, Karole, Larolina, Karoly, Karyl, Kerril, Lola, Loleta, Lolita, Lotta, Lotte, Lotti, Lottie, Sharleen, Sharlene, Sharline, Sharyl, Sherrie, Sherry, Sherye, Sheryl. *Latin:* "strong, womanly"; *Old French:* "song of joy". *A feminine form of* Carl and Charles. Fun, but more often serious, intelligent, very able leader, leads without degrading others, tends toward overbearing, energetic, good team person, non athletic or light athletic, try recreational snow skiing, often own small business, great with kids. *Carol Channing*, (born 1923), U.S. singer, actress, and comedienne. *Caroline Norton*, (1808-77), British novelist and poet. *Carolyn Haywood*, (born 1898), U.S. illustrator and author of children's books, noted for portraits of children. *Carlotta Grisi*, (1819?-99), Italian ballerina. Totals: (12) author-poet-novelist-children's 58%, scientist, librarian, politician, illustrator, actress. *Carol Alt*, *Carol Lynley*, *Carole Bouquet*, *Carole Lombard*, *Carol Burnett* - Actresses.

Caroline // Carolyn. *Latin:* "little and womanly". *Forms of* Carol. See Carol. Feminine *forms of* Carl or Charles.

Carrie // Carey, Cari, Carie, Cary, Carree, Carri, Carry, Kari, Karrie. *Form of* Carol and Caroline. Likely out going and leader. *Carrie Chapman Catt*, (1859-1947), woman suffrage activist who founded the League of Women Voters. *Carrie Perry*, (born 1931), U.S. politician. *Carry Nation*, (1846-1911), vehement and destructive foe of alcoholic beverages and bars. *Carre Otis*, *Carrie Fisher* - Actresses.

Casey // Casi, Casie, Kacey, Kacie, Kacy, Kasey, Kaycee. *Gaelic:* "brave".

Cassandra // Cass, Cassady, Casandra, Cassie, Cassey, Cassi, Cassidy, Kassey, Kassi, Kassie, Sandy. *Greek:* "helper of men, disbelieved by men". Mythological: a prophetess of ancient Greece. Non-athlete, very feminine, cute, fairly intelligent student, occasional sharp tongue, opinionated.

Catherine // Caitlin, Caitrin, Caren, Cari, Carin, Caron, Caryn, Cass, Cassi, Cassie, Cassy, Catalina, Catarina, Cate, Caterina, Catha, Catharina, Catharine, Cathe, Cathee, Catherin, Catherina, Cathi, Cathie, Cathleen, Cathlene, Cathyleen, Cathrine, Cathryn, Cathy, Cati, Catie, Catina, Catlaina, Catrina, Catriona, Caty, Caye, Ekaterina, Kathleen, Katrina. *Greek:* "pure". *English form of* Katherine. More studious and scholarly, intelligent, insightful, managerial, often manager of both males and females, efficient, good with details, honest, quick witted, more dominant and likely to marry a less dominant and less authoritarian male whom easily shares leadership, may find difficulty in finding an acceptable spouse, can seem a bit severe when dealing with others, Kathleens may be somewhat less dominant than Catherines, leader. Cathy's tend to be perfectionistic, more critical including of possible mates, dominant, somewhat bossy. Totals: (15)

writer-novels-children's 47%, dancer-choreographer 13%, religious group founder 13%, charming-intelligent-empress 13%, ascetic-mystic-martyr-saint 13%, teacher, naturalist, philanthropist. *Cate Blanchett*, *Catherine Bach*, *Catherine Bell*, *Catherine Deneuve* - Actresses.

Cecilia // Cacilia, Cacilie, Cecil, Cecile, Ceciley, Cecily, Ceil, Cele, Celia, Celie, Cicely, Cicily, Ciel, Cilka, Cissie, Cissy, Kilelia, Sile, Sileas, Sisely, Sisile, Sissie, Sissy. *Latin:* "blind". *A feminine form of* Cecil. Able leader, not dominating, medium soft appearance, often manager of females, does not appear forceful, socializes easily in large mixed group, good representative, good at public relations. Historical: *Saint Cecilia*, patroness of musicians and the blind. *Cecilia Bohl de Faber*, (1796-1877), German-born Spanish novelist. *Celia Laighton Thaxter*, (1835-94), U.S. poet.

Celeste // Cele, Celena, Celene, Celesta, Celestia, Celestina, Celestine, Celestyn, Celestyna, Celia, Celie, Celina, Celinda, Celine, Celinka, Celisse, Celka, Selestina. *Latin:* "heavenly". Feminine, may get frusterated by others not taking her leadership seriously, fairly serious, follower, co-leader or leader of four.

Celia. *Short form of* Cecilia.

Chantal // Chana, Chandler, Chanel, Chanell, Chanelle, Chandal, Chantalle, Chantel, Chantelle. *French:* "song".

Charity // Carissa, Carita, Charis, Charissa, Charita, Cherri, Cherry, Sharity. *Latin:* "charity or brotherly love".

Charlene // Charleen. *Familiar form of* Caroline and Charlotte.

Charlotte // Carla, Carleen, Carlene, Carline, Carlota, Carlotta, Carly, Chara, Charil, Charla, Charleen, Charlene, Charline, Charlotta, Charmain, Charmaine, Charmian, Charmion, Charo, Charyl, Cherlyn, Cheryl, Karla, Karleen, Karlene, Karlotta, Karlotte, Lola, Loleta, Lolita, Lotta, Lotte, Lotti, Lottie, Sharleen, Sharlene, Sharline, Sharyl, Sherrie, Sherry, Sherye, Sheryl. *French:* "little and womanly". *French form of* Carol. *Feminine form of* Charles. Also see Carol and Caroline. Historical: *Charlotte* (1896-1985), grand duchess of Luxembourg. *Charlotte Corday*, (1768-93), assasinated Jean-Paul Marat, radical leader of the French Revolution and a strong supporter of the Reign of Terror. *Charlotte Gilman*, (1860-1935), U.S. writer and lecturer on labor and feminism. *Charlotte Yonge*, (1823-1901), English novelist and writer on religious and educational subjects. *Charlotte Cushman*, (1816-76), U.S. tragic actress. *Charlotte Crabtree*, (Lotta) (1847-1924), U.S. actress, retired in 1891 with $2,000,000 fortune made by astute investments in real estate. *Charlotte Ross* - Actress.

Charmaine // Charmain, Charmane, Charmian, Charmion. *French form of* Carmen or Charlotte.

Chastity // Chasity. *Latin:* "purity".

Chelsea // Chelsae, Chelsey, Chelsie, Chelsy, Cheslie. *Old English:* "a ship port". Historical: daughter of U. S. President William Clinton.

Cherie // Cher, Cherice, Chere, Cherey, Cheri, Chérie, Cherice, Cherise, Cherish, Chery, Cherye, Sher, Sherry, Sherye. *French:* "beloved, dear". Singer: *Cher* (originally Cherilyn Sakasian La Pierre) (born 1946), U.S.

folk-rock singer, actress, 'Sonny and Cher'.

Cheryl // Charyl, Cherianne, Cherilyn, Cherilynn. *Form of* Charlotte and Shirley. Moldable, somewhat nieve or gullable, attractive but cold to new comers, reliable, faithful, honest, hard worker, executive secretary, project lead in science related field, judging, expectation of other's prudence, cool to strangers and new acquaintances, takes awhile to warm up to another and let into her group of friends, fiercely protective, hardly adventurous. Marries: somewhat adventurous type who's willing to submit to her way, i.e. Jay. *Cheryl Ladd*, Actress. Singer: *Cheryl James* of 1988 U.S. rap group Salt-N-Pepa. Supermodel: *Cheryl Tiegs*.

Cheyenne // Cheyanne, Chyenne. *Native American:* "our people".

China // Chyna, Chynna. *English:* an Eastern Asian country or its delicate pottery.

Chloe. Chloë, Clo, Cloe. *Greek:* "young leaves".Literary: 'Daphnis and Chloe', Greek pastoral romance by Longus and basis for ballet by Ravel. *Chloe Annett* - Actress.

Chloris. Cloris. *Greek:* "pale". Greek Mythology: *Chloris*, daughter of Amphion and Niobe; often confused with Chloris, the wife of Zephyrus and goddess of flowers.

Chris. Chrissy. *Short forms of* Christine.

Christine // Cairistiona, Cristen, Crystie, Chris, Chrissie, Chrissy, Christa, Christan, Christean, Christen, Christi, Christian, Christiana, Christiane, Christie, Christin, Christina, Christy, Christye, Christyna, Chrysa, Chryste, Cris, Crissie, Crissy, Crista, Cristi, Cristie, Cristin, Cristina,

Cristine, Cristiona, Cristy, Kirsten, Kirstin, Kris, Krissie, Krissy, Krista, Kristen, Kristi, Kristie, Kristin, Kristina, Kristy, Krysta, Krystyna, Tina. **Greek:** "Christian, anointed". Christina - resembles father and close with father, doesn't have problems with school, hard working, kind, social, but gets offended easily, which is why she has few friends - for example one girl-friend; perseverance, stubbornness and self-determination characterize her; get married early and often unsuccessfully; her authoritative and jealous nature causes bumps in her marriage; likes to dress brightly and uniquely; may wear trinkets or bobbles; likes new experiences, likes far trips; good housekeeper, not wasteful. Christys are often bubbly, strong, leaders, come across as self confident, expect to share leadership with spouse, cute, usually medium to overwieght - rounded, loving and loyal mate, love children, often writer especially for children, often have weight problem, marriage ready, takes boy-friend and marries sooner than average. Christines tend to be more emotionally steady and thoughtful, tend to be independent and thinner (also true of Kristine). Historical: _Christine Ladd-Franklin_, (1847-1930), U.S. scientist, first woman student at Johns Hopkins University and at Universities of Gottingen and Berlin in Germany; distinguished career in mathematics, physics, and psychology; famous for her theory of color perception. _Christine Weston_, (born 1904), U.S. author. _Chris Evert_, (born 1954), tennis great. _Chrissie Hynde_, (born 1951), U.S. rock 'n' roll musician, lead vocalist The Pretenders. _Christie Brinkley_, supermodel. _Christa Miller_, _Christina Applegate_, _Christine Cavanaugh_, _Christine Lahti_, _Christine Lakin_, _Christy Chung_ - Actresses.

Cindy // Cindie, Cyndie. _Short form of_ Cynthia and Lucinda. Often teacher, executive secretary, reliable, efficient, fun in family and relationship orientated mode, cold and hard in business mode, often co-leads with husband or leads own group; holds opinion but not an idealist, love to lead children and do it well; need relationships, often impudent/wild before married. marries: often Rons. Supermodel & actress: _Cindy Crawford_. _Cyndi Lauper_, (born 1953), U.S. pop singer, video performer, wacky persona.

Clara // Chiarra, Clair, Claire, Clarabelle, Clare, Claresta, Clareta, Claretta, Clarette, Clarey, Clari, Clarice, Clarie, Clarinda, Clarine, Clarissa, Clarita, Clary, Klara, Klarika, Klarrisa. **Greek:** "clear, bright". Tender, caring, little trouble for her parents, obiedient, good grades, friendly, many think she takes after her father, has a lot of friends; not very talkative, good listener and doesn't force her opinion, so she's liked by her friends, she doesn't discuss her problems broadly, but keeps them close, her children are her best friends - to whom she is very devoted, she is withdrawn from handsome boys because she values character above looks, dresses modestly with taste, seldom shops for clothes - but shops with careful choices, uses makeup conservatively - judiciously and tastefully; chooses occupations of: teacher, engineer, doctor, hairdresser, musician, sales; likes stability in everything, good marrages because she chooses an independent and good provider; she pursues education and chooses occupation - not by what she likes - but by its good income; good worker - but family is her first priority; she would quit her job in order to pick up her child from school, in a poor marriage - she is long-suffering. *Clara (Clarissa) Barton*, (1821-1912), nurse, founder of the American Red Cross, called the "angel of the battlefield". *Clara Schumann*, a talented concert pianist. *Saint Clare of Assisi*, (1194-1253), Italian nun, co-founder of the Order of Poor Clares. *Clare Luce*, (1903-87), U.S. writer and diplomat, edited Vogue, Vanity Fair, turned to writing plays, later became a war correspondent, member U.S. Congress, U.S. ambassador to Italy. *Clara Judson*, (1879-1960), U.S. writer of children's books. *Clara Morris*, (1848-1925), U.S. emotional actress, wrote about stage life, author of novels. *Clare Newberry*, (1903-70), U.S. artist and writer, famous for paintings of cats, author-illustrator of children's books. *Claire Danes*, *Claire Forlani*, *Clara Bow* - Actresses.

Clarissa // Clerissa. ***Latin-Greek:*** "most brilliant". Form of Clara. See Clara.

Claudia // Claude, Claudelle, Claudetta, Claudette, Claudie, Claudina, Claudine, Clodia, Gladys. ***Latin:*** "lame". *Feminine form of* Claude. *Claudia Schiffer*, supermodel & actress. *Claudia Cassidy*, (born 1899), music, dance, and drama critic. *Claudia Muzio*, (1892-1936), opera star in U.S. and abroad. *Claudette Colbert*, *Claudia Cardinale*, *Claudia Christian* - Actresses.

Cody // Codee, Codi, Codie. ***Old English:*** "a cushion".

Colette // Collete, Coletta, Collette. ***Greek-French:*** "victorious in battle". Familiar form of Nicole. *Colette*, (1873-1954), outstanding French woman writer, describe sights, sounds, tastes, smells, and feelings in unique ways that allow a reader almost to experience them.

Colleen // Coleen, Colene, Collie, Colline, Colly. ***Gaelic:*** "girl". Often short or pudgy, able follower, personnel manager. Connie. *Short form of* Constance. *Connie Francis*, singer & actress.

Constance // Conni, Connie, Conny, Constancia, Constancy, Constanta, Constantia, Constantina, Costanza, Konstance, Konstanze. ***Latin:*** "constancy, firmness". *Feminine form of* Constantine. Also see Constantine. Supportive, tows the line, does the work requested, often writer. *Constance Rourke*, (1885-1941), U.S. historian, pioneered the study of American character and culture. *Constance Holme*, (1880-1955), British novelist. *Constance Skinner*, (1879-1939), U.S. writer, stories for boys and girls. *Constance Motley*, (born 1921), U.S. public official.

Consuelo // Consolata, Consuela. ***Spanish:*** "consolation". Religious: the name honors Santa Maria del Consuelo, "Mary of Consolation".

Cora // Corabel, Corabella, Corabelle, Coraima, Corella, Corena, Corenda, Corene, Coretta, Corette, Corey, Cori, Corie, Corilla, Corina, Corinna, Corinne, Coriss, Corissa, Corrina, Corrine, Corry, Kora. ***Greek:*** "maiden". *Forms of* Kora. Also see Kora. Average to over weight, moderately artistic. *Coretta Scott King*, (born 1925), U.S. lecturer and writer, noted for her work with civil rights and peace organizations, wife of Martin Luther King, Jr.

Coral // Coralie, Coraline, Koral, Koralie. ***Latin:*** "coral".

Corey // Cory, Cori, Corie, Correy, Corri, Corrie, Corry,

Kori, Korrie, Korry. *Gaelic:* "hollow".

Corrina // Coreen, Corine, Corinna, Corinne, Correna, Corrianne, Corrine, Corrinne. Perhaps means: "Bubbling brook". *Forms of* Cora. Cute, bubbly, very relational; as a child she's constantly in motion, stubborn, easily offended and often sick; her parents often spoil her as they try to please her, good student, may study music or dance, resembles her father's features, resembles mother's character, she can manipulate with almost professional acting, almost always reaches the goal she sets, demonstrative person, liking to draw attention to herself, her need to be in the center of things has no boundaries, people interpret this as her desire to accepted and valued for her abilities, but it is really caused by her impatience; selfish, jealous, marries early following her passion, first marriage is seldom successful, many can't adjust to married life, hate to wash dishes, loves sweets, usually attractive, loves a lot of money, lives as a queen, wants glamour and prestige, like handsome men, has good intuition, understands individual's psychology and adjusts to their communication level, would be good in any area which deals with people. *Corinna*, (fl. 500 BC), Greek lyric poet, famous for her beauty and victory over Pindar in 5 poetic contests.

Cornelia // Cornela, Cornelie, Cornelle, Cornie, Corny, Neely, Nelia, Nelie, Nell, Nellie, Nelly. *Latin:* "yellow, horn-colored". *A feminine form of* Cornelius. Loves children and writing. *Cornelia Skinner*, (1901-79), U.S. actress, monologist, and writer. *Cornelia* (2nd century BC), Roman matron. *Cornelia Meigs*, (1884-1973), U.S. writer of historical adventure stories for young people.

Courtney // Cortney, Courtenay, Courteney, Courtnay, Kortney. *Old English:* "from the court". *Courteney Cox*, *Courtney Love* - Actresses.

Crystal // Cristal, Crysta, Christal, Christalle, Christel, Chrystal, Crystal, Kristel, Krystal. *Latin:* "transparent quartz". Cute, attractive, intelligent, thin, social worker, pacifistic, musical? *Crystal Eastman*, (1881-1928), U.S. social worker, feminist, and pacifist. *Crystal McKellar* - Actress.

Cybil. A form of Sibyl. *Cybill Shepherd* - Actress.

Cynthia // Cinda, Cindee, Cindi, Cindie, Cindy, Cynde, Cyndia, Cyndie, Cynthea, Cynthie, Cynthy, Kynthia, Sindee. *Greek:* "moon, from Mount Cynthus". Mythological: the moon goddess. Also see Cindy. *Cynthia Ozick*, (born 1928), U.S. novelist. *Cynthia Gregory*, (born 1946), U.S. ballet dancer. Czarina. *Russian:* "Empress". *Russian feminine form of* Caesar.

Dahlia // Dalia. *English:* A Central American flower. Dalai, *Mongolian:* "vast sea". *Dahlia Salem* - Actress

Daisy // Daisey, Daissy, Daysi, Daysy. *English:* A flower known in Old English as the "day's eye". *Daisy Bates*, (born 1922) U.S. civil rights figure.

Dakota // Lakota. *Sioux Indian:* "friends" or "allies".

Dale // Dael, Daile, Dalena, Dayle. *Old English:* "valley". Attractive, subdued, stable. *Dale Evans Rogers* - Actress.

Dalila // Dallana, Lila. *African:* "gentle". French form of Delilah.

Dallas. *Gaelic:* "wise".

Damara // Damaris, Damariz, Mara, Maris. *Greek:* "gentle girl".

Dana // Dania, Danica, Danika, Danna, Dayna, Tana. *Scandinavian-Slovic:* "from Denmark". Thin, leader, manager, often reserved. *Dana Delany* - Actress.

Danae. Greek mythology: the beautiful daughter of Acrisius, king of Argos.

Danielle // Danella, Danelle, Danette, Dani, Danice, Daniel, Daniela, Daniele, Daniella, Danila, Danit, Danita, Danna, Danni, Dannie, Dannielle, Danny, Dannye, Danya, Danyel, Danyell, Danyella, Danyelle. *Hebrew:* "judged by God". *Feminine form of* Daniel. Quite attractive, reserved, tactful, judicious. Model: *Daniela*.

Daphne // Daffi, Daffie, Daffy, Daphna. *Greek:* "laurel tree". Greek mythology: nymph turned into a laurel tree. Reserved, shy, writer. *Daphne Du Maurier*, (Lady Browning) (1907-89), British novelist. *Daphne Rubin-Vega* - Actress.

Darby // Darb, Darbie. *Gaelic:* free man"; *Norse:* "deer estate".

Darcie // Darcee, Darcey, Darcie, Darcy, Darice, Darsey. *Gaelic:* "dark". Likable leader, amiable, genial, not over-baring, adventurous, intelligent-expect college, likes reading, bubbly personality, avoids showing dislike of another, would rather avoid disliked person, diplomatic, thin? social.

Daria // Dari, Dausha. *Old Persian:* "conquerer"; *Greek:* "queenly". *Feminine form of* Darius. Smart, bit impulsive, always leading peers in games, puts the offender in his place quickly and often with fists, don't like to be alone, enjoys loud fun games with children, even when not taught to be housekeeper as child - grows up as a neat tidy person who organizes and likes cleanliness, good student but not from hard studying, spends little time studying, likes knitting, dresses tastefully, falls in love easily, good as: journalist, psychologist, insurance agent; energetic, active, lives for today and not in the past, will forgive any dirty past of her husband to make a good marriage, frugal, sensitive to husbands ego, wouldn't degrade her husband in before others.

Darian // Darien. *Form of* Doria.

Darlene // Dareen, Darelle, Darla, Darleen, Darlin, Darline, Darling, Darlleen, Darlyn, Darrelle, Darryl, Daryl. *Old French:* "little darling". Daring, adventurous, talkative, tells negative behavior of another, prone to gossip, fiercely loyal, committed to friend or family.

Davita // Daveen, Daveta, Davida, Davina, Davine, Devina, Veda, Vida, Vita, Vitia. *Hebrew:* "beloved". *A feminine form of* David.

Dawn. *English:* "dawn." Cute, pretty, do what they set to do, sees world with blinders, sees only her path or goal. Possibly marries: John. *Dawn Fraser*, (born 1937) first woman swimmer to win gold medals in three consecutive Olympic Games. *Dawn French*, *Dawn Zulueta* - Actresses.

Deanna // Dayana, Deana, Deandra, Deanne. *Form of* Dena or Diana. A *feminine form of* Dean. Writer, *Deanna Durbin*, *Deanna Dunagan* - Actresses.

Deborah // Deb, Debi, Debbee, Debbi, Debbie, Debby, Debi, Debor, Debora, Debra, Devora. *Hebrew:* "bee". Very strong personality, determined, leader, sometimes pushy, dominant, forceful, stubborn, loyal, can be very playful, energetic, often overweight, often marries someone she can control or will concede to her will, hard working, reluctant or unlikely to initiate divorce. Biblical: Hebrew heroine, prophetess, judge. Historical: *Deborah Sampson*, (1760-1827), U.S. soldier and lecturer; assumed a man's identity and entered the Continental Army to participate in the American Revolution (1782). *Debbe Duning*, *Debbie Harry*, *Debbie Reynolds*, *Deborah Foreman*, *Deborah Kerr*, *Debrah Farentino* - Actresses.

Dee // Dede, Dedie, Dee Dee, DeeAnn, Didi. *Welsh:* "black, dark". *Short form of* Deirdre, Delia and Diana.

Deirdre // Dede, Dedee, Dedra, Dee, Dee Dee, Deerdre, Deidre, Deisy, Deisi, Didi, Dierdre. *Gaelic:* "sorrow, complete wanderer". Celtic mythology: beautiful woman fated to cause misfortune. Literary: heroine of Cuchulain Cycle and dramas by Yeats, James Stephens, and Synge. *Dedee Pfeiffer*, *Deidre Hall* - Actresses.

Deja // Daija, Daja, Dajah. *French:* "already" as in déjà vu: "already seen".

Delaney // Delainey, Delainie, Delana, Delanie, Delany, Dulany.

Delia // Dee, Dede, Dee Dee, Dehlia, Dela, Delinda, Della, Didi. *Greek:* "visible, she of Delos (i.e. the goddess Artemis)". Greek mythology: a name for the moon goddess. *A short form of* Cordelia.

Delilah // Dalila, Delila, Lila, Lilah. *Hebrew:* "brooding". Biblical: treacherous mistress of Samson.

Della // Delana, Delina. *Familiar form of* Adelaide and Delia.

Demetria // Demetra, Demetris, Demi. *Greek:* "belonging to Demeter." Greek mythology: Demeter was goddess of agriculture and marriage. *Feminine form of* Demetri or Dimitri. **Demi Moore** - Actress.

Dena // Deana, Deane, Deanna, Deena, Deeyn, Dene, Denna, Denni, Dina. *Hebrew:* "vindicated"; *Old English:* ley". *Feminine form of* Dean which is Arabic: "faith". *Greek:* Dinomis, "strength, power". Also see Diana and Dinah. Often sharp behaviors as child, sharp tongued, sharp-sudden movements, irritable, she requires additional effort by her parents, moody, quick mood changes from her sensitive spirit, sacrificing, will help anyone who needs her — even if they don't ask, she can stand-up for herself, often have poor first marriage and often poor second also, often single mothers, these problems are based in her personality, with age she often becomes more thorny stubborn judgemental and absolute, gives no regard to authority figures, can offend people easily, like a lighted explosive — any simple frustration can set her off, hard working, practical, she knows exactly what she wants and what will benifit her, people find her to be cunning and they're right, she will find a way, men avoid her because of her straight-forwardness and harshness, actually she is a nice person and has many caring qualities, she's a creative chef, underneithe she often believes that she is fighting for what is right, she's sacreficing and caring for her family, faithful wife, good worker, often a hard and determined worker.

Denise // Deni, Denice, Denisse, Dennis, Dennise, Denys, Denyse. *French:* "adherent of Dionysus". Greek mythology: Dionysus was the god of wine. *Feminine form of* Dennis. Energetic, hard worker, hair stylist, secretary, often imprudent, husband hungary, small business owner, poor judgement in picking spouse. Historical: *Eve Denise Curie*, (born 1904), French author, lecturer, and musician. *Denise Crosby* - Actress.

Desiree // Deserae, Deseree, Deserie, Desirae, Desire, Desirea, Désirée, Desiri, Dessery. *French:* "desired". Historical: *Desiree Clary*, former fiancee of Napoleon Bonaparte.

Destiny // Destany, Destenie, Desteny, Destine, Destinee, Destiney, Destini, Destinie. *English:* "destiny".

Devin // Devan, Devine, Devinne, Devon, Devyn. *Gaelic:* "poet".

Diamond // Dyamond, Dymon, Dymond. *English:* "diamond".

Diana // Diane, Deana, Deane, Deanna, Deanne, Dede, Dee, Dee Dee, Dena, Di, Diahann, Dian, Diandra, Diane, Dianna, Dianne, Didi, Dyan, Dyana, Dyane, Dyann, Dyanna, Dyanne. *Latin:* "divine". Roman mythology: virgin huntress and moon goddess, identified with Greek Artemis. Helpful, kind, sensible, no nonsense, careful, attractive, gentle manner, judgmental of unsensiblity and wild behavior, reserved, not generally a risk taker, marries: hardworking, sensible, stable, careful, leader, grows up as calm kind obiedient child, easy going, sensitive to others pain, compasionate, often get in trouble for bring home stray kittens, firm, even stubborn, able to achieve a lot in life, good intuition, good housekeeper, hospitable. *Princes Diana*, formerly *Lady Diana Spencer*. *Diana Adams*, dancer. *Diana Ross*, singer and actress. *Diana Rigg*, *Diane Keaton*, *Diane Lane* Actresses.

Dinah // Dina, Dyna, Dynah. *Hebrew:* "judged, vindicated". Also see Dena and Diana. Emotional, impulsive, therefore often makes mistakes, hard working, diligence, good follow through, reaches goal, quick temper, in hot temper behaves offensively, but temper dies down quickly, good housekeeper, tasty cook, may be manipulated with words, fantasizer, creates interesting stories, quickly rises in carreer through determination and good work, optimistic, failure doesn't disturb her. Biblical: daughter of Jacob and Leah. *Dinah Maria Craik*, (pen name Dinah Maria Mulock) (1826-87), British children's novelist. *Dinah Shore*, actress-singer. *Dinah Washington*, singer.

Dionne // Deonne, Dion, Dione, Dionis. *Greek:* "divine queen". Greek mythology: the mother of Aphrodite. Singer: *Dionne Warwick*.

Dixie // Dix, Dixy. *French:* "ten". Geographical: nickname for the U.S. Southeast. *Dixy Lee Ray*, (born 1914), Washington state's first woman governor, outspoken, not reelected.

Dolly // Dolley, Dollie. *English:* child's form of "doll". Familiar form of Dorothy. *Dolley "Dolly" Madison* was a popular Washington hostess; she was plump, pretty, and lively. *Dolly Parton*, country singer & actress.

Dolores // Delora, Delores, Deloria, Deloris, Dolorita, Doloritas, Lola, Lolita. *Spanish:* "sorrows". Name honors Santa Maria de los Dolores, "Mary of the sorrows". *Lola Ridge*, (1883-1941), U.S. poet with intense sympathy for the laboring and oppressed classes. *Lola Rodriguez de Tio* (1854-1924), early Puerto Rican poet.

Dominique // Domenica, Domeniga, Domenique, Dominga, Domini, Dominica, Dominika, Dominque, Domonique. *Latin:* "belonging to God, God's day". *A feminine form of* Dominic. Writer, painter, artistic, healthy and calm child, fearless, stubborn, easily offended, independent, hates social games, would rather play dolls by herself in her corner, character from mother, resembles father, initially difficult adjustment to school, after adjustment to school she makes progress, good memory, easily learns poetry, likes to resite poetry for others, presonality changes after puberty, she becomes more difficult, her relationship with her mother becomes strained, she tries to achieve in life, she has good intuition, doesn't get decieved easily, sensitive to the opinions of others, hospitable, likes to visit people, she often pick occupation of nurse, teacher, artist, doctor, journalist, hairdresser, sales, chef, singer.

Donna // Dona, Donella, Donelle, Donetta, Donia, Donica, Donielle, Donnell, Ladonna. *Latin:* "lady". Thin, desires attention, often marries early, somewhat naïve, energetic, bit irritable, tom-boyish child, dresses like boy as child, fearless, sporty, sharp tongued, may be sacastic child to those she doesn't want as friends, easily gets aquanted, and likewise moves on from friends easily, likes big parties and partying, likes to be the dynamo of the party, computer programmers, accountants, detectives, culinary, music teachers, hair dressers. *Ina Donna Coolbrith*, (1843-1928), U.S. poet & librarian. *Donna D'Errico*, *Donna Reed* - Actresses.

Dora // Dore, Doreen, Dorena, Dorene, Dorey, Dori, Dorie, Dorree, Dory. *Greek:* "gift". Also see Doris & Dorothy. Writer, architect, designer.

Doris // Dori, Doria, Dorice, Dorisa, Dorise, Dorita, Dorri, Dorrie, Dorris, Dorry, Dory. *Greek:* "sea". Also see Dora & Dorothy. Puts interest into writing, artistic. *Doris Gates*, (born 1901), U.S. author of children's books & librarian. *Doris Humphrey*, (1895-1958), U.S. modern dancer, choreographer & author. *Doris May Lessing*, (born 1919), British writer. *Doris Emrick Lee*, (born 1905), U.S. modernist painter, muralist, and book illustrator. *Doris Day* - Actress.

Dorothy // Dolley, Dolli, Dollie, Dolly, Dora, Dori, Dorotea, Doroteya, Dorothea, Dorothee, Dorthea, Dorthy, Dory, Dot, Dotti, Dottie, Dotty. *Greek:* "gift of God, goddess of gifts". Also see Dora and Doris. Possible author, works with children, activist. *Dorothy Lamour* - Actress.

Dottie // Dotty. *Familiar forms of* Dorthy.

Drusilla // Drew, Dru, Druci, Drucie, Drucill, Drucy, Drusi, Drusie, Drusy. ***Latin:*** "descendent of Drusus, the strong one". *Drew Berrymore* - Actress.

Dulcie // Delcina, Delcine, Dulce, Dulcea, Dulcee, Dulci, Dulcia, Dulciana, Dulcine, Dulcinea, Dulcy, Dulse, Dulsea. ***Latin:*** "sweetness".

Dusty. *Feminine form of* Dustin. Discerning, perceptive.

Ebony // Ebonee. ***Greek:*** "a jet-black hard-wood".

Eden // Edin. Babylonian: a plain; ***Hebrew:*** "delight". Biblical: a garden paradise on earth.

Edith // Dita, Eadith, Eadie, Eda, Ede, Edi, Edie, Dedita, Editha, Edithe, Ediva, Edy, Edyth, Edythe, Eyde, Eydie. ***Old English:*** "rich gift". *Edith Wharton*, (1862-1937), writer.

Edna // Eddi, Eddie, Eddy, Edwina. ***Hebrew:*** "rejuvenation". Apocryphal: the wife of Enoch. *Edna St. Vincent Millay*, (1892-1950), career poet. *Edna Ferber*, (1887-1968), U.S. novelist, dramatist, and short-story writer, wrote "Show Boat".

Eileen. *Irish form of* Helen. *Eileen Farrell*, (born 1920), U.S. dramatic soprano. *Eileen Daly* - Actress.

Elaine // Elaina, Elana, Elane, Elayne, Lainey, Layney.

French form of Helen. In Arthurian legend, who with Sir Lancelot births Sir Galahad. *Elaine L. Konigsburg*, (born 1930), U.S. children's author and illustrator. *Elaine May*, comic in 1950s and 1960s.

Eleanor // Eleanora, Eleanore, Elénore, Elenore, Eleonore, Elianora, Elianore, Elinor, Elinore, Ella, Elladine, Elle, Ellen, Ellene, Elli, Ellie, Elly, Ellyn, Elna, Elnora, Elnore, Elora, Elyn, Leanor, Leanora, Lena, Lenora, Lenore, Leonora, Leonore, Leora, Nell, Nellie, Nelly, Nora. ***Greek:*** "light". *Form of* Helen. Author, singer, works for children, confident, goal reaching, strong character, leader. *Eleanor (Anna) Roosevelt*, (1884-1962), reformer and humanitarian, wife of U.S. President, suspected lesbian. *Eleanor of Aquitaine* (1122?-1204), wife and mother of kings, beautiful, strong-willed, tenacious, and powerful, dominant political force in Europe.

Electra. ***Greek:*** "shining, brilliant". Greek mythological: daughter of Agamemnon and Clytemnestra.

Elena // Elia, Eliana. Form of Helen.

Elisa // Alyssa, Elicia, Elise, Elissa, Eliza, Ellissa, Elyssa, Lissa, Lissie, Lissy. *Familiar forms of* Alice & Elizabeth. Architectial abilities.

Elizabeth // Belle, Bess, Bessie, Bessy, Beth, Betsey, Betsy, Betta, Bette, Betti, Betty, Elisa, Elba, Elisabet, Elisabeth, Elisabetta, Elise, Elissa, Eliza, Eliza, Elizabet, Elsa, Else, Elsey, Elsi, Elsie, Elsy, Elyse, Helsa, Isabel, Lib, Libbey, Libbi, Libbie, Libby, Lisa, Lisabeth, Lisbeth, Lise, Lisette, Lissa, Lissie, Lissy, Liz, Liza, Lizabeth, Lizbeth, Lizzie, Lizzy, Lusa, Yelizaveta, Ysabel. ***Hebrew:*** "oath of God". Biblical: the mother of John the

Baptist. Faithful friend, gentle but not weak, as a leader in control, personnel manager, not over-bearing, noble bearing, love children, writer, playful, always doing-busy, may often cross into disobedience because of her constant activity, easy to love because of her friendly adventurous personality, always wants to appear better than she is, this pushes her to extravagant actions, soon she regrets each, proud and impulsive, she suspects people are not treating her as well as she deserves, therefore she often gets into conflicts, prefers exact sciences, tries to be leader among women, soft and sensitive with friends and family, peace in the family is very important to her well being for which she will do anything, she's never irritated by her In-laws, at peace with her neighbors, family is first priority and work-friends-recreation is second, not lucky with love when young, happiness usually comes later in life - often with a second marriage. *Queens Elizabeth I & II* of England. *Elizabeth Blackwell*, (1821-1910), first woman doctor in the U.S. *Elizabeth Cady Stanton*, (1815-1902), women's rights pioneer. *Elizabeth Barrett Browning*, (1806-61), the ethereal English poet. *Elizabeth Fry*, (1780-1845), a chief advocate of prison reform in Europe. Supermodel: *Elizabeth Hurley*. *Elisabeth Shue*, *Elizabeth Berridge*, *Elizabeth Montgomery*, *Elizabeth Taylor* - Actresses.

Ella // Ellette, Elli, Ellie, Elly. *Old English:* "elf, beautiful fairy woman". Nurse, writer, poet, educator, signer. *Ella Fitzgerald*, (born 1918), U.S. jazz singer. *Ella T. Grasso*, (1919-81), U.S. public official. *Ella Flagg Young*, (1845-1918), U.S. educator, first woman president of the National Education Association.

Elle. *French:* "she, her". Supermodel: *Elle MacPherson*.

Ellen // Ellene, Ellie, Elly, Ellyn. *English form of* Helen. Author, writer, actress, activist, feminist. *Ellen Glasgow*, (1874-1945), U.S. novelist & feminist. *Ellen Key*, (1849-1926), Swedish social writer & feminist. *Ellen DeGeneres,* openly homosexual actress.

Eloise // Eloisa, Héloïse. *French form of* Louise. Loves children and writing. *Eloise Lownsbery*, (1888-1967), U.S. medieval history writer for children.

Elsa // Else, Elsie, Elsy, Elza, Ilsa, Ilse. *German:* "noble." *Familiar form of* Elizabeth. Independent, strong personality, fearless, enduring, determined, sporty, her sensitivity requires a sensitive approach; teacher, waitress, designer, actress, model, engineer. *Elsa Beskow*, (1874-1953), Swedish writer & illustrator of charming children's books. *Elsie Janis*, (1889-1956), U.S. actress noted for clever impersonation. *Elsie Worthington Clews Parsons*, (1875-1941), U.S. sociologist and anthropologist, first woman elected president of American Anthropological Association.

Elvira // Elva, Elvera, Elvina, Elwira, Lira. *Germanic:* "elf-counsel, excelling"; Elva means "elf". Teacher, tutor, engineer; first impression of her is calm, balanced and even-tempered; she can be stubborn, cunning, adaptable yet stay can stay displeased with everything; hard working, she is busy doing a lot of things and does them well; while in a leadership position, she insights one against another; doesn't like slow or unconfident people, therefore prefers friendship with men over women; those who know well don't share secrets with her because she doesn't keep them; good housekeeper; first marriage is usually not long, it usually takes the second marriage to be happy; those who surround her consider her strong and courageous; more usually has sons more than daughters; quick tempered but quick forgiving; finishes her work, likes traveling, a bit untrusting. *Elvira de Hidalgo* once voice instructor at the Athens Conservatory.

Elysia // Elicia, Elise, Elisha, Elyse, Elysha, Iesha, Ilise, Ilysa, Ilyse. *Latin:* "sweetly blissful". Mythological: after-life paradise called Elysium. Also see Alicia & Elise.

Emily // Em, Ema, Emalee, Emalia, Emelda, Emelia, Emelina, Emeline, Emelita, Emelyne, Emera, Emilee, Emili, Emilia, Emilie, Emiline, Emmalee, Emmaline, Emmey, Emmi, Emmie, Emmy, Emmye, Emyle, Emylee, Milka. *Old German:* "industrious"; *Latin:* "flatterer". *Form of* Amelia. *Feminine form of* Emil. Also see Amy and Emma. Flower: Emilia, also called Flora's paintbrush. Industrious, determined, individual accomplishments, respected leader, doctor, lawyer, executive, executive secretary, writer. *Emily Dickinson*, (1830-86), among U.S.'s finest poets, exciting imagination, spinster. *Emily Kimbrough*, (1899-1989), U.S. author and editor. *Emily Blackwell*, (1826-1910), U.S. physician. *Emily Balch*, (1867-1961), U.S. economist and sociologist, teacher Wellesley College, executive in Women's International League for Peace and Freedom. *Emily Post*, (1873-1960), U.S. author, novelist. *Emily Neville*, (born 1919), U.S. journalist and author. *Emily Carr*, (1871-1945), Canadian artist and writer.

Emma // Em, Ema, Emelina, Emeline, Emelyne, Emmaline, Emmalyn, Emmalynn, Emmalynne, Emmi, Emmie, Emmy, Emmye. *Old German:* "universal, nurse". *Short form of* Emily. Also see Amelia & Amy. Ideologue, possibly feisty, bit stubborn, writer, dreamer; always self-critiquing which complicates her life, but does not make her unconfident; mostly not pleased with herself, you might say she eats at herself; spends a long time picking between options - both on important matters and trivial; once she has decided, she doesn't change her mind; she doesn't listen to good advice; independent in everything; her choices are not always wise; often have good artistic taste; painter, designer, art critic. *Emma Willard*, (1787-1870), advanced womens's educational opportunities and coeducation in the U.S. *Emma Goldman*, (1869-1940), international anarchist. *Emma Lazarus*, (1849-87), U.S. poet, worked for Jewish nationalism. *Emmeline Pankhurst*, (1858-1928), British militant suffrage leader. *Emma Samms*, *Emma Thompson* - Actresses.

Emmanuelle. *Feminine form of* Emmanuel. *Hebrew:* "God with us." Actress: Emmanuelle Beart.

Enid. *Welsh:* "purity, woodlark". *Enid La Monte Meadowcroft*, (1898-1966), U.S. teacher and author. *Enid Bagnold*, (1889-1981), British novelist; wrote 'National Velvet'.

Erica // Aarika, Enrica, Enrika, Ericha, Ericka, Erika, Ricki, Rickie, Ricky, Rikki. *Scandinavian:* "ever powerful". *Feminine form of* Eric. Focused, fairly determined, good student, leader, goal orientated; straight forward, egotistical, jealous, very social, knows how to approach people and get aquainted easily, values people with whom she can rely on completely; clings to good friends; in partners, values good taste and ability to give good advice and assistance; predisposed to stress and depression; many have deep philosophical faith; often attractive. *Erica Jong* (born 1942), feminist author of 'Fear of Flying' and 'Fanny'.

Erin // Aaren, Aryn, Eran, Erina, Erinn, Erinna, Eryn. *Gaelic:* "peace". Literary: colloquialism for Ireland. Reserved, restrain, constrained, inhibited, undemonstrative, fairly serious, concerned, cut-up and silly with close friends, peaceful, fairly determined, nurse. *Erin Gray* - Actress.

Ernestine // Erna, Ernaline, Ernesta. *Old English:* "earnest". *Feminine form of* Ernest.

Esmeralda // Esma, Esmaria, Esme, Ezmeralda. *Greek:* "emerald". Literary: character in Victor Hugo's 'The Hunchback of Notre Dame.'

Essence. *English:* "essence".

Estefany // Estee, Estefani, Estefania, Estefauni, Estefawni, Estephanie, Estephany, Esti. *Greek:* "crown". *Feminine form of* Stephen.

Estelle // Estel, Estele, Estell, Estella, Stella. *Latin:* "star". Also see Esther & Stella. *Estelle Sylvia* (1882-1960), activist daughter of British militant suffrage leader.

Esther // Essa, Essie, Essy, Esta, Ester, Etti, Ettie, Etty, Hester, Hesther, Hettie, Hetty. *Persian:* "star". Biblical: Jewish heroine queen of Persians who saved her people from destruction. *Esther Birdsall Darling*, (1879-1965), U.S. author who bred Alaskan sled dogs. *Esther Morris*,

(1814-1902), U.S. woman suffrage leader, appointed world's first woman justice of the peace. *Esther Forbes*, (1894?-1967), award winning U.S. author of 'Paul Revere and the World He Lived In' and 'Johnny Tremain'.

Ethel // Ethelda, Ethelin, Etheline, Ethelyn, Ethyl. *Old English:* "noble". *Ethel Mary Smyth*, (1858-1944), British composer, prominent in militant suffrage movement. *Ethel Barrymore*, (1879-1959), U.S. actress (stage, screen, radio, and television). *Ethel Greenglass Rosenberg*, (1915-53) with husband, first U.S. civilians to be sentenced and put to death for espionage. *Ethel Waters*, (1896-1977), U.S. actress and singer.

Eudora // Dora. *Greek:* "honored gift". *Eudora Welty*, (born 1909), Pulitzer prize winning author.

Eugenia // Geena, Gene, Genia, Jean, Jena, Jenny. *Greek:* "well-born". *Feminine form of* Eugene.

Eunice. *Greek:* "happy victory". Biblical: the mother of Timothy.

Eva. *A short form of* Evangeline *and a form of* Eve. *Eva Le Gallienne*, (1899-1991), U.S. actress. Supermodel: *Eva Herzigova*. *Eva Habermann*, *Eva Herzigova* - Actresses.

Evangeline // Eva, Evangelia, Evangelina, Evangeline, Eve. *Greek:* "bearer of good news". *Evangeline C. Booth*, (1865-1950), U.S. Salvation Army commander and daughter of founder.

Eve // Eba, Ebba, Eva, Evaleen, Evelina, Eveline, Evelyn, Evey, Evie, Evita, Evonne, Evvie, Evvy, Evy, Yeva. *Hebrew:* "life". Biblical: the wife of Adam. Also see Evelyn and Yvonne. Very capable, full of life, self-seeking, manipulative, kind character from father, stubbornness from mother, perseverance and her own ideals characterizes her as an adult, jealous, not predictable, creates conflicts, men like her because she is not boring, she never forgives a man's unfaithfulness, she looks for a husband with the same temperament as hers, some never get married, good cook especially of sweets if married, hospitable, enjoys socializing especially with men, takes good care of her appearance, favorite colors may be black and red, usually has few or one child, doesn't like to stay in one place, she likes travel, swimming skiing, usually she's a thin blond or bleached blond, because she thinks that men prefer blondes, often chooses her occupation as a typist, doctor, seamstress, translator, hairdresser, teacher. *Eve Denise Curie*, (born 1904), French author, lecturer, and musician.

Evelyn // Aveline, Evalyn, Eveleen, Evelia, Evelin, Evelyne, Evelynn. Combination of Eve and Helen.

Evette // Evet, Evett. *Form of* Yvette and Yvonne.

Fabiola. Origin and meaning unknown.

Fabrice. *Fabrice Luchini* - Actress.

Faith // Fae, Fay, Faye, Fayth, Faythe. **Middle English:** "fidelity". Tenaciously faithful even under personal

difficulty, gentle, friendly, tendency to choose husband poorly.

Fairuza. Fairuza Balk - Actress.

Famke. Famke Janssen - Actress.

Fanny // Fan, Fanni, Fannie. *Familiar form of* Frances. Musically artistic, creative, word smith, actress. *Fanny Brice*, (1891-1951), U.S. singer, dancer and comedienne. *Fannie Merritt Farmer*, (1857-1915), U.S. cookbook author. *Fanny Elssler*, (1810-84), Austrian dancer remarkable for beauty and skill. *Fannie Bloomfield Zeisler*, (1863-1927), U.S. concert pianist, born in Austrian Silesia; a foremost woman musician. *Fanny Cerrito*, (Francesca Cerrito) (1817-1909), Italian ballerina. *Fanny Mendelssohn*, (1805-47), German pianist and composer. *Fanny Lily Gypsy Davenport*, (1850-98), U.S. actress. *Fanny Kemble*, (Frances Anne Kemble) (1809-93), British actress and author. *Fanny Crosby*, (Frances Jane Crosby) (1820-1915), U.S. hymn writer. *Fannie Hurst*, (1889-1968), U.S. author. *Fanny Ardant* - Actress.

Farrah // Fara, Faraah, Farah, Farra, Fayre. **Middle English:** "beautiful, pleasant". *Farrah Fawcett* - Actress.

Fatima // Fatma. Name honors the Virgin Mary apparition, Our Lady of Fatima. Name also honors *Fatima*, (606?-632), favorite daughter of Muhammad and wife of Ali.

Faviola. Meaning and origin unknown.

Fay // Fae, Faye, Fayette, Fayina. **Old French:** "fairy, elf". Also see Faith. *Faye Dunaway* - Actress.

Felicia // Felecia, Felice, Felicidad, Félicie, Felicity, Félise,

Felisha, Felita, Feliza, Iesha. *Latin:* "happy". *Feminine form of* Felix. *Felicia Dorothea Hemans*, (1793-1835), British poet with sentimental lyrics.

Fern // Ferne. *English:* "fern". *Short form of* Fernanda.

Fernanda // Ferdinanda, Ferdinanda, Ferdinande, Fern, Fernande, Fernandina. *Old German:* "adventurer". *Feminine form of* Ferdinand.

Fidelity // Fidela, Fidelia. *Latin:* "faithfulness". Also see Faith.

Fifi // Fifine. *Familiar form of* Josephine.

Fiona // Fionna. *Gaelic:* "fair". Fiona Cameron, co-author of children's book 'We Live in Belgium and Luxembourg'.

Flora // Fiora, Fiore, Fleur, Flo, Flor, Flore, Florella, Floria, Florie, Floris, Florri, Florrie, Florry. *Latin:* "flower, plant life". Roman mythology: goddess symbolizing flowers and spring blooming". *Short form of* Florence. Inspired personality with a rich inner world; interested by serious literature such as ancient history, philosophy; often keeps a diary, writes poetry, likes music and theater, all that she sees or hears is perceived emotionally, she relives the lives of heroes - especially romances; quickly gets acquainted, she prefers boys over girls as friends, easily associates with others, doesn't like proud or boastful people, good listener, knows how to convince others, her opinion always carries weight, gets married late, has created the ideal man in her mind - which takes her a long time to find, tries and succeeds to subject her husband, good housekeeper when inspired only, successful on the career ladder.

Florence // Florenza, Flo, Flor, Flora, Florance, Flore, Florencia, Florentia, Florenza, Flori, Floria, Florida, Florie, Florina, Florinda, Florine, Floris, Florri, Florrie, Florry, Floss, Flossi, Flossie, Flossy. *Latin:* "blooming, prosperous". Also see Flora. Soft hearted, cares about others, determined. *Florence Nightingale*, (1820-1910), she established nursing as a profession, devoting her life to improving hospital care. *Florence Means*, (born 1891), U.S. writer for younger readers, books reveal deep interest in persons of various races. *Florence Chadwick*, (born 1918), U.S. swimmer, first woman to swim English Channel both ways (1950), first to swim from Catalina Island to Los Angeles. *Florence Mills*, (1895-1927), U.S. entertainer. *Florence Kelley*, (1859-1932), U.S. social worker. *Florence Harriman*, (1870-1967), U.S. public official. *Florence Sabin*, (1871-1953), U.S. anatomist, first woman elected to National Academy of Sciences. *Florence Griffith-Joyner*, (1960-1998), 1988 Seoul Olympic track medelist, 3 Golds, 1 Silver.

Fran // Frannie. *Short forms of* Frances. *Fran Drescher* - Actress.

Francis // Fan, Fanchette, Fanchon, Fancie, Fancy, Fanechka, Fania, Fanni, Fannie, Fanny, Fanya, Fran, Francesca, Franci, Francie, Francine, Francisca, Franciska, Francoise, Francyne, Frank, Frankie, Franky, Franni, Frannie, Franny. *Latin:* "free, from France". *Feminine form of* Francis. Loves children, idealist, romanticist, optimist, radical, freethinker, not grounded in truth, unrealistic, friendly, likable, very expressive, when drunk may flirt with men, good housekeeper, educator, teacher, children's writer, author, librarian. *Frances Willard*, (1839-98), lecturer, educator and temperance crusader. *Frances Wright*, (1795-1852), U.S. social reformer; socialist, women's rights; denounced religion, slavery, and marriage. *Frances Horwich*, (born 1908), U.S. television star, educator, and writer. *Frances Olcott*, (1873?-1963), U.S. librarian and children's writer.

Francine. *French familiar form of* Frances.

Frieda // Frayda, Freda, Fredella, Freida, Frida. **Old German:** "Peaceful". *Short form of* Frederica. Appears at peace with self, energetic, fun, friendly, quite social, intelligent, hard worker, often good student, singer, may be social worker. *Frieda Hempel*, (1885-1955), U.S. coloratura soprano.

Gabrielle // Gabbey, Gabbi, Gabbie, Gabby, Gabey, Gabi, Gabie, Gabriel, Gabriela, Gabriell, Gabriella, Gabriellia, Gabrila, Gaby, Gavra, Gavrielle, Gay. **Hebrew:** "God is my strength." *Feminine form of* Gabriel. *Gabrielle Roy*, (1909-83), French Canadian novelist & schoolteacher, studied the poor. *Gabrielle Anwar* - Actress.

Gardenia. *French:* "gardenia flower".

Gail // Gael, Gale, Gayla, Gayle, Gayleen, Gaylene. **Old English:** "gay, lively." *Form of* Abigail and Gay. Very good student, friendly to all, befriending, logical, wise, sensible, balanced, capable, thoughtful, well liked, often good at math, chooses husband well, pretty, leader, calm, good teacher, interior design, musician, often doctor or nurse. *Gail E. Haley*, (born 1939), U.S. author and illustrator. *Gail Kubik*, (born 1914), U.S. Pulitzer prize winning composer. *Gail Corbett*, (1873-1952), U.S. sculptor. *Gail Harris*, *Gale Storm* - Actresses.

Galina. *Greek:* "calmness". Daddy's daughter, prefers the company of boys as a child, but she realizes she is a girl, likes to dress-up, looks at her self in front of mirror, she just feels more comfortable around guys, even after she is grown-up she still avoid women's problems and tricks, active by nature, likes camping, plays sports, likes various activities, good worker, makes time to do everything and still stay attractive, calculating business woman, reaches her business goals, people interest her as much as they are useful to her, very friendly and helpful to useful people, but politly cold to those who don't benifit her, quick mood swings, plenty of men are interested in her, often she'll pick a most handsome capable man who will submit to her lead and not fight her authority. *Galina Ulanova*, (born 1910), Russian prima ballerina.

Gay // Gae, Gaye. **Old French:** "merry". *Form of* Gail. Also see Abigail. Very nice, friendly positive attitude.

Gem // Gema, Gemma. **English:** "gem, jewel".

Gena // Geena, Genna, Gina. **Russian:** "wife". *Form of* Gina. *Geena Davis*, *Geena Lee Nolin*, *Geena Lisa*, *Gena Rowlands* - Actresses.

Genesis // Genecis, Genesi, Genessis, Gennesis. **Hebrew:** "the begining".

Geneva // Gena, Genevra, Janeva. *Old French:* "juniper tree." *Short form of* Genevieve. Also see Jennifer.

Genevieve // Gena, Geneva, Genevra, Gennie, Genny, Genovera, Gina, Janeva, Jennie, Jenny. *Old German:* "white wave". *Form of* Guinevere. Also see Jennifer. *Sainte Genevieve*, (422?-512), a patron saint of Paris. *Genevieve Foster*, (1893-1979), U.S. author-artist, books for older children. *Genevieve Taggard*, (1894-1948), U.S. poet.

Georgia // George, Georgeanna, Georgeanne, Georgena, Georgetta, Georgette, Georgiana, Georgianna, Georgianne, Georgie, Georgina, Georgine, Giorgia. *Latin:* "farmer". *Feminine form of* George.

Geraldine // Deena, Dina, Geralda, Geraldina, Gerhardine, Geri, Gerianna, Gerianne, Gerri, Gerrie, Gerrilee, Gerry, Giralda, Jeralee, Jere, Jeri, Jerrie, Jerry. *Old German:* "spear-mighty". *Feminine form of* Gerald. *Geraldine Ferraro*, (born 1935), U.S. official. *Geraldine Page* (1924-87), *Geraldine Farrar* - Actresses.

Geri // Gerri, Gerrie, Gerry. *Short forms of* Geraldine.

Germaine // Germaigne, Germain, Germana, Jermaine. *Germaine Greer*, (born 1939), Australian ultra feminist author.

Gertrude // Gerda, Gert, Gerta, Gerti, Gertie, Gertrud, Gertruda, Gertrudis, Gerty, Trude, Trudi, Trudie, Trudy. *Germanic:* "spear strength". Determined, strong, competent, able, goal directed, get sick often when young, shyish, good student, quiet character, as a child likes to follow the boys, appear not as soft and gentle as some might like, a bit straight forward and lacking in tenderness, but they are in fact kind and charitable, some never marry, devoted and faithful wife, teachers, engineers, translators, psychologists, literary scholar. *Saint Gertrude*, (1256-1302), *German Cistercian*, nun and mystic writer. *Gertrude Ederle*, (born 1906), swimming star and Olympic medalist. *Gertrude Stein*, (1874-1946), author and hostess to celebrities. *Gertrude Vanderbilt Whitney*, (1877-1942), U.S. sculptor. *Gertrude Lawrence*, (1898-1952), British actress.

Gigi. *Familiar form of* Gilberte. *Gigi Leung* - Actress.

Gilberte // Berta, Berte, Berti, Bertie, Berty, Gigi, Gilberta, Gilbertina, Gilbertine, Gill, Gilli, Gillie, Gilly. *Old German:* "brilliant pledge". *Feminine form of* Gilbert.

Gilda. *Old English:* "covered with gold." *Gilda Radner*, actress & comedianne.

Gillian. *Latin:* "youthful". *Form of* Juliana and *feminine form of* Julius. *Gillian Anderson* - Actress.

Gina // Gianna, Jena. *Form of* Angelina, Genevieve, Jena and Regina. Relationship centered, determined, friendly. *Gina Bachauer*, internationally acclaimed pianist. *Gina Lollobrigida* - Actress.

Ginger. *Latin:* "ginger". *Familiar form of* Virginia. *Ginger Rogers* - Actress.

Ginny. *Familiar form of* Virginia.

Giovanna // Giovana, Giovanny, Giovonni. *Italian feminine form of* John.

Giselle // Gisel, Gisela, Gisele, Gisell, Gissel, Gissell, Gisselle, Gizelle. *Germanic:* "pledge". Dance: ballet role.

Giulietta. *Form of* Juliette. *Giulietta Masina* - Actress.

Gladys // Glad, Gladi, Gladiola, Gladis, Gladiss, Gleda. *Celtic:* "princess"; *Latin:* "small sword, gladiolus flower". *Welsh form of* Claudia. *Gladys Swarthout*, (1904-69), U.S. mezzo-soprano. *Gladys Bronwyn Stern*, (1890-1973), English novelist. *Gladys Knight*, popular Motown soul singer. *Mary Pickford* (originally *Gladys Smith*) (1893-1979), U.S. motion-picture starlet.

Glenda // Glenda, Glen, Glenn, Glenna, Glennie, Glennis, Glyn, Glynis, Glynnis. *Gaelic:* "valley, glen". *Feminine form of* Glenn. Calm, gentle, sweet. *Glenn Close, Glynis Barber* - Actresses.

Gloria // Glori, Gloriana, Gloriane, Glory. *Latin:* "glory". Beauty industry, energetic, character of mother, but appearance resembles father, talented, inquisitive, well read, has poetic gift, communicative, but prefers to communicate with men, confident in her abilities, she'll start any new activities, but may not finish them,often architect, teacher, journalist, lawyer, interpreter, actress, make-up artist, art critic. *Gloria Swanson*, 1920's starlet. *Gloria Jahoda*, author: 'Florida: A History'. *Gloria Danziger*, author: 'Women's Movements in America'. *Gloria Stinum*, U.S. feminist. *Gloria Vanderbuilt*, U.S. fashon queen.

Golda // Goldie. *Old English:* "gold". *Golda Meir*, (1898-1978), a founder and prime minister of the state of Israel. *Goldie Hawn* - Actress.

Grace // Engracia, Gracia, Gracie, Graciela, Grata, Gratia, Gratiana, Grayce, Grazia, Grecia. *Latin:* "favor, grace". Social work, intelligent, determined, educated. *Grace Murray Hopper*, (1906-92), U.S. mathematician, computer scientist, and former U.S. Navy rear admiral. *Grace Hoadley Dodge*, (1856-1914), U.S. social worker, introduced industrial education into public schools. *Grace Lee Whitney* - Actress. *Princess Grace of Monaco*, (1929-82) formerly actress *Grace Kelly*.

Greer // Grier. *Scottish short feminine form of* Gregor(y). *Greer Garson* - Actress.

Greta // Gretchen , Grete, Gretel, Gretna, Gretta. German *short form of* Margaret. Also see Gretchen. *Greta Garbo*, (1905-90), actress, known for haunting beauty and desire for privacy. *Greta Scacchi* - Actress.

Gretchen. *German form of* Margaret. Also see Greta. Conscientious, good student, attractive, reserved, teacher.

Griselda // Gricelda, Grisel. Literary: a patient, humble, loving and noble wife in Chaucer's 'Canterbury Tales'.

Guinevere // Genevieve, Genna, Genni, Gennie, Gennifer, Genny, Ginevra, Guenevere, Guenna, Guinna, Gwen, Gwenora, Gwenore, Janifer, Jen, Jenifer, Jennee, Jenni, Jennie, Jennifer, Jenny, Winifred, Winni, Winnie, Winny. *Welsh:* "white, fair". See Gwen. English mythology: the wife of King Arthur.

Guadalupe. Refers to the Shrine of Our Lady of Guadalupe in Mexico City, most famous shrine in country, pilgrimages made to modern basilica.

Gwen. *Short form of* Guinevere & Gwendolyn. Friendly, helpful, well liked leader, diplomatic, teacher, wise, intelligent, hard working, smart working, often starts as nurse.

Gwendolyn // Guendolen, Guenna, Gwen, Gwendolen, Gwendolin, Gwenette, Gwenni, Gwennie, Gwenny, Gwyn, Gwyneth, Gwynne, Wendi, Wendie, Wendy, Wynne. *Welsh:* "white, white-browed". See Gwen. Literary: the wife of Merlin in Arthurian legend. *Gwendolyn Brooks*, (born 1917), Pulitzer prize winning poet and poet laureate of Illinois.

Gwyneth // Gwynne, Winnie, Winny, Wynne, Wynnie, Wynny. *Welsh:* "white, blessed". See Gwen. *Gwyneth Paltrow* - Actress.

Haley // Hailee, Hailey, Haily, Haleigh, Haylee, Hayley, Haylie. *Scandinavian:* "hero". *Hayley Mills* - Actress.

Hallie // Hali, Halie, Halle, Halley, Hallie, Hally. *Greek:* "thinking of the sea".

Hannah // Ann, Anna, Hana, Hanah, Hanna, Hanni, Hannie, Hanny. *Hebrew:* "graceful". Also see Ann. Biblical: the mother of Samuel. Emotionally strong, capable. *Hannah More*, (1745-1833), English writer of verse, plays and books on moral and religious subjects. *Hannah Green*, originally Joanne Greenberg (born 1932), U.S. author, work as teacher of the deaf was basis for novel. *Hannah Dustin*, (1657-1736), captured in American Indian raid, escaped after killing her captors.

Harley // Harleigh, Harlene, Harli, Harlie. *Old English:* "long field, army meadow". Honors the Harley-Davison motor cycle.

Harmony // Harmoni, Harmonia, Harmonie. *Latin:* "harmony".

Harriet // Harri, Harrie, Harrietta, Harriette, Harriot, Harriott, Hatti, Hattie, Hatty. *Old French:* "ruler of the home". *Feminine form of* Harry. Also see Henrietta. Determined, problem solver, sculptor, activist, writer, poet. *Harriet Beecher Stowe*, (1811-96), author of 'Uncle Tom's Cabin'. *Harriet Tubman*, (1820?-1913), a handicapped runaway slave and speaker who helped many slaves escape through the "underground railroad". *Harriet Martineau*, (1802-76), British writer, popularized theological speculation, became an agnostic.

Hayden // Haide, Haidee, Haiden, Haidy, Hayde, Haydee. *Old English:* "hedged valley".

Heather // Heath. *Middle English:* "heather shrub". Cute, gentle but determined, feminine, accomplishes goal, domestic, if undisciplined one can be imprudent/ wild, seldom athletic, very social. Often marries Doug, Brian. *Heather Locklear*, *Heather Tom* - Actresses.

Heaven // Heavanlee, Heavenleigh. *English:* "heaven".

Hedda // Heda, Hedi, Heddi, Heddie, Hedy. *Old German:* "strife". *Hedy Lamarr*, 1940's - Actress.

Heidi // Heida, Heidie, Heidy. *Old German:* "noble, kind". *Form of* Adalheid and Adelaide. Often pretty, smart, occasionally imprudent, business woman. *Heidi Lenhart*, *Heidi Lucus* - Actresses.

Helen // Aila, Aileen, Ailene, Aleen, Eileen, Elaine, Elana, Elane, Elayne, Eleanor, Eleanore, Eleen, Elena, Elene, Eleni, Elenore, Eleonora, Eleonore, Elianora, Elinor, Elinore, Ella, Elladine, Elle, Ellen, Ellene, Ellette, Elli, Ellie, Elly, Ellyn, Ellynn, Elna, Elnora, Elora, Elyn, Galina, Helaina, Helena, Helene, Helenka, Hellen, Helli, Helyn, Ileana, Ileane, Ilene, Jelena, Lana, Leanor, Leena, Lena, Leanor, Leena, Lena, Lenka, Lenora, Leonore, Leora, Lina, Lora, Nell, Nelli, Nellie, Nelly, Nora, Norah, Valenka, Yelena. *Greek:* "light". Capable, illustrator of childrens books, artist, scientist, philanthropist, singer, poet, novelist. *Helen of Troy*, according to Greek legend, was the most beautiful woman in the world. *Helen Wills*, (born 1905), tennis star. *Helen Brooke Taussig*, (1898-1986), famed U.S. physician. *Helen Hogg*, (born 1905), famed U.S. astronomer. *Helen Hughes*, *Helen, Hunt*, *Helen Slater*, *Helena Bonham Carter*, *Helen Hayes* (born 1900) - Actresses

Helga. *Scandinavian:* "holy". Form of Olga.

Heloise. *French form of* Eloise. *Heloise* (1101-64), celebrated, talented, devoted French abbess.

Henrietta // Enrichetta, Enriqueta, Etta, Etti, Ettie, Etty, Hatti Hattie, Hatty, Hendrika, Henka, Henrie, Henrieta, Henriette, Henryetta, Hetti, Hettie, Hetty, Yetta, Yettie, Yetty. *French:* "mistress of the household". *Feminine form of* Henry. Also see Harriet. A real tom-boy as a child, may get into fights, likes climbing trees, plays soccer with the neighbor boys, has male personality, strong, stubborn, determined, a doer, not a sitter, doesn't like or relate to weak guys, has interest only in people equal to her strength, whatever she does - she does well, quick-easy housekeeper, good at training her children, treats her parents with respect but not close with her mother, likes reading books, likes theater, likes movies, become good lawyers, judges, journalists, doctors. *Henrietta Swan Leavitt*, (1868-1921), U.S. astronomer. *Henrietta Szold*, (1860-1945), U.S. Jewish social service leader. *Henrietta Maria* (1609-66), French princess.

Hester // Hestia, Hettie, Hetty. *Dutch form of* Esther. "star." *Hester Lucy Stanhope*, (1776-1839), English traveler, famous beauty and wit, traveled Asia, became a power and prophetess among Druses on Mt. Lebanon, Syria.

Hilary // Hillary, Hilliary. *Greek:* "cheerful". Determined, social, friendly, cheerful, friendly front, achiever, leader, controlling, bitchy when unhappy. *Hillary Rodham-Clinton*, wife of U.S. President Bill Clinton.

Hilda // Hilde, Hildy. *Germanic:* "battle, woman warrior". *Short form of* Hildegarde. Strong determination. *Saint Hilda*, (614-680), English abbess, princess of Northumbria. *Margaret Hilda Thatcher*, (born 1925), first woman prime minister of the United Kingdom, first woman to hold such a post in Europe, first prime minister since the 1820s to win three consecutive elections, held office longer than any other 20th-century British leader. *Hilda Doolittle*, (pen name H.D.) (1886-1961), U.S. poet, one of best of imagist school.

Hildegarde // Hilda, Hildagard, Hildagarde, Hilde, Hildegaard. *Old German:* "fortress". Strong determination. *Hildegarde Hawthorne*, (1871-1952), U.S. poet and author, biographical adventure books for children. *Hildegarde Swift*, (1890-1977), U.S. writer, active in work of

Inter-Racial Fellowship of Greater New York, books for children.

Holly // Holli, Hollie. *English:* "holly tree". Friendly, helpful, pretty, good person.

Honey. *Old English:* "honey".

Hope. *Old English:* "hope". *Laura Hope Crews*, (1880-1942), - Actress.

Hunter. *Old English:* "hunter". *Hunter Tyler* - Actress.

Ida // Idalia, Idalina, Idaline, Idell, Idelle, Idette. *Old English:* "prosperous"; *Old German:* "hardworking". *Ida Bell Wells-Barnett*, (1862-1931), U.S. journalist and civil rights advocate. *Ida Lupino*, *Idina Menzel* -   Actresses.

Iesha. *Form of names ending in* "esha" *and* "isha" sounds, especially Aisha, Alicia, Alyssa, Felisha, Latisha.

Ilene // Ilana, Ileana, Ileen, Iliana. *Form of* Aileen. *Ileana Ros-Lehtinen*, first Cuban American elected to the United States Congress in 1989.

Ilse // Ilsa. *Form of* Elsie. Imani. *Swahili:* "faith".

Iman // Imam, Imon. *Arabic:* "mosque priest, prince, successor to Muhammad". Supermodel: *Iman*.

Ina // Inna. Latin feminine suffix added to masculine names. *Form of* Agnes and Inga. Stubborn as a child causes her tears or her mother's tears, doesn't forgive even the smallest weaknesses of her friends, remembers her hurts forever, but does not take revenge, smart, straight forward communication amazes people, independent, opinionated, isn't controlled by her friends, mother's favorite, given the chance she spends a lot of time learning to cook with her mother, journalist, photo-journalist, hairdresser, engineer, her marriage is complicated, jealous, only a man who is completely honest and open keeps her happy, frank and out-spoken, faithful wife, may tend toward having daughters and marry a not completely masculine or less physical man, takes her children's education seriously, her children are given extra-curricular training like music and sports, if she's talented her profession will be first priority and family second, husband may have to do the housekeeping which may cause problems with the In-laws. *Ina Donna Coolbrith*, (1843-1928), librarian, poet laureate of California. *Inia Te Wiata*, Maori musician.

India // Indira. *Old English:* "India".

Inez // Ines, Inessa, Inesita, Ynes, Ynez. *Spanish form of* Agnes. Early on she is calm and smiling, later she becomes more stubborn and difficult, easy learner, reads a lot, good at sports, enjoys socializing, prefers friendships with boys, independent, dislikes living with her parents or In-laws, her house is always open for people although she is not the best housekeeper, her marriage is usually successful, leader in her family, often teachers, journalists, hairdressers, engineers, sales, sound producers, make-up artists, musicians.

Inga // Inge. *A form of* Ingrid.

Ingrid // Inga, Ingeberg, Ingaborg, Inge, Ingeberg, Ingeborg, Inger, Ingunna. *Scandinavian:* "beautiful as the god Ing". More close to her father and tries to please him, often exaggerates, her parents fail in efforts to stop her exaggerations, she gets offended easily, unforgiving, she complicates the simplest matters, jealous of new sibling, contradictory spirit creates unpredictable actions, often doesn't follow advice even if it is good, difficult to be her friend, even though the boys start noticing her early - she is not flirtish, many romances are not her style, usually dates one guy for a long time - testing him, if parents are against her relationship - she will take determined actions like marrying him or running away with him, faithful wife, strict mother, often poor relationship with In-laws because she hates any critiques, usually kind, easily falls under other people's influence, her contrary nature makes a lot of mistakes for which she is to blame, often a single mother. Supermodel: *Ingrid Seynhaeve*. *Ingrid Blekys*, *Ingrid Bergman* - Actresses.

Irene // Eirena, Erena, Erinka, Ira, Irena, Irina, Irinka, Rena, Rina. *Greek:* "peace". Like to be silly or cut-up with close friends, fairly serious, concerned, peaceful, independent and determined from childhood, desires father's attention more than mother's, capable of being a good student which doesn't take great effort, soberly judges her surroundings, sober-minded, may enjoy detective stories and science fiction, involved in sports, not highly sentimental, not swept to tears from characters in movies or books, sociable, communicates with others easily, relaxed in social atmospheres and may even get a bit drunk, feels more relaxed around men, may get bored quickly with women, straight-forward speaker, jealous, falls in love easily by her nature, always keeps her independent spirit, she does not give her life only to her family and domestics, achieving a profession and continuing her growth is very important to her, usually valuable workers, always knows what she wants; she obtains respect from her husband, children, colleagues and neighbors; carefully picks her husband, her husband may not doubt her faithfulness under the condition he constantly assures her of her value, to under-value her is dangerous and can push her to an affair, but unlikely to divorce because she likes stableness and calmness, good cook, she likes to try new techniques of child training, often predisposed to be over-weight, mother-in-law often don't like her independent nature. *Irene* (752?-803), Byzantine empress, first woman to rule Eastern Empire. *Irene Hunt*, (born 1907), award winning U.S. teacher and children's writer. *Irene Pereira*, (1907-71), U.S. abstract painter, teacher, and lecturer, known for innovations. *Irene Jacob* - Actress.

Iris // Irisa, Irita. *Greek:* "rainbow". Greek mythology: rainbow goddess.

Irma // Erma, Irmina. *Latin:* "noble". Cooking, guides, children. *Irma Bombeck*, comedy writer.

Isabel // Belia, Belicia, Belita, Bell, Bella, Belle, Ibbie, Ibby, Isa, Isabeau, Isabelita, Isabella, Isabelle, Iseabal, Isobel, Issi, Issie, Issy, Izabel, Ysabel. *Old Spanish:* "consecrated to God". *Spanish form of* Elizabeth. *Isabel Allende*, (born 1942), fabulist Latin American writer. *Isabel McMeekin*, (born 1895), U.S. author, books for children. *Isabelle Adjani* - Actress.

Isadora // Isidora. *Latin:* "gift of Isis". *Feminine form of* Isador. *Isadora Duncan*, born Angela Duncan (1877-1927), One of the first to raise the status of interpretive dance to that of creative art.

Isamar, **Isaura**, **Isela**, **Izamar**. Unknown origin and meaning.

Isis. Egyptian mythology: moon goddess.

Itzel // Itsel, Itzayana. Unknown origin and meaning.

Ivette // Ivana, Ivania, Ivanna, Ivet, Ivon, Ivonne. *Forms of* Yvonne.

Ivory. *Latin:* "ivory".

Ivy // Ivie. *Old English:* "ivy plant". *Ivy Maude Baker Priest*, (1905-75), former U.S. treasurer. Ivy Compton-Burnett, (1892-1969), polished, witty British novelist.

Often the letter Y is used instead of the letter J in many languages as the English letter J did not exist before the middle ages and is currently not used in many languages. Following this tradition, some parents, especially imagrants, choose to use the letter Y in the spelling of many names which Americans and English usually start with the letter J. Yasmin-Jasmine is a prime example of this practice, but most any letter J in a name may be found with a Y substituting for it.

Jackie. *Short form of* Jacoba and Jacqueline. *Jackie Joyner-Kersee*, (born 1962), U.S. Olympic gold medalist in heptathlon.

Jacqueline // Jackelyn, Jacki, Jackie, Jacklin, Jacklyn, Jackquelin, Jackqueline, Jacky, Jaclin, Jaclyn, Jacquelin, Jacquelyn, Jacquelynn, Jacquenetta, Jacquenette, Jacquetta, Jacquette, Jacqui, Jacquie, Jaquelin, Jaquelyn, Jaquenetta, Jaquenette, Jaquith. *Hebrew:* "supplanter"; *Old French:* "little Jacques". *Feminine form of* Jacob through Jacques. Quiet worker, one of a group, leads as team, pretty. *Jacqueline Cochran*, (1910?-80), record-breaking American aviator. *Jacqueline Du Pre*, (1945-87), brilliant British cellist. *Jacqueline Bouvier Kennedy* Onassis, (born 1929), U.S. editor, widow of President John F. Kennedy and Aristotle Onassis. *Jaclyn Smith*, *Jacqueline Bisset* - Actresses.

Jade // Jada. *Spanish:* "jade".

Jahaira // Jahayra. Unknown origin and meaning.

Jalina, **Jalisa**. Unknown origin and meaning.

Jamie // Jaimie, Jamesha, Jami, Jammie, Jayme, Jaymee. *Feminine form of* James. Energetic, adventurous, very social, ring leader, conspirator often in groups of two, accomplice, quick with ideas, fun, tends to get cheated on. *Jamie Lee Curtis*, *Jamie Rose* - Actresses.

Jamila // Jamilah. *Arabic:* "pretty". *Feminine form of* Jamil.

Janae // Jana, Janay. *Forms of* Jane.

Jane // Jaine, Jan, Jana, Janaya, Janaye, Jandy, Janeen, Janel, Janeia, Janella, Janelle, Janean, Janene, Janessa, Janet, Janeta, Janeth, Janetta, Janette, Janey, Jania, Janice, Janie, Janina, Janine, Janis, Janith, Janka, Janna, Jannel, Jannelle, Janot, Jany, Jayne, Jaynell, Jean, Jeanette, Jeanie, Jeanne, Jeannette, Jeannine, Jenda, Jenica, Jeniece, Jenni, Jennie, Jenny, Jess, Jessie, Jinny, Jo Ann, Jo-Ann, Joan, Joana, Joanna, Joanne, Joeann, Johanna, Joni, Jonie, Juana, Juanita, Sheena, Shena, Vania, Vanya, Zaneta. *Hebrew:* "God is gracious". *Feminine form of* John. Activist, cares for others, intelligent, sincere, speaks her mind, socially aware, journalist, detailed, involved, firm opinion. *Jane Austen*, (1775-1817), famed author of 'Sense and Sensibility' and 'Pride and Prejudice.' *Jane Addams*, (1860-1935), pioneer in the field of social work. *Jane Byrne*, (born 1934), U.S. public official, mayor of Chicago 1979-83. *Jane Austin*, *Jane Fonda*, *Jane Horrocks*, *Jane Seymour*, *Jane Wyatt*, *Janeane Garofalo* - Actresses.

Janet // Janette, Janot, Jessie. *Form of* Jane. Difficulty in finding right husband, business woman. *Janet Guthrie*, (born 1938), first lady race car driver to qualify at Indianapolis 500. *Janet Frame*, (born 1924), celebrated New Zealand writer. *Janet Scudder*, (1873-1940), U.S. sculptor, noted for fountains with playful childish figures. *Janet Taylor Caldwell*, (1900-85), U.S. novelist. *Janet Dibley*, *Janet Leigh* - Actresses.

Janice // Janis. *Forms of* Jane.

Janna // Jana, Janaya, Janaye. *Form of* Jane and Johanna.

Also see Johnna.

Jasmine // Jasmen, Jasmin, Jasmina, Jasmyn, Jasmyne, Jassmin, Jazmin, Jazmine, Jazmyn, Jazmyne, Jazzmen, Jazzmin, Jazzmine, Jess, Jessamine, Jessamyn, Jessie, Yasmeen. *Persian:* "jasmine flower". Heroine of Disney's Aladdin. Supermodel: *Yasmeen Ghauri*.

Jean // Gene, Jeana, Jeane, Jeanelle, Jeanette, Jeanie, Jeanine, Jeanna, Jeanne, Jeannette, Jeannie, Jeannine, Jenette, Jennette, Jennica, Jennine. *Forms of* Jane and Joan. Also a popular French male name. Very openly friendly, optimistic, vocal of opinion, talker, keeps busy, fairly athletic, energetic, physical, daring, bold, fairly modest, writer, reporter. However, most alternate forms are more children oriented and reserved. *Jean Rhys*, (1890-1979), West Indian novelist. *Jean Lee Latham*, (born 1902), U.S. writer. *Jean Collins Kerr*, (born 1924), U.S. writer. *Jean Arthur*. *Jean Harlow*, *Jean Louisa Kelly*, *Jeanne Moreau*, *Jeanne Tripplehorn*, *Jennie Garth*, *Jean Simmons* (born 1929) - Actresses.

Jeanette // Jeannette, Jenet. *Form of* Jean. Children oriented, intelligent, efficient, very studious, straight laced, law abiding, prudent. *Jeanette MacDonald*, (1907-65), U.S. actress and singer. *Jeanette Eaton*, (1886-1968), U.S. author of children's books.

Jena // Genna, Genni, Gennie, Genny, Jen, Jenna. *Arabic:* "a small bird". Also see Johnna. Follower, gentle. *Jenna Elfman*, *Jenna Von Oy* - Actresses.

Jennifer // Genna, Genni, Gennie, Gennifer, Genny, Ginnifer, Jen, Jena, Jeni, Jenifer, Jeniffer, Jenilee, Jenn, Jenna, Jennee, Jenni, Jennica, Jennie, Jennilee, Jenny.

Welsh: "white, fair". *A form of* Guinevere. Also see Jean, Jeanette, Genevieve, Gwendolyn. Tend toward positive attitude, not highly concerned with formal education, quite relational, organizational, leader to a point especially in organizing, usually quite pretty, adventurous, energetic, bouncy, popular with guys, leader. *Jennifer Capriati*, (born 1976), professional tennis player. *Jennifer Lawson*, former vice-president of the Public Broadcasting Service. Supermodel: *Jennifer Flavin*. *Jennifer Aniston*, *Jennifer Connelly*, *Jennifer Ehle*, *Jennifer Jones*, *Jennifer Saunders* - Actresses.

Jenny // Jenni, Jhene. *Form of* Jennifer or Jane. Also see Jennifer and Jeanette. Faithful. *Jenny Lind*, (1820-87), Swedish soprano. *Jenny McCarthy*, *Jhene Erwin* - Actresses.

Jensen. *Norwegian:* "son of Jen". *Jensen Buchanan*, *Jensen Daggett* - Actresses.

Jerrie // Jeri, Jerrilee, Jerrine, Jerry, Jerrylee. *Short forms of* Geraldine.

Jessica // Jess, Jessalin, Jessalyn, Jesselyn, Jessie, Jessika, Jessy. *Hebrew:* "wealthy". *Feminine form of* Jesse. Also see Jessie. Small bit tom-boyish, attractive, able athlete, adventurous, energetic, actress, very social, self-confident. *Jessica Kuper*, political science author. *Jessica Lange*, *Jessica Steen*, *Jessica Tandy* (born 1909) - Actresses.

Jessie // Jessa, Jesse, Jessenia, Jessi, Jessy. *Form of* Jasmine, Jessica and Janet. *Feminine form of* Jesse. Strong, tom-boy, very adventurous, average, often imprudent before married.

Jesus. *Greek form of Hebrew* name Yeshua (Joshua): "God saves". Name honors Jesus Christ.

Jewel // Jewell, Jewelle. *Old French:* "precious gem". Jewel Staite - Actress.

Jill // Gillian, Jillana, Jillane, Jillayne, Jilleen, Jillene, Jilli, Jillian, Jillie, Jilly. *Latin:* "young downy-haired child". *Familiar form of* Gillian. *Short form of* Juliana. Quite pretty, bouncy, popular with guys, academic leader, adventurous, motherly, domestic, teacher, writer, biologist. *Jill Krementz*, children's author. *Jillian Hennessy* - Actress.

Jinny // Jini, Jinni. *Form of* Virginia or Jenny.

Jo. *Short form of* Josephine, Joanna and Joan. *Feminine form of* Joseph. Reserved.

Joan // Jo, Joane, Joanie, Joann, Jo Ann, Jo-Ann, Joanna, Joanne, Jodi, Jodie, Jody, Joeann, Johanna, Johannah, Joni, Jonie. *Hebrew:* "God is gracious". *Feminine form of* John. *Form of* Jane. Also see Johnna. Gentle, motherly, teacher, leader, business woman, owner of small business. *Joan of Arc*, (1412?-1431), a peasant girl who saved the kingdom of France. *Joan Sutherland*, (born 1926), a leading coloratura soprano. *Joan Rivers*, (born 1933), U.S. comedienne. *Joan Robinson*, (1903-83), British economist. *Joan Littlewood*, (born 1914?), British director. *Joan Finney*, (born 1925), U.S. public official, governor of Kansas. *Joan Allen*, *Joan Collins*, *Joan Crawford*, *Joan Fontaine*, *Joanne Whalley-Kilmer* - Actresses.

Joby // Jobey, Jobi, Jobie, Jobina, Jobye, Jobyna. *Hebrew:* "persecuted". *Feminine form of* Job. *Jobyna Ralston* - Actress.

Jocelyn // Jocelin, Joceline, Joscelyn, Joselin, Joseline, Joslyn, Josselyn, Joyce, Joycelin. *Latin:* "merry"; *Old English:* "just". Also see Joyce and Justine. Leader, teacher, formal, self-motivated, doer, pusher, strives, serious, warm and cold, goal minded, hard worker, planner, lacks humor.

Jody // Jodee, Jodi, Jodie. *Form of* Joan or Judith. Very cute, energetic, intelligent, very relational, physically fit, sexy, flighty, chooses her mate, attraction to man obvious, group of friends, ignores others, requires great deal of attention; marries young. *Jodie Foster* - Actress.

Joelle // Joela, Joell, Joella, Joellen, Joelly, Joelynn. *Hebrew:* "God is willing". *Feminine form of* Joel. gentle, feminine but not fragile, thin, uniformly liked, not pushy, relational, follower, able, sensitive, often smaller than others.

Joey. *Form of* Joe and Joseph. *Joey Lauren Adams* - Actress.

Johnna // Giana, Gianna, Johna, Johnath, Jonell, Jonis. *Feminine form of* John. *Form of* Johanna. Determine, leader among women, "spearhead", organizer, attractive, business woman, owner of small business, likes to play sports - skiing, basketball, swimming, good at exact sciences, good friend with boys, good friend, very close best friend, very loyal to her friend, can do men's occupation well, may seldom dress in feminine clothes, may be very attractive but doesn't use it for her benefit or advancement, quick wit and mouth, energizes people and activities, doesn't try to get married early, usually finishes college and works for a while before marrying, often marries a long time friend or buddy, leader in the marriage, she raises her children to be emotionally strong and not delicate, many of them smoke and like partying.

Jolene // Joleen, Joline, Jolyn. *Middle English:* "he will increase". *Feminine form of* Joseph.

Jolie // Jolee, Joli, Joly. *French:* "pretty".

Jordan // Jordain, Jordana, Jordanna, Jordyn, Jorey, Jori, Jorie, Jorrie, Jorry, Jourdan. *Hebrew:* "descending".

Josephine // Fifi, Fifine, Fina, Jo, Joette, Joey, Joline, Josee, Josefa, Josefina, Josepha, Josephina, Josey, Josi, Josie, Josy. *Hebrew:* "he shall increase". *Feminine form of* Joseph. attractive, intelligent, humorous, fun loving, hard worker, leader. *Josephine Johnson*, (born 1910), U.S. novelist and poet. *Josephine Baker*, (1906-75), French entertainer, 1960s U.S. civil rights demonstrator. *Josephine Peary*, (1863-1955), U.S. Arctic traveler and children's writer. *Josephine Lawrence*, (1890-1978), U.S. author and journalist. *Josefin Nilsson*, *Josie Bissett* - Actresses.

Jovana // Jovanna. *Form of* Giovanna.

Joy // Joya, Joyan, Joyann, Joye. *Latin:* "joy". Also see Joyce. Joyful, fun, helpful.

Joyce // Joice, Joyous. *Latin:* "joyous". Also see Jocelyn and Joy. Leader, teacher, formal, self-motivated, doer, pusher, strives, serious, warm and cold, goal minded, hard worker, planner, lacks humor. *Joyce Anne Marriott*, (born 1913), Canadian poet. *Joyce Carol Oates*, (born 1938), U.S. author.

Juanita // Juana, Waneta. *Spanish familiar form of* Joan. *Juanita M. Kreps*, (born 1921), U.S. educator and appointed official.

Judith // Giuditta, Jodi, Jodie, Judy, Judi, Judie, Juditha, Judy, Judye. *Hebrew:* "of Judah". Efficient, manager, determined, even stubborn, goal orientated, mathematical, mechanical, leader, planner, sometimes indifferent and self-seeking. *Judith*, Jewish heroine. *Judith Resnik*, (1949-86), U.S. astronaut, killed in space shuttle explosion. Model: *Judit Masco*. *Judi Evans Luciana*, *Judy Garland* - Actresses.

Julia // Giulia, Giulietta, Joletta, Julee, Juli, Juliana, Juliane, Juliann, Julianne, Julie, Julienne, Juliet, Julieta, Julietta, Juliette, Julina, Juline, Julissa, Julita, Yulia. *Latin:* "youthful". *Feminine form of* Julius. Also see Julie and Yulia. As a child her not easy character is herited from her mother, she resembles her father, closer attachment to her father, pretty good student, also likes to do music and dancing, likes to read romance novels, sometimes keeps a diary, kind, doesn't remember evil or hold a grudge, sometime she's unpredictable, can sever a relationship for no appearent reason, some get married late eventhough popular with guys, she tends to be a choosy bride, usually picks spouse wisely and well, likes socializing, generally optimistic, friendly and positive attitude, enjoys visiting and being a guest even more than inviting and hostessing, good cook, big lover of sweets, may be moody. *Julia Agrippina*, (AD 16?-59), Roman empress. *La Julia Rhea*, (1908-92), U.S. classical soprano. *Julia Mood Peterkin*, (1880-1961), U.S. novelist. *Julia Margaret Cameron*, (1815-79), British photographer. *Julia Clifford Lathrop*, (1858-1932), U.S. social worker. *Julia Marlowe*, (1866-1950), U.S. Shakespearean actress. *Julia Ward Howe*,

(1819-1910), U.S. writer and reformer. *Julia Hammond*, 19th-century U.S. inventor. *Julia Duffy*, *Julia Ormond*, *Julia Roberts*, *Julianna Margulies*, *Julianne Moore*, *Juliette Binoche* - Actresses.

Julie. *Form of* Julia. Often quite attractive, composed not Noble, resolute, calm, joker, laugher, deep thinker, gentle, patient, determined. flaky, competent leader, especially under others, reaching other's goals well, fun, friendly, attractive, good sense of humor, faithful, serious. *Julie Jeanne Eleonore de Lespinasse*, (1732-76), French letter writer and social leader, noted for her love letters. *Julie Recamier*, (1777-1849), French society leader, famed for beauty and intelligence. *Julie Andrews*, *Julie Christie*, *Julie Condra*, *Julie Deply*, *Julie Harris* (born 1925) - Actresses.

June // Junette, Junia, Junieta, Junina. *Latin:* "June". Capable leader in small groups, often secretary or assistant, not large group leader, friendly, spirited. *June Meyer Jordan*, (born 1936), U.S. poet, teacher, children's author. *June Allyson* - Actress.

Juno. Roman mythology: Juno/Hera, wife of Zeus/Jupiter. See Winona for possible personality.

Justine // Giustina, Justina, Justinn. *Latin:* "just". *Feminine form of* Justin. *Justine Bateman* - Actress.

Kacie // Kacee, Kacey, Kaci. *Forms of* Casey.

Kaila // Kaela, Kaelyn, Kai, Kailee, Kailey, Kala, Kalani, Kaleigh, Kaley, Kali, Kalia, Kalie, Kalila, Kalli, Kally, Kaylee, Kaylil, Kylila. Form of Katherine.

Kaitlyn // Kaitlin, Kaitlynn. Form of Katherine. Kali. *Sanskrit:* "energy". Indian mythology: a goddess of murder, death, and plague. *Philippine:* a very old martial art, also called Arnis. *Latin:* "salsola kali" or Russian thistle.

Kalinda // Kaleena, Kalina, Kalindi. *Sanskrit:* "sun". *Latin:* kalendae, "calendar".

Kara // Karalee, Karrah. *Form of* Cara. *Familiar form of* Katherine. The Kara Sea (also called Karskoe More), arm of Arctic Ocean. Gentle, capable, able follower, a bit reluctant to lead, stable, a little shy.

Karen // Caren, Carin, Caron, Caryn, Karena, Kari, Karin, Karissa, Karna, Karon, Karyn, Kerrin. *Danish form of* Katherine. Gentle, capable, able follower, able leader, stable, determined, stubborn, would like to deny her mistakes but is still quick to admit them to others. *Karen Horney*, (1885-1952), German-born psychoanalyst. *Karen Christence Dinesen*, (1885-1962), Danish writer, wrote 'Out of Africa' (1937). *Karen Allen*, *Karen Lynn Gorney* - Actresses.

Kari // Karee, Karie, Karilynn, Karry, Kary, Karylin. *Familiar form of* Katherine. Feminine form of Kerry. Fun loving, bright, leader, amiable, social, energetic. *Kari Wuhrer* - Actress.

Karla // Karley, Karli, Karlie, Karly, Karol. *Form of* Caroline or Charlotte. Fun, quite intelligent, very able leader, leads without degrading others, energetic, great team person, often own small business. Marries sensitive relational leader.

Kate // Katarina, Katelyn, Katelynn, Katerina, Kattie. *Short form of* Katherine. More adventurous than Katherines, upbeat. Supermodels: *Kate James* & *Kate Moss*. *Kate Beckinsale*, *Kate Jackson*, *Kate Mulgrew*, *Kate Winslet* - Actresses.

Katherine // Caitlin, Caitrin, Caren, Carin, Caron, Caryn, Cass, Cassie, Cassy, Catarina, Cate, Caterina, Catha, Catharina, Catharine, Cathe, Cathee, Catherina, Catherine, Cathi, Cathie, Cathleen, Cathlene, Cathrine, Cathryn, Cathy, Cati, Catie, Catlaina, Catriona, Cathyleen, Caty, Caye, Ekaterina, Kakalina, Karen, Karena, Kari, Karin, Karna, Kass, Kassi, Kassia, Kassie, Kata, Katalin, Kate, Katerina, Katerine, Katey, Kath, Katha, Katharine, Katharyn, Kathe, Katheryn, Kathi, Kathie, Kathleen, Kathryn, Kathryne, Kathy, Kathye, Katie, Katina, Katinka, Katrina, Katrine, Katrinka, Katti, Kattie, Katuscha, Katushka, Katya, Kay, Kaye, Ketti, Kettie, Ketty, Kit, Kitti, Kittie, Kitty, Yekatarina. *Greek:* "pure". Attractive, studious, intelligent, administrator, manager of people, goal reacher, fairly serious, bit of perfectionist, writer especially for children, bit proud, she one of the best students, may be difficult emotionally when others excel her, competes with them, chooses as her friends those who excel, she may doubt herself, she often acts extravagant, doesn't marry quickly even though she has a lot of admirers, she picks a guy who is close to her psychological type, her inner anxiety increases for insignificant reasons which lead to actions which appear impulsive, she needs a husband who helps her feel more confident in life, usually quite successful in life, often not good at proper disciplining of her children, successful at any area of work, may believe in astrology and metaphysical. _Katherine Mansfield_, (1888-1923), story writer gifted with keen insight into human character. _Katherine Dunham_, (born 1910), dancer, choreographer, and anthropologist. _Katherine Milhous_, (born 1894), U.S. author and illustrator of children's books. _Katharine Hepburn_ - Actress.

Kathleen // Kathlin, Katlee, Katlin. _Form of_ Katherine. Slightly lighter personality than Katherine. _Kathleen Turner_ (born 1954?), _Kathleen Quinlan_ - Actress.

Kathy // Cathy. _Form of_ Katherine, Kathleen or Kathryn. More fun loving but otherwise a Katherine. _Kathy Whitmire_, (originally Kathryn Jean Niederhofer) (born 1946), Texas' first major woman mayor. _Kathy Whitworth_, (born 1939), major professional U.S. golfer. Supermodel: _Kathy Ireland_.

Katie // Katee, Kati, Kattie, Katty, Katy. _Short form of_ Katherine. Same as Katherine but a bit less serious.

Katrina // Catrina, Katine, Yekatarina. _Greek form of_ Katherine.

Kay // Caye, Kai, Kaia, Kaja, Kaya, Kaye. _Short form of_ Katherine. _Spanish:_ "reef, low island".

Kayla // Cayla, Kaela, Kaila, Kaylah, Kaylee, Kayleigh, Kaylie, Kaylin, Kaylyn, Keyla. Form of Kay and Katherine.

Kelly // Kelley, Kellen, Kelli, Kellia, Kellie, Kellina. _Gaelic:_ "warrior woman". Cute, light, energetic, bouncy, determined, organizer, organizing leader, gullible when young. _Kellie Martin_, _Kelly Packard_, _Kelly Preston_, _Kelly Rowan_, _Kelly Willis_ - Actresses.

Kelsey // Kelsea, Kelsi, Kelsie. _Scandinavian:_ "ship island".

Kendall // Kendal. _Old English:_ "bright valley".

Kendra // Kendre, Kenna, Kinna. _Old English:_ "knowledgable". Knowledgeable, self-restrained, focused, independent soul.

Kennedy. _Gaelic:_ "helmetied chief".

Kenya // Kenia. An African republic.

Kerry // Keri, Keriann, Kerianne, Kerri, Kerrie. _Gaelic:_ "dark, dark-haired". A county in Ireland. Gentle, capable, able follower, able leader, stable, fun-loving, bouncy. _Keri Russell_, _Kerri Green_ - Actresses.

Khadijah // Khadija. _Arabic._ _Khadijah_ (d. 619), wealthy first wife of the Prophet Muhammad, the founder of Islam.

Kiana // Keana, Keanna, Kianna. _Hawian._ Kiana, hostess of Kiana's Flex Appeal, fitness show.

Keira // Keyra, Kiara, Kiarra, Kiera, Kierra, Kira, Kyra. _Old Greek:_ "lady, Miss". _Female form of_ Keir. Stubborn, overly sensitive to herself, conceited, good athlete, not generally lucky in life, principled and goal directed, directly pursues goal, a little withdrawn and quiet, failure affects her deeply even though she tries to hide this fact, chaste, unfaithfulness to husband is nearly impossible; ideal wife for a reserved and sexually undemanding husband, likes housekeeping, likes to hostess, she enjoys to be liked.

Kimberly // Kim, Kimberlee, Kimerley, Kimberli, Kimberlyn, Kimbra, Kimmi, Kimmie, Kimmy, Kym. *Old English:* "royal fortress meadow". Emotional, very relational, fun-loving, always apparently friendly except when confronting another then very sober, intelligent but avoids mathematics, acting, public relations. Model: Kim Alexis. *Kim Basinger*, *Kim Cattrall*, *Kim Delaney*, *Kim Novak*, *Kim Thomson*, *Kimberley Davies*, *Kimberly McCullough*, *Kimberly Williams*, *Kym Wilson* - Actresses.

Kirsten // Kiersten, Kirsteni, Kirsti, Kirstie, Kirstin Kirstyn, Kyrstin. *Scandinavian form of* Christine. Thinner than Christine, energetic, more self-confident. *Kirsten Flagstad*, (1895-1962), Norwegian dramatic soprano. *Kirstie Alley* - Actress.

Kitty. *Familiar form of* Katherine.

Kora // Cora, Corabel, Corabella, Corabelle, Corella, Corena, Corene, Coretta, Corette, Corey, Cori, Corie, Corina, Corinna, Corinne, Coriss, Corissa, Corrina, Corrine, Corry, Kore, Korella, Koren, Koressa, Kori, Korie Korina. *Greek:* "maiden". Also see Cora. Leader, steady, stable, average to over weight, friendly to all, hardworking, conscientious.

Kristen // Krista, Kristan, Kristi, Kristin, Kristina, Kristine, Kristy, Kristyn, Krysta, Krystyna. *Scandinavian form of* Christine and Christy. Kristines tend to be more emotionally steady, thoughtful, independent and thinner than Christys. *Kristen Cloke*, *Kristen Johnston*, *Kristin Lehman*, *Kristin Scott Thomas*, *Kristina Malandro Wagner*, *Kristy McNichol*, *Kristy Swanson*, *Kristy Wright* - Actresses.

Krystal // Kristal, Krystalle, Krystie, Krystle. *Forms of* Crystal.

Kyla // Kyle, Kial, Kiele, Kiley, Kylen, Kylie, Kylynn. *Gaelic:* "pretty, near the chapel".

Kyra. *Kyra Sedgwick* - Actress.

Lacy // Lacee, Lacey, Lacie, Lacya. *English:* "lacy". *Familiar form of* Larissa. Musical talent, good at drawing, enjoys reading, smart, many girl-freinds, quite egotistical, hospitable, avoids strangers, self relient, chooses steps carefully, takes time to pick husband, usually marries a man she has known for many years, marriage is usually successful, likes to gossip with her friend on the phone, likes to sleep late, good doctors and pediatricians, teachers, clothes designers, singers, artists.

Ladonna. *French:* "the Lady". Intelligent, thinking, rounded.

Lainey. *Familiar form of* Elaine. A softer more feminine Elaine.

Lana // Lanae, Lanette, Lanna, Lanny. *Form of* Helen and form of Alanna. Also see Lane and Linette. *Lana Turner* (born 1920) - Actress.

Lane // Laina, Laney, Lanie, Lanni, Lanny, Layne.

Lani // Lanita. *Hawaiian:* "sky."

Lara. *Latin:* "shining". *Also forms of* Laraine, Laura and Lorraine.

Laraine // Larina, Larinae, Larine. *Latin:* "gull". *Form of* Lorraine. Also see Lara and Laura.

Larissa // Lacey, Larisa, Laryssa, Lissa. *Greek:* "cheerful". A city in Greece. Popular, leader, good sence of humor, adventurous, bit athletic, loyal freind, liked by everyone, popular with guys, likes to dress nice, maybe dress a bit sexy, likes parties, good worker, patient, doesn't try to change her husband, bares with his unfavorable attitude, good relationship with In-laws, caring, she can not forgive her husband's unfaithfulness, devoted mother, very caring toward her children. *Larissa Latynina*, (born 1934), gymnast, first competitor of any sport to win 18 Olympic medals.

Laurie // Lari, Lauralee, Laure, Laureen, Laurel, Laurella, Lauren, Laurena, Laurene, Lauretta, Laurette, Lauri, Laurice, Laurie, Lora, Loree, Loreen, Loren, Lorena, Lorene, Lorenza, Loretta, Lorette, Lori, Lorinda, Lorita, Lorna, Lorri, Lorrie, Lorry. *Latin:* "laurel leaf crown". *Feminine form of* Lawrence. Academic achiever, thin, organizer, beautiful, elegant, less sporty, coura-geous, brave, sensible, leader, philosophical thinker, calm, manager, works well alone, less interested in athletics, writer, actress. Marries: can overlook character of man because of his physical and leadership appearance, but usually picks a loyal man; Lori - rounded; Laura: bit proud, first marriage is often not successful - seems to choose husband poorly the first time, busy, energetic, bit stub-born, hard working, fairly strong opinion but usually open to learn and change it. *Laura*, (1308-48), woman loved by Petrarch and celebrated in his poems. *Laura Ingalls Wilder*, (1867-1957), celebrated U.S. author of nine children's books, basis for 'The Little House on the Prairie' TV series. *Laura Ashley*, (1925-85), English fashion designer. *Laura Bertram*, *Laura Leighton*, *Laura Wright*, *Lauralee Bell*, *Lauren Bacall*, *Laurie Beechman*, *Laura Keene* (1826?-73), *Laura Hope Crews* (1880-1942) - Actresses.

Lauren // Lauryn, Lorne, Lorrin. *Form of* Laura. Slightly less attractive than Laura.

Laverne // Laverna, La Verne, Verna. *Old French:* "grove of alder trees".

Leah // Lea, Leandra, Lee, Leia, Leigh, Leigha, Lia. *Hebrew:* "wild cow". Biblical: the unloved first wife of Jacob. Solemn, intelligent, introvert, responder. *Lea Thompson* - Actress.

Leann // Leanna, Leanne, Lee, Leeann, Leeanne, LeeAnn, Leigh, Liana. *Gaelic:* "poetic"; *Old English:* "pasture meadow". *Form of* Lee + Ann. *Form of* Leah. Egotistical, concealed personality, a bit nervous, musically talented, good artist, sexy and feminine, able to take revenge on a rival stealthily, kind but jealous, struggles with her jealousy, falls in love easily, prefer men's social company, often marry late, some are single mothers. *Lee Remick* - Actress.

Leila // Layla, Leela, Leelah, Leilah, Lela, Lelah, Lelia, Leyla. *Persian:* "dark as night".

Lena // Lenee, Lenette, Lina, Yelena, Ylena. *Latin:* "temptress". *Short form of names ending in* "leen," "lena," "lina," and "line". As child enjoys fairy tale, reserved child, trusting child but takes revenge, she enjoys to do a little of everything, doesn't like to do homework, good student through her good memory, often resembles her father and takes after his personality, emotional, gives the impression of shy and reserved but as you get to know her you'll learn that she is optimistic cheerful and a lover of life, excels in occupations which require communication, the feeling of love is a secondary impulse, her love grows as a consequence of her compassion, she would prefer and marry the one she has compassion for over the rich and successful man, her love is sacrificing and she expects it in return, jealously sensitive toward everything which takes her husband's time, being in her own world - she doesn't care if her domestic life is imperfect, she can live without amassing stuff, she is not overly difficult to please, nor does she show or demand excessive delicacy or care, keeps peace in her house, likes to stay home, caring mother, finds cooking boring, cooks out of necessity.

Lenora // Leanora, Lenore, Leonor. *Russian form of* Eleanor. Slim and very beautiful, draws attention by her appearance, uses her beauty when necessary to get something, marries a man with money, calm personality, even tempered, balanced; often marries twice, often marries much older man, talented, lots of friends, hospitable, not judgmental, spends a lot of money on herself; likes music, flowers and sleeping late; although egotistical and stubborn - she is simultaneously also kind and compassionate. *Judge Lenore Prather* becomes the first female State Supreme Court Justice in Mississippi, 1983.

Leona // Leoine, Leola, Leone, Leonelle, Leonie. *Feminine form of* Leo. From purring kitten to roaring lion, very able. Leona Mitchell, opera stars.

Leonora // Leonore, Nora, Norah. *Form of* Eleanor. *Leonora O'Reilly*, (1870-1927), U.S. labor leader and reformer, organized factory reforms, enforced safety standards, unionized female garment workers, delivered numerous speeches, active in civil rights, socialist, and women's suffrage movements, founding member of NAACP. *Leonora Speyer*, (1872-1956), U.S. poet.

Leslie // Lesley, Lesli, Lesly, Lezlie. *Gaelic:* "gray fortress". Usually cheerful, energetic, hopeful, accepting of others. Leslie Charteris, (born 1907), U.S. writer. *Lesley-Anne Down*, *Leslie Caron*, *Leslie Mann*, *Leslie Carter* (1862-1937) - Actresses.

Letitia // Iesha, Laetitia, Latashia, Latia, Latisha, Leda, Leisha, Leshia, Leta, Lethia, Leticia, Letisha, Letizia, Letta, Letti, Lettie, Letty, Lida, Loutitia, Tish, Tisha. *Latin:* "gladness".

Libby // Lib, Libbey, Libbie. *Familiar form of* Elizabeth.

Lida // Leda, Lyda.

Lillian // Lil, Lila, Lilas, Lili, Lilia, Lilian, Liliane, Lilias, Lilla, Lilli, Lillie, Lilly, Lily, Lilyan, Liuka. ***Latin:*** "lily flower". Planner, schemer, marries poor early, borrower, often appear pretty and fragile as child, seem calm, stubborn, uncontrollable, little tyrant, likes to appear weak or a victim, may pretend sickness in conflicts, as a youth her relationships become more stable, may fight with parents to let her wear the most current fashions, many admirers who like her charm and flirting and nice dressing, kind, doesn't hold a grudge; at gatherings she's relaxed, likes to laugh and have fun; temperamental and flirtatious, falls in love easily -but not with completely sacrificial loyalty, often successful in marriage, she does better with older and wiser husband who will be patient with her capricious or impulsive behavior, her husband usually loves her and gives her unlimited clothes and gifts, he doesn't care that she is not a good housekeeper, she may be unfaithful in marriage but may break off the affair to save her own marriage, her little faults are compensated by her kind and compasion-ate character. *Lillian Nordica*, opera star. *Lillian Hellman*, (1905-84), an American playwright. *Lily Emily Langtry*, (1852-1929), English actress noted for her beauty. *Lillian D. Wald*, (1867-1940), U.S. social worker. *Lillian Russell*, (1861-1922), U.S. actress and singer noted for her beauty. *Lila Cockrell*, (born 1922), first woman elected mayor of one of top-ten U.S. cities, San Antonio. *Lili Taylor*, *Lillian Gish*, *Lilyan Tashman* - Actresses.

Lina. *Short form of names ending in* "leen," "lena," "lene," "lina," and "line". *Lena Horne*, (born 1917), U.S. actress and nightclub singer. *Lina Wertmuller*, (born 1928), Italian movie director and screenwriter.

Linda // Lind, Lindi, Lindie, Lindy, Lynda, Lynde, Lyndy. ***Spanish:*** "pretty". Attractive, highly efficient; business minded; organizer, relational; strong determination, forceful, will not stand for disrespect, expects equality in relationships, no bums for this lady. Marries: highly expectant of husband to share decision-making and plead his case. *Lynda Carter*, *Linda Dano*, *Linda Hamilton*, *Linda Wong* - Actresses.

Lindsey // Lind, Lindsay, Lindsy, Linzy, Lyndsay, Lyndsey, Lyndsie, Lynsey. ***Old English:*** "linden tree island". Attractive. *Constance Lindsay Skinner*, (1879-1939), U.S. children's writer.

Linette // Lanette, Linet, Linnet, Lynette, Lynnet, Lynnette. ***Celtic:*** "graceful". Bright, energetic, thin, discerning.

Lisa // Leesa, Liesa, Liesl, Lise, Lisetta, Lisette. *Familiar form of* Elizabeth. *Short form of names ending in* "lisa" or "lise". Pretty/beautiful, intelligent, energetic, always a leader among equals, however follows authority well, outspoken; strong minded, a bit stubborn, judgmental, social, loyal, marries nearly equally strong male. *Liza Lehmann*, (1862-1918), British soprano and composer. *Liza Minnelli*, (born 1946), U.S. brassy singer-dancer-actress. Model: Talisa Soto. *Lisa Darr*, *Lisa Gay Hamilton*, *Lisa Howard*, *Lisa Kudrow*, *Lisa Ryder* - Actresses.

Lisha // Lishe. ***Arabic:*** "darkness of midnight". Also forms of Alisha and Lisa.

Liz // Liza, Lizbeth, Lizet, Lizeth, Lizette, Lizzie. *Familiar form of* Elizabeth. See Lisa.

Lois. *Form of* Louise.

Lola. *Familiar form of* Dolores and Louise.

Lolita // Lita, Lulita. *Spanish form of* Lola. *Lolita Davidovich* - Actress.

Loni // Lona, Lonee, Lonna, Lonni, Lonnie. **Mid-English:** "solitary". *Loni Anderson* - Actress.

Lora // Loree, Lorelle, Lori, Loria, Lorianna, Lorianne, Lorie, Lory. *Forms of* Laura. *Lori Hallier*, *Lori Loughlin* - Actresses.

Loretta. *Familiar form of* Laura. Slightly more forceful-determined type of Laura. *Loretta Swit* - Actress.

Lorraine // Laraine, Lorain, Loraine, Lori, Lorine, Lorrayne. *French:* "from Lorraine, France". Also see Lara and Laura. More quiet-sedimentary type of Laura. *Lorraine Hansberry*, (1930-65), U.S. playwright.

Lottie // Lotta, Lotte, Lotti, Lotty. *Short form of* Charlotte. *Lotte Lehmann*, (1888-1976), U.S. soprano.

Lou. *Short form of* Louella and Louise.

Louise // Aloise, Aloisia, Aloysia, Eloisa, Eloise, Heloise, Lois, Loise, Lola, Lolita, Lou, Louisa, Louisette, Loyce, Lu, Luisa, Luise, Lulu. **Old German:** "famous woman warrior". *Feminine form of* Louis. Pretty, calm, stable, supportive, gentle, observant of people's behaviors, medium to overweight, rounded, novelist. *Marie Louise* (1791-1847), 2nd wife of Napoleon I. *Louise Rankin* (1897-1951), U.S. children's author. *Louise, queen of Frederick William III of Prussia* (1776-1810), her beauty and goodness and the fortitude with which she bore the hardships of the Napoleonic Wars made her a popular

heroine. *Louise Homer* (1871-1947), U.S. dramatic contralto singer. *Louis Couperus* (1863-1923), Dutch novelist. *Louise Brooks* - Actress.

Lourdes. Refers to the shrine at Lourdes in France, the location of Saint Bernadette's visions of the Virgin Mary.

Lucia // Lucero. Form of Lucy.

Lucille // Lucila, Lucilla. *Familiar form of* Lucy. *Lucile Grahn*, (1821?-1907), Danish ballerina. *Lucille Ball* - Actress.

Lucinda // Cindy, Lucky. *Familiar form of* Lucy.

Lucy // Lu, Luce, Luci, Lucia, Luciana, Lucie, Lucienne, Lucilla, Lucille, Lucina, Lucinda, Lucine, Lucita, Luz. Latin: "light." *Feminine form of* Lucius and Luke. Determined, capable, fun-loving, social, social activist, feminist. *Lucy* (or Lucia) (283?-304?), saint noblewoman of Syracuse. *Lucy Stone* (1818-93), one of the first feminists in the United States, by the 1890s the term Lucy Stoner was used for any female crusader in the women's rights movement particularly for a married woman who kept her own name as her surname. *Lucy Page Gaston* (1860-1924), U.S. anti-cigarette reformer. *Lucy Maud Montgomery* (1874-1942), Canadian romantic novelist, journalist and schoolteacher; achieved international success with novel 'Anne of Green Gables' (1908). *Lucy Larcom* (1824-93), U.S. poet of life in New England. *Lucy Lawless* - Actress.

Lupita // Lupe. Latin.

Luella // Loella, Lou, Louella, Lu, Luelle, Lula, Lulu. *Old English:* "elf". *Louella Parsons*, early Los Angeles radio broadcaster.

Luz. *Form of* Lucy.

Lydia // Lidia, Lydie. ***Greek:*** "from Lydia". See both Linda and Lynn. Geographical: ancient kingdom in Asia Minor; early seat of Asian civilization with important influence on Greeks. Organizer, serious, manager, writer, a curious girl while growing up, obedient, careful, tries to be around adults - especially her mother, listens to advice, not fully confident - so may tend to follow other's influence, energetic, but doesn't focus her energy on substantial results, busy at a lot of little and inconsequential activities, at best - her energy helps herself and her family, often her energy is simply scattered, friendly, compassionate, comforting, will get involved and help in some cases, people like her at every gathering - but don't notice immediately when she leaves, good worker, works without questioning, her boss values her a lot, she's good at occupations which involve interaction with others, she takes advise when picking a husband, married - she works hard making her home comfortable, doesn't boast or try to get attention for herself, her husband usually respects her for her devotion to the family and house-keeping, her children don't give her full respect due and they slightly ashamed of her old-fashionedness, seeks mother-in-law for advice. *Lydia Child* (1802-80), U.S. author and abolitionist, published first monthly for children in U.S. *Lydia Nikolaevna Seifullina* (1889-1954), Soviet short-story writer and novelist.

Lynn // Lin, Linell, Linn, Linnell, Lyn, Lyndel, Lyndell, Lynelle, Lynette, Lynna, Lynne, Lynnell, Lynnelle, Lynnett, Lynnette. ***Old English:*** "waterfall, pool below a fall". *Short form of names containing* "lin," "line," or "lyn." Efficient, strong leadership, helpful, very cut and dry, direct, tends toward serious side, can be fun but only thinly covering the serious goal side, not very playful, administrator, spokeswoman. *Lynn Riggs* (1899-1954), U.S. playwright and poet, 'Green Grow the Lilacs', basis of musical comedy 'Oklahoma!'. *Lynn Rachel Redgrave* (born 1943), British actress. *Lynn Fontanne* (1887?-1983), U.S. actress, jointly awarded Presidential Medal of Freedom 1964.

Lynnette. *Familiar form of* Lynn. Somewhat more playful and adventurous type of Lynn.

Mabel // Amabel, Mab, Mabelle, Mable, Mae, Maible, Maybelle. ***Latin:*** "lovable". *Mabel Hunt* (1892-1971), U.S. author of children's books. *Mabel Staupers* (born 1890), U.S. registered nurse, won 1951 Spingarn Medal.

Mackenzie. *Gaelic:* "son of the wise leader".

Madeline // Madalyn, Madeleine, Madelyn. ***Greek:*** "Magdalene, woman from Magdala".

Madison // Maddi, Maddison. ***Old English:*** "son of the powerful soldier".

Madonna. ***Latin:*** "a representation of the Virgin Mary". Also see Donna. *Madonna* (Madonna Louise Ciccone) (born 1958), U.S. singer, actress, pop icon, wrote catchy, often overtly sexual, rock songs.

Mae. *Form of* May. <u>*Mae West*</u> (1892?-1980), actress set the standard for voluptuous, seductive blondes. <u>*Mae C. Jemison*</u> (born 1956), first black woman astronaut.

Magali // Magaly. *Form of* Megali. **Greek:** "great".

Maggie // Maggee, Maisie, Mamie, Meg. *Familiar form of* Margaret. <u>*Mag Ruffman*</u>, <u>*Maggie Cheung*</u> - Actresses.

Mallory // Mallorie, Malorie, Malory. **French:** "armored".

Mandy. *Familiar form of* Amanda or Melinda. Athletic, adventurous, pretty.

Manisha. <u>*Manisha Koirala*</u> - Actress.

Manon. Model: <u>*Manon*</u>.

Mara // Maira, Mari. *Form of* Mary, Amara and Damara.

Marcella // Marcela, Marcelle, Marcellina, Marcelline, Marchelle Marcile, Marcille, Marcy, Maricela, Marquita, Marsiella. **Latin:** "belonging to Mars, warlike". *Feminine form of* Mark. Also see Marcia. Quite pretty, determined, gentle, good student, motherly. <u>*Marcella Sembrich*</u> (originally Praxede Marcelline Kochanska) (1858-1935), Polish operatic soprano, noted for purity and brilliance of her voice. <u>*Maricel Soriano*</u> - Actress.

Marcia // Marcelia, Marcie, Marcile, Marcille, Marcy, Marquita, Marsha. **Latin:** "warlike". *Feminine form of* Mark. Also see Marcella. Energetic, intelligent, hard-working, competent. <u>*Marcia Joan Brown*</u> (born 1918), U.S. children's author-artist. <u>*Marcia Cross*</u> - Actress.

Margaret // Greta, Gretal, Gretchen, Gretel, Grethel, Gretta, Madge, Mag, Maggi, Maggie, Maggy, Maiga, Maisie, Marga, Margalo, Margareta, Margarete, Margaretha, Margarethe, Margaretta, Margarette, Margarita, Marge, Margery, Marget, Margette, Margie, Margit, Margo, Margot, Margret, Marguerita, Marguerite, Marquita, Margy, Marji, Marjie, Marjorie, Marjory, Marketa, Meg, Megan, Meggi, Meggie, Meggy, Meghan, Meta, Peg, Pegeen, Peggi, Peggie, Peggy, Rita. **Greek:** "pearl". Energetic, competitive, competent, friendly, bit reserved, well focused to task at hand, enjoys watching or partici-pating in sports with friends, enjoys group participation, group player, willing to try new things, not afraid to try, often first to succeed in new activities among women, possibly understands human motivation better than most, fairly prudent; very independent, an opinion on every-thing which she doesn't feel restricted to tell, straight forward, her opinions sometimes embarrass her parents, at school age she is already known for her ability in logic, can plays chess well, intelligent, smart, a bit cunning, bit unconfident at getting new friends, normal relationship with peers, spends a lot of time in sports, likes biology, practical, good leader, bit impatient, often marries the first man she likes, often poor first marriage, takes divorce hard, may marry again to prove to others or herself - maybe to get rid of feeling not valuable, likes to be among men and have admirers, her behavior provokes her husband's jealousy, doesn't enjoy cooking, cooks well for guests, doesn't enjoy yard-work, caring to children, seldom satisfied with her marriage, capricious. <u>*Margaret Sanger*</u> (1883-1966), a U.S. nurse among the poor and the founder of the birth-control movement. <u>*Margaret Mitchell*</u> (1900-49), wrote Pulitzer prize winning 'Gone with the Wind'. <u>*Margaret Thatcher*</u> (born 1925), first woman to be elected prime minister of the United Kingdom, first woman to hold such a post in the history of Europe, held office longer than any other 20th-century British leader. *Margaret Fuller* (1810-50), first woman to serve as a foreign correspondent in the United States, also a social reformer, critic, and teacher. Many others famous. *Margaret O'Brien*, *Margot Finley* - Actresses.

Maria // Mariah, Mariam, Marian, Mariana, Maribel, Marie, Mariel, Marietta, Marilyn. Forms of Mary. Attaches to man too quickly ignoring negative character, out-going, often career in music or science, kind, sensitive, calm, when young she likes to care for children, keeps her word, likes justice, responsible with school and homework, peers like her for her diligence and compassion; as an adult - she always attracts people who need attention, affection, compassion or help; devoted mother, adores her children, good relations with in-laws, stoic in daily difficulties, unfaithfulness of her husband is the only thing which makes her deeply unhappy, she's very loved by her children, her children always side with her. *Maria Callas* (1923-77), most exciting opera singer of her generation. *Maria Mayer* (1906-72), won the 1963 Nobel prize for physics. *Maria Montessori* (1870-1952), a pioneer in modern education whose method bears her name. *Maria Mitchell* (1818-89), first U.S. professional woman astronomer. *Mariah Carey*, popular singer. *Maria Bello*, *Maria Grazia Cucinotta* - Actresses.

Marian // Mariam, Mariana, Marianna, Marinne, Marion, Maryann, Maryanne. Form of Mary + Ann. More like Mary than Ann. *Marian Anderson* (1897-1993), U.S. contralto and pioneer in overcoming racial discrimination.

Mariana Hill, *Marion Davis* - Actresses.

Maribel. *Form of* Mary + Belle.

Marie // Mari. *French form of* Mary.

Mariela // Mariel, Marilena. Dutch form of Mary.

Marilyn // Marilee, Marilin, Marylin, Merrili. *Form of* Mary + Lynn. Pretty, fairly determined, educator, teacher, active in society, possible writer. *Marilyn French* (born 1929), feminist writer. *Marilyn Monroe* - Actress.

Marina // Marena, Marinna, Maris, Marna, Marne, Marni, Marnie. *Latin:* "from the sea". Cute, thin when younger, social, loves to be in groups, high opinion of herself, beautiful, she over values herself, can control her emotions, pre-thinks her action, men are magnetized by her, smart, fearless, relaxed, doesn't forgive unfaithfulness; marriage will be a success if her husband is calm, easy-going, good income and admires her; talented cook, impulsive and inconsistent in child rearing, first marriage is often difficult. *Marina Sirtis* - Actress.

Maris // Marisa, Marisela, Marisol, Marissa, Maritza, Marris, Marrissa, Meris, Merissa, Morissa. *Latin:* "of the sea". Short form of Damara. Also see Marina and Mary. *Marisa Tomei* - Actress.

Marjorie // Marje, Marjie. Form of Margery. Energetic, bouncy, friendly. *Marjorie Kinnan Rawlings* (1896-1953), U.S. writer of 'The Yearling', won 1939 Pulitzer prize. *Marjorie Flack* (1897-1958), U.S. author and illustrator of children's books. *Marjorie Lowry Christie Pickthall* (1883-1922), Canadian poet and novelist. *Marjorie Stewart Joyner* (born 1896), African American civic leader in cosmetology.

Markie. *Feminine form of* Mark. *Markie Post* - Actress.

Marlene // Marla, Marlane, Marlee, Marleen, Marlena, Marley, Marlyn, Marna. *Form of* Madeline. Also see Marilyn. Calm. *Marlene Dietrich* (1901-1992) - Actress.

Marla. *Form of* Marlene. Often marries dominating man, her man often has abusive adictive or adulturous behavior.

Marlo. *Form of* Mary. *Marlo Thomas* (born 1938) - Actress.

Marnie // Marna, Marne, Marney, Marni. *Familiar form of* Marina. Also see Marlene. Usually a positive-up attitude about life, energetic, energising, buddy, companion.

Marsha. *Form of* Marcia.

Martina // Marti, Martie, Marty, Martynne. *Feminine form of* Martin. *Martina Navratilova* (born 1956), tennis star.

Martha // Marta, Martelle, Marthe, Marthena, Marti, Martie, Martina, Martita, Marty, Martynne, Matti, Mattie, Matty, Pat, Patti, Pattie, Patty. *Aramaic:* "lady". Concerned, hard working, diligent, determined, stubborn, emotional, likable, self-confident, persevering and long-suffering, remembers offences and makes no effort to reconsile, loves to be with groups, likes and knows how to dress attractive, likes to attract the attension of men, intelligent, usually choose the more intellectual occupations, usually marry late even though plenty of admirers, often marries twice, faithful to her family, loyal to her man, jealous but tries to hide it, handy at repares around the home; favorite colors may be red, blue and green; enjoys books and skiing, likes sweets. Biblical:

sister of Mary and Lazarus and friend of Jesus. *Martha Graham* (1893-1991), innovative choreographer and teacher. *Martha Van Rensselaer* (1864-1932), U.S. expert in home economics. *Martha McChesney Berry* (1866-1942), U.S. educator, founded schools for children. *Martha Ostenso* (1900-63), U.S. novelist. *Martha Layne Collins* (born 1936), Kentucky's first woman governor, former high school teacher. *Martha Stuart*, modern U.S. expert on home economics. *Martha Hackett*, *Martha Raye* - Actresses.

Mary // Mair, Maire, Malia, Mame, Mamie, Manon, Manya, Mara, Marabel, Maren, Maria, Mariam, Marian, Marianna, Marianne, Marice, Maridel, Marie, Mariel, Marieta, Marilee, Marilin, Marilyn, Marin, Marion, Mariquilla, Mariska, Marita, Maritsa, Marja, Marje, Marla, Marlo, Marnia, Marya, Maryann, Maryanne, Marylin, Marysa, Masha, Maura, Maure, Maureen, Maurene, Maurine, Maurise, Maurita, Maurizia, Mavra, Meridel, Meriel, Merrili, Mimi, Minette, Minnie, Minny, Miriam, Mitzi, Moira, Mollie, Molly, Muire, Murial, Muriel, Murielle. *Hebrew:* "bitter". Gentle but capable/ strong, firmly faces life's difficulties, only devistated by husband's unfaithfulness, can be a lot of fun/easy-going with close friends, not fighter/violent, calm, traditional/ prudent, very motherly, main goal: to be married and have children, good at many things such as singer or writer, artistic, loves rural areas, simple personality, accomplish goals but not driven toward them, driven toward marriage & children, compasionate, loyal, faithful, emotional, arbitrary, not sound in doctrine, bit radical(simplistic) ideas often not shared because of her reserved personality, very romantic notions, hard working. Marries: medium dominant male such as Joseph, Ford, Dwayne. Biblical: the mother of Jesus. Traditionally the most popular female name in the Western hemisphere. *Mary McLeod Bethune* (1875-1955), U.S. pioneer in Black American education. *Mary Baker Eddy* (1821-1910), founder of the religious cult Christian Science. *Mary Cassatt* (1844-1926), American painter. Several nobles of the British Isles by this name often linked with persecutions of Protestants. Totals: (36) writer 36%, social worker 17%, artist 11%, educator 11%, clergy 6%, nurse 6%, singer 6%, reformer 6%, actress, hostess, flagmaker, athlete, politician, dancer-choreographer. *Mary Astor*, *Mary Vivian Pearce*, *Mary-Louise Parker* - Actresses.

Maryann // Mariann, Marianne, Maryanna. Mary + Ann, see both.

Marybeth // Maribeth. Mary + Elizabeth, see both.

Marycruz // Maricruz. Mary + Santa Cruz.

Maryellen // Mariellen. Mary + Ellen, see both.

Maryjane. Mary + Jane, see both.

Maryjo // Marijo. Mary + Jo, see both.

Marylin. Mary + Lynn, see both.

Marylou // Maryl, Meryl. Mary + Louise, see both.

Marzena. *Marzena Godecki* - Actress.

Matilda // Maitilde, Matelda, Mathilda, Mathilde, Matilde, Matti, Mattie, Matty, Maud, Maude, Tillie, Tilly. *Old German:* "powerful in battle".

Mattie // Matty. *Short form of* Martha or Matilda.

Maud // Maude. *Familiar form of* Madeline or Matilda. *Maud Slye* (1879-1954), U.S. pathologist, cancer researcher. *Maud Gonne* (1865-1953), Irish patriot and actress. *Maud Hart Lovelace* (1892-1980), U.S. author, known for books for girls. *Maude Adams* (1872-1953) - Actress.

Maura. *Irish form of* Mary or Maureen. *Maura Tierney* - Actress.

Maureen // Maura, Maurene, Maurine, Maurise, Maurita, Maurizia, Moira, Mora, Moreen, Morena, Moria. *Old French:* "dark skinned". *Feminine form of* Maurice. *Irish form of* Mary. Intelligent, capable leader, fun-loving, friendly, out-going, average attractive. *Maureen Catherine Connolly* (1934-69), U.S. tennis star. *Maureen Flaherty*, *Maureen O'Hara*, *Maurine Watkins*, *Maureen O'Sullivan* - Actresses.

Maxine // Max, Maxi, Maxie, Maxy. *Latin:* "greatest". *Feminine form of* Max. Decisive, personable, friendly, business type, organizer, relational leader, average attractive.

May // Mae, Maia, Maya, Maye, Mei. *Latin:* "great". Greek mythology: Maia, goddess of springtime, daughter of Atlas and mother of Hermes. Roman mythology: Maia, cult partner of Vulcan. Feminine, decisive, loves children. Cunning without being mean, she can be very obedient to get what she wants but once she gets it - again doesn't care, her parents adore her and think she is better than the other children, she is not taught to work diligently, she'll be good student for a soft caring and complementing teacher, if teacher is strict - she may loose interest in learning, usually a good leader, her business blooms and her workers respect and fear her, energetic and social, she easily finds a husband, likes beautiful expensive things so her she's often in debt or husband working extra, jealous and doesn't hide it, very determined in her interests, she fights for what is hers, flirtative, a jealous husband will find it difficult. *Maia Wojciechowska* (born 1927), award winning U.S. children's author. *Maya Deren*, *Mayim Bialik* - Actresses.

Mayra. *Form of* Myra.

Meg. *Familiar form of* Margaret or Megan. *Meg Ryan* - Actress.

Megan // Maegan, Meagan, Meaghan, Meg, Megen, Meggi, Meggie, Meggy, Meghan, Meghann. **Greek:** "great". *Irish form of* Margaret. Type of Margaret, sporty, a little heavier than Margaret. *Megan Terry* (born 1932), playwright. *Megan Follows*, *Megan Gallagher* - Actresses.

Melanie // Malanie, Mel, Mela, Melania, Melany, Mella, Melli, Mellie, Melloney, Melly, Melonie, Melony, Milena. **Greek:** "blackness". Also see Melina. Not interested in playing athletics, hostess, home-body, secretarial. *Melanie Klein*, psychoanalyst worked with children. *Melanie Griffith* (born 1957), *Melanie Lynskey* - Actresses.

Melba // Melva. English: "from Melbourne, Australia". *Feminine form of* Melvin.

Melina. *Latin:* "canary-yellow colored". Also see Madeline, Melinda,and Melanie. Spoiled child, as child she lacks independence since she's accustomed to adult direction, she remains babyish in school with her friends watching over her, not usually a leader in the family she creates, her husband leads her, usually not emotional, seldom shares other's joy or sorrow, usually lives near her parents since she needs their help. *Melina Mercouri* - Actress.

Melinda // Linda, Lindy, Linnie, Lynda, Malina, Malinda, Malinde, Malynda, Mandy, Melinde. **Greek:** "dark, gentle". Gentle, hard working, reliable, caring, easy going, conservative, traditional, very relational, dissuadable from ideal for relationship, not particularly athletic. *Melinda S. Meade*, professor of geography. *Melinda McGraw* - Actress.

Melissa // Lissa, Malissa, Mallissa, Mel, Melesa, Melessa, Melicent, Melisa, Melisandra, Melise, Melisenda, Melisent, Melisse, Melita, Melitta, Mellicent, Mellie, Mellisa, Melly, Melosa, Milicent, Milissent Milli, Millicent, Millie, Millisent, Milly, Misha, Missie, Missy. **Greek:** "honey bee". Very similar to Lisa, artistic, managerial. *Melissa Hayden*, (originally Mildred Herman) (born 1923), U.S. dancer. *Melissa Etheridge*, *Milissa Gilbert*, *Melissa Joan Hart*, *Melissa Reeves* -Actresses.

Melody // Melodie. **Greek:** "song".

Mercedes. *Spanish:* "mercies". Business woman.

Mercy // Merci, Mercie, Mersey. **Middle English:** "mercy".

Meredith // Meredithe, Meridith, Merridie, Merry. **Welsh:** "guardian from the sea". *Meredith Bishop*, *Meredith Salenger* - Actresses.

Meryl // Merl, Merla, Merle, Merlina, Merline, Merola, Myrle, Myrlene. *Latin:* "blackbird". *Merle Oberon, Meryl Streep* - Actresses.

Merry // Marrilee, Marylee, Merrie, Merrielle, Merrile, Merrilee, Merrili, Merrily. *Middle English:* "merry". *Short form of* Meredith and Marilyn.

Mia. *Italian:* "mine, my". *Familiar form of* Michelle. *Mia Kirshner, Mia Farrow* (born 1946) - Actresses.

Michelle // Mechelle, Micaela, Michaela, Michaelina, Michaeline, Michaella, Michal, Michel, Michele, Michelina, Micheline, Michell, Micki, Mickie, Micky, Midge, Miguela, Miguelita, Mikaela, Mikayla, Miki, Misha, Miquela. *Hebrew:* "who is like the Lord?". Feminine form of Michael. Very social, spirited, adventurous; competent, goal/accomplishment minded, organizer, command control when leading, tend to have emotional fulfillment goals, people persons, very competent, leader, make good business leader, willing to change, very conscientious of getting work done, hard working, will take her leader's goal and work very diligently on it, loyal, stubborn, very able at sports once started, willing to learn, works toward self betterment through education, tend to lean toward traditional mindset & not quick to change, easily frustrated when goal blocked but not quick to give up trying. *Michelle Ferdinande Pauline Viardot* (1821-1910), illustrious mezzo-soprano also taught and composed. *Michelle Phillips*, singer of the Mamas and the Papas. *Michele Monique Reis, Michelle Forbes, Michelle Pfeiffer* - Actresses.

Mildred // Mil, Mildrid, Milli, Millie, Milly. *Old English:* "gentle strength". *Mildred Helen McAfee* (born 1900),

American educator and commander of WAVES during World War II. *Mildred Walker* (born 1905), U.S. novelist. *Mildred Taylor* (born 1943), U.S. author, awarded 1977 Newbery Medal. *Mildred Zaharias*, (1914-56), most outstanding American woman athlete of the 20th century.

Millie // Milly. *Short forms of* Camille, Emily, Melissa, Mildred and Millicent. Gentle, unique. *Milla Jovovich* - Actress.

Mimi. *French familiar form of* Miriam. Energetic, focused. *Mimi Rogers* - Actress.

Mindy // Mindi. *Familiar form of* Melinda, Minda and Minna. Sporty, good student, attractive.

Minerva. Roman mythology: goddess of wisdom, Greek counterpart is Athena.

Minna // Mina. *Old German:* "tender affection". *Short from of* Wilhelmina.

Minnie. Form of Minna and Wilhelmina. *Minnie Maddern Fiske* (1865-1932) - Actress.

Mira // Mireille, Mirella, Mirelle, Mirielle, Mirilla, Myra, Myrilla. *Latin:* "wonderful". *Short form of* Mirabel and Miranda. Resembles father in both features and personality, sensitive, gets offended easily, bit shy, squeamish, responsible, keeps her word, persevering, persistent, musical talents, good at following rhythm, physically flexible, doctors, hairdresser, music teacher, teach kindergarten, sales, accountant. *Mira Furlan, Mira Sorvino* - Actresses.

Mirabel // Mira, Mirabella, Mirabelle. *Latin:* "admirable, of extraordinary beauty".

Miranda // Mira, Miran, Myra, Myranda, Randa. *Latin:* "admirable". The heroine of Shakespeare's 'The Tempest'. Cute, sporty, feminine, not a strong leader, relational.

Miriam // Mimi, Mirian, Mirna, Mitzi. *Hebrew:* "bitter". *The "original" Hebrew form of* Mary. Energetic, friendly, out-going, poet. Biblical: Hebrew prophetess, sister of Moses and Aaron. *Miriam Amanda Ferguson* (1875-1961), governor of Texas 1925-27, 1933-35, second woman to be governor of a U.S. state.

Missy. *Familiar form of* Melissa. Energetic, efficient, friendly, motherly, sporty, fun, positive attitude.

Misty // Misti. *Old English:* "misty". Calming, gentle, motherly, nuturing, supportive, companion, submissive, teasable.

Mitzi // Mitzy. *Familiar form of* Miriam.

Molly // Mollee, Molli, Mollie. *Irish familiar form of* Mary. Opinionated, stubborn, talented talker. *Molly Pitcher* (Mary Ludwig Hays McCauly) (1754-1832), The battle of Monmouth during the American Revolutionary heroine. *Molly Brown* (Margaret Tobin Brown) (1873?-1932), U.S. "unsinkable" heroine of Titanic. *Molly Holden* (born 1927), poet. *Molly* (Marian Jordan 1898-1961), early radio vaudevillians.

Mona // Monae, Monet, Moina, Monah, Moyna. *Greek:* "solitary"; *Gaelic:* "noble". Short form of Monica. *Mona Shafer*, Fashion Design writer. *Mona Van Duyn*, poet laureate U.S. Library of Congress 1992-93.

Monica // Mona, Monika, Monique. *Latin:* "advisor". Helpful, sometimes tom-boyish and one of the guys, adventurous, sporty, gentle, respected, leader, writer, loves children. *Monique Corriveau* (born 1927), French-Canadian author, 1966 Canadian Book of the Year for Children Award. *Monica Shannon* (1898?-1965), U.S. poet and author of children's books, 1935 Newbery Medal. *St. Monica*, St. Augustine's mother.

Montserrat // Monserrat, Monserrath, Monzerat, Monzerrat, Monzerrath. Refers to Our Lady shrine at Montserrat near Barcelona, Spain.

Montana // Montanna. *Latin:* "mountain".

Morgan // Morgana, Morganica, Morganne, Morgen, Morgiana. *Welsh:* "edge of the sea". *Feminine form of* Morgan. Composed, attractive. English legend: sorceress *Morgan le Fay*, sister of King Arthur. *Morgiana*, Heroine in Ali Baba story.

Moriah. *Form of* Mary.

Muriel // Murial, Murielle. *Arabic:* "myrrh"; *Gaelic:* "sea-bright". *Form of* Mary. *Muriel Spark* (born 1918), British writer of novels about females and critic. *Muriel Rukeyser* (1913-80), U.S. feminist poet.

Mylene. *Mylene Farmer* - Actress.

Myra. *Old French:* "quiet song". *Form of* Mira and Miranda. *Myra Hess* (1890-1965), British pianist.

Myrna // Merna, Mirna, Moina, Morna, Moyna. *Gaelic:* "polite". *Myrna Loy* (born 1905) - Actress

Nadia // Nadejida, Nidia. *Old Slavic from* **Greek:** "hope". *Form of* Nadine. Friendly, optimistic, cute, relational, social, artistic, emotional, bit stubborn, musically talented, likes dancing, likes noisy games, likes to be leader among other girls, self-controlled, firm, goal directed, not highly affectionate, motivated by calculated benefit, becomes more organized and neat after marriage, lives by "time is money" attitude, picks organized and reserved mannered husband, she leads her husband in a guiding manner, she will be self-centered if her parents don't teach her altruism when young, hard working, her children grow up educated and with a reserved manner - knowing the value of money and showing respect to her. *Nadia Boulanger* (1887-1979), French composer regarded as the leading teacher of composition in the 20th century. *Nadia Comaneci* (born 1962), Romanian gymnast, Olympic multi-gold medalist.

Nadine // Nada, Nadean, Nadeen, Nadia, Nadiya, Nady, Nadya, Natka. *French from* **Russian:** "hope". *Feminine form of* Nathan. Friendly, optimistic, cute, relational, social, artistic. *Nadine Gordimer* (born 1923), South African novelist and short-story writer, fought relentlessly to expose South Africa's system of apartheid, founder of Congress of South African Writers, longtime member of African National Congress, won 1991 Nobel prize for literature.

Nailah // Nala, Nalah, Naila, Nyla. Unknown meaning and origin.

Nallely // Nalley. Unknown meaning and origin.

Nancy // Nance, Nancee, Nancey, Nanci, Nancie, Nanice, Nannie, Nanny. *Familiar form of* Ann. Friendly, traditional, conviction of opinion, involved mother, trains her children, from fun to preachy, fairly serious, hard working. *Viscountess Nancy Astor* (Nancy Witcher Langhorne) (1879-1964), American who became British political and social leader. *Nancy Hart*, American heroine of Revolutionary War, captured of six Tories. *Nancy Hanks Lincoln* (1784?-1818), mother of Abraham Lincoln. *Nancy Landon Kassebaum* (born 1932), U.S. senator (Republican) from Kansas 1979. *Nancy Grace Roman* (born 1925), U.S. astronomer, NASA chief of astronomy 1964-79. *Nana Visitor*, *Nancy McKeon*, *Nancy Travis, Nancy Valen* - Actresses.

Nanette // Netti, Nettie, Netty. *Familiar form of* Ann. Cuter type of Nancy but essentially the same.

Nani. *Hawaiian:* "beautiful". Expect the same as Nancy.

Naomi // Naoma, Noami, Noemi, Nomi. *Hebrew:* "pleasant". Biblical: Mother-in-law of Ruth. Pleasant, gentle. Supermodel: *Naomi Campbell*.

Natalie // Nat, Nata, Natala, Natalee, Natali, Natalia, Natalina, Nataline, Nataly, Natalya, Natasha, Nathalia, Nathalie, Nathaly, Natividad, Natty, Netti, Nettie, Netty. *Latin:* "ralated to birth, especially Jesus birth, Christmas". Independent, initiator of games as child, active in school, finds time to do everything, likes to be noticed, complements of her bring forth double effort, cheerful, energetic, determined manner, actively kind, likes to protect those weaker, bit straight forward, bit impulsive, impatient with criticism of her, maybe best student and certainly not among the worst, marries early, not choosy at picking a spouse, her cheerfulness makes her husband and children feel loved, guests enjoy her hospitality, likes to travel, likes to draw, needy for complements, complements increase her energy, even mild criticism devastates her, remembers her hurts for her life, if her husband wants a happy marriage - he must learn to not criticize small things. *Natalie Savage Carlson*, Canadian folktale writer. *Natalia Makarova*, ballet dancer. *Natalia Ginzburg* (1916-1991), Italian writer. *Natalie Cole* (singer), *Natalie Wood*, *Natanya Ross* - Actresses.

Natasha // Nastassia. *Russian form of* Natalie. Beautiful/ cute, intelligent, reserved. *Natasha Henstridge* - Actress.

Nayeli // Nayelly, Nayely. Unknown meaning and origin.

Neala // Nelida. *Celtic:* "like a chief". *Feminine form of* Neal. Bit subborn and cunning, active but calm, adaptable, likes comfort and coziness, weakness for beautiful things and jewelry, after finishing her education she often doesn't pursue her carrer in favor of devoting herself to her family and staying home with her children.

Neda // Nedda, Nedi, Neida. *Slavic:* "born on Sunday". *Feminine form of* Edward. Also see Nadine.

Nelia // Neely. *Short form of* Cornelia.

Nell // Nellie, Nelly. From *Greek:* Nyosa, "young, new". *Familiar form of* Cornelia and Eleanor. Confidence, determination, intelligent, relational, friend to everyone, cannot keep a secret, usually her mother's favorite daughter, often mother seldom refuses her anything, gets irritated easily and is quickly back to normal, capable in various areas, good grades in school without much effort, hard to call her stubborn or pressing, but she will smoothly prove her point without irritating people, compassionate and caring to those weaker, she nearly always has a cat or dog, she may have several when she's older, she's not a money saver, she spends her money on clothes and expensive things, she has good taste and tries to follow current fashions, always busy, housekeeping gets in the way of her plans, she's glad to let another do the housekeeping, her relationship with her husband in more like a good friendship than passionate love, her egotism causes her to behave jealously and often cross the boundary, her children often prefer their father, she can be infatuated with obviously more intelligent men than herself, but her marriage's stability is more important to her, often artistic work, medicine, teaching, often get advanced degrees. *Nellie Melba*, (1861-1931), Australian coloratura soprano, Melba toast and peach Melba named after her. *Nellie McClung*, (1873-1951), Canadian novelist, wife, mother, feminist, social reformer, and politician. *Nellie Tayloe Ross*, (1876-1977), first woman U.S. state governor (Wyoming), first woman to head the United States Mint. *Nelly Sachs*, (1891-1970), Swedish poet, received 1966 Nobel prize.

Nessie. *Familiar form of* Agnes.

Nettie // Netty. *Familiar form of* Natalie and *short form of names ending in* "netta," "nette".

Nia. *Form of word ending in* "nia".

Nicole // Colette, Cosetta, Cosette, Nechelle, Nichol, Nichole, Nicholle, Nicki, Nickie, Nicky, Nicol, Nicola, Nicolea, Nicolette, Nicoli, Nicolina, Nicoline, Nicolle, Nicollette, Niki, Nikki, Nikoletta, Nikolia. *Greek:* "victory of the people". Feminine form of Nicholas. Quite pretty, actress, gets married young, easy going, often poorly picks a dominating abusive guy. Actresses: *Nichelle Nichols, Nicholle Tom, Nicole Eggert, Nicole Kidman, Nicolette Krebitz, Nikki Cox.*

Nikki // Niki. *Familiar form of* Nicole.

Nina // Ninetta, Ninette, Ninnetta, Ninnette, Ninon. Russian: form of Ann; *Spanish:* "girl"; *Greek:* Ninos, the founder of Ninevah. *Familiar form of* Ann. Fun-loving, motherly, strong headed, stubborn, egotistical, opinionated, doesn't usually take into account the opinion of elders, strongly persevering in reaching her goal, good student on account of her ego, often not showing self-control, other's opinion of her is very important, good relation with peers but not a close friend, pretentiousness and moralizing get in the way of her friendships, responsible worker, punctual; knows how to be likable, feminine and gentle; finds husband without difficulty, loves her family but takes her emotions out on them; since she is hard working, she demands it from her children and husband, they slightly fear her; she wants everything improved to her ideal, she's a perfect housekeeper, accumulates things which will benefit them in the future; since her mother-in-law suspects that Nina is the leader of the family, often poor relations with her; she's the boss in the family and doesn't try to hide her striving to lead; she may rather divorce her husband than take a submissive role. *Ninette De Valois*, (originally Edris Stannus) (born 1898), Irish dancer, teacher, choreographer, and ballet director.

Noel // Noell, Noella, Noelle, Noellyn, Noely, Noelyn, Nohely, Novelia. *Latin:* "Christmas". Shy, withdrawn, not leader. *Noel Streatfield*, (1901-86), English actress and author, especially childrens books.

Nona // Nonah, Noni, Nonie, Nonna, Nonnah. *Latin:* "ninth." Mythological: one of the three Roman Fates. Energetic, friendly, leader, out-going, open.

Nora // Norah. *Short forms of* Eleanor, Honora and Leonora. Artist type, diligent worker, constant, planner, often reserved, behind the scenes, unruffled, her calmness can drive people crazy or cause them to think she is strange, but behind her coolness lay embers ready to sparkle with warmth and friendliness, she has many admirers, she warms and cools toward people quickly, often attractive with uniquely beautiful eyes, picks husband with good finances and secure position, lives long and may outlive several husbands, she keeps attractive into old age, usually gets a good education; if able to not work, she wont work. *Nora Kaye*, (originally Nora Koreff) (1920-87), U.S. ballerina. *Nora Spicer* Unwin, (1907-82), British artist and illustrator of children's books. *Nora Waln*, (1895-1964), U.S. writer. *Nora Archibald Smith*, (1859-1934), U.S. writer, kindergarten work, author and compiler of poetry and folklore for children.

Noreen // Norina, Norine. *Gaelic. Form of* Nora. Confident, diligent worker, peer leader, teacher.

Norma // Noreen. *Latin:* "model". Confident, diligent

worker, peer leader, teacher. *Norma Redpath*, among Australia's leading female sculptors. *Norma Gleason*, book 'Cryptograms and Spygrams.' Actress: *Norma Jean Mortenson* (Marilyn Monroe 1926-62). *Norma Shearer*. Singer and actress Peggy Lee (born *Norma Dolores Engstrom* 1920).

Nubia. A location of North Africa and its people, Nubians.

Ocsanna // Ocxanna, Oczanna, Oxanna, Oxzanna. See Auxanna.

Odelia // Odalys, Odele, Odelinda, Odella, Odelle, Odetta, Odette, Odilia, Odille, Otha, Othelia, Othilia, Ottilie, Uta. *Hebrew:* "I will praise god"; *Old French:* "little and wealthy". *Feminine form of* Odell.

Olga // Elga, Helga, Olenka, Olia, Olva. *Russian form* of Helga: "holy". *Feminine form of* Oleg. Artistic, serious, easily gets offended, sensitive, withdraws after small remark, stubborn - even when wrong, prideful, won't ask for forgiveness, equally good friend with boys as girls, capable but not motivated student, does not seek attention as leader or delinquent; not without ambition but seldom achieves great success because of her unproductive activity; tends to be over critical and unforgiving of her failings, her failures can eat on her; jealous of greater successes of friends which she tries to hide with her

helpfulness; feminine, takes care of her appearance, always busy; if she doesn't marry her first love, she compares others to him and is slow to marry; good wife, good cook, likes family outings, doesn't try to be the primary leader of the family, husband upsets her when he gives advise in her domestic activities. *Olga Koklova*, a young Russian ballerina Picasso married. *Olga Korbut*, (born 1956), gymnast won 6 Olympic medals. *Olga Maria Elisabeth Friederike Schwarzkopf*, (born 1915), internationally renowned operatic soprano.

Olivia // Liv, Liva, Livia, Livvie, Livvy, Nola, Nolana, Nollie, Olive, Olivette, Ollie, Olly, Olva. *Latin:* "olive tree". Beautiful, intelligent, versatile, popular. Actresses: *Olivia Hussey* (originally Olivia Osuna) (born 1951), *Olivia Mary De Havilland* (born 1916), *Olivia d'Abo, Olivia Newton-John* (also singer).

Opal // Opalina, Opaline. *Hindu:* "precious stone".

Ophelia // Filia, Ofelia, Ofilia, Ophelie, Phelia. *Greek:* "serpent". Literary: character in Shakespeare's 'Hamlet'.

Oprah. *Oprah Winfrey*, talk-show host.

Page // Paige. *French:* "useful assistant"; *Old English:* "child, young". Supportive friend.

Paloma. *Spanish:* "dove".

Pamela // Pam, Pamelina, Pamella, Pammi, Pammie, Pammy. *Greek:* "all-honey". Energetic, generalist, usually positive, fun loving, appearance of easy going, light hearted, but takes life seriously, determined, set on her desire or goal, relaxed attitude, managerial, quick to make decisions, does not agonize over decisions, likes to lead or co-lead, doesn't much like to follow, wants to stay in control of her destiny, seldom interested in competing, opinionated but doesn't push it on others, has two speeds - managerial and fun loving, enjoys people who are also fun loving and not too serious; personality seems similar to Gwens. *Pamela Travers* (born 1906) British author of 'Mary Poppins' books. Actresses: *Pamela Anderson, Pamela Franklin.*

Paola. A city in Italy. Saint Francis of Paola, (1416?-1507), Italian saint, founder of Minims mendicant order of Roman Catholicism.

Paris. The capital city of France.

Patience. *French:* "enduring expectations". *Patience Sewell Latting,* mayor of Oklahoma City 1971, at that time the largest city in the nation with a woman mayor.

Patricia // Pat, Patrica, Patrice, Patrizia, Patsy, Patti, Patty, Tricia, Trish. *Latin:* "of the nobility". *Feminine form of* Patrick. Reserved, friendly, attractive, receptive, teacher, golfer. *Patricia Ireland*, feminist. *Patricia Hearst*, (born 1954), U.S. newspaper heiress who joined her kidnappers after "brain-washing." *Patricia Highsmith*, (born 1921), U.S. mystery writer, known for exploration of character's motivation. *Patricia Roberts Harris*, (1924-85), U.S. lawyer, educator, diplomat and first black woman in U.S.

President's Cabinet. *Pat Nixon*, (Thelma Catherine Patricia Ryan Nixon) (born 1912), teacher and wife of former President Nixon. *Patty Berg*, (Patricia Jane Berg) (born 1918), outstanding U.S. golfer. *Pat Bradley*, (born 1951), U.S. professional golfer. *Patti Page*, singer. *Patsy Cline*, Country-Western singer. Actresses: *Patricia Arquette, Patricia Ford, Patricia Richardson, Patricia Routledge, Patricia Tallman, Patty Duke*. Supermodel: *Patricia Velasquez.*

Paula // Paola, Paolina, Paule, Pauletta, Paulette, Pauli, Paulie, Paulina, Pauline, Paulita, Pauly, Pavla, Polly. *Latin:* "small". *Feminine form of* Paul. Also see Paulina. Outgoing, intelligent, fairly logical, less emotional, pursues talent or hobby, attractive, easy going, determined, humorous, fun, adventurous, sense of justice in equality. *Paula Abdul*, (born 1962), U.S. pop singer and choreographer. *Paula Fox*, (born 1923), U.S. author and educator, adult novels, children's books, awarded 1974 Newbery Medal. *Paula Hawkins*, U.S. Senator from Florida.

Paulette. More feminine slightly more reserved type of Paula. Actress: *Paulette Goddard.*

Pauline. More serious type of Paula.

Paulina. More thin/feminine appearence but determined and focused type of Paula. Compassionate, helpful, cries with those who cry, rejoices with those who rejoice, appears to love all creatures and all people, very diplomatic, tries to not offend people, very neat, likes to dress beautifully with taste, frugal, may prefer to make than to buy; responsible, trustworthy, people take advantage and over-load her, helps without expecting something in return; believes in the brotherhood of mankind, usually believes communism and socialism work and should be done; innocent and believes the best of others, she will look for justification of her husband even when caught flirting with her best friend; career and professional success seldom interest her, family comes first, she seeks job which gives her more time with her family, faithful, good mother, first marriage is not always successful. *Paulina W. Davis*, (1813-76), U.S. editor and suffragist. Supermodel: *Paulina Porizkova.*

Pearl // Pearla, Pearle, Pearline, Perl, Perla, Perle. *Latin:* "pearl". *Pearl S. Buck,* (1892-1973) won Nobel prize for books about Chinese peasants. *Pearl Bailey*, (1918-90), U.S. singer, actress, recording star, and diplomat.

Peggy // Peg. *Familiar forms of* Margaret. Out-going, very diligent worker, consistent, often somewhat heavy, roundish, out of shape. *Peggy Bacon*, (1895-1987), author and illustrator of books for children. *Peg Woffington*, (1714?-60), celebrated Irish comic and tragic actress. *Peggy Gale Fleming*, (born 1948), U.S. ice skater, Olympic gold medalist, professional TV and ice-show star. *Peggy Lee*, singer. *Peggy Guggenheim*, (1898-1979), U.S. art collector. Singer and actress *Peggy Lee* (born Norma Dolores Engstrom 1920).

Penelope // Pen, Penny. *Greek:* "weaver".

Penny. *Short form of* Penelope. Reserved, follower, opinionated, hard worker, very mothering, peace and security orientated.

Perla. Unknown meaning and origin.

Perry // Peri, Perri. *French:* "pear tree"; *Welsh:* "son of

Harry". Actress: *Peri Gilpin.*

Petra // Peta, Petrina. *Greek:* "little rock". *Feminine form of* Peter. Actress: *Peta Wilson.*

Phoebe. *Greek*: "shining". Greek mythology: moon goddess. Feminine form of Phoebus. *Phoebe Apperson Hearst,* (1842-1919), U.S. philanthropist, mother of William Randolph Hearst, gifts included kindergartens, kindergarten training schools, public libraries. *Phoebe Cary* (1824-71), U.S. poet. *Phoebe Anne Oakley Moses* (Annie Oakley) (1860-1926), U.S. best-known markswoman. Actress: *Phoebe Cates.*

Phyllis // Philis, Phillis, Phylis. **Greek:** "green leaf". *Phillis Wheatley*, (1753?-84), U.S. slave and poet, born in Africa. *Phyllis Schlafly*, (born 1924), U.S. syndicated columnist and noted spokeswoman for conservative causes. *Phyllis Ayame Whitney*, (born 1903), U.S. author of books for older girls. *Phyllis Reid Fenner*, (1899-1982), U.S. children's author, librarian, and teacher. *Phyllis McGinley,* (1905-78), U.S. author, books for children and poems for adults, awarded Pulitzer prize for poetry 1961. *Phyllis Diller*, comedian.

Pilar. *Spanish*.

Piper. *Old English:* "pipe player".

Polly. *Familiar form of* Molly or Paula. Friendly, reserved. *Polly Finley*, married Davy Crockett.

Pollyanna. Polly + Anna, see both.

Pooja. Actress: *Pooja Bhatt.*

Precious. *English:* "precious".

Priscilla // Pricilla, Pris, Prisca, Priscella, Priscila, Prissie. *Latin:* "from ancient times".

Prudence // Pru, Prudi, Prudy, Prue. *Latin:* "foresight, intelligence". *Prudence Crandall,* (1803-90), U.S. school-teacher, attempted to educate black girls against the dominate culture.

Rachel // Rachael, Rachele, Rachelle, Rae, Rahel, Rekel, Raquel, Raquela, Ray, Raychel, Rayshell, Rey, Rochell, Shell, Shelley, Shellie, Shelly. *Hebrew:* "ewe". Biblical: the wife of Jacob and mother of Joseph. Beautiful, feminine, gentle not pushy, thin, quality person, supportive, daddy's girl and mommy's girl, good student, devoted, courage, generosity, and fine simple manners, organized, steady, diligent, loves to work with young children. *Rachel Field,* (1894-1942), award winning U.S. writer, known for children's verses, picture books, one-act plays and later adult fiction. *Rachel Carson*, (1907-64), biologist, conservationist and scientific writer. *Rachel Crothers*, (1878-1958), U.S. playwright, produced own plays, chiefly comedies with satirical touch. *Rachel* (Elisa Rachel Felix) (1821-58), French actress. *Rachel Korn*, Yiddish poet. Margaret and *Rachel McMillan* established nursery schools in the slum districts of London shortly before World War I. *Rahel Varnhagen von Ense*, (1771-1833), German author remembered for her letters and for her influence on literary men. Supermodel: *Rachel Hunter.*

Rae // Raeann, Ralina, Raylene, Rayna. *Old English:* "doe". *Familiar form of* Rachel. *Feminine form of* Ray. Also see Ray. *Rae Bains*, author of scientific works 'Forests and Jungles' and 'Light'.

Ramona // Ramonda, Romona, Romonda. *Spanish:* "mighty or wise protectress". *Feminine form of* Raymond. Determined, busy, intelligent.

Randi // Randa, Randee, Randene, Randy. *Feminine form of* Randy and Randolph. Cute, beautiful, average-poor student, very relational, chooses overly dominating man, sales. *Randi Londer*, co-authored young adult book, 'The Coevolution of Climate and Life'.

Rani // Raina, Raine, Rana, Ranique, Ranee, Rania, Ranice, Rayna, Raynell. Sanskrit: "queen".

Raquel. *Spanish form of* Rachel. Beautiful, thin, calm, gentle, motherly. Actress: *Raquel Welch*.

Raven // Raveena. *Old English:* "raven". Actress: *Raveena Tandon*.

Reba // Rheba. *Short form of* Rebecca. *Reba McEntire*, Country singer.

Rebecca // Becca, Becka, Becki, Beckie, Becky, Bekki, Reba, Rebbecca, Rebecka, Rebeka, Rebekah, Rebekkah, Ree, Reeba, Rheba, Riva, Rivalee, Rivi, Rivkah, Rivy. *Hebrew:* "bound". Biblical: the wife of Isaac. Also see Becky. Nice, gentle, excitable, often bouncy, cute, pretty, not generally thin, rounded, compassionate, caring, love children, generally strong desire for children, may choose to work with children or else some type of socially active or relational work, less athletic, doesn't push to lead but offers opinion, tend to be weak at mathematics and very strong relationally, teacher, social worker, reporter, children's writer, inner and outer beauty, organized, organizer, administrative, efficient, potentially good at training others and potential leader, office manager. *Rebecca Caudill*, (born 1899), U.S. children's writer, taught in Rio de Janeiro, Brazil. *Rebekah Baines Johnson*, graduate of Baylor University, taught school before her marriage, mother of U.S. President Lyndon B. Johnson. *Rebecca Boone*, wife and companion of Daniel Boone. *Rebecca Stefoff*, biographical writer of U.S. Presidents. Actresses: *Rebecca Callard, Rebecca Gayheart*. Model: *Rebecca Romijin*.

Regan. *Form of* Regina. Type of Regina but slightly less ladylike, athletic, most any team sport, fairly logic orientated, friendly but not highly gregarious, well liked, well behaved, able leader but often refrains, not attention seeking, composed.

Regina // Raina, Regan, Reggi, Reggie, Regine, Reina, Reine, Reyna, Rina. *Latin:* "queen". Girlish, social, sometimes attention seeking, weak at mathematics, very relational, avoids contact sports, possible gymnast; distinguished by her kindness and goal directedness, stubborn, persistent, relies on her good intuition, imaginative, works with enthusiasm, very neat but doesn't like to wash dishes, very good cook, likes traveling and far trips, like to sleep-in; likes to spends money, does so wisely, not frugal, determined; not lucky with marriage, if marriage going poorly, may break marriage quickly, strong but not organized, she learns self-discipline out of a very stressful situation, likable, charming.

Rena // Reanna, Reanne, Reena, Reina, Reyna. *Hebrew:* "song".

Renata // Renae, Renate, Rene, Renée, Renie, Rennie. *Latin:* "reborn".

Renée // Renae, Rene, Renee, Renell, Renelle, Renie. *French:* "reborn". Work in one to one relationships well and in small groups, in larger groups they tend to follow another's lead, thin, opinionated, social, fairly athletic, determined, adventurous. *Renee Jeanmaire*, ballerina performed 'Carmen' (1949). Actresses: *Renee O'Connor, Renee Zellweger.*

Reta // Reeta, Rheta, Rhetta. *African:* "to shake". *Rheta Childe Dorr,* (1872-1948), U.S. writer and suffragist.

Rhea // Rea, Reanne, Rheanna, Rhiannon. *Greek:* "earth, rivers".

Rhonda // Rhondda, Ronda. Cities of Ronda, Spain and Rhondda, Wales.Quite social, somewhat gregarious, friendly, not hardly athletic, office manager.

Riane // Ryann. *Feminine form of* Ryan.

Ricki // Rickie, Riki, Rikki. *Short forms of* Frederica. Social, often attention seeking, short term drive, low achievement. Ricki Lake, TV talk-show hostess.

Riley // Ryley. *Gaelic:* "valiant".

Rita // Reeta, Rheta. *Short form of* Margaret. *Rita Levi-Montalcini,* (born 1909), Italian neurologist, received 1986 Nobel prize. *Saint Rita Margarita de Cascia*, (1386-1456), patroness of impossibilities. *Rita M. Johnston*, (born 1935), Canadian public official, the first woman to be premier of a Canadian province. *Rita Stevens*, writer biographer of U.S. Presidents. *Rita Kramer,* author of 'At a Tender Age: Violent Youth and Juvenile Justice.' *Rita Angus*, New Zealand artist. Actresses: *Rita Hayworth, Rita Moreno.*

Roberta // Bobbe, Bobbette, Bobbi, Bobbie, Bobby, Bobbye, Bobina, Bobine, Bobinette, Robbi, Robbie, Robby, Robena, Robenia, Robin, Robina, Robinett, Robinette, Robinia, Ruperta. *Old English:* "shining with fame". *Feminine form of* Robert. Also see Bobbie, Robin and Robbi. Pretty, rounded, feminine, reserved, gentle, nice, well behaved. *Roberta Flack*, (born 1940), popular singer, Grammys for smash singles 'The First Time Ever I Saw Your Face' and 'Killing Me Softly with His Song'. *Roberta Stalberg*, author of book on puppets in China. Model: *Roberta Little.*

Robbi // Robby. *Form of* Roberta. Also see Bobbie. Quite pretty, graceful, feminine, gentle, quite social, seldom a bit impudent/wild, usually down to earth.

Robin // Robyn. *Old English:* "robin". Also *familiar form of* Roberta. Very social, pretty, friendly, good student, good behavior, flighty, may through herself at man, looking for security, goes for older guys. Actresses: *Robin Mattson, Robin Strasser, Robin Tunney.*

Rochelle // Roch, Rochell, Rochella, Rochette, Roshelle, Shell, Shelley, Shelly. *French:* "little rock". Also a *form of* Rachel but less careful. Pretty.

Rocio. Unknown meaning and origin.

Rona // Rhona, Ronalda, Ronisha. *Scandinavian:* "mighty power". *Feminine form of* Ronald. Liked, a friend to all, helpful.

Ronni // Ronnie, Ronny. *Familiar forms of* Roanna, Rowena and Veronica.

Rosalie // Rosalia, Rosalind, Rosalinda, Rosalyn. *Latin:* "festival of roses". *Forms of* Rose. Rose + Lee and Rose + Lynn, see all. Very goal oriented, makes the impression of frivolity, seems destined for no-where, but may receive her doctorate in ten years, charming, pleasant looking, quite good psychologist - discovering the psyche of others; idealizes her man and doesn't see his faults, this helps her marriage; likes and possessed by neatness or cleanliness, may be very disappointed with those who don't share this passion; talented, hard working, achieves success, good in occupation; watches all the fashionable movies or plays.

Rose // Rasia, Rhoda, Rhodia, Rhody, Rois, Rosa, Rosaleen, Rosalia, Rosalie, Rosario, Rosella, Roselle, Rosene, Rosetta, Rosette, Rosie, Rosina, Rosio, Rosita, Rosy, Rozalie, Roze, Rozele, Rosela, Rozina, Zita. *Greek:* "rose". Also see Rosalie. Very relational, weak logically, poor at mathematics, artistic type, verse writer, singer, idealist, sometimes prefers to live fantasy, not pragmatist, stuborn, animal lover especially cats. *Rosa Bonheur,* (1822-99), successful French painter, kindly, devoted to animals. *Rosa Luxemburg*, (1871-1919), a foremost theoreticians of the Socialist and Communist movements in the early 20th century, believed in the violent overthrow of the capitalist system. *Rose Mofford,* (born 1922), U.S. public official, Arizona secretary of state 1977-88 (Democrat), succeeded to governorship (1988-91) when Governor Evan Mecham was impeached. *Rose O'Neal Greenhow*, (1817-64), spied for the Confederacy during Civil War, arrested, tried for treason and exiled. *Rose Macaulay*, (1881-1958), British author of novels, verse, essays, humorous, satirical touch. *Rosa L. Parks*, (born 1913), U.S. civil rights advocate, refused to give up bus seat to a white man. *Rose Franken*, (1898-1989), U.S. writer. *Rose Cecil O'Neill*, (1874-1944), U.S. illustrator and writer, created the Kewpie doll 1909. *Rosalia de Castro*, (1837-85), Spanish poet. *Rose Fyleman*, (1877-1957), English writer of children's stories and poems, chiefly about fairies; also singer and lecturer. Actresses: *Rose McGowan, Rosie O'Donnell.*

Roseanne // Ranna, Roanna, Roanne, Rosanna, Rosanne, Roseann, Razanna. Rose + Anne, see both. *Roseanne Arnold,* (formerly Roseanne Barr) (born 1952), U.S. actress, abrasive stand-up comedian. *Rosanne Amberson*, author of 'Raising Your Cat'.

Rosemary // Rosemaria, Rosemarie. *English:* "rosemary". Rose + Mary, see both.

Roshumba. Supermodel: *Roshumba.*

Roxanne // Roxane, Roxanna, Roxanne, Roxi, Roxie, Roxine, Roxy. *Persian:* "dawn". Literary: heroine in novel 'Cyrano de Bergerac'. Stubborn and persisting child, also very sensitive; charming, talented; her capricious behavior causes trouble for her parents, especially her mother; good housekeeper, hospitable, loves her house, cooks tastily; marriage is not usually smooth since most men don't like a woman always trying to press a point; most are very active in the evening, but not morning people; she loves to drive her car; usually musically talented, many musicians, doctors, teachers, nurses, painters; may

tend toward over weight. *Roxane*, chieftain's daughter whom Alexander the Great married. Actress: *Roxann Biggs-Dawson.*

Ruby // Rubetta, Rubi, Rubia, Rubie, Rubina. *Old French:* "ruby".

Ruth // Ruthe, Ruthi, Ruthie. *Hebrew:* "friend of beauty". Character doesn't stand out in group, blends in, pretty, intelligent, basically good person, nearly always chooses to do right, follows safe traditional route, non-assertive, mellow, nice but not definitively out-going, tend toward arts, graphic arts, writing, dance, social service, non-sportsman, does not enjoy competing, follower, loyal friend, may follow group peer pressure to do questionable activity without dissension, influenced by surroundings, if taught well will have good life, if not she'll have a tough start, enjoys travel. Marries: leader. Biblical: daughter-in-law of Naomi. *Ruth Benedict*, (1887-1948), U.S. anthropologist of native societies. *Ruth Crawford Seeger,* (1901-53), U.S. musician and teacher. *Ruth Page*, (1905-91), U.S. ballet dancer and choreographer. *Ruth Draper,* (1884-1956), U.S. monologist. *Ruth Chrisman Gannett*, (1896-1979), U.S. lithographer, illustrator of books for children. *Ruth Cheney Streeter,* (born 1895), director of Women's Reserve, U.S. Marine Corps 1943-45, social worker, held commercial airplane pilot's license. *Ruth Bryan Owen*, (1885-1954), U.S. political leader and lecturer, congresswoman from Florida 1929-33, minister to Denmark 1933-36. *Ruth Saint Denis*, (1877-1968), U.S. dancer, choreographer, teacher, and lecturer. *Ruth Sawyer*, (1880-1970), award winning U.S. children's writer and storyteller.

Ryan // Ryann, Ryanna, Ryanne. *Gaelic:* "little king".

Sabina // Sabine, Savina. *Latin:* "woman from Sabine, woman from Sheba". *Poppaea Sabina* (died AD 65), mistress, later wife, of Nero; beautiful but unscrupulous.

Sabrina // Brina, Zabrina. *Latin:* "boundry line".

Sadie // Sada, Sade, Sadye, Saidee, Sydel, Sydelle. *Familiar form of* Sarah.

Sally // Sal, Sallee, Salli, Sallie. *Familiar form of* Sarah. Relational, group leader, planner, good student, writer of non-fiction. Marries: cooperative leader, also relational. *Sally Kristen Ride*, (born 1951), first U.S. woman astronaut. Actresses: *Salli Richardson, Sally Field*.

Salome // Saloma, Salomé, Salomi. *Hebrew:* "peace". Biblical: daughter of Herodias. *Salome Urena de Henriquez* (1850-96), 19th-century romantic poet of the Dominican Republic.

Samantha // Sam, Sammy. *Aramaic:* "listener". Actresses: *Samantha Fox, Samantha Mathis, Sammi Cheng*.

Samara // Sam, Samarah, Samaria, Samira, Sammy. *Hebrew:* "ruled by God".

Sandra // Sandi, Sandy, Sandye, Zandra. *Short form of* Alexandra. Also see Sandy. *Sandra Day O'Connor,* (born 1930), first woman United States Supreme Court Justice. *Zandra Rhodes*, (born 1940), British fashion designer,

exponent of punk. *Sandra Hochman* (born 1936), feminist writer. Actresses: *Sandra Bullock, Sandra Dee*.

Sandy // Sandi, Sandie, Sandye. *Familiar form of* Sandra. Pretty, energetic, hard worker, fairly strong personality, but willing to follow under, questioning of authority, teacher, leader, fun, humorous, playful, adventurous, wants to be at home when kids are and at work when they're not. Marries: looks for someone she can follow, support, care for and rank just under. Marriage: a team effort with different roles. *Sandy Dennis*, (1937-92), U.S. actress.

Sarah // Sadella, Sadie, Sadye, Saidee, Saira, Sal, Salaidh, Sallee, Salli, Sallie, Sally, Sara, Sarahi, Sarai, Saray, Sarena, Sarene, Sarette, Sari, Sarina, Sarine, Sarita, Sayre, Shara, Sharai, Shari, Sharon, Sharona, Sher, Sheree, Sheri, Sherie, Sherri, Sherrie, Sherry, Sherye, Sorcha, Sydel, Sydelle, Zara, Zarah, Zaria. *Hebrew:* "princess". Biblical: the wife of Abraham and mother of Isaac. Very pretty, intelligent, logical, good student, strong leader, easy to like, not much into sports but able, very relational, achiever, teacher, fun but not especially humorous, serious. *Sarah Bernhardt*, (formerly Henriette Rosine Bernard) (1844-1923), celebrated French actress, performed throughout Europe and the United States. *Sarah Gertrude Millin*, (1889-1968), penetrating South African writer. *Sarah Josepha Hale*, (1788-1879), U.S. editor and author, editor Boston Ladies' Magazine and Godey's Lady's Book, credited with Thanksgiving Day as national holiday and 'Mary Had a Little Lamb'. *Sara Teasdale*, (1884-1933), U.S. poet, love lyrics admired for their feeling, simplicity, and melody. *Sarah Caldwell,* (born 1924), U.S. opera conductor, first woman to conduct Metropolitan Opera, New York City 1976. *Sarah Siddons*, (1755-1831), English tragic actress. *Sarah Orne Jewett*, (1849-1909), U.S. short-story writer and novelist. *Sarah Fielding*, (1710-68), English writer. *Sarah Vaughan*, influential 1940's jazz singer. Actresses: *Sarah Jessica Parker, Sarah Michelle Gellar.*

Saree // Sari. *Arabic:* "most noble". Much like Sarah, but slightly more playful.

Sasha // Sacha, Sascha, Sashenka, Sashinca. *Russian familiar form of* Alexandra. Sporty, energetic, adventurous, pretty, co-leader. *Sasha Sokolov*, Russian fiction writer.

Savannah // Savana, Savanah, Savanna. *Spanish:* "savanna".

Scarlett // Scarlet. *Middle English:* "scarlet". Literary: Scarlett O'Hara is the heroine of 'Gone with the Wind'.

Selena // Celene, Celie, Celina, Celinda, Celine, Salina, Sela, Selene, Seline, Selia, Selie, Selina, Selinda, Seline, Sena. *Greek:* "moon". *Selena*, famous Hispanic singer. *Celine Dion*, popular singer.

Selma // Anselma, Zelma. *Scandinavian:* "divinely protected". Quiet, good student, loyal. *Selma Lagerlof,* (1858-1940), first woman to win the Nobel prize for literature, folklore, magic, her family, and the her countryside. Actress: *Salma Hayek.*

Sequoia. *Latin:* "sequoia".

Serena // Reena, Rena, Sarina, Serene, Serina. *Latin:* "calm, serene".

Shaina // Shaine, Shanie, Shayna, Shayne. *Hebrew:* "beautiful".

Shanelle. *Form of* Chanel.

Shannon // Channa, Shana, Shandy, Shane, Shannen, Shanon, Shanna, Shannah, Shannen, Shauna, Shawna. *Gaelic:* "small, wise". Appear self-confident sometimes arrogant, friendly, leader and follower, hard worker, love parties and appearances, in-crowds and trendy, "small-picture" orientation, good at accomplishing tasks, cliquish, unbalanced in perspective of others/subjectively talking down to some and pedestaling others, undue belief in the surface image of others can make marriage and relationships a gamble. Actress: *Shannen Doherty*.

Shantal // Shantel. *Form of* Chantal.

Shari. *Form of* Sarah.

Sharon // Charin, Cherin, Shara, Sharai, Shari, Sharla, Sharona, Sherri, Sherrie, Sherry, Sherye. *Form of* Sarah. Calm, gentle, hard-worker, even temperament, steady, follower or co-leader among friends, managerial leader, attractive. *Sharon Pratt Kelly*, (born 1944), U.S. political activist and first African American woman to head the government of a major city. *Sharon Harris Hart,* fashion designer. *Sharon Scranage*, spy. Actress: *Sharon Stone*.

Shawn // Sean, Seana, Shaun, Shauna, Shawna, Shawnee, Siana, Sianna. *Feminine form of* Sean and John. Somewhat athletic, Shauna tends to be more attractive and more feminine than Shawn, often weaker on mathematics, model, secretary, cashier, clerk, entrepreneur. Actress: *Shawnee Smith.*

Sheena. *Irish form of* Jane. Cute, very pretty, calm, imprudent/wild, dancer, similar to Shawn/Shauna. *Sheena Easton*, singer/actress.

Sheila // Selia, Sheela, Sheelagh, Sheelah, Sheilah, Shela, Shelagh, Shelia, Shelley, Shelli, Shellie, Shelly. *Irish form of* Cecilia. Cute, pretty, sporty, energetic, popular, active, trendy, appearance conscience, initial shallow judgment of men. *Sheila Kaye-Smith*, (1887-1956), British novelist, wrote chiefly of country life. *Sheila Burnford*, (born 1918), award winning Canadian author, 'The Incredible Journey'. *Sheila A. Scoville*, former Lecturer, Middle East History. *Sheila Sancha*, author of book on 'Crafts and Trades in the Middle Ages'.

Shelby // Shel, Shelbi, Shelli, Shellie, Shelly. *Old English:* "ledge estate".

Shelley // Shell, Shelli, Shellie, Shelly. *Old English:* "meadow on the ledge". *Familiar form of* Rachel, Sheila, Shelby and Shirley. Energetic, bouncy, one of the group, intelligent, weak at math, manager. *Shelley Berman*, 1950's nightclub comic. Actress: *Shelley Hack*.

Sherry // Shari, Sheeree, Sheree, Sheri, Sherie, Sherri, Sherrie, Sherye. Sherry: a type of wine. Shari, a river flowing through Chad, Africa. *Familiar forms of* Charlotte, Cher, Sarah, Sher and Shirley. Often bouncy, serious, upbeat, sometimes strict-biting, focused, determined, leader, manager, organizer, boss, intelligent, teacher. Marries: someone gentle, not severe, not forceful but coaxing, often marries Scott or Edward. *Shari Lewis*, puppeteer of Lamb Chop.

Sheryl // Cheryl, Sherilyn, Sherrill. *Form of* Shirley. Very hard worker, serious, usually very conscientious student or worker, loyal, calm, bottles anger, inhibited, protective, eventually open among friends, can be fun, introvert, non-athlete, thinner, manager, organized. *Sherrill Whiton*, wrote 'Interior Design and Decoration'.

Shina. *Japanese:* "good, virtue". See Sheena.

Shirley // Sher, Sheree, Sheri, Sherill, Sherline, Sherri, Sherrie, Sherry, Sherye, Sheryl, Shir, Shirl, Shirlee, Shirleen, Shirlene, Shirline. *Old English:* "bright meadow". Similar to Sheryl, hard worker, conscientious worker, calm, loyal, fun, protective, a little athletic, leader, manager, organized. *Shirley Chisholm*, (born 1924), first black woman ever elected to the United States Congress. *Shirley Verrett*, (born 1933), U.S. mezzo-soprano. *Shirley Graham*, (born 1906), U.S. writer and composer. *Shirley Hufstedler*, (born 1925), U.S. judge and public official. *Shirley Jackson*, (1919-65), U.S. writer, noted for macabre tales. *Shirley MacLaine*, actress and New Age Movement author. Actresses: *Shirley Jones, Shirley Temple*.

Shoshana. *Hebrew:* "rose". *Hebrew form of* Susan.

Sibyl // Cybil, Cybill, Sib, Sibbie, Sibby, Sibeal, Sibel, Sibella, Sibelle, Sibilla, Sibley, Sibylia, Sibylle, Sybil, Sybila, Sybilla, Sybille. *Greek:* "prophetess", sibyls were women who were believed to predict the future inspired by the gods. *Cybill Shepherd*, (born 1950), U.S. model and actress. *Sibyl Marcuse*, author of 'Musical Instruments: A Comprehensive Dictionary'. *Sibyl Hancock*, author of 'Famous Firsts of Black Americans'.

Sidney // Cyd, Cydney. *Old Fench:* "Saint Denis". Actress: *Cyd Charisse*.

Siena // Sienna. *Italian:* a city in Italy.

Sierra // Ciara, Ciera, Cierra. *Spanish:* "saw, saw-toothed mountains".

Silvia // Silvie. *Form of* Sylvia.

Simone // Simona, Simonette, Simonne, Symone. *Hebrew:* "one who hears". *Feminine form of* Simon. Focused. Actress: *Simone Buchanan*.

Skye // Sky, Skylar, Skyler. *Old English:* "sky".

Sondra. *Short form of* Alexandra. Also see Sandra.

Sonia // Sonja, Sonni, Sonnie, Sonny, Sonya, Sunny. *Slovic and Scandinavian Form of* Sophie. Pretty, rounded, energetic, a bit shy. *Sonja Henie*, (1912-69), U.S. ice skater, three Olympic gold medals, actress. *Sonia Terk*, Ukrainian painter.

Sophie // Sofia, Sofie, Sophey, Sophi, Sophia. *Greek:* "wisdom". Refined, gentle, not a whiner, kind, distant with new acquaintances, although not open with family and friends - they can count on her, if they are in need - she will give her last; principled - always ready to fight for her ideals; good student, likes dainty hand work, musically talented, enjoys involvement in theater, valuable adaptive worker, quickly reaches success in her sphere of work; diplomatic, good cook, hospitable, enjoys having guests in her house; good attitude toward her in-laws; follows current fashion, but doesn't like extravagance. Catherine the Great, (1729-96), born Princess *Sophie Auguste Friederike*. *Sophie Karp*, the first woman to act professionally in Yiddish theater. Actresses: *Sophia Loren, Sophie Marceau.*

Stacy // Stace, Stacee, Stacey, Staci, Stacia, Stacie. *Short form of* Anastasia. Bubbly, relational, very social, secretary, assistant, sales, usually quite pretty. Actress: *Staci Keanan.* Supermodel: *Stacey Williams.*

Stella // Star. *Latin:* "star". *Short form of* Estelle. Complex and stubborn personality, always follows her ideals, sociable and inquisitive, reads a lot, interested in politics, hospitable, her greatest joy is her relationship with friends and people with a similar spirit; most are talented and very hard working, may work several jobs simultaneously; likes traveling, responsible at keeping her word; can not be called open as she is a bit careful with people; quick temper but forgiving; kind for kindness sake; unselfish, likes fun and noisy gatherings, materialist, independent, dresses tastefully, likes warm colors, often not successful in marriage, often have daughters. *Stella M. Morice*, author of children's story of Maori life. Actress: *Stella Adler.*

Stephanie // Stafani, Stefa, Stefanie, Steffane, Steffi, Steffie, Stepha, Stephana, Stephani, Stephannie, Stephenie, Stephi, Stephie, Stephine, Stesha, Stevana, Stevena. *Greek:* "crowned". *Feminine form of* Stephen. Chooser, energetic, set into action by emotional response, over responds, follows her group, not bubbly but determined, fairly serious, appears to be follower but willing adventurer. *Stephanie comtesse de Genlis*, (1746-1830), French author and educator. *Stephanie Feeney*, author 'Hawaii Is a Rainbow'. Model/actress: *Stephanie Seymour.* Actresses: *Stefanie Powers, Stephanie Cameron, Stephanie Zimbalist.*

Sue. *Short form of* Susan.

Summer. *Old English:* "summer". Attractive, cute, mild.

Susan // Sue, Susana, Susann, Susanna, Susannah, Susanne, Susette, Susi, Susie, Susy, Suzanna, Suzanne, Suzette, Suzi, Suzie, Suzy, Zsa Zsa. *Hebrew:* "lily". Also see Anne. Heroine of apocryphal book, 'The History of Susanna'. Nice enough, fairly serious about life, organizer, leader of organizing, daring/courageous, appears confident, business type, often secretary, actress, biographer, writer, teacher; resembles her father and has his stubbornness, independent, many talents, good student, reads a lot, involved in music and dancing, finds it difficult to get acquainted, finds separation difficult from her friends, her married life is closed to outsiders knowledge, she doesn't share her private feelings with her friends, sexual topics are very uncomfortable, can not hide that she has been offended, works to climb the ladder of success and may be given a position unrelated to her education because of her hard work. *Susanne Langer,* (1895-1985), U.S. philosopher. *Suzanne Vega*, (born 1959), U.S. singer and songwriter, folk music. *Susanne Salter,* (1860-1961), first woman mayor in U.S. *Suzanne Lenglen,* (1899-1938), French tennis player. *Sue Hastings*, U.S. producer and director of marionette shows. *Susan Butcher*, (born 1954), U.S. sled-dog racer. *Susan L. Picotte*, (1865-1915), U.S. physician and reformer. Actresses: *Susan Egan, Susan Hayward, Susan Sarandon.*

Susanna // Susannah, Susie, Susy. *Hebrew:* "lily". *Forms of* Susan.

Svetlana // Sveta. *Slovic:* "bright". High regard for herself, middle student, likes social activities, likes to give orders, reaches her goals, easily trusts people, kind, not impudent or insolent, tactful, diplomatic, will help another even if a big inconvenience, neat, takes good care of her appearance, may dress bit extravagant when young, coquettish; if failures occur in her life, she analyzes it and makes the necessary changes for improvement; adapts to life well, independent, hard working, you can be confident her success is caused by her, she won't marry if she is not confident that her fiancé deserves her and that his feelings are sincere; feminine, gentle; very devoted to her children, gives them good education, loyal friend.

Sybil. *Greek:* "sibyl".

Sydney // Cyd, Sidney, Sydnee. *Old French:* "Saint Denis". Actress: *Cyd Charisse* (dancer).

Sylvia // Silva, Silvana, Silvia, Silvie, Zilvia. *Latin:* "she of the forest". Writer. *Sylvia Beach*, (1887-1962), U.S. bookseller and publisher. *Sylvia Townsend Warner,* (1893-1978), English fantasy writer. *Sylvia Field Porter*, (1913-91), U.S. journalist and financial author. *Sylvia Thompson*, (1902-68), English novelist and lecturer.

Tabitha // Tabatha, Tabbi, Tabbie, Tabbitha, Tabby. *Aramaic:* "gazelle". *Tabitha*, disciple of Jesus at Joppa, full of good works.

Talia // Tallie, Tally, Talyah, Thalia. *Greek:* "blooming".

Greek mythology: *Thalia* (bloom), one of the three Graces, goddesses of grace and charm. Also see Thalia. Actress: *Talia Shire*.

Tallulah. *Native American:* "leaping water". *Tallulah Bankhead,* (1903-68), U.S. stage and screen actress.

Tamara // Tamar, Tamarah, Tamarra, Tamera, Tamma, Tammi, Tammie, Tammy, Tamra. *Hebrew:* "palm tree". A more composed and more serious Tammy, can not stand monotony, can not concentrate for a long time even though her nature is curious and ready to learn; artistic, likes to perform before people, likes to do theatrical sketches, friendly and nice to people she knows well, bit tense and suspicious around those she doesn't know well, tends to be critical of peers, almost always leader in her family, she relies only on herself; her husband's efforts to change her lead to conflicts, and if he persists it can lead to divorce, which is why she often marries a younger man, she controls the family budget and does it well, jealous, quick tempered, may scream and cry but quickly calms down; knowledgeable cook and cooks well; likes to keep her house clean and organized and involve her husband and children in this; likes traveling; likes meeting new people, likes to rearrange her home's interior, good leader at work; her suspicious nature requires that she date only those she gets to know slowly over time, especially those she is put together with through life's situations, communications. *Tamara Karsavina,* (1885-1978), Soviet ballerina. Actress: *Tamera Mowry, Tamlyn Tamita.*

Tammy // Tammi, Tammie, Tami. *Short form of* Tamara. Bubbly, outgoing, very social, helpful, ready to participate as part of a group, will try anything, daring, fun, friendly, ready for marriage young, mommy. *Tammy Faye Bakker,* televangelist with husband Jim Baker. *Tammy Wynette,* country musician with ex-husband George Jones.

Tanya // Tanhya, Tania, Tatiana, Tatiania, Tatianna, Tatyana, Tawny, Tawnya, Tiana, Tianna. *Slavic form of* Tatiana. *Greek:* "founder, constituent, organizer". *Latin:* "Tatios", the name of a Sabine king. Energetic, pretty, shares her opinion, determined, sporty, emotional, pragmatic, principles moody, tries to be peer leader, like dancing, routine bores her, stubborn, strong willed, knows what she wants and doesn't like objections, can do any work, manager, keeps underlings in there place, appears artistic, likes to be around men, bit despotic at home, but likes strong man, quick tempered with children, not sentimental, pragmatic approach to relationships, likes to dress fashionably, but lacking some fashion sense, initiates changes in family, becomes more patient with age which benefits her marriage, loves travel, will always try to prove her view, good worker - especially in front of boss, often unhappy at home because she likes wants her man to submit to her, her children are a bit afraid of her, she can scold them without apparent reason, doesn't have many friends - at least not close ones, pragmatic with her mother-in-law, buys expensive clothes, rearranges furniture often, doesn't like to complain, jealous but stubbornly hiding her jealousy. Suggested for marriage: Mark. *Tanya Moiseiwitsch*, theater, designed the thrust stage. *Tana Hoban*, wrote book on colors. Actress: *Tanya Roberts.*

Tara // Tarah, Tarra, Tarrah, Taryn, Terra. *Gaelic:* "rocky pinnacle". Mythology: the home of the ancient Irish kings. *Latin:* terra, "earth". Hard worker, fun loving, intelligent, energetic, cute, thin, outgoing, friendly, ambitious. *Tara Lipinski,* 1998 Olympic gold medal figure skater.

Tasha. *Familiar form of* Natasha or Anastasia. *Tasha Tudor,* (born 1915), U.S. author and illustrator of children's books, won Regina Medal 1971.

Taylor // Tayler. *Old English:* "tailor"; *Latin:* "cutting".

Teresa. Form of Theresa. Actress: *Teresa Wright.*

Terra // Tiera, Tierra. *Latin:* "earth, land".

Terry // Tera, Teri, Terra, Terri, Terrie, Terrye. *Short form of* Theresa or a *feminine form of* Terence. Less prudent, less careful and a less calculating risk taker than Theresa, questionable judge of character of potential mate, friendly, cheerful. Actress: *Teri Garr, Teri Hatcher, Terri Nunn, Terry Farrell.*

Tess // Tessi, Tessie, Tessy. *Short form of* Tessa or *familiar form of* Theresa.

Tessa // Tess, Tessi, Tessie, Tessy. *Greek:* "fouth, fourth child". *Familiar form of* Theresa or *shortened form of* Countessa or Countess.

Thalia. Mythological: Thalia (comedy), one of the nine Muses. Greek mythology: Thalia (bloom), one of the three Graces. Also see Talia. *Thalia Mara,* wrote ballet instruction books.

Thea // Tea. *Greek:* "goddess". Mythology: one of the 12 Titans. *Short form of* Dorothy and Timothea. Actress: *Tea Leoni.*

Theresa // Tera, Teresa, Terese, Teresina, Teresita, Teressa, Teri, Terri, Terrie, Terry, Terrye, Terza, Tess, Tessa, Tessi, Tessie, Tessy, Therese, Tracey, Tracie, Tracy, Tresa, Tressa, Trescha, Zita. *Greek:* "reaper". Noble leader, often head nurse or head social worker, intelligent, business like, hard worker, fairly serious, friendly and kind but strong and efficient, management, very conscientious, often rather study than play. *Theresa Elmendorf,* (1855-1932), U.S. librarian, first woman president American Library Association 1911-12. *Saint Theresa,* (1515-82), Spanish Carmelite nun and mystic; founder of reformed order of Barefoot Carmelites. *Saint Theresa,* (1873-97), French Carmelite nun, promised "to spend my heaven doing good upon earth". *Maria Theresa* (1717-80), archduchess of Austria and queen of Hungary and Bohemia.

Thomasina // Tomasina. *Greek:* "little twin". *Feminine form of* Thomas.

Tia. *Spanish:* "little". Actress: *Tia Mowry.*

Tiara // Tiare, Tiarra. *Greek:* "headdress, crown". Also see Terra.

Tiffany // Tiff, Tiffani, Tiffanie, Tiffi, Tiffie, Tiffy, Tiphani. *Greek:* "appearance of God". Actresses: *Tiffani Amber-Theissen, Tiffany Brissette.*

Tina // Teena, Tiena, Tine. *Short form of names ending in* "tina" or "tine". Daring, forward, flirtatious, very fun-loving, social, talker, average to shorter stature. *Tina Turner,* (formerly Anna Mae Bullock) (born 1938), U.S. rock singer and actress. Actress: *Tina Caspary.*

Toni // Tonia, Tonie, Tony. *Familiar form of* Antoinette. Relaxed, not high strung, follower.

Tory // Torey, Tori, Torie, Torrie. *Short form of* Victoria. Actress: *Tori Spelling*.

Tracy // Tracee, Tracey, Traci, Tracie. *Gaelic:* "battler"; *Latin:* "courageous". *Familiar form of* Theresa. Attractive, appears easy going, but determined, organizer, administrator, fun-loving. *Tracy Chapman*, (born 1964), U.S. plaintive folksinger-songwriter. Actress: *Tracey Gold, Tracey Needham, Traci Bingham.*

Treasure. *Greek:* "store, treasure".

Tricia // Trish, Trisha. *Short form of* Patricia. Writer. *Trish Shannon* authored 'Express Yourself'. *Trish Durbin* authored 'Collected Classics of Soaring'. *Tricia Haynes* authored 'Let's Visit Honduras'.

Trina // Trenna. *Familiar form of* Katherine from Katrina. Actress: *Trini Alvarado*.

Trinity // Trinidad. *Latin:* "unit of three".

Trista. *Feminine form of* Tristan.

Trixie // Trix, Trixy. *Familiar form of* Beatrice.

Trudy // Truda, Trude, Trudey, Trudi, Trudie. *Old German:* "beloved". *Short form of* Gertrude. Organized, energetic, leader, serious, severe, teacher, wants it orderly, friendly, sociable. *Trudy Hanmer* wrote about Nicaragua. *Truda Kaschmann,* dance teacher.

Twila // Twyla. *Middle English:* "woven of double thread". *Twyla Tharp,* (born 1942), U.S. modern dancer and choreographer. *Twila Paris*, Christian singer.

Tyler. *Old English:* "maker of tiles".

Tyra. Supermodel/actress: *Tyra Banks*.

Unique. *Latin:* "sole, only".

Unona. *Russian form* of Juno. See Winona for character.

Ursula // Ursala, Ursela. *Latin:* "little she-bear".

Valentina // Teena, Tina, Val, Vale, Valeda, Valene, Valencia, Valentia, Valentine. *Latin:* "Strong, healthy". Strong, healthy, bold, sensitive, charitable, very kind, she will give away her only candy, shares with everyone, sacrifical kindness, often causes problems for herself in her giving by ignoring her own needs, does not expect reciprical giving, easy-going, may fight-argue with best friend but will reconsile in minutes, people who know her forgive her lapses in kindness, hospitable, likes to be invited as guest, excitedly enjoys competition in card and board games, marries for love, dedicates her free-time to her husband and children, remembers and cares for her parents, no enemies, her marriage is not always successful - so blames ex-husband. *Valentina Tereshkova*, (born 1937), first woman to travel in space, member of the Supreme Soviet Presidium, awarded the Order of Lenin twice.

Valerie // Val, Valaree, Valarie, Valaria, Vale, Valeria, Valérie, Valery, Valerye, Valli, Vallie, Vally, Valry. *Latin:* "strong". Strong, bold, energetic, co-leader, liked, pretty, teacher, unpredictable, may hold grudge a long time as child, complex, contradictory at judging people and events, not steady in her plans; insecure; if you are patient enough to get her favor or if you are lucky enough to be liked by her you will find a loyal friend, even when you don't deserve it; if you can discover the depths of her character you will see that her unreasonable behaviors are caused by her easily wounded sensitive personality; she notices her man's glance at another female and is quick to be hurt and seemingly unexplainably change her behavior, jealous, good house keeper, caring wife, prefers to stay home with family over partying, her jealous nature often destroys the good relationship with her man. *Valerie Illingworth*, wrote a dictionary of astronomy. *Valerie Wilmer*, wrote about jazz. Actress: *Valerie Bertinelli*.

Vanessa // Nessa, Nessi, Nessie, Nessy, Van, Vanesa, Vania, Vanna, Vannessa, Vanni, Vannie, Vanny. Literary: poetical name invented by Jonathan Swift for Esther Vanhomrigh. Pretty, energetic, friendly, intelligent, model, teacher, actress. Actresses: *Vanessa Redgrave* (born 1937), *Vanessa Angel, Vanessa Marcil, Vanessa Paradis, Venesa Talor, Vanna Bonta, Vanna White.*

Vendela. Supermodel: *Vendela Kirsebom*.

Venus // Venera, Venita, Vin, Vinita, Vinnie, Vinny. *Latin:* "love" Roman mythology: Venus, the goddess of spring, beauty and love; also Aphrodites in Greek mythology. Often weak as a child, multi-capable, musically able, physically flexible, sporty, argues with teachers, fall in love easily, makes a lot of mistakes in love, good housekeeper, devoted mother, likes to dress extravagant, may profer red and violet, may be engineer, programmer, clothes design, nurse, actress, accountant.

Vera // Veradis, Vere, Verena, Verene, Verina, Verine, Verla. *Latin:* "true"; *Slovic:* "faith". *Short form of* Veronica. Faithful, true, very relational, conscientious, hard-working, manager, translator, logical, stable-minded, not loud and not a winer, organized and practical, quick concreate thinker, analytical, judges without undue emotion, artistic ablities, knows what she wants from life and stays on her goal, even when emotionally discouraged, does not live in fanciful or overly romantisied world, she understands both her needs and life's needs, she seldom picks her future husband from her peers, prefering older man, strict toward her children, good relationship with mother-in-law out of practicality, usually successful in marriage. *Vera Bock*, U.S. artist, illustrator. *Vera Fokina*, ballerina in early 1900's. *Vera Caslavska*, (born 1942), Czech gymnast, won 22 medals in Olympic, world, and European champion-ships. Actress: *Vera Miles*.

Veronica // Ranna, Ronica, Ronna, Ronni, Ronnica, Verenice, Veronika, Veronike, Véronique. *Greek:* "true image". *Form of* Bernice. A type of perennial flower. Also see Vera. Shy child with laking of confidence, later adds stubborness and iritability, falls in love very easily, men are attracted to her like bees to honey, easily falls out of love, her favorite colors may be red, violet and black. Actress: *Veronica Lake*.

Vi // Vie, Vianca, Vianey, Vianney, Vita, Viva. *Latin:* "life".

Vicki // Vicky. *Short form of* Victoria. Energetic, up-beat/positive, adventurous, leader, manager, hard-worker, marries very energetic man.

Victoria // Vicki, Vickie, Vicky, Vitoria, Vittoria. *Latin:* "victory". *Feminine form of* Victor. Also see Vicki. More staid, serene, settled, sober, composed, solemn, quiet, not so adventurous, hard working, pretty, often resembles her father, fairly silent, withdraws without reason, becomes more active as teen but still unsure of herself and shy, her efforts to distinguish herself may come-off inappropriate, may use too much prefume or overly short skirt, may behave over-the-top, often chooses jobs and careers which let her do individual activities, slow to choose husband but not from high expectations, very conscientious in choice of husband, doubting in her descisions even after she makes them, sensitive a caring husband will give her confidence in her marriage but an insensitivity from him will reignite her doubts, she is a caring and faithful wife, generally attractive, she may be an ideal model. *Queen Victoria,* (1819-1901), born Alexandrina Victoria. *Victoria de los Angeles*, (born 1923), Spanish soprano. *Victoria Sackville-West*, (1892-1962), British author. *Victoria Ocampo*, (1891-1979), Argentine writer, founded literary review Sur 1931, known as Argentina's "queen of letters." *Victoria Woodhull*, (1838-1927), U.S. reformer, nominated by Equal Rights party 1872 as first woman U.S. presidential candidate. Actress: *Victoria Wyndham.*

Viola. *Latin:* "violet". Stringed instrument. *Viola Spolin*, improvisational acting teacher.

Violet // Vi, Viola, Viole, Violeta, Violette. *Latin:* "violet flower". Fearless and strong woman, stubborn and determined, not attentive, if she offends she may not ask for forgiveness even if she knows she was wrong, emotional, likes to stay up at night and sleep in the morning, diligent, she only does well what she likes, good taste in dressing, enjoys designing clothes, attractive, husbands often jealous, strong leader, but not very fortunate. *Violet Oakley*, (1874-1961), U.S. painter

Virginia // Ginelle, Ginger, Ginni, Ginnie, Ginny, Jinny, Virgie, Virginie. *Latin:* "virginal, maidenly". Attractively thin, calm, novelist, children's writer, artistic. *Virginia Woolf,* (formerly Adeline Virginia Stephen) (1882-1941), British novelist and critic. *Virginia Haviland*, (born 1911), U.S. children's author, librarian, awarded 1976 Regina Medal. *Virginia Eggertsen Sorensen*, (born 1912), U.S. Morman novels and children's writer, awarded Newbery Medal 1957. *Virginia Hamilton*, (born 1936), U.S. author, awarded 1975 Newbery Medal. *Virginia Crocheron Gildersleeve*, (1877-1965), U.S. women's educator and author. *Virginia Lee Burton*, (1909-68), U.S. artist, illustrator, and author of children's books.

Viridiana // Viridian. *Latin:* "green, blue-green".

Vivian // Vevay, Vi, Vitalia, Vitalina, Viv, Vivi, Vivia, Viviana, Vivianne, Vivie, Vivien, Vivienne, Vivyan, Vivyanne. *Latin:* "full of life". English legend: Viviane, the Lady of the Lake in Arthur legend. Full of life, energetic, pretty, leader, friendly, combination of soft feminine gentleness and daring courage, usually get married early, may not pick peer as mate, her mature mind prefers education and ability and steadiness in a man, often has difficulty in communication with mother-in-law, often very trusting and easily deceived, when she learns that she has been deceived she grieves heavily, economical housekeeper, takes good care of her family, however, her husband helps a lot and you may find him doing the dishes, confident energetic and determined in business, feels more comfortable working with men, she is always a leader when she works with women. *Vivian L. Thompson* wrote 'Polynesian Myth and Legend.' *Vivian Faulkner-King*, Professor in Art and Design. Actress: *Vivian Chow, Vivien Leigh* (originally Vivian Mary Hartley) (1918-67) British actress of stage and screen, twice won Academy award.

Wanda // Wandie, Wandis. *Old German:* "wanderer". *Form of* Gwendolyn. Wanders from moral moorings, adventurous, daring, promiscuous, manager, intelligent, not usual. *Wanda Landowska*, (1879-1959), harpsichordist and educator. *Wanda Gag*, (1893-1946), U.S. writer and illustrator of children's books.

Wendy // Wendeline, Wendi, Wendie, Wendye. *Familiar form of* Gwendolyn and Wanda. Busy with an interest, easily liked, trying to improve someone's life, socially active, talkative. *Wendy Rydell* wrote 'All About Islands' for children. *Wendy Cooper* wrote 'Hair: Sex, Society, Symbolism'. Actress: *Wendy Makkena*.

Whitney. *Old English:* "white island, fair water". *Whitney Houston*, Pop Singer.

Wilhelmina // Billi, Billie, Billy, Minni, Minnie, Minny, Valma, Velma, Vilhelmina, Vilma, Wilhelmine, Willa, Willi, Willie, Willy, Wilma, Wylma. *Old German:* "determined guardian". *Feminine form of* William. Determined.

Wilma. *Short form of* Wilhelmina.

Winnie // Winni, Winny. Short form of Gwyneth or Winona or Winnifred. *Winnie Mandela*, (born 1936), South African anti-apartheid political activist.

Winnifred // Freddi, Freddie, Freddy, Winifred, Winnie, Winne, Winny. *Old German:* "peaceful friend". *Form of* Guinevere.

Winona // Wenona, Wenonah, Winnie, Winny, Winonah. *Native American:* "first-born daughter". Easy-going, calm, leader; alway desires the center of attention, artistic nature, creates an atmospher of holiday joy, organizer of different events, likes to organize gatherings, be the center and talk to them; kind, compasionate toward people, her trusting nature brings her frustration or sadness; not choosy at picking friends, so may be surrounded by insincere or dishonest people; little interest in domestic activities; usually good worker; fights for her ideals of justice; marriage is not usually stable. *Winona Ryder*, actress.

Xenia // Xena, Zena, Zenaita, Zenia. *Greek:* "hospitable". Puts herself above others, cold, often quarrales with her girlfriends, likes to be first in everything, tyranical to her parents - especially her grandparents, tries to be the teachers pet and hand, respects authority, gossips, good student, developes good taste, flurtative, knows how to hide her sharp edges, likes dancing, seldem beautiful, knows how to present herself to be liked, usually has enough admirers and dates, leader by her nature, but she knows how to hide this by being submissive, after marriage the despot comes out, often leads the family's finances, controlling of her husband and children, has a hard stubborness, likes to fix her house, a bit frugal, but willing to pay anything for something she really wants, she doesn't mind to drink alcohol when she has the chance and predisposed to alcoholism.

Xiomara. Unknown meaning and origin.

Xochitl, Xochilt. *Aztec:* meaning unknown.

Often the letter Y is used instead of the letter J in many languages as the English letter J did not exist before the middle ages and is currently not used in many languages. Following this tradition, some parents, especially imagrants, choose to use the letter Y in the spelling of many names which Americans and English usually start with the letter J. Yasmin-Jasmine is a prime example of this practice, but most any letter J in a name may be found with a Y substituting for it. I will only include some of the very most common occurences of this in the Y section of this guide.

Yadira. Probably variation of *Hebrew:* Hadera.

Yahaira, Yajaira. Unknown meaning and origin. Probably Spanish or Arabic variation of Hegira: "Muhammad's flight from Mecca (AD 622), from which Muslim dates are calculated".

Yanina // Yana. Additional *Slavic form* of Iyon, Yvonne, Ivon and Ivan. *Feminine Slovic form of* John. Stubborn child, throws hysterical tantrums, likes to show of before peers with dress or toy, favorite of her father and spoiled by him, she expects her husband to treat her this way, not all husbands can bare her capricious behavior; likes to be around men, understands their psychology and manipulates them; theatrical mannerism, emotionalism helps her get what she wants; spends money freely; attractive; in certain situations where she wants something, she can be very soft, friendly and likable to gain favor; mother-in-law does not have a very good relation with her since Yana controls the man and he tolerates the capricious behavior; husband is content with marriage.

Yasmin // Yasmeen, Yasmine, Yazmin. *Arabic:* "jasmine". *Yasmeen Ghauri* , model. *Yasmine Bleeth*, actress.

Yesenia // Yecenia, Yessenia. Probably Latin.

Yetta. *Old English:* "to give, giver". *Short form of* Henrietta. Giver.

Yeti. *Nepalise:* "abominable snowman".

Yolanda // Yolande, Yolane. *Greek:* "violet flower". *French form of* Violet from Violante.

Yulia. *Latin:* "curly, fluffy". *Slovic form* of Julia. Wild imagination as girl, sensitive, easily offended girl, mood swings, accumulates as an adult, takes good care of her possessions, good cook, spends most of her time for her family; work and professional advancement doesn't interest her, so she may be viewed as a bit lazy; successful or determined in marriage; her house is always open for friends and relatives; altruistic, open-handed; likes to talk about things of life with friends a bit; sincerely rejoices over her friend's successes; not envious; bit stubborn and won't follow other's advice even when she knows it is reasonable; her stubbornness gets in the way of good relationships with her mother and mother-in-law, so prefers to live away from them; her favorite activity is reading; she keeps her husband form being bored; her husband loves her and concedes to her; sacrificially loves her children.

Yvette // Evetta, Ivett, Ivette, Veta, Yevette. *Familiar form of* Yvonne. Sporty, somewhat athletic, fortune seldom spoils her, many ablities, unstable emotionally, very impressonable, gets overly disheartened, determined arguer, not trusting, overly sensitive, takes offence overly easily, doesn't trust her husband, therefore difficult marriage, her desire to rule her husband often destroys the marriage, has a loyal close friend. *Yvette Guilbert*, (1869-1944), French singer, unsurpassed in her day for dramatic and humorous rendition of old ballads.

Yvonne // Evona, Evonne, Ivana, Ivonne, Yevette, Yvette. *Old French:* "archer". *Feminine form of* Ivar or Ives. Calm, peaceful, internalizes, sullen. *Yvonne Burke*, (born 1932), practiced law in Los Angeles, member California legislature 1967-72, U.S. House of Representatives (Democrat) 1973-79. *Yvonne Grozny* wrote 'The Fables of Phonecius'. *Ivana Trump*, first wife of Donald Trump. Actresses: *Yvonne Craig, Yvonne Zima.*

The letter "Z" is used in some cultures instead of the letter "S". Parents desiring a name which starts with the letter "S" may give the name a unique twist while retaining personality characteristics by substituting the letter "Z".

Zalina. *Slovic form* of Xenia. Zalina, Russian pianist & singer.

Zara // Zarah, Zaria. **Hebrew:** "dawn". *Form of* Sarah. Courageous, leader.

Zena // Zenia. *Form of* Xenia.

Zita. *Short form of names ending in* "sita" *or* "zeta". Also see Xenia.

Zoe // Zoya. **Greek:** "life". Grows up as an obedient friendly child, not a fighter, believes in fairy tales and is distressed when she learns that there is no Santa Claus, friends with girls, big help to her mother, she is better with humanistic sciences, likes animal and growing flowers, she can be a good zoologist or biologist, usually good relationship with all people, almost no conflicts with her husband, warm relationship with colleges and neighbors, sensitive to people, can read peoples thoughts by voice intonation and facial expressions, she takes life's difficulties as inevitable and normal, often religious even if she doesn't attend church, her faith and religion brings comfort to her marriage which is not always successful, she's a faithful sacrificing wife.

Zsa Zsa. *Hungarian familiar form* of Susan. *Zsa Zsa Gabor,* actress.

Zulema // Zuleima, Zulma. **Semitic:** "peace".

WARNING: It is very important to read the first chapters of this book. Failure to heed the first chapters may cause serious detrimental consequences in your hopes and dreams for the person who's name you intend to choose!

Male Names

WARNING: It is very important to read the first chapters of this book. Failure to heed the first chapters may cause serious detrimental consequences in your hopes and dreams for the person who's name you intend to choose!

Aaron // Aharon, Ari, Arin, Arnie, Arny, Aron, Arron, Erin, Haroun, Ron, Ronnie, Ronny. **Hebrew:** "enlightened". Biblical: Aaron, first high priest of Israel and brother of Moses. Calm, athletic, manly, intelligent, lawyer, actor, handsome. _Aaron Burr_, (1756-1836), American soldier and statesman. _Aaron Copland_, (1900-90), U.S. composer, leader in the development of modern American music. _Aaron Klug_, (born 1926), British chemist, 1982 Nobel prize for work on the structure of viruses and other particles. _Aaron Spelling_, (born 1928), U.S. television producer. _Aaron Montgomery Ward_, (1843-1913), U.S. merchant, grew into present Montgomery Ward and Co. _Aaron Douglas_, (1899-1988), U.S. artist. _Abbott Lawrence_, (1792-1855), U.S. manufacturer and diplomat. _Aaron Lohr_ - Actor

Abdul // Ab, Abdel, Del. **Arabic:** "son of". _Abdul Pazhwak_, (born 1919), Afghani diplomat, president of UN General Assembly.

Abe // Abey, Abie. _Short form of_ Abelard, Abraham and

Abram. Calm, noble, resolute. _Abe Fortas_, (1910-82), U.S. lawyer, public official, associate justice U.S. Supreme Court.

Abel // Abe. **Hebrew:** "breath". Biblical: brother killed by Cain. _Also a Short form of_ Abelard. _Abel Tasman_, (1603?-59?), foremost 17th-century Dutch explorer, discovered the island of Tasmania, New Zealand, Tonga, and the Fiji Islands. _Abel Gance_, (1889-1981), French director, best known for extravagant historical spectacles. _Abel Upshur_, (1790-1844), U.S. Secretary of the Navy, secretary of state.

Abelard // Ab, Abbey, Abby, Abe, Abel. **Old German:** "noble and resolute".

Abner // Ab, Abbey, Abbie, Abby, Avner, Eb, Eb, Ebbie, Ebby, Ebner. **Hebrew:** "father of light". Biblical: the commander of King Saul's army. _Abner Doubleday_, (1819-93), U.S. Army officer, inventor of baseball.

Abraham // Abe, Abrahan, Abram, Abramo, Abran, Avram, Avrom, Bram, Ibrahim. **Hebrew:** "father of the multitude". Biblical: the first Hebrew patriarch. Noble, resolute, calm, joker, laugher, deep thinker, gentle, patient, determined. _Abraham Lincoln_, U.S. President during civil war, all children who knew him loved him, people who knew him admired him and called him "honest Abe". _Abraham Cahan_, (1860-1951), a founder of the Jewish

Daily Forward, turned it into the most-read Yiddish newspaper in the world, writer, activist, socialist, educator. *Abraham Ortelius*, (1527-98), Flemish cartographer, map dealer, published first modern atlas. *Abraham Jacobi*, (1830-1919), U.S. physician, called founder of American pediatrics. Totals: politician 38%, writer 31%, lawyer 15%, businessman 15%, educator 15%, socialist, cartographer, physician, watchmaker-inventor, philosopher-psychologist, commander. Actor: *Abraham Benrubi*.

Abram // Abe, Abramo, Avram, Avrom, Bram. *Hebrew*: "the lofty one is father". Also see Abraham. Determined. *Abram Ryan*, (Father Ryan) (1838-86), U.S. Roman Catholic priest and poet. *Abram Chasins*, (1903-87), U.S. pianist and composer. *Abram Hewitt*, (1822-1903), U.S. capitalist and political leader. *Abram Markoe*, (1729-1806), Danish merchant, formed troop to fight in Revolutionary War. *Abram Lincoln Harris* (1899-1963), U.S. economist, author.

Adam // Adamo, Adams, Adan, Addie, Ade, Adhamh. *Hebrew*: "from the ground". Biblical: the first person created by God. Quiet, internalizes, sensitive, writer, bit artistic, romatisist; as a child: often don't look like mother or father, emotional, stubborn, persevering, predisposed to lieing; likes sports and can do well; as adult becomes more calm, not very lucky in marriage eventhough a good father, very complicated relationship with wives, often incompatable with wife, likes animals and nature, spends time outside, jealous, will not be subjugated to wife, not career oriented, achieves a lot because of patients, thinks before he speaks, doesn't distain doing any housework, he often marries late because he is fickle, coach, agraculturist, vetrinarian, computer programmer, cook,

artist, pastor, writer. *Adam Smith*, (1723-90), the single most influential figure in the development of modern economic theory, Capitalism. *Adam Gordon*, (1833-70), one of most popular and distinctive of Australian poets. *Adam Wagnalls*, (1843-1924), U.S. Lutheran minister, publisher, one of founders of Funk and Wagnalls Co. *Adam Mickiewicz*, (1798-1855), Polish poet, chiefly famous for epics based on folk tales and legends. *Adam Oehlenschlager*, (1779-1850), Danish poet and dramatist of wide influence. *Adam Krafft*, (1455?-1509), principal German sculptor of late Gothic period. Actors: *Adam Arkin, Adam Baldwin.*

Adan // Aden. Unknown origin and meaning. City of Aden, the capital of Yemen.

Addison // Ad, Addie, Addy. *Old English*: "son of Adam". *Addison Verrill*, (1839-1926), U.S. natural scientist.

Adlai // Ad, Addie, Addy. *Hebrew*: "my witness". *Adlai Stevenson*, (1900-65), U.S. statesman, orator, writer.

Adolph // Ad, Adolf, Adolfo, Adolphe, Adolpho, Adolphus, Dolf, Dolph. *Old German*: "noble wolf, noble hero". Artistic personality type, seeks power and adventure, complicated and stubborn personality from early childhood, looks like mother as child, later resembles father physically and in character, good student; likes chess, soccer, table tennis, reading or watching adventures; courageous although sensitive; picks his friends; coin collecting, likes to fix things, responsible and can not stand irresponsibility in others, compulsive, knows how to convince people but won't beg or entreat; hungers for knowledge, developed imagination, fantasizes, marries late, chooses a calm woman, can not stand someone tempestuous attempt to prove, likes to do only what is pleasant for him, leads a monotonous life, very talented, successful in various areas, banker, engineer, jeweler, driver, doctor, writer, chemist, perfectionist, psychiatrist, music, painter, sculptor, artist. *Adolph Zukor*, (1873-1976), U.S. motion picture mogul, founded Paramount Pictures. *Adolph Gottlieb*, (1903-74), U.S. painter. Adolphe Max, (1869-1939), Belgian public official. *Adolph Weinman*, (1870-1952), U.S. sculptor. *Adolph Bolm*, (1884-1951), U.S. dancer and choreographer. *Adolph Ochs*, (1858-1935), U.S. newspaper publisher. *Adolph Rupp*, (1901-77), U.S. basketball coach, University of Kentucky with great win record. *Adolph Borie*, (1809-80), U.S. public official, merchant, and financier. *Adolf Hitler*, (1889-1945), dictator of Germany, started WWII.

Adonis // Adonnis. *Semitic*: "my lord, my master". Greek / Phoenician mythology: the handsomest of the gods.

Adrian // Ade, Adriano, Adrien, Hadrian. *Latin*: "dark" or "from Hadria, Italy". Sensitive type, bit artistic; resembles mother, character like father - stubborn and egotistical; quite good student, busy, likes pets, brings strays home, some have high achievements in sports; punctual - always on time and don't like when others are not; engineer, programmer, mechanic, teacher, electrician, jurist, administrator, military, doctor, scientist; marriage not always successful, but patiently tries to improve married life: helps wife around house, spends time with children. *Adrien Stoutenburg*, (born 1916), U.S. author, writer of fiction and poetry for children. *Adrian Kantrowitz*, (born 1918), U.S. heart surgeon, first U.S. heart transplant.

Adrian Ostade, (1610-85), Dutch painter. *Adrian Joss*, (1880-1911), U.S. baseball player. *Adrien Marie Legendre*, (1752-1833), French mathematician. *Adrien de Jussieu*, (1797-1853), French botanist. Actors: *Adrian Pasdar, Adrian Paul.*

Agustin. See Augustus.

Ahmed // Ahmad. *Arabic*: "most highly praised". *Ahmed Ben Bella*, (born 1918), cofounder and leader of the Algerian liberation movement, Algeria's first prime minister, elected president of the Algerian Republic. *Ahmed Ali Pasha Fuad I*, (1868-1936), king of Egypt. *Ahmed Zaki Yamani*, (born 1930), Saudi Arabian petroleum minister, former chief spokesman and strategist for OPEC.

Aidan // Aiden. *Aiden Ripley*, (1896-1969), U.S. painter.

Al. Also *Short form of* names beginning with "al" with characteristics of: Sensitive, gentle, liked, handsome, cheerful, friendly, opinionated, easy-going, liked, loner/ leader, able, helping, bit shy, not fearful. Competitor, sports. See names starting with "al" for likely similar characteristics. *Al Barlick*, (born 1915), U.S. baseball umpire. *Al Davis*, (born 1929), U.S. football coach and executive. *Al Kaline*, (born 1934), U.S. baseball player. *Al Unser, Sr.* (born 1939), U.S. auto racer. Actor-musician: *Al Jolson.*

Alan // Ailin, Al, Alain, Aland, Alano, Alanson, Allan, Allen, Allyn, Alon. *Celtic, Gaelic*: "handsome, cheerful". See names starting with Al for likely similar characteristics. Handsome, healthy, cheerful, friendly, social, multitalented, energetic, romanticist, strategist, studies how things work, inquisitive, philosophizer, scheming, crafty, inventive, writer, poet, businessman?, diplomat, politician, lawyer, newsman, studies social interaction, loves language, doctor, scientist, foreign traveler, adventurer, archeologist, sensitive, busy, entrepreneurial, not always logical, opinionated, holder of unsubstantiated beliefs, but easy going, liked, loner/leader, able, helping, marries apparently strong female. *Alain Locke*, (1886-1954), writer and teacher. *Alan Paton* (1903-88), South Africa novelist, presents religion, not politics, as the potential healer of his homeland. *Allen Ginsberg*, (born 1926), poet of the "beat generation", poems adopted by 1960s youth revolution. *Alan Bean*, (born 1932), former U.S. astronaut. *Allan Wilson*, (1934-91), New Zealand-born American biochemist and zoologist, evolutionist. *Allen Whipple*, (1881-1963), U.S. surgeon. *Alan Brooke,* (1883-1963), British military officer, strategist for Winston Churchhill. *Alan Hodgkin*, (born 1914), British biophysicist. Totals: writer 53%, politician 28%, scientist 12%, commander 9%, lawyer 9%, astronaut 6%, businessman 6%, educator 6%, economist 6%, adventurer 6%, surgeon, detective, cabinet maker, inventor, zoologist, archaeolgist, lyricist, athlete, Egyptologist. Actors: *Alan Alda, Alan Bates, Alan Rickman.*

Alastair // Al, Alasdair, Alasteir, Alaster, Alastor, Alistair, Alister, Allister, Allistir. *Scottish form* of Alexander. See names starting with Al for likely similar characteristics. *Alistair Cooke*, (full name Alfred Alistair Cooke) (born 1908), U.S. journalist and essayist.

Albert // Al, Alberto, Albie, Aubert, Bert, Bertie, Berty, Elbert. *Germanic*: "illustrious through nobility". Also see Al. See names starting with Al for likely similar characteris-

tics. Thinker, anti-violence, charitable, philanthropic, peace loving, friend of all, courageous, adventurous, pioneer, engineer, writer; finishes projects which he starts with strong determination, organizes his work well, taking into account time and schedule, has these military qualities from birth, many leaders, but not perfect leaders; sometimes too emotional, straight forward, creating conflict situations, over careful - perhaps a bit fearful when making important decisions; avoids critiques. *Albert Einstein*, (1879-1955), internationally known brilliant physicist. *Albert Namatjira*, (1902-59), Australian watercolor landscape artist. *Albert Schweitzer,* (1875-1965), noted clergyman, musician, theologian and medical missionary. *Albert Luthuli*, (1898-1967), nonviolent activist against racial discrimination in South Africa. *Alberto Giacometti*, (1901-66), Swiss abstract sculptor. *Albert Camus*, (1913-60), writer of novels, essays, and plays against indifference and meaninglessness and for truth and justice. *Albert I* (1875-1934), King Albert of Belgium was well educated in engineering and mechanics and widely traveled, courageous, pioneer flier, enthusiastic mountain climber, and a patron of artists, writers, and musicians. *Albert Michelson*, (1852-1931), among the world's most distinguished physicists, established the speed of light as a fundamental constant. Totals: writer 25%, politician 21%, artist 13%, scientist 13%, educator 11%, musician 11%, commander 11%, businessman 9%, lawyer 7%, clergy 5%, doctor 5%, missionary 4%, historian 4%, engineer 4%, aviator 4%, athlete 4%, economist 4%, philosophy, psychologist, architect, photographer, coach, sociologist, ecologist.

Alden // Aldin, Aldo, Aldwin, Elden, Eldin. *Old English*: "old friend, wise protector". Also see Al. See names starting with Al for likely similar characteristics. "old, wise protector", gentle, strong, fairly quiet.

Aldrich // Al, Aldric, Aldridge, Alric, Eldridge, Rich, Rich ie, Richy. *Old English*: "old wise ruler". *Eldridge Cleaver*, (born 1935), former Black Panther party leader, who became Christian and Republican.

Alec // Alex. *Short forms of* Alexander. Handsome, friendly, easy-going, playful, entrepreneurial, scheming, crafty. *Alex La Guma*, (1925-85),South African anti-racial segregation novelist. *Alec Douglas-Home*, (born 1903), Britain's 44th prime minister. *Alec Guinness*, (born 1914), British actor, director, and writer. *Alec Waugh*, (1898-1981), English writer. Actor: *Alec Baldwin*.

Alexander // Al, Alasdair, Alastair, Alaster, Alec, Alejandro, Alejo, Alek, Aleksandr, Alessandro, Alex, Alexandr, Alexandre, Alexandro, Alexandros, Alexio, Alexis, Alic, Alick, Alisander, Alistair, Alister, Alix, Allister, Allistir, Sander, Sandro, Sandy, Sascha, Sasha, Saunder. *Greek*: "defender of men" Also see Al and Alec. Handsome, friendly, easy-going but directed, humorous or witty, multi-talented, energetic, become involved in sports, strong, goal directed, capable of great achievements, good leader who gives credit to talented and capable workers, reputation of being fair or just; predisposed to drinking too much but a traumatic event can change this; tries to be charming toward women, seldom is there a more attentive and considerate man: habitually opens doors, gives hand for support, buys gifts of flowers, his main device is complements, all this is done sincerely; however his sincere promise to love forever will be sincerely repeated to another woman in a while; writer, entrepreneurial, businessman, adventurer, strategist, engineer, inventor, diplomat, public speaker, statesman, military officer, poet, novelist, artist. *Alexander the Great*, (356-323 BC), conquered almost all the then known world before he died at age 32. *Alexander Nevski*, (1220?-63), Russian prince and outstanding military commander. *Alexander Calder*, (1898-1976), American engineer trained sculptor created the abstract constructions known as "stabiles" and "mobiles". *Alexander von Humboldt*, (1769-1859), German scholar and explorer, laid the foundations for modern physical geography, geophysics, and biogeography and helped to popularize science. *Alexander Pope*, (1688-1744), English poet, master of satire and epigram. *Alexander Graham Bell*, (1847-1922), inventor and father of the electric telephone. *Alexander Solzhenitsyn*, (born 1918), exiled Soviet novelist and historian. Three Romanov rulers of Russia were named Alexander. Totals: writer 38%, politician 27%, musician 14%, artist 13%, commander 11%, businessman 8%, clergy 5%, scientist 5%, inventor 5%, historian 3%, communist 3%, doctor 3%, lawyer 3%, missionary, philanthropist, psychologist, explorer. Actor: *Alexander Siddig*.

Alexis // Alexi. *Greek*: "defender". *Familiar form of* Alexander. As a child he perceives himself as the defender of his mother; when older he perceives himself as defender of those around him; although not leading the other boys, they come to him for advice and respect him; conscientious worker; likes work that requires patients; good worker in any area; ambitious and becomes successful; talented, painter, writer, actor, engineer, physicist, surgeon, criminologist; gives wife her way in little matters, but firm in big matters; easily offended, values a woman's neatness the highest; not jealous, usually faithful because of his uncomfort with untidiness; caring toward children; stays attached to his parents throughout life.

Alfonso // Alfonzo. Form of Alphonse

Alfred // Al, Alf, Alfie, Alfredo, Alfy, Avery, Fred, Freddie, Freddy. *Old English*: "wise counsel, elf counsel". Also see Al and Fred. Popular name. See names starting with Al for likely similar characteristics. Multi-talented, easy-going, often playful or witty, bends the rules, fast effective worker, stubborn from early childhood, good grades, obedient; at first he doesn't stand-out from his peers, but later becomes a leader; fearless, courageous, able to reason well; avoids forcing his opinion on others; relatively large percentage of writers philosophers and psychologists, thinker, commander, writer, novelist, poet, inventor, statesman, orator, musician, photographer, painter, scientist, engineers, doctors, actors, composers, administrators, military, journalist, writer; often changes his profession until he finds his talent. *Alfred T. Mahan*, (1840-1914), naval officer and historian. *Alfred Adler*, (1870-1937), the founder of individual psychology. *Alfred North Whitehead*, (1861-1947), 20th-century giant in philosophy, thinker, interest in all science and human experience, educational reformer, profound analyst of religion. *Alfred Korzybski*, (1879-1950), Polish-born scientist and philosopher. *Alfred Nobel*, (1833-96), invention and manufacture of high explosives, left much of his fortune for the Nobel prizes to promote world peace, advance scientific knowledge, and encourage literary

achievement. *Alfred C. Kinsey*, (1894-1956), Zoologist-psychologist noted student and interpreter of human sexual behavior. *Alfred the Great*, (848?-899), statesman and warrior. *Lord Alfred Tennyson*, (1809-92), considered England's greatest poet of later 19th century. Totals: writer 39%, scientist 15%, commander 10%, artist or photographer 10%, politician 10%, philosopher 9%, psychologist 7%, musician 6%, businessman 6%, inventor 4%, doctor 4%, pacifist 3%, theatrical director 3%, educator 3%, engineer 3%, craftsman, dandy, actor, scholar, astronaut-test pilot, naturalist, lawyer-jurist, traitor, historian, zoologist.

Ali. *Arabic*: "greatest". *Ali* (600?-661), 4th Muslim caliph, reign characterized by unrest and civil strife.

Allan // Allen. *Forms of* Alan. See Alan.

Allard // Al, Alard. *Old English*: "noble and brave". See names starting with Al for likely similar characteristics. Noble and brave, leader, fair, easy-going, delegates.

Alonzo // Alonso. *Forms of* Alphonse. Also see Al. See names starting with Al for likely similar characteristics. *Alonso Cano*, (1601-67), Spanish architect, painter and sculptor of great ability. *Alonzo de Ojeda*, (1465?-1515), Spanish explorer.

Alphonse // Al, Alf, Alfie, Alfons, Alfonso, Alfonzo, Alonzo, Alphonso, Fons, Fonsie, Fonz, Fonzie. *Old German*: "noble and eager". See names starting with Al for likely similar characteristics. Fairly quiet, noble, eager, helping, volunteer, handsome, composed, patient with others, hard working. *Alphonse de Lamartine*, (1790-1869), Honored today as the first of the French Romantic poets.

Alphonse Daudet, (1840-97), novelist, dramatist, and short story writer. Thirteen rulers of Spain have borne the name Alfonso.

Alvaro. *Spanish:* "just, wise".

Alvin // Al, Alvan, Alwin, Elvin. *Germanic:* "beloved by all". See names starting with Al for likely similar characteristics. Sensitive side, entrepreneurial, founder, daring(?). *Alvin York*, (1887-1964), In WW I, Sgt. York single-handedly captured or killed an entire German battalion, in later life founded a school to improve rural education. *Alvin Adams*, (1804-77), U.S. pioneer express mailman. *Alvin Ailey*, (1931-89), U.S. modern dancer and choreographer, founded dance company. *Alvan Clark*, (1832-97), U.S. astronomer and astronomical instrument maker.

Amir // Aamir, Emir. *Arabic:* "lord, ruler". Muslim title used to denote ruling power or distinct office; also title of honor given to descendants of Muhammad through his daughter Fatima. Actor: *Aamir Khan*.

Ambrose // Ambie, Ambroise, Ambros, Ambrosi, Ambrosio, Ambrosius, Amby, Brose. *Greek:* "immortal". *Ambrose Shea*, (1815-1905), Canadian political leader. *Ambrose Burnside,* (1824-81), U.S. Army general and politician. *Ambrose Hill,* (1825-65), U.S. soldier, lieutenant general. *Ambrosio O'Higgins,* (originally Ambrose Higgins) (1720?-1801), soldier and govenor. *Ambroise Pare*, (1510-90), French army physician, the father of modern surgery. *Ambroise Thomas,* (1811-96), French composer.

Amory // Amery. *Form of* Emery.

Amos. *Hebrew:* "burden". Biblical: a Hebrew prophet and book. *Amos Lawrence*, (1786-1852), U.S. merchant and philanthropist. *Amos Adams*, (1814-86), chief founder of Lawrence College. *Amos Rusie*, (1871-1942), U.S. baseball player, pitcher. *Amos Stagg*, (1862-1965), U.S. football coach. *Amos Akerman*, (1821-80), U.S. lawyer. *Amos Alcott*, (1799-1888), U.S. philosopher, educator, and writer. *Amos Tutuola*, (born 1920), Nigerian writer. *Amos Kendall*, (1789-1869), U.S. newspaper editor and public official. *Amos Dolbear*, (1837-1910), U.S. inventor and physicist.

Anatole // Anatol, Anatoli, Anatolia, Anatolii, Anatolio, Anatoliy, Anatoly. *Greek:* "man from the east". As child: not very communicative or confident, likes to read science-fiction and adventure novels, imagining himself to be a super-hero, bit "moma's boy"; As Adult: stops being "moma's boy", peers respect him for his intelligence and knowledge, stays a romanticist inside, compliant, good relationship with people; in an extreme situation can become out of control, unsociable and difficult; developed sense of justice, he leads respectfully, diplomatic, sensible, stable, easily trusted by women, prefer blondes, quickly develops a good relationship with in-laws, may like to drink to much, may get addicted easily, his wife tries and often succeeds to be the family's leader often becoming a dictator, which causes him to abandon home, usually difficult to communicate at his children's level, easily offended, good money earner. *Anatole France*, (Jacques Anatole Thibault) (1844-1924), major French novelist. *Anatoly Filipchenko*, (born 1928), Soviet cosmonaut. *Anatoly Lunacharski*, (1875-1933), Soviet political leader, author and revolutionary. *Anatoliy Lukyanov*, (born 1930), Soviet hard-line politician, mastermind behind 1991 failed coup. *Anatolii Dobrynin*, (born 1919?), Soviet diplomat.

Anders // Anderson. *Swedish form* of Andrew. Scientist. *Anders Zorn*, (1860-1920), Swedish artist. *Anders Celsius*, (1701-44), Swedish astronomer. *Anders Ekeberg*, (1767-1813), Swedish mineralogist. *Anders Dahl*, (1751-89), Swedish botanist.

Andre // Andras, Andres, Andris. *Greek:* andros, "man". *French form* of Andrew. As child: bit cunning and mischievous, dreamer, not obedient, likes sweats, doesn't obey mother, argues back to father, good friendship with brother, jealous and selfish toward sister, not prominent or distinguished as teenager among peers, but later in life becomes more successful than them, girls complain of his instability, one day he can declare his love for a girl and the next he doesn't even notice her as he is hand-in-hand with another girl; actor adventurer, romantic, artistic, poet, relational, statesman, chemistry, biologist, doctor, military, singer, composer, producer; good worker, unpredictable and impulsive; picks an attractive, beautiful and emotional wife; almost no interest in her character or inner-self; ignores warnings from others about hurrying marriage; egotistical, artistic, demands high attention, may be jealous of his wife's time with the children, bit thrifty, spends money wisely, accumulates things, complicated relationship with mother-in-law. *Andre-Frederic Cournand*, (1895-1988), U.S. physician. *Andre Messager,* (1853-1929), French composer and conductor. *Andre de Chenier*, (1762-94), French poet. *Andre Breton*, (1896-1966), French poet, novelist, and critic. *Andre Tardieu*, (1876-1945), French statesman. *Andre de Segonzac*, (1884-1974), French painter and illustrator.

Andrew // Anders, Andie, Andonis, Andre, Andrea, Andeas, Andrej, Andres, Andrey, Andy, Drew, Dru. *Greek:* "strong, manly". Greek view of a whole man included being sensitive. Biblical: one of the twelve Apostles. Also see Andre. Handsome, a bit mischievous, romantic, artistic, relational, strong, manly, quick learner, diplomat, politician, physician, sympathetic to religion, military, poet. *Andrew Carnegie*, (1835-1919), industrialist and philanthropist. *Andrew Wyeth*, (born 1917), realistic painter, widely acclaimed U.S. artist. *Andrew Marvell*, (1621-78), politician, political satirist, wit, nature mystic, fine amateur English poet. *Andrew Jackson*, fiery, iron-willed General, 7th U.S. president, charmer, gambler. *Andrew Mellon*, (1855-1937), U.S. financier, ambassador to England, philanthropist. *Andrew Lloyd Webber*, (born 1948), British musical comedy writer. Totals: politician 32%, commander 21%, writer poet 18%, businessman 15%, scientist 9%, artist 6%, clergy 6%, lawyer 6%, educator 6%, philanthropist, physician, missionary, hero, adventurer, landscaper, engineer-inventor. Actor: *Andrew McCarthy.*

Andy // Andie. *Form of* Andrew. A bit more fun seeking than Andrew, has not accepted the formality that "Andrew" represents. See Andrew and Andre. *Andy Warhol*, (1930?-87), the top name in Pop art. *Andy Williams,* popular singer. Actors: *Andy Garcia, Andy Griffith*.

Angelo // Angel. *Italian from Greek:* "angel, messenger". *Angelo Patri*, (1877-1965), U.S. author and educator, specialist in child training. *Angelo Heilprin*, (1853-1907), U.S. naturalist and traveler. *Angelo Bartlett Giamatti*, (1938-89), U.S. scholar, university president, and baseball executive.

Ansel // Ancell, Ansell. *Old French:* "loyal follower of a nobleman". *Ansel Adams*, (1902-84), U.S. photographer, technical innovation, dramatic Western landscapes, pioneer preservationist, promoted photography as an art form.

Anthony // Antoine, Anton, Antone, Antoni, Antonin, Antonino, Antonio, Antonius, Antons, Antony, Tony. *Latin:* "priceless"; *Old Greek:* "engaging in battle". Charming, friendly, a lover, ladies man, excellent at romancing/wooing, good looking, sexy, kind with women, may be very jealous and uncontrollable, has many girlfriends when young, slow to marry, not a perfect family man, doesn't like to stay home, falls in love too quickly, his kindness and compliant nature help avoid big family conflicts, resembles mother's personality, very attached to father, acts respectful to both parents, very hard working, master of his job, may read a lot, talented scientist, politician, statesman, businessman, actor, diverse successes. *Anthony Trollope*, (1815-82), human behavioral novelist. *Anthony Wayne*, (1745-96), American Revolution general, displayed the most reckless bravery and boldness, calculated risks carefully and won. *Anthony Eden*, (1897-1977), prime minister of Great Britain, highly competent statesman and a brilliant diplomat. *Anthony van Leeuwenhoek*, (1632-1723), extraordinary ability to grind lenses, vast amount of innovative research on bacteria, protozoa. *Anthony Van Dyck*, (1599-1641), Flemish painter, known for his portraits of Europe's kings and queens and other dignitaries. *Anthony Hope Hawkins*, (1863-1933), British romantic comedies novelist. *Anthony Overton*, (1864-1946), U.S. manufacturer, banker, life-insurance executive, and publisher. *Anthony Drexel*, (1826-93), founder of Philadelphia banking house. Totals: politician 19%, writer 11%, scientist 11%, artist 7%, businessman 7%, judge 7%, actor 7%, reformer 7%, commander, engineer, clergy, athlete, athlete, auto-racer, lawyer, philanthropist, librarian, philosopher, inventor, choreographer. Actors: *Anthony Clark, Anthony Edwards, Anthony Head, Anthony Hopkins, Anthony Quinn, Anthony Rapp, Antonio Banderas, Antonio Sabato Jr.*

Antoine. *French form* of Anthony. Totals: artist 40%, writers 27%, commander, scientist, clergy, jurist, politician, adventurer, scholar, inventor, craftsman.

Antonio. *Italian form* of Anthony. Totals: politician 26%, writer poet dramatist 19%, artist 15%, musician 11%, architect 11%, commander 11%, engineer 7%, craftsman, dictator, heavy-handed, communist, scientist, traveler, businessman, explorer, librarian, jurist.

Archer. *English:* "bowman". *Short form of* Archibald. *Archer Martin*, (born 1910), British biochemist.

Archibald // Arch, Archaimbaud, Archambault, Archer, Archibaldo, Archibold, Archie, Archy. *Old German:* "genuinely bold". Totals: (11) writer 81%, educator 36%, librarian, physician, commander, geologist, lawyer, politician, orator, inventor-engineer, physiologist, orientalist.

Archie // Archy. *Familiar forms of* Archer and Archibald. *Archie Shepp*, (born 1937), U.S. avant-garde saxophonist, pianist, composer, educator, and playwright.

Ariel. *Hebrew:* "lion of God".

Aristotle // Ari, Arie, Aristarkh, Arri. *Greek:* "the best". Firm, persevering, active; as a small child, he is busy and irritable; in everything and everywhere he likes to be first; reaching his goals, more compliant with years, doesn't take anything on faith, has an opinion on everything, enduring, not afraid of difficulties, love adventures. *Aristotle*, (384-322 BC), ancient Greek philosopher, among the greatest thinkers of all time, his work in the natural and social sciences greatly influenced virtually every area of modern thinking. *Aristotle Onassis*, (1906-75), Greek businessman and shipping magnate, married Jacqueline Kennedy.

Arlo. *Spanish:* "the barberry". *Arlo Guthrie*, (born 1947), U.S. folksinger and composer.

Armand // Arman, Armando, Armen, Armin. *Old German*: "army man". *French form* of Herman. *Armin Henry Meyer*, (born 1914), U.S. diplomat. *Armando Palacio Valdes*, (1853-1938), Spanish novelist and critic. *Armand Hammer*, (1898-1990), U.S. industrialist, oil executive, philanthropist, art patron. *Armand Hippolyte Louis Fizeau*, (1819-96), French physicist. Actor: *Armin Shimerman*.

Armon // Armen, Armin. *Hebrew:* "tower fortress". Also see Armand.

Armstrong. *Old English:* "strong arm". *Armstrong Sperry*, (1897-1976), U.S. author and illustrator of children's books.

Arne. Arney, Arni, Arnie, Arno. *Old German:* "eagle". Also see Arnold. *Arne Carlson*, (born 1934), U.S. public official, governor of Minnesota. *Arne Garborg*, (1851-1924), Norwegian novelist and lyric poet. *Arne Tiselius*, (1902-71), Swedish biochemist, professor and researcher. *Arno Penzias*, (born 1933), U.S. astrophysicist. *Arno Luckhardt*, (1885-1957), U.S. physiologist, professor. *Arno Holz*, (1863-1929), German poet and critic.

Arnold // Arnaldo, Arnauld, Arney, Arni, Arnie, Arnoldo, Arnulfo, Arny. *Old German:* "strong as an Eagle". Stubborn, irritable and always wants to be first as child; quite good student, best subjects are mathematics and physics, very straight forward which causes conflicts with teacher, secluding personality, doesn't let people become close, able hands, good imagination, whatever he starts - he finishes, first marriage often doesn't last very long, the second marriage is more successful. *Arnold Gesell*, (1880-1961), child development researcher and writer. *Arnold Schoenberg*, (1874-1951), influential composer, founder of school of musical composition. *Arnold Bennett*, (1867-1931), English novelist, journalist and playwright. *Arnold Toynbee*, (1889-1975), major researcher historian. *Arnold Palmer*, (born 1929), professional golfer with many golf first. *Arnold Rothstein*, (1882-1928), U.S. crime overlord. *Arnold Schwarzenegger*, (born 1947), U.S. actor and former bodybuilding champion. Totals: (13) writer 54%, athlete 23%, educator 23%, musician, historian, naturalist-geographer-geologist, actor, hero, sociologist-economist, crime boss, newscaster.

Arsien // Arseni, Arsenio. *Old Greek:* "couragious". Not a problematic child for parents, good grades, seldom conflict with peers, out-going, choosy at picking a friend, likes animals - especially dogs - but doesn't like to take care of them; only puts effort into what he likes to do, can lie to be able to do what he likes; coach, doctor, cook, artist, architect, jurist, driver, priest; like to collect antiques. *Arsenio Hall*, (born 1959), U.S. entertainer, actor, comedian, talk show host.

Art. *Short form of* Arthur. Art Buchwald, (born 1928), U.S. author, humorist, political commentator, and syndicated newspaper columnist. *Art Shell,* (born 1946), U.S. football player and first black NFL head coach. *Art Pepper,* (1925-82), U.S. jazz saxophonist, clarinetist, and composer. *Art Tatum,* (1910-56), U.S. jazz pianist.

Artemae // Artemea. As child: very persevering, even stubborn, like to be around adults more than peers, parents may be strict, limber becoming a good athlete, what he does goes well, finishes what he starts, independent personality, doesn't naturally adjust to others.

Artemus // Artemae, Artemas, Artemea, Artemis, Artie, Artome, Arty, Artyome. *Greek:* "safe and healthy, gift of Artemis". Greek mythology: Artemis, daughter of Zeus and Leto, twin sister of Apollo; virgin huntress and moon goddess; Roman counterpart Diana. See Artemae and Artome. *Artemas Ward,* (1727-1800), American Revolutionary War general, jurist and politician.

Artome // Artyome. *Greek:* "healthy". As a child: calm, never pushy with opinion, usually don't get into trouble in school, likes to read, objective, tells only the truth which sometimes is disadvantageous, resemble mother, friendly, social; when adult: compliant, goal directed, but not career directed, all achievement is from hard work, faithful, can keep secrets, various professions, jeweler, doctor, electrician, artist, journalist, architect, teacher; good husband, likes animals, hard working, likes traveling, usually own mechanic, not leader in the family, likes to host guests and cook for them.

Arthur // Art, Arte, Arther, Artie, Artur, Arturo, Arty, Aurthur. *Celtic:* "noble". *Welsh:* "bear-hero". Often calm stable and obedient child; sensitive, squeamish, jealous, friendly, likable, novelist, writer, composer, thinker, engineer, architect, scientist, artist, illustrator, music, creator, military man, sales, dentist, surgeon, jurist, tailor, lower dominance, very attached to his children, may not assist wife domestically, hospitable, likes business trips, attracted to strong female more stubborn than himself, relational, he feels need to share his power, does his woman's beckoning, often marries determined woman: Cathy, Melissa. *Arthur Fiedler,* (1894-1979), conductor of the Boston Pops Orchestra. *Arthur Meighen,* (1874-1960), Prime Minister of Canada, conservative politician. *Arthur Phillip,* (1738-1814), British naval commander, established and governed first European colony in Australia. *Artur Rubinstein,* (1887-1982), international virtuoso pianist. *Arthur Conan Doyle,* (1859-1930), British physician, historical novelist, creator of detective Sherlock Holmes. *Arturo Toscanini,* (1867-1957), Italian opera and symphony conductor. *Arthur C. Clarke,* (born 1917), British science-fiction writer, underwater explorer, and photographer. Total: writer 44%, politician 21%, educator 13%, scientist 8%, musician 8%, commander 8%, businessman 8%, lawyer 6%, artist-illustrator 5%, dancing teacher 2%, historian 2%, economist 2%, engineer 2%, physician, philosopher, architect, scholar, archaeologist, anthropologist, athlete, entertainer, jurist. Actor: *Arthur Lake*.

Asa // Ase. *Hebrew:* "physician". *Asa Randolph,* (1889-1979), U.S. labor leader. *Asa Whitney,* (1791-1874), U.S. inventor. *Asa Gray,* (1810-88), U.S. botanist, professor, prolific writer on botany.

Asher // Ash. *Hebrew:* "happy, blessed". *Asher Durand,* (1796-1886), U.S. portrait and landscape painter and engraver.

Ashley // Ash, Ashland, Ashlin. *Old English*: "ash tree meadow".

Ashton // Ash. *Old English:* "ash town".

Aubrey // Alberik, Aube, Auberon, Avery, Aberon. *Germanic:* "blond ruler, elf ruler". *Aubrey DeVere,* (1814-1902), Irish poet. *Aubrey Beardsley,* (1872-98), British artist.

August // Agosto, Aguistin, Agustin, Augie, Auguste, Augustin, Augustine, Augusto, Augustus, Augy, Austen, Austin, Gus. *Latin:* "majestic dignity". Historical: honors *Augustus Caesar* and *Saint Augustine.* Wordsmith, artistic, dramatist, poet, writer, politician, artist, scientist especially biologist, clergy, detailed studies in his interest. *August Strindberg*, (1849-1912), noted Swedish dramatist. *Auguste Escoffier,* (1846-1935), "king of chefs and the chef of kings". *Auguste Comte,* (1798-1857), French philosopher, father of Sociology. *Auguste Rodin,* (1840-1917), French artist, his works include distress, moral weakness, passion and beauty. *Augustus Saint-Gaudens,* (1848-1907), monumental American sculptor. *August Kiss,* (1802-65), German sculptor. *August von Kotzebue,* (1761-1819), German playwright. *Auguste Beernaert,* (1829-1912), Belgian statesman.

Augustine // Agostino, Aguistin, Agustin, Augie, Augustin, Augy, Austen, Austin, Gus. *Latin:* "belonging to Augustus". The name honors *St. Augustine.* Also see August. *St. Augustine of Hippo,* (354-430), bishop of Hippo, great church Father, helped doctrinalize Christian theology. *Augustine of Canterbury,* (died 604?), founder of the Christian church in England, first archbishop of Canterbury. *Augustin Fresnel,* (1788-1827), French physicist. *Augustin Daly,* (1838-99), U.S. dramatist and theatrical manager. *Augustin de Candolle,* (1778-1841), Swiss botanist. *Augustin Cauchy,* (1789-1857), French mathematician, wrote successful poetry. *Augustin Scribe,* (1791-1861), French dramatist. *Augustin Thierry,* (1795-1856), French historian.

Austin // Austen. *Form of* August and Augustine. *Austin Harbutt MacCormick,* (1893-1979), U.S. penologist/criminologist. *Austen Henry Layard,* (1817-94), British diplomat, archaeologist, and writer. *Austen Chamberlain,* (1863-1937), British states- man, received 1925 Nobel peace prize. Actors: *Austin Peck, Austin St. John.*

Avery. *English form* of Alfred and Aubrey. Actor: *Avery Brooks.*

Avram. *Hebrew form* of Abraham or Abram.

Axel. *Scandinavian form* of Absalom. *Axel Theorell,* (1903-82), Swedish biochemist. *Axel Munthe,* (1857-1949), Swedish physician and author. *Axel Cronstedt,* (1722-65), Swedish chemist and mineralogist. *Count Axel Oxenstjerna,* (1583-1654), noted Swedish statesman, chancellor. *Axel Holst,* (1860-1931), Norwegian chemist and physician.

Barnabas // Barnabe, Barnaby, Barnebas, Barneby, Barney, Barnie, Barny, Burnaby. *Greek:* "son of prophecy". Biblical: fellow laborer with the Apostle Paul. Friendly, accepting of others, easy-going, relational, willing to follow, but can lead. *Barnabe Googe*, (1540-94), English poet.

Barnett // Barn, Barney, Barron, Barry. *Old English*: "nobleman". *Barnett Newman*, (1905-70), painter and sculptor of abstract.

Barney. *Familiar form of* Barnabas, Barnett and Bernard. *Barney Oldfield*, (Berna Eli Oldfield) (1878-1946), U.S. automobile racer. *Barney Bigard*, jazz musician. *Barney Nagler*, boxing writer.

Baron. *Old English:* "nobleman, baron". *Baron Noel-Baker*, (1889-1982), British statesman, campaign for disarmament, won silver medal in 1920 Olympics.

Barret // Bar, Barrett, Bear. *Old German*: "mighty as a bear". *Barrett Wendell*, (1855-1921), U.S. author and educator.

Barry // Barri, Barrie, Barris, Bary. *Gaelic:* "spearlike, pointed". *Familiar form of* Barnett and Bernard. Tend to be less physical, more cerebral, friendly, easy going. *Barry Commoner*, (born 1917), U.S. biologist, ecologist, and educator. *Barry Leger*, (1737-89), British soldier. *Barry Goldwater*, (born 1909), U.S. department store executive

and political leader.

Bart. *Short form of* Bartholomew, Barton and Bertram. Entrepreneur, friendly, helps when asked, businessman, tends toward heavy.

Bartholomew // Bart, Bartel, Barth, Barthélemy, Bartholomeus, Bartlet, Bartlett, Bartolomé. *Hebrew:* "farmer's son". Biblical: one of the Twelve Apostles. Also see Bart. Explorer, missionary. *Bartholomew Diaz*, sea captain/explorer, the first European to round the Cape of Good Hope, 1488. *Barthelemy Thimonnier*, (1793-1859), French tailor, inventor of first sewing machine. *Bartolome de Las Casas*, (1474-1566), missionary and theologian, first person to oppose the enslavement and oppression of the American natives by Spanish. *Bartolome Murillo*, (1617-82), artist whose many religious paintings emphasized the peaceful, joyous aspects of spiritual life. *Bartholomew Columbus,* (1445?-1515?), Italian explorer and cartographer. *Bartholomew Gosnold*, (died 1607), English navigator and explorer. *Bartolome Mitre*, (1821-1906), Argentine soldier and statesman. *Bartolome de Torres Naharro*, (1476?-1531?), Spanish playwright.

Bartram. Form of Bertram.

Basil // Base, Basile, Basilio, Basilius, Vasilis, Vassily. *Greek:* "kingly, royal". *Saint Basil the Great*, (329-379), early father of Greek church. *Basil Zaharov*, (1850-1936), Turkish international financier. *Basil King*, (1859-1928), Canadian poet and novelist. *Basil Spence*, (1907-76), British architect. Actor: *Basil Rathbone*.

Bayard // Bay. *Old English*: "red-brown haired". *Bayard Taylor*, (James Bayard Taylor) (1825-78), U.S. translator, traveler, and poet. *Bayard Rustin*, (1910-87), U.S. civil rights leader, a founder of CORE, assistant to Martin Luther King Jr.

Beau // Beaufort, Bo. *French:* "beautiful, handsome". *Short form of* Beauregard. Bo: short form for Brother and Boyfriend. *Bo Jackson*, (Vincent Edward Jackson) (born 1962), U.S. baseball and football player. Actor: *Beau Bridges.*

Beauregard // Beau, Bo. *Old French*: "beautiful in expression".

Beck. *Scandinavian:* "brook". Strong, manly, capable, respected.

Ben // Benn, Bennie, Benny. *Hebrew:* "son of". *Short form of* names beginning with "ben", especially Benjamin. Composed, manly, strong, leader, humorous, determined, brave, sensitive, performer, actor, musician, writer. *Benny Goodman,* (1909-86), U.S. clarinetist, orchestra conductor. *Benny Carter*, (full name Bennett Lester Carter) (born 1907), U.S. alto saxophonist, jazz composer, arranger, trumpeter, and pianist. *Benny Leonard*, lightweight boxing champion, 1917-24, retired undefeated. *Ben Shahn*, (1898-1969), artist. *Ben Jonson*, (1572?-1637), English poet, playwright, bricklayer, soldier, and actor. *Ben Milam*, (1791?-1835), Texan patriot. *Ben Williams*, (1889-1953), U.S. writer. *Ben Johnson*, (born 1961), Canadian track star, stripped of gold medal after testing positive for steroids. *Ben Vereen*, (born 1946) U.S. entertainer. *Ben Turpin*, (1874-1940), U.S. actor. *Ben E. King*, (originally Benjamin Earl Nelson) (born 1938), U.S. soul singer. *Ben Mottelson*, (born 1926), Danish physicist, shared 1975 Nobel prize.

Ben Fuller, (1870-1937), U.S. major general, head of U.S. Marine Corps. *Ben Hecht*, (1894-1964), U.S. author. *Ben Nicholson*, (1894-1982), British artist. *Ben Hogan*, (born 1912), U.S. professional golfer. *Ben Nelson*, (born 1941), U.S. public official. Totals: (14) writer 21%, actor 14%, artist 14%, commander 14%, athlete 14%, bricklayer, soldier, scientist, businessman, politician, singer, entertainer. Actor: *Ben Bass, Benicio Del Toro.*

Benedict // Ben, Bendick, Bendict, Bendix, Benedette, Benedetto, Benedick, Benedicto, Benedikt, Bengt, Benito, Bennie, Benny, Benoit. *Latin:* "blessed". As child: kind, calm, involved, balanced development, likes animals; engineer, artist, journalist, accountant, electrician, teacher, auto mechanic, scientist, clergy, historian; doesn't always choose wife wisely, becomes good father, master at home remodeling, excellent work with his hands, hospitable, good at entertaining friends, does his own auto work, often like fishing. *St. Benedict of Nursia*, (480?-547?), founder of 12 monastaries, wrote the rules on monastic order. *Benedetto Croce*, (1866-1952), eloquent historian, philosopher, humanist, and patriot. *Benedict Arnold*, (1741-1801), American Revolutionary War general and traitor. *Benedict Vilakazi*, (1906-47), South African Zulu educator and writer. *Benedict Flaget*, (1763-1850), French missionary.

Benjamin // Ben, Beniamino, Benjamen, Benji, Benjie, Benjy, Benn, Bennie, Benny, Benyamin, Jamie, Jim. *Hebrew:* "son of the right hand" implying "son of strength". Composed, manly, strong, determined, humorous, leader, brave, sensitive, performer, actor, musician, writer, doctor, serious thinker, hard-worker, high percentage of educators inventors and social reformers. *Benjamin Disraeli*, (1804-81), clever novelist and brilliant statesman, twice Great Britain prime minister. *Benjamin Harrison*, former U.S. president and lawyer. *Benjamin Cardozo*, (1870-1938), inovative U.S. Supreme Court Justice. *Benjamin Spock*, (1903-1998), all-time best-seller author of 'The Common Sense Book of Baby and Child Care', also known for his involvement in the peace movement. *Benjamin Rush*, (1746-1813), eminent physician, social reformer attacking slavery, capital punishment, alcohol, tobacco, war and promoting free public schools, the education of women, and a national university. *Benjamin Franklin*, printer, diplomat, a scientist, an inventor, a philosopher, an educator, and a public servant. *Benjamin West*, (1738-1820), artist. *Benjamin Banneker,* (1731-1806), mathematician, astronomer, and inventor. *Benjamin Britten*, (1913-76), renown English opera composer, outstanding pianist and conductor. *Benjamin Lee Guinness*, (1798-1868), best known from "The Guinness Book of World Records", expanded the Guinness brewery sales throughout the English world, elected first lord mayor of Dublin, Parliament representitive, baronet. Totals: (54) author 26%, politician 24%, lawyer 19%, scientist 19%, educator 19%, businessman 17%, commander 13%, inventor 11%, judge 9%, social reformer 9%, physician 7%, musician 6%, clergy 6%, phychiatrist 4%, scholar 4%, historian 4%, anti-war, philosopher, artist, naturalist, explorer, architect-engineer, philanthropist. Actor: *Benjamin Bratt.*

Benson // Ben, Benn, Bennie, Benny. "son of Ben". *Benson John Lossing*, (1813-91), U.S. historical writer.

Bernard // Barnard, Barney, Barnie, Barny, Bear, Bearnard, Bern, Bernardo, Bernarr, Berne, Bernhard, Bernie, Berny, Burnard. *Old German*: "bold as a bear". Strong, sometimes dominant, respected, physical, friendly, maybe aggressive to try to prove manhood, high percentage of famous authors, soldier, patriot, scientist. However, forms of these names ending with long E sound "ey, ie, y, e" are not associated with agressive behavior. *Bernhard Berenson*, (or Bernard Berenson) (1865-1959), U.S. art critic. *Bernard Malamud*, (1914-86), award-winning author. *Bernardo O'Higgins*, (1778-1842), dictator of Chile's first independent government, brilliant soldier. *Bernhard Riemann*, (1826-66), mathematician. *Bernard Montgomery*, (1887-1976), noted British general in WW II. *Bernard Baruch*, (1870-1965), remarkable investor, 40 year economic adviser to American presidents. *Sir Bernard Katz*, (born 1911), British biophysicist. *Barnard Bee*, (1824-61), Confederate general. *Bernard Lovell*, (born 1913), English radio-astronomer. *Bernhard Kellermann*, (1879-1951), German novelist. *Bernard Kroger,* (1860-1938), U.S. grocer. *Bernard Wagenaar*, (1894-1971), U.S. composer. *Bernard Herrmann*, (1911-75), U.S. composer and conductor. *Bernard Hubbard,* (1888-1962), U.S. Jesuit geological scientist. *Bernardo Houssay*, (1887-1971), Argentine physiologist. *Saint Bernard of Clairvaux*, (1090-1153), French monk. Totals: (20) author 45%, scientist 25%, commander 10%, musician 10%, clergy 10%, investor, businessman, artist-naturalist-potter, athlete-coach, lawyer, educator.

Bert // Burt. *Old English*: "bright". *Short form of* names containing "bert". *Bert Taylor*, (1866-1921), U.S. newspaperman. *Bert Williams*, (Egbert Austin Williams) (1876-1922), U.S. comedian. *Bert Sakmann*, (born 1942), German scientist. *Burt Lancaster*, (born 1913), U.S. magnetic he-man performer acrobatic and actor. Actor: *Bert Convy*, *Burt Reynolds.*

Bertram // Bart, Bartram, Bert, Bertie, Berton, Bertrand. *Germanic:* "bright raven". *Bertrand Russell*, (1872-1970), scholar of philosophy, logic, mathematics, science, sociology, education, history, religion, and politics. *Bertram Goodhue*, (1869-1924), U.S. architect. *Bertrand Goldberg*, (born 1913), U.S. architect. *Bertrand Du Guesclin*, (1320?-80), French general. *Bertram Dobell*, (1842-1914), British bookseller and poet.

Bill // Billy. Familiar forms of William. Also see William. Courage, physical skill, competitive, bit-unrestrained, daring, zealous, energetic, athlete, theatrical, businessman, orator, artistic ability but usually too busy to be an artist, typically male pursuits. *Bill Cosby*, (born 1937), U.S. actor, comedian. *Bill Clinton*, 42nd U.S. president, presidency embroiled in sexual scandal. *Wild Bill Hickok*, (James Butler Hickok) (1837-76), scout, stagecoach driver, and marshal, courage and skill with a gun. *Billy (William) Mitchell*, (1879-1936), air power advocate, army private to brigadier general, after insubordinations reduced to colonel and later resigned. *Bill (William) Shoemaker*, (born 1931), horse jockey celebrity. *Bill (William) Tilden*, (1893-1953), tennis champion, outstanding athlete. *Buffalo Bill (William) Cody*, (1846-1917), folk hero, scout, legendary frontiersman. *Billy (William) Graham*, (born 1918), worldwide Christian evangelist and pastor to U.S. presidents. Totals: (22) athlete 41%, businessman 18%, orator 14%, actor 14%, politician 9%, clergy 9%, musician 9%, author 9%, lawyer, corrupt, commander, zealot, jockey, scout-marksman, memory, designer, outlaw, cowboy, journalist, comedian. Actors: *Bill Cosby, Bill Murray, Bill Paxton, Bill Pullman, Billy Barty, Billy Crudup, Billy Wirth, Billy Zane.*

Bing. *Old German:* "kettle-shaped hollow". *Bing Crosby*, actor/singer.

Birch // Birk, Burch. *Old English:* "birch tree". *Birch Bayh, Jr.* (born 1928), U.S. politician, studied agriculture and law.

Bjorn. *Scandinavian form* of Bernard. Friendly. *Bjorn Borg*, (born 1956), tennis star, imperturbable manner.

Blaine // Blane, Blayne. *Gaelic:* "thin, lean".

Blair. *Gaelic:* "plain". Actor: *Blair Underwood*.

Blake // Blakely. *Old English*: "attractive, dark".

Bo. *Short form of* Beau, Beauregard, Bogart, Brother and Boyfriend. *Bo Jackson*, (Vincent Edward Jackson) (born 1962), U.S. baseball and football player.

Bob // Bobby, Bobbie. Familiar forms of Robert. See Robert. Word-smith, athlete, gentle. *Bob Hope*, (born 1903), well-known comedian and comic actor. *Bobby Jones*, (1902-71), greatest amateur golfer of modern times. *Bob Dylan*, (born 1941), American singer-songwriter with complex literary lyrics. *Bobby Hull*, (born 1939), ice hockey star. *Bob Hawke*, (born 1929), Australia's longest-serving prime minister. *Bob Woodward*, (born 1943), U.S. newspaperman and author. *Bob Waterfield*, (born 1920), U.S. football coach and quarterback. *Bob Geldof*, (born 1951),

Irish rock musician, given honorary knighthood. *Bob Gibson*, (born 1935), U.S. baseball pitcher. *Bob Feller*, (born 1918), U.S. baseball pitcher. *Bob Fosse*, (1927-87), U.S. dancer, choreographer and director. *Bobby Orr*, (born 1948), Canadian ice-hockey player. *Bob Mackie*, (born 1940), U.S. costume designer. *Bob Marley*, (1945-81), Jamaican reggae singer and composer. *Bobby Fischer*, (born 1943), U.S. chess master. Totals: (24) athlete 54%, musician 17%, politician 8%, coach 8%, author 8%, actor, comedian, journalist, dancer-choreographer, designer, businessman, chess master. Actors: *Bob Denver, Bobby Darin, Bobby Deol.*

Boone // Bone, Boonie, Boony. *Old French:* "good". *T. Boone Pickens, Jr.* (born 1928), U.S. petroleum executive and "corporate raider".

Booth // Boot, Boote, Boothe. *Old English:* "hut". *Booth Tarkington,* (1869-1946), U.S. award winning novelist. *Booth Gardner,* (born 1936), U.S. politician.

Boris // Borislav. *Slavic:* "battler, warrior". Leader, businessman, strong, competitive, physical, buddy, relational, entrepreneur, determined, word-smith, politician; good boy, grow to independence, likes to be out with friends or girl friends until late, secretive, mother doesn't get introduced to friends, mother may not meet his girl friend for a long time, mother learns about his impending marriage on the last week, usually intelligent, many are very successful, sense of humor, interested in politics and sports, achieves through his own effort and determination, not greedy, likes to appear generous, caring toward parents, nearly fanatical pride of his land, may like to do his own home repairs; faithful to his work, may be so involved at work that he forgets about family, his wife will have to abide this since every thing he does is for the well being of the family; family is his quiet haven where he regains his strength to accomplish his ambitious goals; may not watch television to relax; attending wife, helping around the house and helping children with studies is his relaxation; his hard working personality often leads to a nervous breakdown; falls in love easily, jealous, may have multiple marriages. *Boris Yeltsin*, first freely elected president of Russia, flamboyant. *Boris Pasternak*, (1890-1960), Russian poet and novelist, wrote 'Doctor Zhivago'. *Boris Volynov*, (born 1934), Soviet cosmonaut. *Boris Yegorov*, (born 1937), Soviet physician and cosmonaut. *Boris Artzybasheff*, (1899-1965), U.S. illustrator and writer. *Boris Pyankov,* (born 1935), Soviet politician, coup attempt. *Boris D. Pankin*, (born 1931), Soviet politician, writer, and literary critic. *Boris Pugo*, (1937-91), Soviet politician, coup attempt. *Boris Bugaev*, (1880-1934), Russian poet and novelist. *Boris Godunov*, (1551?-1605), Russian czar.

Bowie // Bow, Bowen, Boyd. *Gaelic:* "yellow-haired". *Bowie Kuhn*, (born 1926), U.S. lawyer, commissioner of baseball.

Brad. *Old English:* "broad". *Short form of* names beginning with "brad". Fun-loving, adventurous, relational, busy, hobbyist, physical. Actors: *Brad Maule, Brad Pitt, Braden Matthews.*

Bradley // Brad, Bradly, Bradney, Lee, Leigh. *Old English:* "broad meadow". Also see Brad. More refined Brad. *Bradley Allen Fiske*, (1854-1942), U.S. Navy officer and inventor. *Bradley Walker Tomlin*, (1899-1953), U.S. painter.

Bram // Bran. *Gaelic:* "raven". *Old English:* "fierce, famous". *Short form of* Abraham and Abram. Form of Brand. *Bram Stoker*, (Abraham Stoker) (1847-1912), British writer, 'Dracula'.

Brand // Bran, Brander, Brandt, Brandy, Brant, Brantley. *Old English:* "firebrand". *Short form of* Brandon. *Brand Whitlock*, (1869-1934), U.S. diplomat and author. *Brander Matthews*, (James Brander Matthews) (1852-1929), U.S. writer, professor, critic, essays, plays.

Brandon // Bran, Brand, Branden, Brandy, Brandyn, Brannon, Bren, Brendan, Brenden, Brendin, Brendis, Brendon, Brennan, Brennen, Brennon. *Old English:* "beacon hill". Actors: *Brandon Lee, Brendan Fraser.*

Brent // Bret, Brett, Brit, Britt. *Old English:* "steep hill". Athletic, thin, handsome, energetic. *Bret Harte*, (1836-1902), writer, originator of the American local-color story. *Brett Whitely*, Australian painter. *Brent Ashabranner*, wrote book about farming life. *Bret Watson*, co-wrote book about police life. *Brent Gale*, co-wrote manual on home satellite TV installation. Actor: *Brent Spiner.*

Brian // Brayan, Briano, Briant, Brien, Brion, Bryan, Bryant, Bryon. *Gaelic:* "Strength, virtue". Helping, family man, sensitive. *Brian* (or Brian Boru) (941-1014), Irish high king. *Brian O'Nolan* (1911-66), outstanding 20th-century Gaelic writer. *Brian Freemantle* and *Bryan Forbes* each wrote an outstanding spy novels in the 1980s. *Brian Mulroney*, (born 1939), prime minister of Canada 1984. *Bryan Starr*, (Bart) (born 1934), U.S. football player. *Brian D. Josephson*, (born 1940), British physicist, superconductivity and tunneling. *Brian Dennehy*, (born 1942), Ameri-

can actor in films "Cocoon" ,"10", and "Silverado". *Brian Aldiss*, (born 1925), British writer. *Brian Boitano*, (born 1963), U.S. athlete. *Brian De Palma*, (born 1940), U.S. film director, gore-obsessed. *Bryan Grimes*, (1828-80), Confederate soldier, major general. *Bryant Gumbel*, (born 1948), U.S. television personality. *Brian Moore*, (born 1921), Canadian novelist. Totals: (11) writer 27%, athlete 18%, scientist, actor, film director, commander, TV host, politician-lawyer-businessman. Actors: *Brian Keith, Brian Lane Green, Brian Thompson, Brian Wimmer.*

Brigham // Brig, Brigg, Briggs. *Old English:* "village seaport". *Brigham Young*, (1801-77), founder of Utah and patriarch of the Mormon church.

Brock // Brockie, Brocky, Brok. *Old English:* "badger". *Brock Adams,* (born 1927), U.S. public official.

Broderick // Brod, Broddie, Broddy, Broderic, Rick, Rickie, Ricky. *Old English*: "broad ridge".

Brody // Brodie. *Gaelic:* "ditch". Form of Broderick.

Bronson // Bron, Bronnie, Bronny, Son, Sonny. *Old English:* "son of the dark skinned man". *Bronson Howard*, (1842-1908), U.S. journalist and playwright.

Brook // Brooke, Brooks. *English:* "brook". *Brook Taylor,* (1685-1731), English mathematician noted for Taylor's theorem.

Bruce // Brucie, Bruis. *Old French*: "brushwood thicket". Composed, friendly, noble demeanor, calm, hard working, easy-going, manly, handsome. *Bruce Springsteen,* (born 1949) 1980's pop-music superstar. *Bruce Catton,* (Charles Bruce Catton) (1899-1978), U.S. journalist and writer, books about Civil War. *Bruce Rogers*, (1870-1957), U.S. typographer. *Bruce McCandless II*, (born 1937), U.S. astronaut, U.S. Navy officer. *Bruce King*, (born 1924), U.S. public official, governor (Democrat) of New Mexico. *Bruce Sundlun*, (born 1920), U.S. public official, captain, U.S. Air Force, attorney, governor (Democrat) of Rhode Island. Actors: *Bruce Abbott, Bruce Boxleitner, Bruce Campbell, Bruce Greenwood, Bruce Lee, Bruce Willis*.

Bruno. *Italian:* "brown-haired". *Bruno Bettelheim*, (1903-90) psychologist, pioneer in the treatment and education of emotionally disturbed children. *Bruno Walter*, (Bruno Walter Schlesinger) (1876-1962), U.S. conductor. *Bruno Frank*, (1887-1945), German writer and poet. *Bruno Kreisky*, (1911-90), Austrian public official, chancellor of Austria, known for policy of "active neutrality", allowed Austria to serve as a gateway to the West for Soviet and eastern European refugees.

Bryan // Bryant. Forms of Brian.

Bryce // Brice. Form of Price. Similar to Bruce but less masculine. *Bryce Nathaniel Harlow*, (1916-87), U.S. government official.

Buck // Buckie, Bucky. *English:* "male deer ". *Buck Buchanan*, (Junious Buchanan) (1940-92), U.S. football player.

Bud // Budd, Buddie, Buddy. *Old English:* "herald, messenger". Friendly, accepting of others, not a nerd but "out of step", leans toward hobbies, relational, gentle, wisdom, insightful, non-forceful manner, non-dominating, musician. *Buddy Bolden*, the first improvising jazz musician, band leader. *Buddy Holly*, (1936-59), U.S.

musician, outstanding early rock and roll performer. *Bud Freeman,* (Lawrence Freeman) (1906-91), U.S. jazz musician. *Buddy Rich*, (Bernard Rich) (1917-87), big band musician. *Bud Powell,* created long, uninterrupted streams of bop piano melody. Actor: *Bud Cort*.

Burgess // Burg, Burr. *Old English:* "citizen of a fortified town". *Burr Tillstrom*, (1917-85), U.S. puppeteer.

Burl // Burlie, Byrle. *Old English:* "cupbearer". *Burl Ives*, (born 1909), U.S. stage, screen, radio, and television singer and actor, renowned ballad singer.

Burt. Form of Bert. *Short form of* Burton.

Burton // Burt. *Old English:* "fortress". *Burton Holmes,* (Elias Burton Holmes) (1870-1958), U.S. traveler and lecturer. *Burton Wheeler*, (1882-1975), U.S. politician, U.S. senator from Montana, maintained isolationist policy during WW II. *Burton Hendrick*, (1870-1949), U.S. writer, biographer, historian. *Burton Richter,* (born 1931), U.S. physicist, head of group that discovered the subatomic J (psi) particle.

Byron // Biron, Byram, Byran, Byrann, Byrom. *Old French:* "cottage". Warm, friendly, relational, intelligent, productive worker, businessman. *Byron White*, (born 1917), U.S. jurist, played professional football, Rhodes scholar, associate justice of the U.S. Supreme Court. *Byron Johnson,* (1864-1931), U.S. baseball organizer and first president of American League.

Caesar // Casar, Cesar, Cesare, Cesaro, Kaiser. *Latin:* "long-haired". Used as title for Roman emperors. *Cesare Beccaria,* (1738-94), celebrity at the age of 26 for a critical study of criminal law 'Crimes and Punishments'. *Cesar Franck*, (1822-90), Belgian-born French composer and organist. *Cesare Siepi*, (born 1923), Italian operatic basso, concert, television, and radio. *Cesare Lombroso*, (1836-1909), Italian criminologist, originated theory of "criminal type" marked by physical signs, 'The Criminal'. *Cesar Pelli*, (born 1926), U.S. architect. *Cesar Ritz*, (1850-1918), founder of the Ritz Hotel in Paris, France, his name became a synonym for luxury and elegance. *Cesar Chavez*, (born 1927), U.S. labor leader. *Cesar Milstein,* (born 1926), British immunologist. *Cesar Cui*, (1835-1918), Russian composer and military engineer. *Cesar Sandino*, (1893-1934), Nicaraguan leader and popular hero. *Cesar Gaviria*, (born 1947), Colombian politician, anti-crime campaign. *Caesar Rodney*, (1728-84), U.S. patriot, early advocate of independence and signer of the Declaration, general in Revolutionary War, president of Delaware 1778-82. *Caesar Augustus Rodney*, (1772-1824), U.S. public official. Totals: (13) politician 31%, musician 23%, anti-crime agenda 23%, author, architect, businessman, labor leader, scientist, engineer, commander.

Cal. *Short form of* names beginning with "cal". Outgoing, friendly, salesman, businessman, sportsman, energetic.

Cal Hubbard, (1900-77), U.S. pro-football player and pro-umpire.

Caleb // Cal, Cale, Kaleb. Biblical: Joshua's associate and brave warrior. Bold, entrepreneurial, friendly, composed, playful, adventurous. *Caleb Cushing,* (1800-79), U.S. diplomat. *Caleb Heathcote*, (1666-1721), New England colonial merchant and public official. *Caleb Blood Smith*, (1808-64), U.S. public official. *Caleb Gattegno*, British mathematics professor. *Caleb D. Bradburn*, pharmacist, invented Pepsi-Cola.

Calvin // Cal, Calv, Kalvin, Vin, Vinnie, Vinny. *Latin:* "bald". Honors: John Calvin. Daring, adventurous, energetic. *John Calvin*, (1509-64), the second of the great 16th-century reformers whose work and teachings had a profound impact on the development of Christianity and European history. *Calvin Coolidge*, 30th U.S. president, stood for economy, caution, and self-respect. *Calvin Woodward*, (1837-1914), U.S. educator. *Calvin Peete*, (born 1933), U.S. pro-golfer. *Calvin Verity*, (born 1917), U.S. public official and business executive. *Calvin Goddard*, (1891-1955), U.S. ballistics expert, physician, and military historian.

Cameron // Cam, Camey, Cammy. *Gaelic:* "crooked nose".

Carey // Care, Cary. *Welsh:* "near the castle". Liked by all, group activities, team sports. *M. Carey Thomas*, (1857-1935), U.S. educator and writer. Actors: *Cary Elwes, Cary Grant, Cary-Hiroyuki Tagawa.*

Carl // Karl. *Old German:* "farmer". Swedish form of Charles also a *Short form of* names beginning with "carl". Also see Charles. Thin, adventurous, athletic, competitive, talker, relational leader, buddy, educator, bit pretentious, talented in many artistic areas, hard to influence him, strong personality, can be convincing and influential, one woman type of man and hurt if she doesn't return affection, good household manager, calculating, frugal, saver of money. *Carl Menger,* (1840-1921), Austrian economist. *Carl Sagan*, (born 1934) American astronomer, scientist, evolutionist. *Karl Landsteiner,* (1868-1943) Austrian immunologist and pathologist. *Carl Maria von Weber*, (1786-1826), German composer, conductor, and pianist. *Carl Zeiss*, (1816-88), inventor and industrialist, name synonymous with optical equipment. *Carl Jung,* (1875-1961), Swiss psychologist and psychiatrist. *Carl Karl von Clausewitz*, (1780-1831), writer and theorist on military strategy. *Karl Barth*, (1886-1968), leading Protestant theologian. *Karl Marx*, (1818-83), founder of communist theory. *Carl Schurz*, (1829-1906), lawyer, ambassador, American Civil War general, writer, editor. Totals: (94) educator 31%, scientist 30%, author 44%, musician 11%, politician 11%, commander 7%, inventor 6%, businessman 6%, engineer 6%, philosopher 5%, psychologist 3%, explorer 3%, artist 3%, athlete 3%, zoologist 3%, lawyer 2%, sociologist 2%, reformer 2%, theologian-clergy, communist, film director, pacifist, traveler, typographer, philologist, taxidermist, aviator.

Carleton // Carl, Charlton, Karl. *Old English:* "farmer's town". Also see Carl. *Carleton Wiggins*, (1848-1932), U.S. artist. *D. Carleton Gajdusek*, (born 1923), U.S. virologist and medical anthropologist. *Carleton Coon*, (1904-81), U.S. anthropologist. *Charlton Heston*, (born 1923), U.S. actor of screen, stage, and television.

Carlos // Carlo. *Spanish form* of Charles. Also see Charles. Artistic, politically active, outspoken. *Carlo Maratti*, (1625-1713), Italian painter. *Carlos Merida*, (1893-1984), Mexican artist. *Carlo Blasis,* (1797-1878), Italian choreographer and dancer. *Carlos Antonio Lopez,* (1790-1862), dictator of Paraguay, teacher and lawyer. *Carlos Saul Menem,* (born 1930), Argentine politician. *Carlos Juan Finlay,* (1833-1915), Cuban physician, scientist. *Carlo Gozzi*, (1720-1806), Italian dramatist. *Carlos Manuel de Cespedes*, (1819-74), Cuban patriot and revolutionist. *Carlo Sforza*, (1873-1952), Italian statesman. *Carlo Maria Giulini*, (born 1914), Italian opera and orchestra conductor. *Carlos Chavez*, (1899-1978), Mexican composer and conductor. *Carlos Pena Romulo*, (1899-1985), Philippine diplomat. *Carlo Crivelli*, (1430?-95), Venetian painter. *Dolci, Carlo* (1616-86), Italian painter. *Carlos Salinas de Gortari,* (born 1948), Mexican politician and economist. *Carlos P. Garcia*, (1896-1971), Philippine political leader. *Carlos Fuentes*, (born 1928), Mexican author and editor. *Carlo Goldoni*, (1707-93), Italian dramatist. *Carlo Farinelli*, (Carlo Broschi) (1705-82), Italian singer. *Carlos Saavedra Lamas*, (1878-1959), Argentine lawyer and diplomat. *Carlo Rubbia*, (born 1934), Italian physicist, 1984 Nobel prize. Totals: (22) politician 32%, artist 18%, writer 14%, musician 14%, educator 9%, lawyer 9%, choreographer, businessman, physician, commander, author, economist, scientist.

Carmine // Carman. *Latin:* "song". Energetic, artistic, imaginative, musical, singer.

Carroll // Carol, Carolus, Carrol, Caryl. *Gaelic:* "champion". *Familiar form of* Charles. Also see Charles. *Carol II*

(1893-1953), king of Romania, "divorced" twice. *Carol Ryrie Brink,* (1895-1981), U.S. author, 1936 Newbery medal. *Carroll A. Campbell, Jr.* (born 1940), U.S. public official, governor of South Carolina. *Carroll Davidson Wright,* (1840-1909), U.S. statistician and economist. Actor: *Carroll O'Conner.*

Carter // Cart. *Old English:* "cart driver". *Carter Glass,* (1858-1946), U.S. political leader. *Carter Woodson,* (1875-1950), U.S. editor, author, and educator. *Carter Braxton,* (1736-97), signer of Declaration of Independence.

Cary. *Short form of* Carey and Carroll.

Casey // Case. *Gaelic:* "brave". Adventurous, relational, out-going. *Casey Stengel,* (Charles Dillon Stengel) (1890-1975), U.S. baseball outfielder and manager.

Caspar // Casper, Cass, Cassie, Cassy, Gaspar, Gaspard, Gasparo, Gasper, Jasper, Kaspar, Kasper. *Persian:* "treasurer". *Caspar Weinberger,* (born 1917), U.S. lawyer and government. *Caspar Olevianus,* (1536-87), German theologian, founder of German Reformed Church. *Kaspar Wolff,* (1733-94), German embryologist. *Caspar Wistar,* (1696-1752), North American colonial glassmaker. *Caspar Wistar,* (1761-1818), U.S. physician and anatomist. *Caspar Friedrich,* (1774-1840), pioneer German Romantic painter.

Cassius // Cash, Cass, Cassie, Cassy Caz, Cazzie. *Latin:* "vain". *Cassius Clay,* (1810-1903), U.S. abolitionist and politician. *Muhammad Ali,* (born 1942, Cassius Clay), a great United States heavyweight boxing champion, flamboyant personality, motto was "I am the greatest!". *Cass Gilbert,* (1859-1934), U.S. architect.

Cecil // Cece, Cecile, Cecilio, Cecilius, Celio. *Latin:* "blind". *Cecil Rhodes,* (1853-1902), successful British fortune seeker in South Africa became its prime minister. *Cecil Taylor,* (born 1933), U.S. jazz musician. *Cecil Andrus,* (born 1931), U.S. politician. *Cecil Powell,* (1903-69), British physicist. *Cecil B. De Mille,* (1881-1959), U.S. motion-picture producer. *Cecil Forester,* (1899-1966), English journalist and novelist.

Cedric // Cad, Caddaric, Ced, Rick, Rickie, Ricky. *Old English*: "battle chieftain". *Cedric Hardwicke,* (1893-1964), British actor. *Cedric Gibbons,* Hollywood art director, sketched Oscar statuette 1928. *Cedric* founder of Wessex in S. Britain, 519.

Cesar. Form of Caesar.

Chad // Chadd, Chaddie, Chaddy, Chadwick. *Old English:* "warlike". *Short form of* names beginning with "chad". *Familiar form of* Charles. Bit reserved, easy-going, universally liked, team player. *Chad Mitchell,* popular 1960s folksinger. Actors: *Chad Allen, Chad Lowe.*

Chaim // Hayyim, Hy, Hyman, Hymie, Mannie, Manny. *Hebrew:* "life". *Chaim Weizmann,* (1874-1952), first president of modern Israel, chemist, head of the World Zionist Organization. *Chaim Soutine,* (1894-1944), painter. *Hyman Rickover,* (1900-86), U.S. Navy officer. *Chaim Potok,* modern novelist. *Hyman Saunders,* European illusionist.

Chance. *Old English*. Form of Chancellor and Chauncey.

Chandler. *Middle English:* "candle maker" from *French*: "candle".

Charles // Carl, Carlo, Carlos, Carrol, Carroll, Cary, Caryl, Chad, Chaddie, Chaddy, Charley, Charlie, Charlot, Charlton, Chas, Chaz, Chic, Chick, Chick, Chicky, Chip, Chuck, Karel, Karl, Karoly. *Old German:* "man of the common people". Very competitive, strategist, physical, discrete, humorous but serious about the goal, use humor well during serious issues to accomplish goal, determined, relational, liked, adventurous, athletic, competitive, strong willed, talker, stubborn but relational leader, able leader, expect to lead, buddy, not rough, more subtle than Bills, tend to be insightful & knowledgeable, intelligent, quick learner, energetic, accomplishes goal. Many European kings with this name. Seven rulers of the Holy Roman Empire were named Charles. *Charlemagne* (Charles the Great), founded an empire. *Charles Schulz*, (1922-1999), U.S. cartoonist, 'Peanuts'. *Bonnie Prince Charlie* (popular name of *Charles Edward Stuart*) (1720-88), military genius, but stubborn insistence on war, studied and admired great military leaders, liked to hunt and to play rough games, ate simple coarse food, followed a Spartan life to build up his own strength and endurance, intelligent but self-willed. *Charles V*, (1500-58), ruled nearly half the world, skilled of monarchs, frail as boy, strong willed, excellent rider and hunter. *Charles Martel*, (688?-741), his Frankish army stopped intended world conquest of Muslims. *Charles Lamb*, (1775-1834), essayist, critic, and poet. *Charles de Gaulle*, (1890-1970), twice lead France through times of trouble, general, military leader and statesman. *Charles Babbage*, (1792-1871), mathematician, inventor of the modern computer. *Charles Dickens*, (1812-70), one of the world's most celebrated writers. *Charles the Bold* (1433-77), the last great duke of Burgundy, strong, industrious, pious, proud and ambitious. *Charles Evans Hughes*, (1862-1948), 11th U.S. chief justice, secretary of state, governor of New York state, and judge of the World Court. *Charles Darwin*, (1809-82), primary proponent of controversial theories of biological evolution. *Charles Lyell*, (1797-1875), founded science of geology. *Charles Lindbergh*, (1902-74), first one-man flight across the Atlantic Ocean, fished, hunted, and deep interest in machinery. *Charles Spurgeon*, (1834-92), British nonconformist preacher. *Charles Finney*, (1792-1875), U.S. Congregational minister, famous revivalist preacher. Totals: (98) politician 26%, author 24%, scientist 16%, businessman 15%, educator 9%, lawyer 6%, commander 6%, judge 5%, clergy 4%, inventor 4%, explorer 4%, musician 3%, engineer 3%, artist 3%, athlete 3%, aviator 2%, philosopher 2%, social reformer 2%, cult founder, physician, actor, economist, philanthropist, dressmaker, choreographer. Actors: *Charles Bronson, Charles Keating, Charles Laughton, Charlie Chaplin, Charlie Sheen, Charlton Heston, Chazz Palminteri. Musician: Chuck Barry*.

Charlton. Form of Carleton and Charles. Actor: *Charlton Heston.*

Chase. *Old French:* "hunter". *Chase Osborn*, (1860-1949), U.S. political leader.

Chauncey // Chance, Chancey, Chancy, Chaunce, Chauncy. *Middle English:* "chancellor, church official". *Chauncey Depew*, (1834-1928), U.S. lawyer, politician and witty orator. *Chauncey Rose*, (1794-1887), U.S. businessman and philanthropist.

Chen. *Chinese:* "great". *Chen Ning Yang*, (born 1922), Chinese-born American theoretical physicist. *Chen Cheng* (1897-1965), Chinese general and statesman, premier of Taiwan. *Chien-shiung Wu*, (born 1912), Chinese-born physicist.

Chester // Ches, Cheston, Chet. *Old English:* "fortified camp". *Short from of* Rochester. *Chester A. Arthur,* (1829-86), 21st U.S. President. *Chester William Nimitz,* (1885-1966), U.S. Navy officer, commander in chief U.S. Pacific Fleet 1941-45, chief of naval operations 1945-47. *Chester Bowles,* (1901-86), U.S. public official, cofounder of advertising company. *Chester Harding*, (1792-1866), U.S. portrait painter. *Chester Hall,* (1703-71), British lawyer, mathematician, and inventor.

Chet. *Short form of* Chester.

Chevalier // Chev, Chevy. *French:* "knight". *Chevalier Jackson,* (1865-1958), U.S. laryngologist.

Chico. *Spanish familiar form* of Francis and Francisco.

Chris // Kris. *Short form of* Christian and Christopher. *Kris Kristofferson*, (born 1936), erratic singer, songwriter, actor. Actors: *Chris Elliott, Chris Farley, Chris Isaak, Chris Noth, Chris O'Donnell, Chris Potter.*

Christian // Chrétien, Chris, Christiano, Cristian, Kit, Kris, Krispin, Kristian, Kristo. *Greek:* "follower of Christ Jesus". Artistic, clothes designer, scientist, bit extravagant. For five centuries, until 1972, every other ruler of Denmark was named Christian. *Christian Louis Lange*, (1869-1938), Norwegian pacifist and historian. *Christian Daniel Rauch*, (1777-1857), German sculptor. *Christian Boehmer Anfinsen*, (born 1916), U.S. biochemist, received 1972

Nobel prize. *Christian Dior*, (1905-57), French dress designer. *Christian Lacroix*, (born 1950), French dress designer. *Christian Friedrich Schonbein*, (1799-1868), German chemist. *Christian De Duve*, (born 1917), Belgian biochemist, 1974 Nobel prize. *Christian Winther,* (1796-1876), Danish poet. *Christian Krohg*, (1852-1925), Norwegian painter and author. *Christian Friedrich Hebbel*, (1813-63), German poet and dramatist. *Christian Friedrich Samuel Hahnemann*, (1755-1843), German physician. *Christian Jurgensen Thomsen*, (1788-1865), Danish archaeologist. *Christian Sinding*, (1856-1941), Norwegian composer. *Christian Archibald Herter*, (1895-1966), U.S. government official. *Christian B. Tauchnitz*, (1816-95), German publisher. Totals: (15) scientist 27%, writer 20%, educator 13%, dress designer 13%, artist 13%, musician, historian, pacifist, publisher, physician, politician. Actors: *Christian Bale, Christian Slater, Kristian Ayre, Kristian Schmid.*

Christopher // Chris, Christof, Christofer, Christoffer, Christoforo, Christoper, Christoph, Christophe, Christophrus, Cris, Cristobal, Cristoforo, Christos, Kit, Kristo, Kristofer, Kristofor, Kristoforo, Kristos. *Greek:* "Christ-bearer, Savior-bearer". The name honors *St. Christopher.* Artistic, explorer, printer, poet, lawyer, adventurer, garden nursery, tend toward individualistic, personality often very different between young and mature, fairly calm when mature, focused determination, relational, hard worker, good looking, happily married to another calm determined person. *Kit (Christopher) Carson*, (1809-68), great old West hero, fur trapper, guide, Indian agent, and soldier, fearless, leader of whitemen, protector and friend of several Indian tribes. *Christopher Okigbo*, (1932-67), classical Nigerian poet. *Christoph Willibald Gluck*, (1714-87), father of modern opera. *Christopher Marlowe*, (1564-93), dramatist, most significant predecessor to William Shakespeare. *Christopher Wren*, (1632-1723), great mind, professor of astronomy, England's greatest architect, knighted, Parliamentarian. *Christopher Fry*, (born 1907), playwright, director, dramatist. *Christopher Columbus*, (1451-1506), explorer, discovered the Americas. *Christopher Newport*, (1565?-1617), English sea captain, explorer. *Christopher Isherwood*, (1904-86), U.S. writer. *Christopher Nolan*, (born 1965), Irish writer, paralyzed and speechless. *Christoph von Dohnanyi*, (born 1929), German conductor. *Christoph Amberger*, (1500-61), German artist. Totals: (18) author 33%, businessman 17%, politician 17%, commander 17%, educator 11%, explorer 11%, lawyer 11%, architect, scientist, athlete, inventor, scout, soldier. Actors: *Christopher Lambert, Christopher Lloyd, Christopher Pettiet, Christopher Reeve, Christopher Walken.*

Chuck. *Familiar form of* Charles. *Chuck Yeager*, (born 1923 Charles Elwood Yeager), U.S. Air Force test pilot, WW II ace, shot down and escaped capture, first to break the sound barrier. *Chuck Berry*, very successful early rock singer. Actor: *Chuck Barris, Chuck Conners.*

Clare // Clair. *Latin:* "famous". *Short form of* Clarence. *Claire Bishop*, U.S. writer. *Clare Briggs*, (1875-1930), U.S. cartoonist. *Clare Luce*, (1903-87), U.S. writer, politician and diplomat. *Claire Lee Chennault*, (1890-1958), U.S. aviator, commanded Flying Tigers, chief of U.S. Air Force in China 1942-45, author.

Clancy. Actor: *Clancy Brown.*

Clarence // Clair, Clare. *Latin:* "bright, famous". Artistic, inventive, writer, sketcher, diligent, military. *Clarence Darrow*, (1857-1938), notorious labor and criminal defense lawyer. *Clarence Whitehill*, (1871-1932), U.S. dramatic baritone singer. *Clarence Budington Kelland*, (1881-1964), U.S. writer of novels and short stories. *Clarence Streit*, (1896-1986), U.S. journalist and author. *Clarence Thomas*, (born 1948), U.S. public official, Supreme Court justice. *Clarence Tinker*, (1887-1942), U.S. Army general. *Clarence Birdseye*, (1886-1956), creator of the modern frozen food industry. *Clarence Anderson*, (1891-1971), U.S. illustrator and author. *Clarence (Ace) Parker*, (born 1912), U.S. football quarterback, baseball player. *Clarence Michael James Dennis*, (1876-1938), Australian poet and journalist. *Clarence M. Mitchell, Jr.* (1911-84), U.S. civil rights leader. *Clarence Leo Fender*, (1909-91), guitar designer.

Clark // Clarke, Clerc, Clerk. *Old French:* "scholar". *Clark Wissler*, (1870-1947), U.S. anthropologist. *Clark Gable*, (1901-60), U.S. motion-picture actor. *Clark Howell*, (1863-1936), U.S. journalist. *Clark Clifford*, (born 1906), U.S. government official and lawyer. *Clark Griffith*, (Old Fox) (1869-1955), U.S. baseball pitcher and manager. *Clark Hull*, (1884-1952), U.S. psychologist. *Clarke Hinkle*, (born 1909), U.S. football fullback.

Claude // Claudell, Claudian, Claudianus, Claudio, Claudius, Claus. *Latin:* "lame". Artistic, government. *Claude Debussy*, (1862-1918), French rebel composer. *Claude Levi-Strauss*, (born 1908), social anthropologist. *Claude Monet*, (1840-1926), painter, leader of French impressionist movement. *Claude Bernard*, (1813-78),

French physiologist. *Claude Pepper,* (1900-89), U.S. public official, champion of senior citizens. *Claude Swanson,* (1862-1939), U.S. lawyer and political leader. *Claude Villars,* (1653-1734), one of greatest French generals. *Claude Helvetius,* (1715-71), French encyclopedist and utilitarian philosopher. *Claude Lorrain,* (1600-82), French landscape painter. *Claude Bowers,* (1878-1958), U.S. diplomat and historian. *Claude Rouget de Lisle,* (1760-1836), French soldier and songwriter.

Clay // Claiborn, Claiborne, Clayborn, Clayborne, Clayson, Clayton. *Old English:* "earth". *Claiborne Fox Jackson,* (1807-62), U.S. political leader, governor Missouri, brigadier general in Confederate army. Actor: *Clayton Moore.*

Clement // Clem, Clemens, Clemente, Clementius, Clemm, Clemmie, Clemmy, Clim, Klemens, Klement, Kliment. *Latin:* "mild, merciful". Biblical: a disciple of Paul. Very calm and not a troublesome child, good student, likes adventure books and movies, likes technician work, kind, unpretentious, compliant, engineer, jurist, doctor, teacher, actor, electrician, happy in marriage, not smooth relationship with mother-in-law, hospitable, usually father daughters, patient. *Saint Clement I,* (Clement of Rome), pope 88-97. *Clement Attlee,* (1883-1967), British prime minister, nationalized British industry, begin the welfare state, lawyer, socialist. *Kliment Voroshilov,* (1881-1969), Soviet military and political leader. *Clement Clarke Moore,* (1779-1863), U.S. poet and educator, professor, compiled a 'Hebrew and English Lexicon', wrote poem 'Twas the Night Before Christmas'. *Clemens Winkler,* (1838-1904), German chemist. *Clement Vallandigham,* (1820-71), Ohio congressman, convicted of sedition, banished to Confederate states. *Clement Ader,* (1841-1926), French aircraft designer. *Clements Markham,* (1830-1916), British geographer, active explorer.

Cleveland // Cleavland, Cleve, Clevey, Clevie. *Old English:* "cliffs". *Cleveland Abbe,* (1838-1916), U.S. meteorologist.

Cliff // Clifford. *Old English:* "river crossing at the cliff". Leader, teacher, easy going, gentler, artistic. *Cliff Battles,* (1910-81), U.S. football halfback and coach. *Clifford L. Alexander, Jr.* (born 1933), U.S. lawyer and public official. *Clifford Morris Hardin,* (born 1915), U.S. educator and public official. *Clifford P. Case,* (1904-82), U.S. public official and lawyer. *Clifford Beers,* (1876-1943), U.S. author and humanitarian. *Clifford Webb,* (1895-1972), British illustrator of children's books. *Clifford Sifton,* (1861-1929), Canadian statesman. *Clifton Fadiman,* (born 1904), U.S. editor and literary critic. *Clifford Milburn Holland,* (1883-1924), U.S. engineer. *Clifford Odets,* (1906-63), U.S. playwright. *Cliff Barrows,* Billy Graham Crusades musician. Actor: *Cliff Bemis.*

Clifton // Cliff, Clift. *Old English:* "town at the cliffs". *Clifton Fadiman,* (born 1904), U.S. editor and literary critic.

Clinton // Clint. *Old English:* "headland farm". *Clint Eastwood,* (born 1931), U.S. motion-picture actor and politician. *Clinton Joseph Davisson,* (1881-1958), U.S. physicist. *Clinton Presba Anderson,* (1895-1975), U.S. political leader. *Clinton Hart Merriam,* (1855-1942), U.S. naturalist and writer.

Clive // Cleve, Clyve. *Old English:* "cliff". *C.S. Lewis*, (Clive Staples Lewis) (1898-1963), most widely read author on Christian teaching for thirty years, professor of medieval and Renaissance English at Cambridge University in Cambridge, highly respected teacher and writer, death overshadowed by Pres. Kennedy assasination. Actor: *Clive Robertson*.

Clyde // Cly, Clywd. *Gaelic:* "rocky eminence". *Clyde K. Wells*, (born 1937), Canadian public official. *Clyde Turner*, (Bulldog) (born 1919), U.S. football center. *Clyde Beatty*, (1903-65), U.S. animal trainer. *Clyde William Tombaugh*, (born 1906), U.S. astronomer.

Cody // Codey, Codi, Codie. *English:* "cushion".

Colby. *Old English:* "dark (haired)".

Cole // Coleman, Colman, Colton. *English:* "coal, coalman". *Familiar form of* Nicholas and names beginning with "cole" sound. *Cole Porter*, (1893-1964), U.S. composer and lyricist. *Coleman Hawkins*, (1904-69), U.S. jazz musician.

Colin // Cailean, Colan, Cole, Collin. *Gaelic:* "child". Form of Nicholas. *Colin L. Powell*, (born 1937), U.S. Army general. *Colin Campbell*, (or Baron Colin Campbell Clyde) (1792-1863), British general. *Colin Purdie Kelly, Jr.* (1915-41), U.S. Army aviator. *Colin Maclaurin*, (1698-1746), Scottish mathematician. *Colin Davis*, (born 1927), British conductor.

Conner // Connor, Conor. *Scottish:* "wise".

Conrad // Con, Conn, Conney, Connie, Conny, Conrade, Conrado, Koenraad, Konrad, Kurt. *Old German:* "bold

counsel". Several kings. *Conrad II* (990?-1039), king & emperor temporarily uniting Germany, able & just. *Conrad Gesner*, (1516-65), a founder of modern zoology, a pioneer in mountain climbing, a practicing physician, a student of Latin and Greek classics, and a compiler of encyclopedias. *Conrad Aiken*, (1889-1973), U.S. poet, writer, and literary critic, Pulitzer prize. *Conrad Richter*, (1890-1968), U.S. writer, Pulitzer prize. *Conrad Ferdinand Meyer*, (1825-98), Swiss poet and historical novelist. *Conrad Arnold Elvehjem*, (1901-62), U.S. biochemist. *Conrad Marca-Relli*, (born 1913), U.S. painter.

Constantine // Con, Conn, Conney, Connie, Conny, Constantin, Constantino, Costa, Konstantin, Konstantine. *Latin:* "firm, constant". Historical: honors *Constantine the Great* (AD 280?-337), among greatest Roman emperors, made Christianity a lawful religion in Roman society, and he founded the city of Constantinople (now Istanbul). Serious, leadership, helpful, determined, responsible, cunning, stubborn, puts himself into his work, gentle leader - not commanding, imaginative, can be irritated by a small annoyance, complicated and contradictory personality, sometimes enjoys finding a girl who has no special qualities to help her become special and loved but doesn't marry her, doesn't share the opinions of the majority, divorce is very hard on him, may marry several times, sometimes gloomy, old people like him and he likes them, friend to his oldest son, businessman, artist, scientist. *Konstantin Stanislavsky*, (1863-1938), outstanding Russian director, actor, and producer. *Konstantin Tsiolkovsky*, (1857-1935), Russian research scientist in aeronautics and astronautics, pioneered rocket and space studies. *Konstantin Feoktistov*, (born 1926), Soviet cosmonaut and scientist, spacecraft designer. *Konstantin Simonov*, (1915-79), Soviet author and dramatist. *Constantin Brancusi*, (1876-1957), Romanian artist. *Constantin Meunier*, (1831-1905), Belgian sculptor and painter. *Constantine VII Porphyrogenitus*, (905-959), Byzantine emperor better known as writer and patron of arts than as ruler. *Constantine Caramanlis* (born 1907), Greek political leader, member of Parliament, prime minister, president.

Cooper // Coop. *English:* "barrel maker".

Corbin // Corban, Corben. *Latin:* "raven".

Cordell // Cord, Cordie, Cordy, Cory. *Old French:* "ropemaker". *Cordell Hull*, (1871-1955), U.S. statesman.

Corey // Cori, Correy, Corrie, Cory, Korey, Kory. *Gaelic:* "hollow".

Cornelius // Conney, Connie, Conny, Cornall, Cornell, Corney, Cornie, Corny, Cory, Neel. *Latin:* "horn-colored (hair)". *Cornelius Vanderbilt*, (1873-1942), U.S. capitalist and inventor. *Cornelius Vanderbilt II*, (1898-1974), U.S. journalist, author, and lecturer. *Cornelius Tacitus*, (55?-120?), great Roman historian, senator and consul. *Cornelius Bliss*, (1833-1911), U.S. businessman and public official. *Cornelius Nepos*, (99?-24 BC), Roman historian, wrote love poems and two biographies. *Cornelius Krieghoff*, (1812-72), Canadian painter. *Cornelius Warmerdam*, (born 1915), U.S. athlete.

Cornell // Cornall, Corneal, Corney, Cornie, Corny, Cory. Form of Cornelius.

Cosmo, Cos, Cosimo, Cosme, Cozmo. *Greek:* "order, harmony, the universe". *Cosmo Hamilton*, (1872-1942), English novelist and dramatist. *Cosmo Lang*, (1864-1945), British clergy, archbishop of Canterbury. *Cosimo de' Medici*, (1389-1464), Florentine banker, political leader, art patron.

Courtney // Cort, Court, Courtnay, Curt. *Old French:* "court". *Courtney Hodges*, (1887-1966), U.S. Army officer, from private to 4-star general, commanded U.S. 1st Army in WW II.

Craig // Craggie, Craggy. *Gaelic:* "crag". Strong, determined, valiant, brave, calm, confident. *Craig Breedlove*, (born 1937), U.S. race car driver, designer, and builder, set two world land-speed records (407.45 & 600.601 mph). *Craig Washington*, (born 1941), U.S. politician, lawyer, Democrat.

Crawford // Ford. *Old English:* "river crossing of the crow". *Crawford Long*, (1815-78), surgeon, performed the first operation on an anesthetized patient. *Crawford Greenewalt*, (born 1902), U.S. industrialist and chemical engineer.

Curt // Kurt. *Short form of* Courtney or Curtis. *German form* of Conrad. Friendly, determined, relational, unintimidating manner, easy going, well liked, farely perfectionistic toward self, teacher, researcher. Also see Curtis. *Curt Gowdy*, (born 1919), Sportscaster. *Kurt Waldheim*, (born 1918), Austrian career diplomat, secretary-general of the United Nations, president of Austria. *Kurt Georg Kiesinger*, (1904-88), West Germany chancellor. *Kurt Vonnegut, Jr.*, (born 1922), novelist. *Kurt Godel*, (1906-78), mathematician and logician. *Kurt Wiese* (1887-

1974), U.S. illustrator and writer of children's books. _Kurt Adler,_ (1902-58), German chemist. _Kurt Weill,_ (1900-50), U.S. composer. _Kurt von Schuschnigg_, (1897-1977), U.S. educator. _Kurt Eisner,_ (1867-1919), Bavarian socialist revolutionary. _Kurt Jooss_, (1901-79), German ballet dancer. _Kurt L. Schmoke_, (born 1949), U.S. lawyer and government official. _Kurt Koffka_, (1886-1941), U.S. psychologist. _Kurt Lewin_, (1890-1947), U.S. psychologist. Totals: (15) educator 40%, politician 33%, author 27%, scientist 20%, lawyer 13%, psychologist 13%, artist, musician, dancer, socialist, Nazi, sportscaster.

Curtis // Curt, Curtice, Kurt, Kurtis. _Old French:_ "courteous". "Courteous", determined, relational, friendly, leader, researcher. Also see Curt. _Curtis Wilbur,_ (1867-1954), U.S. public official and judge, started Los Angeles juvenile court. _Curtis LeMay_, (1906-90), U.S. Air Force officer, research and development, 4-star general. _Curtis Marbut_, (1863-1935), U.S. geologist and soil chemist. _Curtis Tarr,_ (born 1924), U.S. educator and government official.

Cy. _Short form of_ Cyril and Cyrus. _Cy Young_, (Denton True Young) (1867-1955), U.S. baseball pitcher, pitching award named for him.

Cyril // Cirillo, Cirilo, Cy, Cyrill, Cyrille, Cyrillus. _Greek:_ "lordly". _Cyril Hinshelwood_, (1897-1967), British chemist, professor of chemistry. _Cyrille Adoula_, (1921-78), Congolese public official, premier of Democratic Republic of the Congo (now Zaire). _Saint Cyril_, (827-69), Greek missionary to the Slavs, name associated with Cyrillic alphabet. _Cyril Joad_, (1891-1953), British philosopher, professor.

Cyrus // Ciro, Cy, Russ. _Persian:_ "sun". Historical: _Emperor Cyrus the Great of Persia_. _Cyrus Field_, (1819-92), businessman promoted the laying of the first transatlantic telegraph cable. _Cyrus McCormick_, (1809-84), invented and marketed mechanical crop reapers. _Cyrus Dallin_, (1861-1944), U.S. sculptor. _Cyrus Vance_, (born 1917), U.S. lawyer and government official. _Cyrus Ching_, (1876-1967), U.S. industrial relations expert. _Cyrus Curtis_, (1850-1933), U.S. newspaper and magazine publisher. _Cyrus Smith_, (born 1899), U.S. businessman and government official. _Cyrus Macmillan_, (1880-1953), Canadian educator and writer.

Dag // Dagny. _Scandinavian:_ "day, brightness". _Dag Hammarskjold,_ (1905-61), Swedish diplomat and financial expert, secretary-general of the United Nations.

Dakota // Dakoda, Dakotah, Lakota. _Sioux Indian:_ "friends, allies".

Dale // Dael, Dail, Dal, Dall, Dayal. _Old English:_ "valley". Less dominant, prefers more dominant spouse. _Dale Carnegie_, (1888-1955), U.S. author, lecturer, and teacher of public speaking.

Dallas // Dal, Dall, Dallis. _Gaelic:_ "wise". _Dallas Lore Sharp_, (1870-1929), U.S. author and educator, Methodist minister, professor English, wrote delightful essays and books on nature.

Dalton. *Old English:* "valley town".

Damon // Dame, Damian, Damiano, Damien. *Greek:* "constant, tamer". Artistic, creative. *Damon Keith*, (born 1922), U.S. judge. *Damon Runyon*, (1880-1946), U.S. journalist, short-story writer, and motion-picture producer. *Damian Domingo* founded the first art school in the Philippines. Actor: *Damian Chapa.*

Dan // Dannie, Danny. *Hebrew:* "judge". *Short form of Daniel and Riordan.* Handsome, relational, sportsman, appears confident, humerous, determined, strong. Biblical: Jacob's first son and patriarch of the Israelite tribe of Dan. *Danny Glover*, (born 1947), versatile actor. *Danny Thomas*, (originally Muzyab Rakhoob) (1912-91), U.S. radio, screen, and television comedian. *Danny Kaye*, (originally David Daniel Kominski) (1913-87), U.S. comedian of stage, screen, radio, and television. *Dan Rather,* (born 1931), U.S. newscaster. *Dan De Quille,* (originally William Wright) (1829-98), U.S. journalist. *Dan Rice*, (1823-1900), U.S. clown. *Dan Quayle*, (James Danforth Quayle III) (born 1947), U.S. public official, reporter, associate publisher, lawyer, politician. Actors: *Dan Aykroyd, Dan Cortese*.

Dana // Dane, Danie. *Scandinavian:* "from Denmark". Comedian, perceptive, bit of loner or soloist. Actor: *Dana Andrews, Dana Ashbrook.*

Dane // Dana, Danie. *Scandinavian:* "from Denmark". Relational, low competitive.

Daniel // Dan, Dani, Dannel, Dannie, Danny. *Hebrew:* "God has judged". Also see Dan. Calm and smiling child, resembles mother, friendly, kind, bit cunning, likes to play soccer, wrestle, tennis gymnastics, as adult: bit short tempered, jealous, often impulsive, handsome, intelligent, creative, imaginative in one fashion or another, do good work, confident, relational, marriage is usually successful, love children, doesn't like to do domestic work, often smooth dancers and good singers, social, hospitable, statesman, writers, scientist, educator, outdoorsman, soldier, lawyer, doctor, musician, surprisingly few actors or clergy. Biblical: *Daniel,* (618-536? BC), Hebrew prophet, central figure of the Book of Daniel, chief Persian administrator. *Daniel O'Connell,* (1775-1847), Irish leader, lawyer. *Daniel Webster*, (1782-1852), U. S. Senator. *Daniel Boone*, (1734-1820), frontiersman, hunter, trapper, guide, tavern store owner, legislator, soldier, magistrate. *Daniel Defoe*, (1660?-1731), writer, businessman, secret agent, journalist. *Daniel Gabriel Fahrenheit,* (1686-1736), German physicist, invented alcohol thermometer. *Daniel Baird Wesson*, (1825-1906), U.S. inventor and manufacturer. *Daniel Pierce Thompson*, (1795-1868), U.S. lawyer, editor, and novelist. *Daniel Berkeley Updike*, (1860-1941), U.S. typographer. *Daniel Carroll,* (1730-96), U.S. Revolutionary War statesman. Totals: (52) politician 33%, author 19%, commander 15%, businessman 15%, scientist 12%, lawyer 12%, educator 12%, explorer-frontiersman-outdoorsman 6%, physician 6%, musician 6%, architect 4%, inventor 4%, actor 4%, secret agent, manager, artist, engineer, socialist, speculator, archaeologist, scholar, clergy, cartoonist, soldier, typographer. Actor: *Daniel Auteuil.*

Dante. *Latin:* "lasting". *Dante Alighieri*, (1265-1321), greatest of Italian poets. *Dante Rossetti,* (originally Gabriel Charles Dante Rossetti) (1828-82), British poet and painter. *Dante Lavelli,* (Glue Fingers) (born 1923), U.S. football player.

Darius // Dare, Darian, Darien, Dario, Derry. *Greek:* "wealthy". *Darius Milhaud*, (1892-1974), French composer, ultramodern.

Darnell // Dar, Darny, Darnel. *English:* "rye grass".

Darrel // Dare, Darrell, Darrill, Darryl, Daryl, Daryle, Derril. *French:* "beloved". Relational, friendly, hobbiest, one of the group, manager, leads by position or suggestion, low competitive, enjoys games through relationship, somewhat scientific, problem solver. Few found with much historical significance; all are listed. *Darrell Duppa*, canal builder, historian. *Darrel Hoff,* astronomy historian. *Darrell Royal,* football coach. *Daryll McDaniels*, rap musician of RUN-D.M.C. *Darryl Zanuck*, (1902-79), motion-picture producer. *Darryl Hutton*, author on ventriloquism.

Darren // Dairen, Dare, Daren, Darien, Darin, Daron, Darrein, Darrin, Derain, Derein, Derren, Derron. *Gaelic:* "great". *Form of* Dorian. Actor: *Darren McGavin*.

Darwin. *Old English:* "Dear friend". Usage may honor Charles Darwin.

Dave. *Short form of* David and Davis. Positive easy going attitude, avoids disputes, friendly. *Davy Crockett*, (1786-1836), frontiersman, Indian fighter, hunter, marksman, congressman, soldier. *Dave Brubeck*, (born 1920), U.S. jazz pianist and composer.

David // Dav, Dave, Davey, Davide, Davidson, Davie, Davin, Davis, Daven, Davon, Davy. *Hebrew:* "beloved". Sensitive, good natured, easy-going, handsome, humorous, learner/teacher, a bit serious, often well organized and disciplined, amiably, diplomatic, well liked by most, charismatic/subtly charming, humorous, capable, able, liberal leanings, bit independent, but enjoys the company of others, explores new thing or ideas, public official, botanist, economist, writer, producer, actor, lawyer, doctor, minister, theologian, philosopher, composer-musician, inventor, court-judge, lawyer, astronomer, businessman, engineer, coach, administrator, artist, cook, journalist, construction, his good looks and interest gets him work as an actor but seldom a celebrated actor or leading man, not aggressive, but can be assertive when supported by his sense of fairness; proud, persevering, pragmatic, social, surrounded by friends - but gets in trouble because of them; resembles mother, can't stand lies, may be short tempered but quickly calmed and doesn't remember offense, kind, hard working, some have success in sports, may have problems in first marriage, the second marriage is more successful, ability to convince people, he never promises what he knows he can't deliver, tries to overcome his weaknesses and does so successfully, good cook. *King David*, early Hebrew king, killed Goliath, great soldier, brave and sensitive. *David Davis*, (1815-86), U.S. Supreme Court justice, U.S. senator. *David Ricardo*, (1772-1823), the second great classical economist, fortune from stockmarket. *David Lloyd George*, (1863-1945), prime minister of Great Britain during World War I. *David Livingstone*, (1813-73), medical missionary to Africa, explorer. *David Garrick*, (1717-79), monumental English actor. *David Hilbert*, (1862-1943), German mathematician. *David Farragut*, (1801-70), U.S. Navel officer, regarded as genius, admiral. *David Hume*, (1711-76), Scottish philosopher and historian. *David Ben-Gurion*, (1886-1973), statesman, political leader, first prime minister and chief architect of the state of Israel. _David Dixon Porter_, (1813-91), celebrated U.S. naval officer. _David Thompson_, (1770-1857), explorer, "Canada's Greatest Geographer." _David Garrick_, One of the three great English tragic actors of all time. Totals: (86) politician 28%, author 16%, educator 14%, scientist 12%, commander 10%, lawyer 9%, businessman 9%, musician 7%, jurist 7%, explorer 6%, artist 6%, physician 5%, inventor 5%, actor 3%, economist 3%, film producer 3%, philosopher 2%, historian 2%, socialist 2%, reformer 2%, film director 2%, liberal theologian 2%, engineer 2%, missionary, clergy, unscrupulous, labor leader, cartoonist, psychologist, athlete, comedian. Actors: _David Canary, David Carradine, David Cassidy, David Copperfield, David Duchovny, David Ferry, David Forsyth, David Hasselhoff, David Hedison, David Hedison, David James Elliott, David Janssen, David Letterman, David Marciano, David McCallum, David Mendenhall, David Morse, David O'Hara, David Schwimmer, David Thewlis._

Dean // Deane, Dene, Dino. _Old English:_ "valley". Bit contemplative, hard worker, friendly, relational, composed, historical interests. _Dean G. Acheson_, (1893-1971), U.S. statesman, policy advisor, writer. _Dino Grandi_, (1895-1988), Italian statesman. _Dean Cornwell_, (1892-1960), U.S. mural painter and illustrator. Actor: _Dean Cain, Dean Martin, Dean Jones._

Deandre // Dandre. _Latin:_ "(son) of André", from De + André. See André.

Delmore // Delmar, Delmer, Delmor. _Old French:_ "the sea". _Delmore Schwartz_, (1913-66), U.S. poet and short-story writer. _Delmer Fahrney_, (born 1898), U.S. Navy officer, pioneer in field of pilotless aircraft and guided missiles, rear admiral.

Demetrius // Demetre, Demetri, Demetris, Dimitri, Dimitry, Dmitri. _Greek:_ "of Demeter, the goddess of fertility". Strong minded, stubborn, complicated to have relationship with him, intelligent, persevering, creative, not afraid of work, colleges value his out going personality, doesn't get bogged down by failures, usually good in areas requiring relating to people, likes comfort, likes beautiful women, likes various of life's pleasures, hard for him to put limits on his likes, very easily falls in love, may get remarried several times, stays attached to his children from previous relationships and continues to support them, wife will have to bear with his nagging nature, respectful toward his mother, not overly jealous, remains romantic toward women through to old age, composer, conductor. _Dimitri Shostakovich_, (1906-75), great modern Soviet composer. _Dimitri Kabalevsky_, (1904-87), Russian composer, pianist, and conductor. _Dimitri Mitropoulos_, (1896-1960), Greek conductor.

Dennis // Deanise, Den, Denis, Dennet, Denney, Dennie, Dennison, Denny, Denys. _Greek:_ "of Dionysus, god of wine and vegetation". Very relational, family man, fairly competitive, casual sportsman, responsible, good grades but trouble maker, lucky, overcomes obstacles easily, often a collector, often pushes his ideas, a little proud and self loving, doesn't just marry for love, thoughtfully considers who he will marry, budgets money wisely, not greedy, if consulted and related with - he can be inclined to buy practically anything, lawyer, public official. _Dennis Conner_, (born 1942), U.S. yachtsman. _Dennis Thomas_

Flynn, (1861-1939), U.S. lawyer and congressman. *Dennis Chavez,* (1888-1962), lawyer, U.S. public official, U.S. senator. *Dennis McLain,* (born 1944), U.S. baseball pitcher. *Dennis Brutus,* (born 1924), U.S. teacher and poet. *Dennis Lee,* (born 1939), Canadian poet and children's author. *Dennis Hopper,* (born 1936), U.S. character actor. *Dennis Davies,* (born 1944), U.S. conductor. *Dennis Gabor,* (1900-79), British physicist. Actor: *Dennis Franz.*

Denzil // Denzel, Denzell. **Germanic:** "Dane's village". *Baron Denzil Holles,* (1599-1680), outspoken British parliamentary leader. Actor: *Denzel Washington.*

Derek // Darrick, Derick, Derrek, Derrick, Derrik, Derk, Dirk. **Old German:** "ruler of the people". *Short form of* Theodoric. Energetic, adventurous, thin, stable, hard working, loyal, calm, accepting of others, caring, helpful, loving husband, not pushy, marries sweet fairly determined female such as Michelle. *Derek Walcott,* (born 1930), West Indian poet and playwright. *Derek Barton,* (born 1918), British chemist. *Dirk Stikker,* (1897-1979), Dutch statesman. *Dirk Coster,* (1889-1950), Dutch physicist. Actor: *Derek Jacobi.*

Desmond // Des, Desi, Desmund. **Gaelic:** "south Munster". *Desmond Tutu,* (born 1931), South African Anglican bishop and outspoken social activist. *Desi Arnaz,* (1917-86), Cuban bandleader, coproducer and actor in 'I Love Lucy.

DeWitt // De Witt, Dewitt, Dwight, Wit, Wittie, Witty. **Flemish:** "blond". *De Witt Clinton,* (1769-1828), U.S. statesman, lawyer, governor of New York. *DeWitt Wallace,* (1889-1981), U.S. editor and publisher, founded The Reader's Digest.

Dexter // Decca, Deck, Dex. **Latin:** "dexterous, on the right hand".

Dick // Dickie, Dicky. *Short form of* Richard. Also see Richard. *Dick Turpin,* (1706-39), notorious English highwayman. *Dick Butkus,* (born 1942), U.S. football player. *Dick Gregory,* (born 1932), U.S. comedian, author, and activist. *Dick Snelling,* (1927-91), U.S. public official, governor of Vermont. Actor: *Dick Van Dyke.*

Diego. *Spanish form* of Jacob and James. *Diego Velasquez,* (1599-1660), Spain's greatest painter. *Diego Rivera,* (1886-1957), Mexican painter. *Diego de Almagro,* (1475-1538), Spanish adventurer, aided conquest of Peru, conquered Chile. Diego Columbus, (1480-1526), eldest son of Christopher Columbus, governor of Indies. *Diego Velasquez,* (1465?-1522?), Spanish soldier, explorer, first governor of Cuba, founded Havana.

Dijon // Dejaun, Dejion, Dejohn, Dejon Dejuan, Deshaun, Deshawn, Deshon. Geographical: Dijon, France. **Latin:** "(son) of John". See Dion, Juan, John and Shawn.

Dion // Deon. *Short form of* Dionysus. Artistic, musical, actor. *Dion Boucicault,* (1820?-90), U.S. playwright and actor.

Dionysus. Greek mythology: the god of wine and later god of vegetation, warm moisture, pleasures and civilization.

Dirk. *Short form of* Derek and Theodoric. *Dirk Coster,* (1889-1950), Dutch physicist. *Dirk Stikker,* (1897-1979), Dutch statesman, secretary-general NATO.

Dmitri. Russian form of Demetrius. See Demetrius.

Dominic // Dom, Domenic, Domenico, Domingo, Dominick,

Dominik, Dominique, Nick, Nickie, Nicky. *Latin:* "belonging to God". *Dominique Pire,* (1910-69), Belgian Dominican priest. *Dominic* (Domingo de Guzman) (1170?-1221), founder of Order of Friars Preachers, or Dominicans. *Domenico Scarlatti,* (1685-1757), harpsichord virtuoso. *Domingo Sarmiento,* (1811-88), president of Argentina, brought educational reforms. *Dom Miguel,* (1802-66), Portuguese prince and pretender. *Domenico Cimarosa,* (1749-1801), Italian composer. *Domenico Fontana,* (1543-1607), Italian architect. *Dominic Lewis,* (1894-1969), English author. *Domenico Ghirlandaio,* (1449-94), Italian fresco painter. *Dominick La Rocca,* (1889-1961), U.S. jazz cornetist.

Don // Donn, Donnie, Donny. *Short form of* names beginning with "don". Also see Donald. Don Bradman, (born 1908), greatest natural batsman in British cricket game history. *Don Carlos Buell,* (1818-98), prominent U.S. Army Major General in Civil War. *Don Cherry,* (born 1936), U.S. jazz musician. *Don Lawson,* (1917-90), U.S. writer and editor. *Don Carlos Seitz,* (1862-1935), U.S. newspaper manager and writer. Actors: *Don Francks, Don Johnson.*

Donald // Don, Donal, Donall, Donalt, Donaugh, Donn, Donnell, Donnie, Donny. *Scotch Gaelic:* "world ruler". By Peter the First's declaration, this name could be given to the children of Russian nobles. "World ruler", resemble mother, personality like father; in certain situations he acts aggressively, friendly, goal directed, efficient, effective, often make good generals, tend toward angry flare-ups, disagreements seen as challenge of an enemy, proud; becomes irate or tyrannical when authority challenged, may tantrum as child, fairly charismatic, writer, lawyer,

public official, five astronauts, scientist, engineer, athlete, biologist, jurist, historian, usually has daughters, greatly enjoys traveling, good child, not ordinary. *Donald Marquis,* (1878-1937), U.S. writer of stories, plays, and verse, humorous bits of wisdom. *Donald Cameron,* (born 1947?), Canadian public official, premier of Nova Scotia 1991. *Donald Cram,* (born 1919), chemist. *Donald Trump,* (born 1946), U.S. real-estate developer and financier. *Donald Payne,* (born 1934), U.S. public official, U.S. congressman. *Donald Kerst,* (born 1911), U.S. physicist. *Donald Hutson,* (born 1913), U.S. football end. *Donald Hornig,* (born 1920), U.S. chemist. *Donald Campbell,* (1921-67), British speedboat and auto racer. *Donald Walsh,* (born 1931), U.S. Navy officer, pilot. *Donald McDonald Dickinson,* (1846-1917), U.S. public official and lawyer. Totals: (27) politician 33%, scientist 19%, author 15%, educator 15%, lawyer 11%, businessman 11%, commander 11%, engineer 11%, inventor 7%, boat & auto racer, athlete, physician, explorer, architect. Actor: *Donald Pleasence.*

Donovan // Donavan. *Scotch Gaelic:* "dark warrior".

Dorian // Dorion. *Greek:* Dorians, one of four great branches of Greek people; took name from Dorus, son of Hellen.

Douglas // Doug, Dougie, Douglass, Dougy, Dugald. *Gaelic:* "dark water". Athletic, adventurous, good student, relational, helps others, intense or determined in accomplishment, non-combative, daring, loyal, family man, not quite pushy but directive leader, problem solver; often marries: sweet, somewhat determined less-athletic female such as Heather. *Douglas Fairbanks,* (1883-1939), motion-picture actor and producer, athletic skill, gallant romanticism, natural sincerity, energetic go-getter. *Douglas Fairbanks, Jr.* (born 1909), U.S. motion-picture and television actor-producer, debonair leading man, decorated American officer WWII. *Douglas MacArthur,* (1880-1964), U.S. WWII General, symbol of American determination and fighting ability. *Douglas Stewart,* (born 1913), Australian poet, playwright, and critic. *Douglas Freeman*, (1886-1953), U.S. editor and author. *Douglas McKay*, (1893-1959), U.S. public official, Oregon state senator and governor. *Douglas Edwards*, (1917-90), U.S. newscaster and anchor. *L. Douglas Wilder*, (born 1931), U.S. public official, Virginia state senate and governor. *Douglas Cockerell*, (1870-1945), British bookbinder and type designer. *Douglas Moore*, (1893-1969), U.S. composer and educator. *Douglas Mawson*, (1882-1958), Australian explorer and geologist. *Douglas Haig*, (1861-1928), British commander. *Douglas Jerrold*, (1803-57), British dramatist and humorist. *Doug Henning*, (born 1947), Canadian magician. *Douglas Hyde*, (1860-1949), Irish scholar and author. Totals: (14) author 29%, commander 14%, actor 14%, producer 14%, politician 14%, educator 14%, businessman, lawyer, newscaster, explorer, scientist, musician, humorist, scholar. Actor: *Doug Hutchison*.

Drake. *English:* "drake".

Drew // Dru, Drud, Drugi. *Old French:* "sturdy". *Old Welsh:* "wise". *Short form of* Andrew. Actor: *Drew Carey*.

Duane // Dewain, Dwain, Dwayne. *Gaelic:* "little and dark". Humorous, businessman, crafty, no non-sense, determined, adventurous. Actor: *Duane Loken*.

Dudley. *Old English:* "people's meadow". *Dudley Allen Sargent*, (1849-1924), U.S. specialist in physical education. *Dudley R. Herschbach*, (born 1932), U.S. chemist. Actor: *Dudley Moore*.

Duke // Dukey, Dukie, Duky. *Old French:* "leader, duke". *Duke Kahanamoku*, (1890-1968), U.S. swimming champion.

Duncan // Dun, Dunc, Dunn. *Gaelic:* "dark-skinned warrior". *Duncan Hines*, (1880-1959), U.S. author and publisher of guides for travelers. *Duncan Grant*, (1885-1978), British painter. *Duncan* (died 1040), Scottish king. *Duncan Campbell Scott*, (1862-1947), Canadian poet and biographer. *Duncan Phyfe*, (1768-1854), U.S. furniture maker. Actor: *Duncan Regehr.*

Dustin // Dust, Dustan, Dustie, Duston, Dusty. *Old German:* "valiant fighter". Valiant fighter, bit of a loner. Actor: *Dustin Hoffman*.

Dwayne. *Form of* Duane.

Dwight. *English form* of De Witt. *Dwight D. Eisenhower*, 34th President of the United States, World War II General, one of the most successful commanders in history. *Dwight Moody,* (1837-99), became the most noted traveling evangelist of late 1800s. *Dwight Davis*, (1879-1945), U.S. statesman. *Dwight Morrow*, (1873-1931), U.S. diplomat and statesman. Actor: *Dwight Yoakam*.

Dylan // Dilan, Dill, Dillie, Dilly. *Old Welsh:* "the sea". *Dylan Thomas*, (1914-53), Welsh poet, boisterous, heavy-drinking man. Actor: *Dylan McDermott*.

Earl // Earle, Errol, Erroll. ***Old English:*** "warrior, noble-man". Noble demeanor, gentle, not pushy, relational, humorous, liked, relational or positional leader. *Earl Butz*, (born 1909), U.S. agricultural economist. *Earl Dorn*, (1820-63), American Confederate general. *Earl Campbell*, (born 1955), U.S. football player. *Earl (Curly) Lambeau*, (1898-1965), U.S. football halfback and coach. *Earle Neale*, (1891-1973), U.S. football end and coach. *Earl Warren*, (1891-1974), U.S. lawyer, California governor, chief justice of the U.S. Supreme Court. *Earl Browder*, (1891-1973), U.S. Communist party leader. *Earle Wheeler*, (1908-75), U.S. Army officer, Army chief of staff, chairman Joint Chiefs of Staff. *Earl Sutherland, Jr.* (1915-74), U.S. physiologist. *Earl (Dutch) Clark*, (born 1906), U.S. football quarterback and coach. *Earle Combs*, (1899-1976), U.S. baseball outfielder. *Earle Page*, (1880-1961), Australian political leader, prime minister. *Earl (Bud) Powell*, (1924-66), U.S. jazz composer and pianist. *Earl (Fatha) Hines*, (1905-83), U.S. jazz pianist and bandleader.

Ebenezer // Eb, Eben, Ebeneser. ***Hebrew:*** "stone of help". *Ebenezer Hoar*, (1816-95), U.S. public official, lawyer and judge.

Ed // Eddie, Eddy. *Short form of* names beginning with "ed". Hard worker, relational, generally seems quiet but gets on talking rolls, loves to have fun, adventurous, athletic, hobbiest, enthusiast, lover of something,, a bit

shy, comedian, athlete, broadcaster, racer, loves speed. *Ed Bradley,* (born 1941), U.S. journalist and television broadcaster. *Eddie Murphy*, (born 1961), U.S. comedian, most successful African American in films in late 1980s. *Eddie Rickenbacker*, (Edward Vernon Rickenbacker) (1890-1973), U.S. aviator, noted as automobile racer; commander first U.S. active aero unit in World War I, U.S. leading ace in World War I. *Eddie Arcaro*, (George Edward Arcaro) (born 1916), U.S. jockey. *Eddie Condon*, (or Albert Edwin Condon) (1904-73), U.S. banjoist and guitarist. *Eddie Cantor*, (originally Edward Israel Iskowitz) (1892-1964), U.S. radio, stage, screen, and television comedian. *Eddie Robinson*, (born 1919), longtime football coach at Grambling State College and most winning coach in college football history. *Eddie Foy*, (originally Edwin Fitzgerald) (1856-1928), U.S. comedian. *Ed Healey*, (1894-1978), U.S. football tackle. *Eddie Mathews*, (full name Edwin Lee Mathews) (born 1931), U.S. third baseman, manager. *Ed Sullivan*, (Edward Vincent Sullivan) (1902-74), U.S. columnist and television emcee. Actors: *Ed Harris, Eddie Cibrian.*

Edgar // Ed, Eddie, Eddy, Edgard, Edgardo, Ned, Neddie, Neddy, Ted, Teddie, Teddy. ***Old English:*** "spear of wealth". *Edgar Allan Poe*, (1809-49), greatest American teller of mystery and suspense tales in 1800s. *J. Edgar Hoover,* (1895-1972), most powerful and feared official in the U.S. federal government for about 50 years, head of the Federal Bureau of Investigation (FBI). *Edgar Degas*, (1834-1917), famed as the "painter of dancers." *Edgar Aulaire,* (1898-1986), U.S. artist. *Edgar Varese*, (1883-1965), U.S. composer. *Edgar Masters*, (1869-1950), U.S. author. *Edgar Guest*, (1881-1959), U.S. writer of verse.

Edgar Adrian, (1889-1977), English physiologist. *Edgar Dewdney*, (1835-1916), Canadian civil engineer and statesman. *Edgar Wallace*, (1875-1932), British writer. *Edgar Cecil*, (1864-1958), British statesman. *Edgar (Sam) Rice*, (1892-1974), U.S. baseball player. *Edgar Snow*, (1905-72), U.S. writer. *Edgar* (944-975), king of England, supported monasteries, improved courts of law, and encouraged commerce. *Edgar Quinet*, (1803-75), French author, professor of literature. *Edgar Mitchell*, (born 1930), U.S. astronaut, U.S. Navy officer. *Edgar Goodspeed*, (1871-1962), U.S. classical Greek and Biblical scholar. *Edgar Howe*, (1853-1937), U.S. author and editor. Totals: (17) author 47%, politician 18%, educator 18%, artist 12%, musician, scientist, athlete, astronaut, scholar.

Edmund // Eadmund, Eamon, Ed, Edd, Eddie, Edmon, Edmond, Edmondo, Ned, Neddie, Neddy, Ted, Teddie, Teddy. *Old English:* "protector of wealth". Artistic, poet, writer, polititian. *Edmund Kean*, (1789-1833), one of the three great English tragic actors of all time. *Edmund Burke*, (1729-97), British parliamentarian noted for equity, wisdom, and justice. *Edmund Hillary*, (born 1919), first to climb Mount Everest. *Edmund Spenser,* (1552?-99), great epic poet. *Edmund Cartwright*, (1743-1823), clergyman-turned-inventor who devised the power loom for weaving. *Edmund Rich*, (1175?-1240), English saint and archbishop of Canterbury. *Edmund Waller*, (1606-87), English poet.

Edsel // Ed, Eddie, Eddy. *Old English:* "rich man's house". *Edsel Ford,* (1893-1943), U.S. automobile manufacturer.

Edward // Ed, Eddie, Eddy, Edik, Edouard, Eduard, Eduardo, Edvard, Ewart, Neddie, Neddy, Ted, Teddie, Teddy. *Old English:* "guardian of wealth". Good student, capable, known as likable and friendly; appears easy-going and possibly appears spineless, but he is not spineless; easy to relate, polite, pleasing, generous but often with calculation; his politeness can quickly evaporate when his interests are crossed, becoming very businesslike; picks a beautiful agreeable wife who is able to live with his weaknesses; he may take control of the finances; easily falls in love; writer, composer, artist, clergy, politician, sculptor, creator, scientist, sociologist, educator, statesman, judge, naval officer, astronaut, few athletes. *Edward Edwards*, (1812-86), English librarian. *Edward Lear*, (1812-88), English humorist made famous the limerick. *Edouard Michelin*, (1859-1940), and brother Andre are world reknown for their revolutionary tires and detailed international travel guides. *Edvard Munch*, (1863-1944), gifted Norwegian painter and printmaker. *Edward R. Murrow*, (1908-65), newscaster. *Edward Hopper*, (1882-1967), American painter. *Edward Albee*, (born 1928), American dramatists and theatrical producer. *Edouard Manet*, (1832-83), French painter. *Edward Weston*, (1886-1958), American photographic artist obsessed with realism. *Edward Hicks*, (1780-1849), American primitive painter and popular preacher. *Edward Gibbon*, (1737-94), writer and author of the 'Decline and Fall of the Roman Empire'. *Edward Hale*, (1822-1909), clergyman and author, wrote "The Man Without a Country." *Edward Teller*, (born 1908), American physicist. *Edward Elgar,* (1857-1934), composer, wrote 'Pomp and Circumstance'. *Edward Jenner,* (1749-1823), physician, developed smallpox vaccination. *Edward Heath*, (born 1916), British Prime Minister. Eight English kings named Edward. *Edward Steichen*, (1879-1973), photographer of early Hollywood stars. *Edward Wakefield*, (1796-1862), promoted colonizing Australia and New Zealand. *Edvard Grieg*, (1843-1907), Norway's greatest composer. Totals: (73) author 38%, politician 18%, clergy 12%, scientist 11%, educator 11%, artist 10%, musician 5%, businessman 5%, commander 5%, judge 4%, athlete 4%, humorist 3%, photographer 3%, lawyer 3%, explorer 3%, sociologist 3%, historian 3%, librarian, physician, producer, newscaster, philanthropist, architect, orator, actor, astronaut. Actors: *Eduardo Palomo, Edward Furlong, Edward Kerr, Edward Norton*.

Edwin // Ed, Eddie, Eddy, Edlin, Eduino, Ned, Neddie, Neddy, Ted, Teddie, Teddy. *Old English:* "friend of wealth". Inventor, scientist, statesman. *Edwin Armstrong*, (1890-1954), American engineer, broadcasting inventor. *Edwin Land*, (1909-91), inventor of optical devices including the Polaroid Land camera. *Edwin Stanton*, (1814-69), able administrator of the U.S. War Department Civil War. *Edwin Robinson*, (1869-1935), poet. *Edwin Forrest*, (1806-72), U.S. tragic actor. Totals: (40) author 35%, scientist 30%, educator 25%, politician 15%, businessman 10%, lawyer 10%, inventor 8%, tragic actor 5%, historian 5%, commander 5%, economist 5%, musician 5%, engineer, tactless & stubborn, administrator, naturalist, artist, athlete, fight corruption, architect.

Efrain // Efrem, Efren. Modern form of Ephraim. See Ephraim.

Elden // Eldon. *Form of* Alden. Also see Alden. "Old, wise protector", gentle, strong, fairly quiet. Actor: *Elden Ratliff*.

Eldridge // El, Eldredge. *Form of* Aldrich. See Aldrich.

Eleazar // Lazarus. *Hebrew:* "God has helped". *Eleazar*, (1000 BC), Hebrew high priest, son of Aaron.

Elias // El, Eli, Elia, Elias, Elihu, Elijah, Eliseo, Ely. Eli is *Hebrew:* "high". *Greek form* of Hebrew Elijah. *Hebrew:* "Jehovah is God". Biblical: *Eli,* Hebrew priest and judge. *Elijah*, Hebrew prophet. Very good manager of his household, enjoys repairing home, doing yard work, fixing car, not very choosy with his friends and easily falls under their influence, weighs the situation before marrying, usually doesn't marry before he is financially stable, faithfully loves his children, although he is attached to his family - he likes to travel; sharp mind, kind, quick temper and quick to regain calm taking responsibility for the conflict, inventor, creator, statesman. *Elias Lonnrot*, (1802-84), folklorist-philologist. *Elias Howe*, (1819-67), invented the sewing machine. *Elias James Corey*, (born 1928), U.S. chemist. *Elias Hicks*, (1748-1830), U.S. minister. *Elias Canetti*, (born 1905), Austrian novelist and playwright. *Elias Boudinot*, (1740-1821), U.S. philanthropist, statesman and Revolutionary War patriot. *Elia Kazan*, (born 1909), U.S. theater and motion-picture director. *Eli Whitney,* (1765-1825), invented the cotton gin, developed the concepts of mass production, interchangeable parts and the assembly line. *Elie Wiesel*, (born 1928), prolific writer, teacher, and philosopher. *Elijah Levita*, (1469-1549), German-born Italian grammarian. *Ely Culbertson*, (1891-1955), U.S. bridge expert and writer. *Elihu Yale*, (1648-1721), English philanthropist. *Elihu Thomson*, (1853-1937), U.S. inventor and electrician. *Elihu Vedder*, (1836-1923), U.S. painter and illustrator. *Elihu Benjamin Washburne*, (1816-87), U.S. statesman. *Elihu Root*, (1845-1937), U.S. lawyer and statesman. *Ely Samuel Parker*, (1828-95), first Native American named commissioner on Indian affairs.

Eli Stanley Jones (1884-1973), U.S. missionary. *Elijah McCoy,* (1843-1929), U.S. inventor. *Eli Hamilton Janney,* (1831-1912), U.S. inventor. *Elijah Parish Lovejoy,* (1802-37), U.S. abolitionist. Totals: (23) inventor 22%, author 22%, educator 13%, clergy 13%, politician 13%, philanthropist 9%, grammarian 9%, scientist, physician, director, philosopher, artist, lawyer, missionary, engineer, reformer.

Elisha. *Hebrew:* "God saves". *Elisha Baxter,* (fl. 1874), U.S. politician, former governor of Arkansas. *Elisha Kane,* (1820-57), U.S. Arctic explorer and scientist. *Elisha,* (1000 BC), Hebrew prophet, successor of Elijah. *Elisha Pease,* (1812-83), U.S. lawyer, governor of Texas. *Elisha Ferry,* (1825-95), U.S. lawyer and public official, first governor of Washington state. *Elisha Gray,* (1835-1901), U.S. inventor, perfected telegraphic devices.

Elliott // Eliot, Eliott, Elliot. *Modern English* form of Elijah. Also see Ellis. Easy-going, constant, relational, amiable, capable, competent. *Elliott Proctor Joslin,* (1869-1962), U.S. physician. *Elliott Daingerfield,* (1859-1932), U.S. figure and landscape painter. *Elliott Coues,* (1842-99), U.S. naturalist, authority on birds. *Elliot McKay See, Jr.* (1927-66), U.S. astronaut candidate. *Elliot Paul,* (1891-1958), U.S. author and journalist. *Eliot Ness,* (1903-57), U.S. Prohibition enforcement officer, "Untouchables". Actor: *Elliott Gould.*

Ellis. *Modern form* of Elijah from Elias. Also see Elliott and Elias. Calm, dignified, wise, friendly, humorous, positive attitude. Actor: *Ellis Moore.*

Ellsworth // Ellsworth, Elsworth. *Old English*: "nobleman's estate". *H. Ellsworth Vines, Jr.* (born 1911), U.S. tennis player. *Ellsworth Kelly,* (born 1923), U.S. artist. *Ellsworth Huntington,* (1876-1947), U.S. geographer and explorer.

Elmer // Aylmar, Aylmer, Aymer. *Old English:* "noble, famous". *Elmer Sperry,* (1860-1930), American engineer and inventor. *Elmer Rice,* (1892-1967), U.S. playwright. *Elmer Apperson,* (1861-1920), U.S. automobile manufacturers. *Elmer Ellsworth,* (1837-61), U.S. soldier, colonel. *Elmer McCollum,* (1879-1967), U.S. biochemist. *Elmer Davis,* (1890-1958), U.S. writer, journalist, and news analyst. *Elmer Flick,* (1876-1971), U.S. baseball outfielder. *Elmer Hader,* (1889-1973), U.S. artist and writer. *Elmer Klassen,* (born 1908), U.S. public official.

Elton // Alden, Aldon, Eldon. *Old English:* "old town". *Elton John,* (born 1947), British musician.

Elvin. *Form of* Alvin.

Elvis // Al, Alvis, El. *Scandinavian:* "all-wise". *Form of* Elwin. *Elvis Presley,* (1935-77), one of the most successful entertainers ever, dominated U.S. popular music, 33 motion pictures, television, live concerts, a one-man industry. *Elvis Jacob Stahr, , Jr.* (born 1916), U.S. lawyer, educator, and government official.

Emerson. *Old German:* "industrious ruler's son". *Emerson Hough,* (1857-1923), U.S. journalist and novelist. *Emerson Whithorne,* (1884-1958), U.S. composer and editor.

Emery // Amery, Amory, Emmerich, Emmery, Emory. *Old German:* "industrious ruler". *Emory Scott Land,* (1879-1971), U.S. Navy officer. *Emery Walker,* (1851-1933), English engraver and printer.

Emil // Emelen, Emile, Emiliano, Emilio, Emlen, Emlyn.
Latin: "flattering". Social studier, researcher. *Emile Durkheim,* (1858-1917), pioneer social scientist. *Emile Zola,* (1840-1902), writer, novelist, social studies. *Emil Nolde,* (1867-1956), German artist. *Emil Adolf von Behring,* (1854-1917), German physician, researcher. *Emil Oberhoffer,* (1867-1933), U.S. musician, conductor. *Emile Vandervelde,* (1866-1938), Belgian Socialist statesman and orator. *Emile Wauters,* (1846-1933), Belgian portrait and historical painter. *Emil Kraepelin,* (1856-1926), German psychiatrist. *Emil Ludwig,* (1881-1948), U.S. author, wrote plays, sketches, and novels, "humanized" historical biographies. *Emil Jannings,* (1886-1950), U.S. actor. *Emil Theodor Kocher,* (1841-1917), Swiss surgeon. *Emil Fischer,* (1852-1919), German chemist. *Emil Gustav Hirsch,* (1851-1923), U.S. rabbi, professor rabbinical literature and philosophy. *Emil Grigoryevich Gilels,* (1916-85), Soviet pianist. *Emile Cammaerts,* (1878-1953), Belgian poet. *Emile Faguet,* (1847-1916), French critic, professor of poetry. *Emile Gaboriau,* (1835-73), French writer of detective stories. *Emile Jaques-Dalcroze,* (1865-1950), Swiss composer. *Emile Loubet,* (1838-1929), French statesman. *Emile Gervais,* (born 1900), Canadian writer and Roman Catholic priest. *Emile Fayolle,* (1852-1928), French general. *Emile Verhaeren,* (1855-1916), Belgian poet and critic, interest in social problems. *Emile Augier,* (1820-89), French dramatist and poet. *Emiliano Zapata,* (1879-1919), Mexican revolutionary, champion of the poor, land reformer, and guerrilla fighter. *Emilio Aguinaldo,* (1869-1964), first Philippine president, revolutionary general and hero. *Emilio Portes Gil,* (1891-1978), Mexican political leader, promoted interests of farmers and laborers.

Emilio Castelar y Ripoll, (1832-99), Spanish liberal statesman, orator, author of histories, essays, novels, travel books. *Emilio Mola,* (1887-1937), Spanish general. *Emilio Gino Segre,* (1905-89), U.S. physicist. Totals: (29) author 34%, politician 21%, scientist 17%, educator 17%, commander 14%, musician 10%, artist 7%, physician 7%, orator 7%, clergy 7%, revolutionary 7%, sociologist, socialist, psychiatrist, actor, philosophy, judge. Actor: *Emilio Estevez.*

Emmanuel // Emanuel, Emanuele, Immanuel, Mannie, Manny, Manuel. *Hebrew:* "God with us". Very relational, leader, determined, energetic. Religious, artistic, general. Biblical: *Immanuel* (or Emmanuel), the divinely appointed deliverer foretold by Isaiah. *Emanuel Swedenborg,* (1688-1772), exceptional scholar and religious mystic, fluent in several languages and in the classics, accomplished craftsman, student of the Bible, mathematics, astronomy, mineralogy, chemistry, hydraulics, botany, and other sciences. *Emanuel Lasker,* (1868-1941), German chess master, wrote books on chess, philosophy, and mathematics. *Emanuel Schikaneder,* (1751-1812), German actor, singer, playwright, and theater manager. *Emanuel Leutze,* (1816-68), U.S. portrait painter. *Immanuel Kant,* (1724-1804), a great philosopher. *Manuel Quezon,* (1878-1944), first president of the Philippines. *Emmanuel Fremiet,* (1824-1910), French sculptor. *Emmanuel Joseph Sieyes,* (1748-1836), leader and pamphleteer in French Revolution. *Manuel Montt,* (1809-80), Chilean statesman. *Manuel Gamio,* (1883-1960), Mexican anthropologist and sociologist. *Manuel de Falla,* (1876-1946), Spanish impressionist composer. *Manuel Avila Camacho,* (1897-1955), Mexican general and political leader. *Manuel Patricio Rodriguez*

Garcia, (1805-1906), Spanish singing teacher. *Manuel Gonzalez*, (1833-93), Mexican general and president. *Emmanuel marquis de Grouchy*, (1766-1847), French marshal. *Manuel Lujan, Jr.* (born 1928), U.S. public official. *Manuel Lisa*, (1772-1820), North American fur trader. *Manuel Vicente Garcia*, (1775-1832), Spanish singer and teacher. *Manuel Noriega*, (born 1938), Panamanian military and political leader, corruption and drug trafficking.

Emmett // Em, Emmet, Emmit, Emmott, Emmy. Name honors Irish patriot Robert Emmett. *Emmett Kelly,* (1898-1979), U.S. clown. *Emmett Matthew Hall*, (born 1898), Canadian Supreme Court justice.

Engelbert // Bert, Bertie, Berty, Englebert, Ingelbert, Inglebert. *Old German:* "bright as an angel". *Engelbert Dollfuss*, (1892-1934), Austrian statesman, chancellor. *Engelbert Humperdinck*, (1854-1921), German composer.

Enoch. *Hebrew:* "dedicated, consecrated". *Enoch*, Hebrew patriarch who "walked with God". *Enoch Pratt*, (1808-96), U.S. capitalist and philanthropist. *Enoch Herbert Crowder*, (1859-1932), U.S. Army, provost marshal general.

Enos. *Hebrew:* "man". *Enos Mills*, (1870-1922), U.S. naturalist. *Enos Slaughter*, (born 1916), U.S. baseball outfielder.

Enrico // Enrique. *Form of* Henry. Scientist, performance artist. *Enrico Fermi*, (1901-54), scientist, first man-made self-sustaining nuclear chain reaction. *Enrico Caruso*, (1873-1921), Italian tenor, all-time opera star. *Enrico Forlanini*, (1848-1930), Italian pioneer of scientific aviation. *Enrico Ferri*, (1856-1929), Italian criminologist, a pioneer in scientific study of criminals and of crime prevention. *Enrico Cecchetti*, (1850-1928), Italian dancer and ballet teacher. *Hank Luisetti*, (Angelo Enrico Luisetti) (born 1916), U.S. college basketball player.

Ephraim // Efrem, Efren, Ephrem. *Hebrew:* "very fruitful". Biblical: the second son of Joseph. Artistic. *Efrem Kurtz*, (born 1900), U.S. conductor. *Efrem Zimbalist*, (1889-1985), U.S. violinist. *Ephraim Chambers*, (1680?-1740), English encyclopedist. *Ephraim McDowell*, (1771-1830), U.S. surgeon.

Erhard // Erhart. *Old German:* "Strong resolution".

Eric // Erek, Erich, Erick, Erik, Errick, Rick, Rickie, Ricky. *Scandinavian:* "ever-ruler, ever-powerful". Leader, business like, friendly, fun, sociable, high percentage of writers, military officer, composer, teacher, behavioral analyzer. *Eric the Red*, colonized Greenland. *Eric Ambler*, (born 1909), highly distinguished writer of spy and crime fiction. *Erich Fromm*, (1900-80), psychoanalyst and social philosopher. *Eric Coates*, (1886-1957), British composer and viola player. *Erich Segal*, (born 1937), U.S. educator and author. *Erik Erikson*, (born 1902), U.S. psychoanalyst and educator. *Erich Kleiber,* (1890-1956), Austrian opera conductor. *Erich von Drygalski*, (1865-1949), German polar explorer, geophysicist, and geographer. *Erich von Ludendorff,* (1865-1937), German general, expert strategist. *Eric Mowbray Knight,* (1897-1943), U.S. author. *Erik Satie*, (1866-1925), French composer. *Eric Geddes*, (1875-1937), British political leader. *Erich von Stroheim*, (1885-1957), U.S. director and actor. *Erik Gustaf Geijer,* (1783-1847), Swedish poet, composer, and historian. *Eric Bruhn*, (1928-86), Danish ballet dancer and choreographer. *Erich* *von Falkenhayn*, (1861-1922), German general. *Erich Kastner*, (1899-1974), German poet, journalist, and author. *Eric Gill*, (1882-1940), English sculptor and stone carver. *Eric Hoffer*, (1902-83), U.S. longshoreman, philosopher, author. *Eric Honeywood Partridge*, (1894-1979), British lexicographer. *Erik Axel Karlfeldt*, (1864-1931), Swedish poet. *Eric Allen Johnston*, (1896-1963), U.S. industrialist. *Erich Leinsdorf*, (born 1912), U.S. conductor. *Eric Philbrook Kelly*, (1884-1960), U.S. writer of children's books and educator. *Erich Raeder*, (1876-1960), WWII commander-in-chief of German navy. *Erich Maria Remarque*, (1898-1970), U.S. novelist. *Erich Wolfgang Korngold*, (1897-1957), U.S. composer. *Erich Mendelsohn*, (1887-1953), architect. Totals: (27) author 56%, musician 22%, educator 19%, commander 15%, pschoanalist 11%, philosopher 7%, actor, director, politician, explorer, scientist, historian, dancer-choreographer, businessman, architect, artist. Actor: *Eric Fleming.*

Ernest // Ernesto, Ernestus, Ernie, Ernst, Erny. *Old English:* "earnest". Eccentric, adventurous, like making own type of adventures like songs, stories, games, etc. fun-loving. *Ernie Pyle*, (Ernest Taylor Pyle) (1900-45), U.S. journalist and war correspondent. *Ernest Roehm*, (1887-1934), German army officer conspired to overthrow Adolf Hitler. *Ernie Nevers*, (1903-76), U.S. football player. *Ernie Lombardi*, (1908-77), U.S. baseball catcher. *Ernie Hare*, U.S. vaudeville actor. *Ernie Banks*, (born 1931), U.S. shortstop and first baseman. *Ernest Hemingway*, (1899-1961), famous writer. *Ernst Mach*, (1838-1916), Austrian physicist and philosopher. Many others. Totals: Wordsmith 15%, physicists 12%, social scientist/theologian/philosopher 12%, composer 9%, artist 7%, physiologist

psychologist 4%, athlete 6%, historian 4%, statesman 6%, labor leader 3%, military officer 6%, chemist 4%, naturalist 4%.

Errol // Erroll, Rollo. *German form* of Earl. *Erroll Garner*, (1921-77), U.S. jazz pianist. *Rollo* (or Rolf, or Hrolf, or Rou) (860?-930?), Norse conqueror of French Normandy. Actor: *Errol Flynn*.

Erskine // Kin, Kinnie, Kinny. *Gaelic:* "cliff height". *Erskine Caldwell*, (1903-87), U.S. writer, had been cotton picker, stagehand, professional football player, book reviewer, and screenwriter, 'Tobacco Road', 'God's Little Acre'.

Ervin // Erwin. *Anglo-Saxon:* "sea friend". *Form of* Irvin. *Erwin Rommel*, (1891-1944), "Desert Fox", brilliant German Field Marshal during World War II. *Erwin Schrodinger*, (1887-1961), award winning Austrian theoretical physicist. *Erwin Neher*, (born 1944), award winning German biophysics scientist. *Erwin Mueller*, (1911-77), U.S. physicist.

Esteban // Estevan. *Spanish form* of Stephan. *Estevan*, (died 1539), African explorer of Southern North America. *Estevan Gomez*, (1470?-1530?), Portuguese explorer, led mutiny.

Ethan // Etan, Ethe. *Hebrew:* "strength". *Ethan Allen*, (1738-89), among the first heroes of the American Revolution. *Ethan Allen Hitchcock*, (1835-1909), U.S. business executive and public official. Actor: *Ethan Hawke, Ethan Phillips.*

Eugene // Eugen, Eugenio, Eugenius, Gene. *Greek:* "well-born, noble". Prince-like, relational, social worker, thinker, quick intellect, may learn to read and write early, big imagination, one of the best student, easily learns foreign languages, hard working, likes to play sports, finds obstacles difficult to overcome, usually moderately successful at his career, predisposed to exact sciences and electronics, values woman's pure heart first, subconsciously looking for a mysterious element in women, created for family life, doesn't mind domestic chores, hates and avoids loud debates, he continues the environment of love even in family power struggles, his wife may take his patients as spineless or weak and it will hurt the relationship, sensitive to the pain of loved ones, but may be unsure what course to take in difficult situations, very jealous, doesn't initiate divorce. *Eugene V. Debs*, (1855-1926), labor union organizer and leader, founder of the Socialist Party of America. *Eugene Ionesco*, (born 1912), French dramatist, helped start the Theater of the Absurd. *Eugene Atget*, (1856-1927), failed painter, influential Paris photographer. *Eugene O'Neill*, (1888-1953), among greatest American dramatists, dealt realistically with psychological and social problems. *Eugene Delacroix*, (1798-1863), among the greatest and most influential French painter. Totals: politician 17%, musician 14%, business exec 10%, actor 10%, writer 10%, painter 10%, athlete 7%, physicist 7%, dramatist 7%, geochemist 3%, astronaut 3%, general 3%, golfer 3%, inventor 3%. Actor: *Eugene Robert Glazer*.

Evan // Ev, Even, Evin, Evyn, Ewan, Ewen, Owen. *Welsh:* "young warrior". *Welsh form* of John. "Young warrior", relaxed, determined, somewhat artistic, somewhat scientific, composed, bit quiet, similar to Eric. *Evan Bayh*, (born 1955), U.S. public official, governor of Indiana. *Evan*

Mecham, (born 1924), former governor of Arizona, businessman. Actor: *Ewan McGregor*.

Evelyn // Evelin. *Old English:* "hazelnut". A surname, often used as a masculine first name in England. *Evelyn Strachey*, (1901-63), English statesman and writer. *Evelyn Baring* first earl of Cromer, (1841-1917), British statesman and diplomat. *Evelyn Arthur Waugh*, (1903-66), English author.

Everett // Eberhard, Ev, Ever, Everand, Everardo, Evered, Eward, Ewart. *Old English:* "strong as a boar". *Everett McKinley Dirksen*, (1896-1969), U.S. congressman and senator, eloquent speaker. *C. Everett Koop*, (born 1916), U.S. surgeon general. *Everett Dean Martin*, (1880-1941), U.S. writer and lecturer on social philosophy and psychology.

Ezekiel // Ezechiel, Ezequiel, Eziechiele, Zeke. *Hebrew:* "God will strengthen." Biblical: Ezekiel major Hebrew prophets. *Ezequiel Padilla*, (1890-1971), Mexican lawyer and statesman, revolutionist. *Ezekiel Reed*, (fl. 18th century), U.S. inventor of first nail-making machine.

Ezra // Esdras, Esra, Ezri. *Hebrew:* "helper". Biblical: *Ezra*, Hebrew priest and reformer. *Ezra Taft Benson*, (born 1899), U.S. public official and Mormon leader. *Ezra Jack Keats*, (born 1916), U.S. author and illustrator. *Ezra Meeker*, (1830-1928), U.S. pioneer, farmer and author. *Ezra Cornell*, (1807-74), U.S. businessman, philanthropist. *Ezra Pound*, (1885-1972), American poet.

Fabian // Fabe, Faber, Fabiano, Fabien, Fabio. *Latin:* "bean grower". *Fabian Gottlieb von Bellingshausen*, (1778-1852), Russian Antarctic explorer and naval officer.

Faust // Faustino, Fausto, Faustus. *Latin:* "fortunate, lucky". *Faust*, (died about 1540), German soothsayer-magician of which legend abounds. *Fausto de Elhuyart*, (1755-1833) one of two brothers, Spanish chemists, who isolated tungsten (1783). *Faustus Socinus*, (1539-1604), Italian theologian, influential in the development of Unitarian theology.

Felipe. *Spanish form* of Phillip. *Felipe Gonzalez Marquez*, Spanish prime minister, socialist.

Felix // Falex, Fee, Felic, Felice, Felicio, Felike, Feliks, Felizio. *Latin:* "fortunate, happy, prosperous". Friendly, very relational, fun, lighthearted; capable student, unstable grades; sensitive, out-bursts as child; complicated nature; insincere-double nature; may be calculating, may be nice to get what he desires; looks for good pay or profitable job; likes to boast a bit; tends over value himself; doesn't always keep his promises; marries not just beauty but also wealth; tries to be the family leader, but respects his wife's opinion; might be an unfaithful husband which doesn't bother him; it helps his marriage for his wife to stay attractive and a bit mysterious; takes stress hard; may have tendency toward alcoholism.

Several Catholic Popes chose this name. *Felix Mendelssohn*, (1809-47), composer, pianist, and conductor. *Felix Bloch*, (1905-83), U.S. physicist and educator. *Felix Andries Vening Meinesz*, (1887-1966), Dutch engineer. *Count Felix von Luckner*, (1881-1966), German naval officer and adventurer. *Saint Felix of Valois*, (1127-1212), French activist monk. *Felix Salten*, (1869-1945), Austrian essayist, novelist, and dramatist. *Felix Octavius Carr Darley*, (1822-88), U.S. illustrator and historical painter. *Felix Weingartner*, (1863-1942), Austrian conductor and composer. *Felix Adler*, (died 1962), U.S. clown. *Felix Riesenberg*, (1879-1939), U.S. writer, engineer, and nautical authority. *Felix Martin*, (1804-86), French Jesuit priest, historian. *Felix Frankfurter*, (1882-1965), U.S. jurist and educator. Several Popes assumed this name. *Felix Mottl*, (1856-1911), German conductor and composer. *Felix Grundy*, (1777-1840), criminal lawyer, U.S. congressman and senator, attorney general. Totals: (16) musician 25%, author 25%, educator 13%, lawyer 13%, engineer 13%, commander 13%, scientist 13%, clergy 13%, jurist, educator, artist, inventor, politician, adventurer, clown, historian, zoologist.

Ferdinand // Ferd, Ferde, Ferdie, Ferdy, Fergus, Fernando, Hernando. *Old German:* "world-daring, life-adventuring". "World-daring, life-adventuring", determined, leader. *Ferdinand Rudolph von Grofe*, (1892-1972), U.S. composer. *Ferdinand Lassalle*, (1825-64), a chief 19th-century theorists of socialism. *Ferdinand Foch*, (1851-1929), French general, marshal of France, great ability and courage. *Ferdinand Magellan*, (1480?-1521), sailing explorer. *Hernando Cortez*, (1485-1547), Spanish soldier, conqueror of Mexico. *Ferdinand Marcos*, (1917-89), thieving president of the Philippines. *Hernando De Soto*, (1500?-42), ruthless soldier, admired horseman, looted Peruvian gold. Ferdinand de Lesseps, (1805-94), French diplomat, built the Suez Canal. Totals: scientist 19%, king 17%, cruel 13%, soldier 11%, statesman 10%, creative 10%, emperor 9%, writer 6%, socialist 6%, thief 4%, human-rights 4%.

Fergus // Ferguson. *Gaelic:* "strong man". *Irish form* of Ferdinand. *Ferguson Jenkins*, (born 1943), baseball pitcher.

Fermin. *Latin:* "strong, firm".

Ferris // Farris. *Irish form* of Peter.

Fidel // Fidele, Fidelio. *Latin:* "faithful". *Fidel Castro*, (born 1926), communist political revolutionary, premier and president of Cuba. *Fidel Ramos*, (born 1928), Philippine president, honorable career army officer.

Flavio. *Latin:* "yellow (hair), blond".

Fletcher // Fletch. *Middle English:* "arrow-featherer". Sensitive side. *Fletcher Christian*, second in ship's command when lead the Bounty mutiny. *Fletcher Henderson*, (1897-1952), U.S. jazz pianist and arranger. *Fletcher (Joe) Perry*, (born 1927), U.S. football fullback and assistant coach.

Floyd. *English form* of Lloyd. *Floyd Bixler McKissick*, (1922-91), U.S. lawyer and organization executive. *Floyd Bennett*, (1890-1928), U.S. aviator and hero. *Floyd Sherman Chalmers*, (born 1898), Canadian publisher. *Floyd Patterson*, (born 1935), U.S. boxer. *Floyd Dell*,

(1887-1969), U.S. author. *Floyd Harold Flake*, (born 1945), U.S. politician and clergy.

Ford. *Old English:* "river crossing". *Ford Madox Hueffer*, (1873-1939), British author. *Ford Madox Brown*, (1821-93), English painter. *Ford Christopher Frick*, (1894-1978), U.S. baseball executive, sportswriter, and sportscaster.

Forest // Forester, Forrest, Forrester, Forster, Foss, Foster. *Old French:* "forest, woodsman". Strong, calm, determined. *Forrest David Matthews*, (born 1935), U.S. public official and educator. Actor: *Forest Whitaker.*

Foster. *Latin:* "keeper of the woods". *Form of* Forest.

Francis // Chico, Fran, Francesco, Franchot, Francisco, Franciskus, François, Frank, Frankie, Franky, Frannie, Franny, Frans, Fransisco, Frants, Franz, Franzen, Frasco, Frasquito, Paco, Pacorro, Panchito, Pancho, Paquito. *Latin:* "Frenchman". Name honors: *Saint Francis of Assisi,* (1182-1226), Roman Catholic saint, founder of Franciscan order. Tends toward two types: artistic or adventurer-soldier. Writer, friendly, easy-going, not forceful, relational, leads through intelligence and knowledge, not gregarious, good worker, loyal, clergy, statesman, word-smith, some scientists. *Frans Hals*, (1580?-1666), Dutch painter. *Francisco Franco*, (1892-1975), soft-spoken and religious dictator of Spain. *Francis Joseph I*, (1830-1916), the last of the Hapsburg emperors. *Francis I,* (1494-1547), French king. *Francisco Ximenes*, (1436-1517), Regent of all Spain, priest, frier, evangelist. *Francis Thompson*, (1859-1907), English writer. *Francis Xavier*, (1506-52), Spanish Jesuit missionary priest. *Francisco de Miranda*, (1750-1816), Venezuelan revolutionist. *Francisco*

Pizarro, (1475?-1541), Spanish adventurer, treacherously conquered Peru. *Francis Marion*, (1732?-95), bold and dashing American revolutionary called "the swamp fox." *Francis Parkman*, (1823-93), brilliant U.S. historian. *Francis Bacon*, (1561-1626), English parliamentarian, famous lawyer, lord chancellor, writer of legal, popular, scientific, historical, philosophical and other books and essays. *Sir Francis Drake*, (1545-96), English privateer, leading part in defeating Spanish sea domination. *Francisco Coronado*, (1510?-54), Spanish gold seeker, adventurer. *Francis Scott Key*, (1779-1843), lawyer, wrote the words to 'The Star-Spangled Banner'. *Francisco de Goya*, (1746-1828), painter. *Francesco Borromini*, (1599-1667), Italian architect. Actor: *Franchot Tone*.

François. *French form of* Francis.

Frank // Frankie, Franky. *German:* "freeman, Frank". *Short form of* Francis. Friendly, slightly quiet, hard-worker, determined worker, strong, writer, publisher, public official, scientist, athlete, engineers. *Frank Harris*, (1856-1931), U.S. author and critic. *Frank Sargeson*, (1903-82), New Zealand author of novels, plays, short stories, and memoirs. *Frank Gilbreth*, (1868-1924), U.S. efficiency expert. *Frank Walker*, (1886-1959), U.S. lawyer and public official. *Frank Whittle*, (born 1907), British aeronautical engineer. *Frank Buck*, (1884-1950), U.S. wild animal entrepreneur, showman and author. *Frank Carlucci III*, (born 1930), U.S. diplomat and public official. *Frank Capra*, (1897-1991), U.S. motion-picture director and producer. *Frank Woolworth*, (1852-1919), U.S. merchant. *Frank Gifford*, (born 1930), U.S. football player. *Frank McNamara*, (1917-57), U.S. businessman, pioneered first universal credit card. *Frank Sinatra*, (1915-1998), superstar singer and actor. *L. Frank Baum*, (1856-1919), wrote 'The Wonderful Wizard of Oz' and other children's stories. *Frank Lloyd Wright*, (1867-1959), most influential architect of his time. Totals: authors 28%, publishers 7%, public official 15%, athletes 8%, engineers 7%, scientists 11%, Navel officer 3%, artists 3%, humorist 3%, businessman 3%, clergy 3%, educator 3%, aviator 3%. Actor: *Frank Whaley*.

Franklin // Francklin, Francklyn, Frank, Frankie, Franklyn, Franky. **Middle English:** "free landowner". Similar to Frank. *Franklin Pierce,* U.S. president, lawyer, shifting views. *Franklin D. Roosevelt*, 32nd U.S. president, deeply hated by many and strongly loved by the others. *Franklin Henry Giddings*, (1855-1931), U.S. sociologist. *Franklin MacVeagh*, (1837-1934), U.S. merchant and political leader. *Franklin Watkins*, (1894-1972), U.S. painter. *Franklin Lane*, (1864-1921), U.S. public official. *Franklin Musgrave*, (born 1935), physician, U.S. astronaut candidate.

Fred // Freddie, Freddy. *Short form of* names containing "fred" such as Frederick and Alfred. Bit adventurous, gregarious, relational, average student, catalystic, energetic, collaborative leader. *Fred Astaire*, (1899-1987), Hollywood dancing movie star. *Freddie Ray Marshall,* (born 1928), U.S. educator and public official. *Fred Zinnemann,* (born 1907), U.S. motion picture director. *Fred Kabotie,* (born 1900), American Indian artist and author. *Fred Lawrence Whipple*, (born 1906), U.S. astronomer. *Fred Biletnikoff*, (born 1943), U.S. football player. *Fred Allan Hartley, Jr.* (1903-69), U.S. congressman. *Fred W. Haise, Jr.* (born 1933), U.S. astronaut, test pilot. *Fred R.*

Harris, (born 1930), U.S. politician. *Fred Andrew Stone*, (1873-1959), U.S. actor, dancer. *Fred Waring*, (1900-84), U.S. bandleader. Actor: *Freddie Prinze Jr.*

Frederick // Frederico, Fred, Freddie, Freddy, Fredek, Frederic, Frederich, Frederico, Frederigo, Frederik, Fredric, Fredrick, Friedrich, Friedrick, Fritz, Ric, Rick, Rickie, Ricky. *Germanic:* "peaceful ruler". See both Fred and Rick. Many Northern European Kings by this name. *Frederick the Great*, (1712-86; ruled 1740-86), plunged Europe into war, rebel, genius soldier, wrote poetry and history, self-seeking. *Frederic Remington*, (1861-1909), painter and sculptor. *Frederick Douglass*, (1817-95), escaped slave, foremost black abolitionists and civil rights leaders. *Frederic Chopin*, (1810-49), musical genius composer. *Frederick William Steuben*, (1730-94), trained George Washington's recruits into well-trained army. Totals: general 19%, artist 11%, author 10%, clergy 8%, chemist 6%, statesman 6%, jurist 5%, educator 5%, historian 5%, designer 3%, manufacturer 3%, publisher 3%, composer 3%.

Freeman // Free, Freedman, Freeland, Freemon. *Old English:* "free man". *Freeman Dyson*, (born 1923), English-born theoretical physicist. *Freeman Fisher Gosden,* (1899-1982), U.S. radio and television writer and actor. *Freeman-Thomas,* first marquis of Willingdon, (1866-1941), British statesman, member of Parliament, governor-general of Canada, viceroy of India.

Fritz. *German Familiar form of* Friedrich and Frederick. Artist with music or brush or words, chemist. *Fritz Kreisler,* (1875-1962), acclaimed violinists. *Fritz Pregl*, (1869-1930), Austrian chemist. *Fritz Albert Lipmann,* (1899-1986), U.S. biochemist. *Fritz Eichenberg*, (born 1901), German artist and illustrator. *Fritz von Unruh*, (1885-1970), German novelist, playwright, and poet. *Fritz Strassmann,* (born 1902), German chemist. *Fritz Lang*, (1890-1976), Austrian film director. *Fritz Kredel,* (1900-73), U.S. artist and illustrator. *Fritz Reiner,* (1888-1963), U.S. musical conductor. *Fritz Reuter,* (1810-74), German novelist and poet. *Fritz Haber*, (1868-1934), German chemist.

Gabriel // Gabbie, Gabby, Gabe, Gabi, Gabie, Gabriele, Gabrieli, Gabriello, Gaby. **Hebrew:** "man of God, devoted to God". Biblical: an outstanding angelic messenger. Masculine, strong, relational, liked, easy-going, tough but not a tough-guy, writer, word-smith, egalitarian, leader, compliant, mother's favorite, much similar character with mother, self-loving, analytical mind, doesn't push his opinion, doesn't like to be ordered around, doesn't panic, patient, likes to collect art and antiques, may speak a foreign language, good family man, usually good intuition, successful. Like the angel, Gabriels are often word-smiths and messengers with the goal to benefit mankind, not the self-seeking typical of politician type. *Gabriel Garcia Marquez,* (born 1928), Colombian fiction author, screen-writer, journalist, publicist. *Gabriel Prosser,* (1775?-1800), U.S. slave insurrectionist. *Gabriel Richard*, (1767-1832),

French Roman Catholic missionary. *Gabriel Jonas Lippman*, (1845-1921), French physicist. *Gabriel Lalemant*, (1610-49), Jesuit missionary. *Gabriel Dumont*, (1838-1906), Canadian rebel. *Gabriel de Tarde*, (1843-1904), French sociologist. *Gabriele D'Annunzio*, (1863-1938), Italian novelist, dramatist, and poet. *Gabriel Duvall*, (1752-1844), U.S. jurist and statesman. *Gabriele Rossetti*, (1783-1854), Italian poet. *Gabriel Urbain Faure*, (1845-1924), French composer. *Gabriel Hanotaux*, (1853-1944), French political leader and historian. *Gabriel Harvey*, (1550?-1631), English poet. *Gabriel Marcel*, (1889-1973), French philosopher and playwrite. *Gabriel Metsu*, (1630-67), Dutch painter. Actor: *Gabriel Byrne, Gabriel Damon*.

Gage. *French:* "pledge".

Galen // Gaelan, Gale, Gayle. *Gaelic:* "intelligent". Galen, (129-199?), extreamly significant physician of the ancient world. *Gale Sayers*, (born 1943), U.S. football player.

Garrett // Gar, Garrard, Garret, Gareth, Garreth, Garrett, Gerrit, Garrot, Garrott, Jarret, Jarrett. *Old English:* "mighty spear". *Garrett Morgan*, (1875-1963), U.S. inventor. *Garret Augustus Hobart*, (1844-99), U.S. lawyer and Republican party leader. *Garret Johnson*, (fl. 1616), Dutch sculptor, tomb maker. Actors: *Garett Maggart, Garret Wang*.

Garth // Gar, Gareth. *Scandinavian:* "grounds keeper". Also see Garrett. Masculine, tough, easy-going, quite relational, helping, quick intellect, creative, artistic. *Garth Brooks*, (born 1962), U.S. country music singer and performer. *Garth Montgomery Williams*, (born 1912), U.S. illustrator, sculptor, cartoonist, and writer.

Gary // Gare, Garey, Garry. *Old English:* "spear-carrier".

Familiar form of Gerald. Quick intellect, determined, striving, easy-going relationally, problem solver, energetic, comedian, acting, public figure, give few problems to his parents, lots of friends at school, talented in many areas, draw well, builds things, play chess, very capable with mathematics and foreign languages, resembles mother, stubborn, his independent character doesn't prevent him form having a good marriage because he has good patients; jealous husband, his wife is usually emotional with a complicated character; gives the impression of calm and enjoying a steady rhythm of life; if he divorces - he don't usually remarry; wife is leader in his family; very hospitable, likes hosting noisy dinner groups, simple to communicate with; remain the same even as the big boss; kind, sometimes suffer from his benevolence and respon-siveness; many get married late. *Garry Kasparov*, (born 1963), Soviet chess champion, artistic style of play, outspoken, lost rematch to IBM Big Blue computer. *Garry B. Trudeau*, (born 1948), U.S. cartoonist and writer, "Doonesbury". *Gary S. Becker*, (born 1930), U.S. econo-mist. *Gary Hart*, (born 1936), U.S. senator. *Gary A. Filmon*, (born 1942), Canadian public official, premier of Manitoba. *Garry Shandling*, (born 1949), U.S. comedian and actor. *Garry Moore*, (born 1915), U.S. comedian, writer, and producer. *Gary Cooper*, (1901-61), U.S. motion-picture actor. *Gary Player*, (born 1935), South African golfer. *Garry Marshall*, (born 1934), U.S. producer, director, screenwriter, and actor. Actor: *Gary Busey, Gary Cole, Gary Oldman, Gary Sinise.*

Gavin // Gavino. *Welsh:* "white hawk". *Gavino Bosch*, (born 1909), Dominican political leader and writer.

Genaro. *Spanish*.

Gene. *Familiar form of* Eugene, see Eugene. Public performer, actor, works with his body. *Gene Autry*, (born 1907), U.S. musician, actor, and business executive. *Gene Wilder,* (originally Jerome Silberman) (born 1935), U.S. actor and screenwriter. *Gene Upshaw*, (born 1945), U.S. football player. *Gene Sarazen*, (born 1902), U.S. professional golfer. *Gene Krupa*, (1909-73), U.S. jazz drummer and bandleader. *Gene Tunney*, (formerly James Joseph Tunney) (1897-1978), U.S. boxer. Actor: *Gene Barry, Gene Hackman, Gene Kelly, Gene Tierney*. *Jeno Hubay*, (or Eugen Hubay) (1858-1937), Hungarian violinist and composer.

Geno // Jeno. *Italian form* of John.

Geoffrey // Geoff, Geoffry, Jeff, Jeffrey. *English form* of Godfrey and Jeffrey. See Jeffrey.

George // Egor, Georas, Geordie, Georg, Georges, Georgie, Georgy, Giorgio, Goran, Jorgan, Jorge. *Greek:* "farmer". Tend to be more practical, dealing with people on a practical even spiritual basis, more down to earth, hard steady working, intelligent, helping, lead from expertise or position; he attracts by his willingness and ability to listen, can keep secrets, eloquent speaking ability, always responsible toward his work, reserved to strangers, easy-going toward friends, kind, friendly, goal directed, a bit cunning, not confident with women, marriage is usually successful, can't stand people lying to him, even the lie of a sweet woman will bend him out of shape, after irritation - calms down quickly, optimistic, enjoys fun with groups, looks for wife who is fun, enthusiastic and ready partici-pant; doesn't try to be the family leader; doesn't hold grudges; those he doesn't like he makes gentle jokes about. *George Balanchine*, (1904-83), very influential ballet choreographer. *Georges Clemenceau*, (1841-1929), premier of France, credited with winning WW I. *George Washington*, general, first U.S. president, liberty, democracy. *George Westinghouse*, (1846-1914), inventor, industrialist. *George Eastman*, (1854-1932), inventor, founded Eastman Kodak Company, philanthropist. *George Armstrong Custer*, (1839-76), leader of "Custer's Last Stand", flamboyant glory seeker. *George Frideric Handel,* (1685-1759), composer, producer, director, wrote "Messiah". *George Washington Carver,* (1860-1943), agriculturist, painter, musician. *George M. Cohan*, (1878-1942), songwriter, actor, playwright, producer, "Yankee Doodle Dandy." *George Patton*, (1885-1945), general, foremost tank specialist of WW II. Totals: politician 23%, commanders 15%, writer 12%, artist 8%, scientist 8%, businessman 7%, clergy 5%, lawyer 5%, inventor 4%, explorer 4%, playwrite 4%, composer 3%, humorist 3%, philosopher 3%, athlete 3%, historian 3%, educator 3%, physician 3%. Actors: *George Burns, George Clooney, George Petrie, George Reeves, George Takei*.

Geovanni // Geovanny, Geovany. *Form of* Giovanni.

Gerald // Garald, Garold, Gary, Gearalt, Gearald, Gerald, Gerek, Gerick, Gerik, Gerold, Gerrard, Gerri, Gerrie, Gerry, Gierek, Giraldo, Giralt, Giraud, Jerald, Jerrie, Jerrold, Jerry. *Old German:* "spear dominion, spear-ruler". Easy going, relational. *Gerald R. Ford*, 38th U.S. president, politician. *Gerald Maurice Edelman*, (born 1929), U.S. molecular biologist. *Gerald McDermott,* (born 1941), U.S. artist, author and illustrator. *Gerald Augustine Regan*, (born 1929), Canadian political leader. *Gerald Emmett Carter*, (born 1912), Canadian Roman Catholic cardinal. *Gerald P. Carr*, (born 1933), U.S. astronaut, Marine Corps officer. *Jerry Voorhis*, (1901-84), U.S. representative. *Jerry L. Falwell*, (born 1933), U.S. clergyman and political lobbyist. *Jerry Lucas*, (born 1940), U.S. basketball player. *Jerry Herman*, (born 1933), U.S. composer-lyricist.

Gerard // Gearard, Gerardo, Géraud, Gerhard, Gerhardt, Gerrard, Gerri, Gerrie, Gerry, Gherardo. **German:** "strong with the spear" or **Old English:** "spearhard". *Gerhard Domagk*, (1895-1964), German physician and research chemist. *Gerard Manley Hopkins*, (1844-89), poet, priest. *Gerhard Herzberg*, (born 1904), Canadian chemist. *Gerard Peter Kuiper*, (1905-73), U.S. astronomer. *Gerardo Machado*, (1871-1939), president of Cuba. *Gerard Terborch*, (1617-81), famous Dutch painter. *Gerhard Scharnhorst*, (1755-1813), Prussian general. *Gerard Schwarz*, (born 1947), U.S. trumpeter and conductor. *Gerard Debreu*, (born 1921), U.S. economist. *Gerard Douw*, (1613-80), Dutch painter. *Gerard De Geer*, (1858-1943), Swedish geologist. *Gerard David*, (1460?-1523), Dutch painter. Actor: *Gerard Depardieu*.

Germain // Germaine, Germayne, Jermain, Jermaine, Jermayne. **Middle English:** "sprout, bud". *Germain Pilon*, (1535?-90), French sculptor.

Gevork // Gevorg.

Gideon. **Hebrew:** "destroyer, feller of trees". Biblical: religious reformer, judge, and warrior; deliverer of Israel from Midianites. Gentle, peaceable, firm willed, honorable,

composed, manly. *Gideon Welles*, (1802-78), U.S. statesman, great executive ability.

Gilbert // Bert, Bertie, Berty, Burt, Burtie, Burty, Gib, Gibb, Gibbie, Gibby, Gil, Gilberto, Gilburt, Gill, Giselbert, Guilbert, Wilbert, Wilbur, Wilburt, Will. **Old English:** "trusted" **German:** "illustrious through hostages". *Gilbert Stuart*, (1755-1828), brilliant portrait painter. *Gilbert Tennent*, (1703-64), U.S. Presbyterian clergyman. *Gilbert White*, (1720-93), English country parson and naturalist. *Gilbert Adrian*, (1903-59), U.S. dress designer. *Gilbert Newton Lewis*, (1875-1946), U.S. chemist. *Gilbert Arthur Highet*, (1906-78), U.S. classicist. *Gilbert Sheldon*, (1598-1677), archbishop of Canterbury. *Gilbert Cannan*, (1884-1955), British novelist and dramatist. *Gilbert Seldes*, (1893-1970), U.S. T.V. critic. *Gilbert Ryle*, (1900-76), British philosopher and editor. *Gilbert Hitchcock*, (1859-1934), U.S. newspaper publisher and political leader. *Gilbert Hovey Grosvenor*, (1875-1966), U.S. geographer. *Gilbert Minto*, (1845-1914), British statesman.

Giles // Gil, Gill, Gilles. **Greek:** "shield bearer". *Gil Vicente*, (1469?-1536?), dramatist and lyric poet. *Giles Fletcher*, (1588?-1623), English poet and clergyman. *Gil Evans*, (1912-88), U.S. jazz musician. *Giles Lytton Strachey*, (1880-1932), English essayist and biographer. *Saint Giles*, (died 712?), hermit and Benedictine abbot of France.

Gino. *Form of* Eugene. *Gino Marchetti*, (born 1927), U.S. football star.

Giovanni // Geovanni, Gian, Gianni, Giovani, Giovanny. *Italian form* of John. *Giovanni Bellini*, (1430?-1516), painter, founder of the Venetian school of painting.

Giovanni Boccaccio, (1313-75), great figure in Italian literature. *Giovanni Pierluigi da Palestrina*, (1525?-94), master of contrapuntal composition. Artists 62%, writers 26%, others 12%.

Glen // Glenden, Glendon, Glenn, Glyn, Glynn. *Gaelic:* "valley". Charismatic, warm and likable, energetic, often hobby is a physical sport which challenges his muscle strength, stamina and mental endurance, therefore physically strong. He gravitates to challenges and enjoys challenges in general. Expect him to enjoy coaching, teaching and managing. *Glenn T. Seaborg*, (born 1912), nuclear chemist. *Glenn Warner*, (1871-1954), U.S. football coach. *Glenn Miller*, (1909-44), U.S. bandleader. *Glenn Gould*, (1932-82), Canadian pianist. *Glenn Martin*, (1886-1955), U.S. airplane manufacturer. *Glenn Hammond Curtiss*, (1878-1930), U.S. pioneer aviator and inventor. Totals: musicians 33%, airplane manufacturer and pilot 33%, scientist 17%, coach 17%. Actor: *Glen Campbell, Glenn Ford.*

Gonzalo // Gonzales, Gonzo. *Spanish:* "wolf". *Gonzalo Pizarro*, (1506?-48), Spanish conquistador. *Gonzalo Jimenez de Quesada*, (1500?-79), Spanish explorer, founded Bogota.

Gordon // Gordan, Gorden, Gordie, Gordy. *Old English:* "hill of the plains". Wily, cunning, highly sociable, perceptive, figures out how things work, innovator; many good characteristics, positive attitude, bit shy, peaceful and compliant personality, optimist; may appear not confident since he doesn't seek the spotlight in fact his very active nature fills people with energy; he's a good speaker, sharp intellect, stable, patient, listens to other's opinions; talented, artistic, dancer, journalist, translators, medicine; lucky and reach secure position. *Gordon Craig*, (1872-1966), English actor, director-designer, producer and especially, theorist. *Gordon Parks*, (born 1912), U.S. photographer, writer, composer, motion-picture director. *Gordon Evans Dean*, (1905-58), U.S. lawyer and government official. *Gordon S. Seagrave*, (1897-1965), U.S. surgeon, author. *Gordon W. Allport*, (1897-1967), U.S. psychologist. *Gordon Bunshaft*, (1909-90), award winning U.S. architect. *Gordon McKay*, (1821-1903), U.S. inventor. *Gordon Gray*, (born 1909), U.S. lawyer, newspaper owner, public official. *Gordon Howe*, (Mr. Hockey) (born 1928), U.S. ice-hockey player.

Graham // Graehme, Graeme, Gram. *Old English:* "gray home". *Graham Greene,* (1904-91), extensive British author, novels, short stories, plays, some nonfiction. *Graham Hill*, (1929-75), British auto racing champion. *Graham Sutherland*, (1903-80), British artist. *Graham Taylor*, (1851-1938), U.S. clergyman, sociologist.

Grant // Grantham, Granthem, Grantley. *French:* "great". Handsome, medium to heavy, a bit reserved speaker, athletic, manly, easily liked. *Grant Wood,* (1892-1942), major Midwestern theme artist. *Grant Devine*, (born 1944), Canadian public official. *Grant Marsh*, (1834-1916), U.S. steamboat captain, pioneer pilot. Actor: *Grant Aleksander*.

Gregory // Graig, Greg, Gregg, Greggory, Grégoire, Gregoor, Gregor, Gregorio, Gregorius, Grieg, Grigori. *Greek:* "vigilant"; *Latin:* "watchman, watchful". Tend to be physical, often stocky, energetic, adventurous, individualist; as child, he tries to be obedient - but finds trouble anyway; very sensitive, cares about other's opinion of him; likes to be liked, may spend time to dress fashionably, gallant, usually good health; photo-journalist, engineer, journalist, driver; doesn't like to be ordered, loves sports; his wife doesn't have to have a prestigious position or be known for beauty, for him a wife should be good house-keeper and easy-going with him; he loves his wife but can't always resist an attractive woman, so his wife should be careful in picking their friends; good relationship with in-laws, children love him very much. *Greg Norman*, (born 1955), charismatic golf champion. *Greg Louganis*, (born 1960), U.S. diver, actor. *Gregory Hines*, (born 1946), U.S. improvisational tap dancer, choreographer, actor, and singer. *Greg LeMond*, (born 1961), U.S. cyclist, won Tour de France back to back. *Grigory Potemkin*, (1739-91), Very influential Russian army officer and statesman, ambitious, talented, detail-oriented administrator. *Gregor Mendel*, (1822-84), discovered the laws of heredity, geneticist, Austrian monk. *Gregory Peck*, (born 1916), 1962 best actor award; played likeable, honest men of measured speech with high moral qualities and honest strength. *Gregorio Sierra*, (1881-1947), Spanish writer of plays of delicacy. *Gregor Piatigorsky*, (1903-75), U.S. concert cellist and teacher of music. *Grigory V. Romanov*, (born 1923), Soviet official. *Grigory Zinoviev*, (1883-1936), Russian Bolshevik leader, active propagandist. Totals: individual sport athletes 24%, clergy 24%, actor 18%, politician 18%, medical researcher 12%, music 12%. Actors: *Greg Evigan, Greg Kinnear, Greg Kramer, Gregg Rainwater.*

Griffin // Griff, Griffie, Griffy. *Latin:* "griffin, a mythical beast". *Griffin Bell*, (born 1918), U.S. judge and public official.

Grover // Grove. *Old English:* "grove". *Grove Karl Gilbert,* (1843-1918), U.S. geologist. *Grover Cleveland*, (1837-1908), 22nd and 24th U.S. president. *Grover Cleveland Alexander*, (Pete) (1887-1950), U.S. baseball pitcher. *Grover Loening*, (1888-1976), U.S. aeronautical engineer.

Guadalupe. Refers to the Shrine of Our Lady of Guadalupe in Mexico City, most famous shrine in country, pilgrimages made to modern basilica.

Guillermo. *Spanish form* of William.

Gunther // Gun, Gunnar, Gunner, Guntar, Gunter. *Scandinavian:* "warrior, army". *Gunnar Karl Myrdal,* (1898-1987), Swedish economist, writer. *Gunnar Gunnarsson*, (1899-1975), Icelandic novelist. *Gunther Gebel-Williams*, wild animal trainer. *Gunther von Huenfeld*, first nonstop westbound flight over North Atlantic.

Gus. *Short form* of Gustave and Augustus. *Gus Savage*, (born 1925), U.S. politician, studied law, worked as journalist, editor-publisher, member U.S. House of Representatives (Democrat), involved in various black power organizations.

Gustave // Gus, Gustaf, Gustav, Gustavo, Gustavus. *Scandinavian:* "Goth's staff". *Gustave Flaubert*, (1821-80), French novelist. *Gustave Courbet*, (1819-77), French painter. *Gustave Dore*, (1832-83), French artist. *Gustav Mahler,* (1860-1911), Austrian symphonist. Totals: novelist 20%, composer 20%, physicists 20%, artist 13%, chemist 7%, engineer 7%.

Guy // Guido. *French:* "guide"; *Old German:* "warrior". Guy (English pronunciation). Like to learn and teach, often teachers, love mental challenges, enjoy being helpful, take relationship building seriously, more composed, formal, official, firm, stratigist, military, statesman. *Guy Johnson*, colonel, first superintendents of Indian affairs. *Guy Chamberlin*, (1894-1967), U.S. football end and coach. *Guy Burgess*, double agent for Soviet Union. *Guy Stanton Ford*, (1873-1962), U.S. historian, educator, editor. *Guy Carleton*, (1724-1808), British general, statesman, governor. *Guy Hunt*, (born 1933), U.S. public official, probate judge, governor of Alabama. *Guy Fawkes*, military man involved in rebellion. *Guy Palmer,* author "Hockey Drill Book." *Guy Albert Lombardo*, (1902-77), U.S. orchestra leader, noted for "sweet" music, national champion speedboat racer. Actors: *Guy Pearce, Guy Williams*.

Guy (French pronunciation) // Guido. *Guy de Maupassant*, (1850-93), great French short story master, special gift for dramatic swiftness and naturalness. *Guy de Chauliac*, (died 1380?), French surgeon. *Guy Pene Du Bois*, (1884-1958), U.S. artist and writer on art, landscape and figure compositions, advocate of realism, children's author and illustrator. *Guy Fourquin*, author of "Lordship and Feudalism in the Middle Ages." *Guido Reni*, (1575-1642), Italian painter. Guido of Arezzo, (995?-1050?), Benedictine monk, introduced modern music notation. *Guido di Pietro*, (1400?-1455), Italian painter, monk, moral virtues.

Hakim // Hakeem. *Arabic:* "ruler". *Al-Hakim bi-Amrih Allah*, the founder of the Druzes sect of Islam, sixth caliph of the Fatimid Dynasty in Egypt, ruled from 996 until 1021, persecutor of Jews, Christians, and Muslims.

Hamilton // Ham, Hamel, Hamil, Tony. *Old English:* "proud estate". Educator, editor, writer, scientist, public official. *Hamilton Fish*, (1808-93), U.S. secretary of state. *Hamilton Fish*, (1849-1936), U.S. public official. *Hamilton Fish,* (1888-1946), U.S. public official. *Hamilton Holt*, (1872-1951), U.S. editor and educator. *Hamilton Lamphere Smith,* (1818-1903), U.S. educator and scientist. *Hamilton O. Smith*, (born 1931), U.S. microbiologist. *Hamilton Wright Mabie,* (1845-1916), U.S. editor, critic, and essayist.

Hank. *Familiar form of* Henry. Team athlete, musician. *Hank Williams, Jr.* (Randall Hank Williams, Jr.) (born 1949), U.S. country musician. *Hank Williams*, (Hiram King Williams) (1923-53), U.S. singer and guitarist. *Hank Luisetti*, (Angelo Enrico Luisetti) (born 1916), U.S. college basketball player. *Hank Aaron*, (Henry Louis Aaron) (born 1934), U.S. baseball outfielder.

Hans. *Short form of* Johannes. *Scandinavian form* of John. *Hans Christian Andersen*, (1805-75), immortal fairy tale writer. *Hans Hofmann*, (1880-1966), German-born painter. *Hans Memling*, (1430?-94), master of Flemish painting. Totals: scientists 38%, writer 18%, artist 18%, musicians 12%, clergy 6%, statesman 6%, physician 3%, historian 3%, philosopher 3%.

Harley // Harleigh, Harlene, Harli, Harlie. *Old English:* "long field, army meadow". Honors the Harley-Davison motor cycle.

Harold // Araldo, Hal, Harald, Harry, Herald, Herold, Herrick. *Old English:* "army dominion"; *Scandinavian:* "army-ruler". Bold, confident, leader, manager, athletic, physical. *Hal Roach*, (Harold Eugene Roach) (1892-1992), Hollywood film producer and director, best known for comedies. *Harald I* (Harold the Fairhaired) (850-933), first king of united Norway; defeated rival earls and established strong kingdom. *Harold Macmillan*, (1894-1986), prime minister of Great Britain. *Harold Clayton Urey*, (1893-1981), U.S. chemist. *Harry S. Truman*, 33rd U.S. president. *Harold Pinter,* (born 1930), powerful playwright. *Harry Houdini,* (1874-1926), 20th century's most famous magician. *Harold Wilson*, (born 1916), Britain's 45th prime minister. *Harry Stack Sullivan*, (1892-1949), psychiatrist. *Harry Blackstone, Sr.* (1885-1965), American magician. *Harry Belafonte*, (born 1927), U.S. entertainer, 'Day-O'. *Harry Reasoner*, (1923-91), U.S. broadcast journalist. *Harold Lloyd*, (1894-1971), U.S. motion-picture actor. Totals: writers 22%, public officials 18%, commanders 7%, educators 7%, scientists 6%, lawyers 6%, baseball players 5%, comedian 4%, musician 4%, jurist 4%, magician 4%, psychologist 4%, explorer 4%, performer 4%, aviator 2%, cartoonist 2%, engineer 2%, yachtsman 2%, businessmen 2%, editors 2%.

Harrison // Harris. *Old English:* "son of Harry". Similar to Harold but more fiery. *Harrison Ford*, (born 1942), U.S.

actor. *Harrison H. Schmitt*, (born 1935), U.S. senator and former astronaut.

Harry. *Old English:* "Soldier". *Short form of* Harold, Henry and Harrison. Actors: *Harry Klynn, Harry Thomas*.

Harvey // Harv, Herve, Hervey. *Old German:* "army-warrior". *Harvey Firestone*, (1868-1938), Firestone tire manufacturer. *Harvey Williams Cushing*, (1869-1939), leading surgeon and physiologist. *Harvey Wiley,* (1844-1930), U.S. chemist. *Hervey Allen*, (1889-1949), U.S. writer. Actor: *Harvey Corman.*

Hayden. *Old English:* "guarded valley".

Haywood // Heywood. *Old English:* "hedged forest". *Heywood Broun*, (1888-1939), U.S. war correspondent, columnist, and labor leader.

Hector // Ettore. *Greek:* "steadfast, holding fast". *Hector,* legendary Trojan warrior hero. *Hector Berlioz*, (1803-69), French composer. *Hector Molina*, (born 1908), president of Dominican Republic. Actor: *Hector Elizondo*.

Helmut. *German:* "helmet courage". *Helmut Kohl,* (born 1930), West Germany's chancellor then head of reunited Germany, a prime force in bringing about the reunification of Germany. *Helmut Schmidt*, (born 1918), chancellor of West Germany, Social Democrat. *Helmut Richard Niebuhr,* (1894-1962), U.S. theologian and educator, authority on theological ethics and American church history, professor Yale Divinity School.

Henri. *French form* of Henry.

Henry // Enrico, Enrique, Hal, Hank, Harry, Heindrick, Heinrich, Heinrik, Hendrick, Hendrik, Henri, Henrik,

Henryk. *Old German:* "ruler of the home". Physical, athletic, strong, sportsman, friendly, leader, active, busy, stock broker. *Henry "Light-Horse Harry" Lee*, (1756-1818), brilliant and daring American Revolution officer. *Heinrich Heine*, (1797-1856), great German writer. *Henry H. Woodring*, (1890-1967), U.S. public official. *Henry (Harry Hotspur) Percy*, (1364-1403), English warden, soldier. *Hank (Henry) Aaron*, (born 1934), U.S. baseball outfielder. *Henry Louis Mencken*, (1880-1956), "Sage of Baltimore," newspaper columnist, essayist, witty, sarcastic. Totals: writer 22%, public officials 20%, scientist 14%, business-man 12%, commander 8%, clergy 8%, athlete 6%, explorer 6%, editor 6%, agriculture 6%, artist 4%, musician 4%, actor 4%. Actors: *Henry Fonda, Henry Winkler.*

Herbert // Bert, Ebert, Eberto, Harbert, Herb, Herbart, Herbie, Herby, Heriberto. *Old German:* "glorious soldier". Energetic, adventurer, a bit lacking in prudence, social liberal, forward, historian, public official, hard science, especially research science, engineer, social science. *Herbert Spencer,* (1820-1903), English philosopher, coined the phrase "survival of the fittest." *Herbert von Karajan*, (1908-89), major conductor. *Herbert Kitchener,* (1850-1916), British field marshal, secretary of state for war. *Herbert Hoover*, 31st U.S. president, engineer. Totals: public official 25%, scientist 25%, engineer 8%, educator 8%, musician 8%, author 8%, philosopher 6%, commander 6%.

Herman // Armand, Armando, Armin, Ermanno, Ermin, Harman, Harmon, Hermann, Hermie, Hermon, Hermy. *Latin:* "high ranking"; *Old German:* "warrior". *Herman Melville*, (1819-1891), novelist, sailor, beachcomber.

Hermann von Helmholtz, (1821-94), scientist, physiologist, optics, electrodynamics, mathematics, and meteorology. *Hermann Hesse*, (1877-1962), novelist, emphasis on self-realization, life's meaning, and Eastern mysticism. *Hermann Ebbinghaus*, (1850-1909), major advance in psychology. *Hermann Wilhelm Goering,* (1893-1946), German Nazi leader. Totals: scientists 50%, authors 32%, artists 9%, philosopher 9%, inventor 9%, statesman 5%, educator 5%.

Hernando // Hernan. *Spanish form* of Ferdinand. *Hernando De Soto*, (1500?-42), Spanish explorer. *Hernando Cortez*, (1485-1547), Spanish soldier, conqueror of Mexico.

Hershel // Hersch, Herschel, Hersh, Hirsch. *Hebrew:* "deer". *Herschel Johnson*, (1812-80), U.S. politician and jurist.

Hiram // Hi, Hy. *Hebrew:* "most noble". *Hiram Maxim,* (1869-1936), U.S. inventor. *Hiram Paulding*, (1797-1878), U.S. admiral. *Hiram Bingham*, (1875-1956), U.S. senator and explorer. *Hiram Powers*, (1805-73), U.S. sculptor. *Hiram L. Fong*, (born 1907), U.S. political leader and businessman. *Hiram*, king of Tyre about 1000 B.C. *Hiram Johnson*, (1866-1945), U.S. lawyer and political leader. *Hiram Revels,* (1822-1901), first black U.S. senator, clergy. *Hiram Maxim*, (1840-1916), British inventor.

Hollis // Holly. *Old English:* "holly trees". *Hollis L. Caswell,* (born 1901), U.S. educator. *Hollis Potter,* (1880-1964), U.S. physician and radiologist.

Homer // Homere, Homerus, Omero. *Greek:* "promise". Names honors renown ancient poet, *Homer*, @800 BC.

Artistic. *Homer Lea*, (1876-1912), U.S. soldier and author. *Homer Martin*, (1836-97), U.S. landscape painter. *Homer Watson*, (1855-1936), Canadian landscape painter. *Homer Davenport*, (1867-1912), U.S. caricaturist. *Homer Rodeheaver*, (1880-1955), U.S. music director, song writer. *Homer Cummings*, (1870-1956), U.S. lawyer and public official.

Horace // Horacio, Horatio, Horatius, Orazio. *Latin:* "keeper of the hours". Name honors: *Horace*, (65-8 BC), great lyric poet of Rome. *Horatio Nelson*, (1758-1805), England's great naval heroes. *Horace Greeley*, (1811-72), New York newspaper editor, advised "Go West, young man, go West!" *Horace Tabor*, (1830-99), silver baron, politician. *Horace Mann*, (1796-1859), "father of the American public school." Totals: authors 30%, politicians 19%, artists 15%, scientists 15%, lawyers 15%, inventor 11%, businessman 11%, commander 7%, jurist 7%.

Howard // Howey, Howie, Ward. *Old English:* "watch-man". Intelligent, idea originator, composed but busy, business minded. *Howard Hughes,* (1905-76), industrialist, aviator, and motion picture producer. *Howard Pyle*, (1853-1911), famous American illustrator and writer. *Howard Christy,* (1873-1952), U.S. painter and illustrator. *Howard M. Temin*, (born 1934), U.S. oncologist. *Howard Hawks*, (1896-1977), U.S. film director. *Howard Hanson*, (1896-1981), U.S. composer and conductor. Totals: writer 27%, public official 18%, director 18%, businessman 14%, artist 14%, inventor 14%, scientist 9%, explorer 9%, producer 9%.

Hubert // Bert, Bertie, Berty, Hobard, Hobart, Hubbard, Hube, Huberto, Hubey, Hubie, Hugh, Hugibert, Hugo,

Humberto, Ugo, Ulberto. *Old German:* "bright in spirit, bright mind". *Humberto Medeiros*, (1915-83), U.S. Roman Catholic prelate, *Cardinal. Hubert Walter,* (died 1205), English archbishop of Canterbury. *Hubert Humphrey*, (1911-78), U.S. political leader, pharmacist and political science teacher. *Saint Hubert*, (died 727), bishop. *Humberto de Alencar Castelo Branco*, (1900-67), Brazilian statesman, army officer, president. *Hubert Gough*, (1870-1963), British general. *Hubert Work*, (1860-1942), U.S. public official and doctor. Totals: clergy 43%, politician 43%, commander 29%, doctor/pharmacist 29%.

Hugh // Hewe, Huey, Hughie, Hugo, Hugues, Ugo. *Germanic:* "mind, spirit"; *Old English:* "intelligence". Also *Short form of* Hubert and Hewett. Intelligence, idea originator. *Hugh Latimer,* (1485?-1555), English priest and Protestant Reformer. *Saint Hugh,* (1024-1109), abbot, clergy reformer. *Hugh Hefner,* (born 1926), founder, editor and publisher of Playboy magazine. *Hugh Duffy,* (1866-1954), U.S. baseball outfielder. Totals: statesman 31%, clergy 14%, writer 14%, commander 14%, athlete 11%, scientist 11%, businessman 11%, jurist 7%, broadcaster 7%, religious reformer 7%, explorer 4%, artist 4%, economist 4%, lawyer 4%. Actors: *Hugh Grant, Hugh O'Brian, Hugh O'Connor.*

Hugo // Ugo. *Latin form* of Hugh. *Hugo Grotius*, (1583-1645), brilliant legal expert, statesman, diplomat, poet, historian, theologian, and dramatist. *Hugo Winckler,* (1863-1913), German Orientalist. *Hugo De Vries,* (1848-1935), Dutch botanist. *Hugo Munsterberg,* (1863-1916), U.S. psychologist. Totals: playwrite 23%, scientist 23%, statesman 15%, businessman 15%, composer 8%, artist

8%, writer 8%, jurist 8%, orientalist 8%.

Humbert // Humberto, Umberto. *German:* "brilliant strength". *Humberto de Alencar Castelo Branco*, (1900-67), Brazilian statesman, career army officer and president. *Humberto Sousa Medeiros,* (1915-83), U.S. Roman Catholic prelate. *Umberto I* (1844-1900), king of Italy, called Humbert the Good because of courage and generosity in plague and earthquake, inaugurated colonial expansion policy.

Humphrey // Humfrey, Humfrid, Humfried, Hunfredo, Onfre, Onfroi, Onofredo. *Old German:* "peaceful Hun". *Humphrey Bogart*, (1899-1957), U.S. motion- picture actor. *Humphrey Gilbert*, (1539?-83), English navigator.

Hunter. *English:* "hunter". *Hunter Liggett*, (1857-1935), U.S. Army officer and author, World War I commanded 1st Army, A.E.F.

Ian // Iain. *Scottish form* of John. *Ian Fleming,* (1908-64), British novelist, creator of James Bond. *Ian Smith*, (born 1919), first native-born prime minister of Southern Rhodesia. *Ian Hamilton*, (1853-1947), British general, author. *Iain Macleod,* (1913-70), British statesman. Actors: *Ian Mckellen, Ian Ziering.*

Ibrahim. *Form of* Abraham. *Ibrahim Pasha* (1789-1848),

Egyptian general and viceroy, commander in Greek war for independence.

Ignatius //, Iggie, Iggy, Ignace, Ignacio, Ignacius, Ignacy, Ignat, Ignaz, Ignazio, Igy, Inigo. *Latin:* "fiery, ardent". Teachers respect him for scholarly knowledge, peers dislike him for his greediness and desire to rule over everyone, capable in all areas, doesn't work with inspiration, only works between the bells, if possible - will pass his work to someone else, keeps pets, likes historical literature, very strict toward children, capable of abuse in the heat of passion, can be severe or harsh when jealous, not taking into account the circumstances; his stormy temperament and emotionalism sometimes turns to gloomy withdrawal, then he can continually nag over unimportant things; he falls in love easily, he controls his fiery side quickly to avoid complications in marriage; seldom divorces because he doesn't like big changes in his life; the leader of his family - he doesn't like his leadership challenged; has no problem with cooking or other domestic tasks for himself; likes to eat a lot. *Ignatius of Loyola,* (1491?-1556), Catholic saint, founder of the Jesuits like a military company to fight heresy, military man. *Ignacy Paderewski,* (1860-1941), popular, but unorthodox concert pianist, composer. *Inigo Jones*, (1573-1652), founder of English classical style of architecture. *Ignaz Semmelweis,* (1818-65), Hungarian physician, pioneer of modern medicine. *Saint Ignatius*, bishop of Antioch, Apostolic Father. Totals: clergy 25%, pianist 17%, composer 17%, painter 17%, writer 17%, statesman 17%, scientists (physician, chemist) 17%, architect 8%. Actor: *Ingo Rademacher.*

Igor. *Russian form* of Inger. Impromptu, energetic, strong determination, bold, businessman, strong leader, idea man, mathematics, stubborn, sportsman, scientist, many close friends, proud, both stepping on others and very friendly to achieve goals, sets his own course, may drop out of school, get and loose friends easily, strong desire of leadership, reach goals through thorough long-term planning, capable, some can become Olympic champions, resemble mother, personality from father, many become successful, good leader, always try to be the leader in marriage, opposing characteristic, adapts easily, makes friends quickly and drops friends suddenly, dreamer, jealous, engineer, lawyer, electrician, jurist, actor, driver, journalist, teacher, musician. *Igor Sikorsky*, (1889-1972), aeronautical engineer pioneered the development of the helicopter. *Igor Stravinsky*, (1882-1971), giant in 20th-century musical composition. *Igor Youskevitch*, (born 1912), U.S. dancer, athlete. *Igor Tamm*, (1895-1971), Soviet theoretical physicist.

Ingemar // Ingamar, Ingmar. *Scandinavian:* "famous son". *Ingmar Bergman*, (born 1918), world famous Swedish film director.

Inger // Igor, Ingar. Also see Igor and Ingemar. *Scandinavian:* "son's army".

Irving // Earvin, Erv, Ervin, Erwin, Irv, Irvin, Irvine, Irwin, Irwinn. *Gaelic:* "beautiful"; *Old English:* "sea friend". Deep thinker, strategist, tactician, scientist, manager, executive. *Irvin Cobb*, (1876-1944), U.S. short-story writer, humorist, and dramatist. *Erwin Schrodinger*, (1887-1961), Austrian theoretical physicist. *Erwin Rommel*, (1891-1944), German Field Marshal, tactician, called "Desert Fox."

Totals: scientists 42%, writer 25%, also commander, philosopher, inventor, producer.

Isaac // Ike, Ikey, Isaak, Isac, Isacco, Isak, Izaak, Izak. *Hebrew:* "he laughs." Biblical: Hebrew patriarch, son of Abraham, and father of Jacob and Esau. *Sir Isaac Newton*, (1642-1727), physicist, mathematician, chief figure of the scientific revolution, discovered the law of gravity. *Isaac Singer*, (1904-91), award winning Yiddish author. *Isaac Asimov*, (1920-92), celebrated author of more than 400 broad ranging books including science facts, science fiction, history and mysteries. Totals: writers 27%, statesman 23%, clergy 23%, commander 19%, educator 12%, scientist 8%, inventor 8%, lawyer 8%, musician 8%, businessman 8%, artist 4%.

Isaiah // Isa, Isai, Isaias, Isiah, Issiah. *Hebrew:* "God is my helper, salvation of God". *Isaiah* (8th century BC), one of greatest of Bible's Old Testament Hebrew prophets. *Isaiah Thomas,* (1749-1831), U.S. publisher. *Isiah Thomas*, (born 1961), U.S. basketball player.

Ishmael // Ishmail, Ishmeal, Ismael. *Hebrew:* "God will hear". *Ishmael*, son of Abraham and Hagar, Sarah's Egyptian handmaid, ancestor of Arabs.

Isidore // Dorian, Isidor, Isidoro, Isidro. *Greek:* "gift of Isis". *Isidor Isaac Rabi*, (1898-1988), award winning U.S. physicist. *Saint Isidore of Seville*, (560?-636), Spanish prelate and encyclopedist. *Isidore Konti,* (1862-1938), U.S. sculptor.

Israel. *Hebrew:* "wrestling with the Lord." Historical: the nation of Israel takes its name from that given to Jacob after he wrestled with an angel. Teacher type. *Israel*

Charles White, (1848-1927), U.S. geologist and teacher.
Israel Putnam, (1718-90), soldier hero of English-speaking colonial America, credited with order "Don't fire until you can see the whites of their eyes." *Israel Zangwill*, (1864-1926), British novelist, dramatist, leader in Zionist movement. *Israel Gollancz*, (1864-1930), British scholar.

Ivan. *Russian form* of John. Also see Ivar. As a child tends to the extremes of obedience or wild, emotional, both tender and angry outrages, goal driven, may abandon goal at its threshold, can be anything because of his internal contradictions, loves family tradition, perhaps tumultuous for wife, diplomatic but stubborn, values marriage but not fidelity, not jealous but may react unpredictably when he sees man's attention for his wife; likes manly work around home, loved by children, often marries twice, likes family gatherings, not greedy, open and responsive personality. *Ivan Turgenev*, (1818-83), one of the great novelists of the world. *Ivan Pavlov*, (1849-1936), brilliant physiologist and a skillful surgeon, known for conditioned reflex. Totals: authors 38%, artists 15%, phisiologist, banker, athlete, engineer, politician, commander, also six Russian rulers.

Ivar // Ive, Iver, Ivor, Yvon, Yvor. Also see Ivan. *Ivar Giaever*, (born 1929), U.S. physicist. *Ivar Kreuger*, (1880-1932), Swedish "match king" businessman and financial wizard. Often the letter Y is used instead of the letter J in many languages as the English letter J did not exist before the middle ages and is currently not used in many languages. Following this tradition, some parents, especially imagrants, choose to use the letter Y in the spelling of many names which Americans and English usually start with the letter J. Yasmin-Jasmine is a prime

example of this practice, but most any letter J in a name may be found with a Y substituting for it.

Jack // Jac, Jackie, Jackson, Jacky, Jock, Jocko. *Familiar form of* Jacob and John. For many, Jack is a nickname, making research difficult. A bit quiet and contemplative, "one of the boys", leader, often co-leader, business owner. *Jackie Robinson*, (1919-72), first black player in major league baseball. *Jackie Gleason*, (originally Herbert John Gleason) (1916-87), U.S. comedian, musician, and television producer. *Jack Dempsey*, (1895-1983), prize fighter. *Jack Nicklaus*, (born 1940), professional golfer. *Jack Benny*, (Benjamin Kubelsky) (1894-1974), comedian. *Jack London*, (John Griffith London) (1876-1916), novelist and short-story writer, wrote "Call of the Wild." *Jack Kerouac*, (Jean-Louis Kerouac) (1922-69), writer and spokesman for the "beat generation." *Jack Johnson*, (John Arthur Johnson) (1878-1946), black prize fighter. Totals: athletes 32%, leader 12%, artists 8%, authors 8%, businessman, musician, actor, producer, killer, astronaut, naturalist. Actors: *Jack Wild, Jackie Chan*.

Jacob // Cob, Cobb, Cobbie, Cobby, Giacobi, Giacomo, Giacopo, Hamish, Iago, Jack, Jackie, Jaky, Jacobo, Jacques, Jaime, Jake, Jakie, Jakob, James, Jamesy, Jamey, Jamie, Jay, Jayme, Jim, Jimmie, Jimmy, Seamus, Seumas, Shamus,

Yakov, Yasha. **Hebrew:** "supplanter". Biblical: _Jacob,_ grandson of Abraham, son of Isaac, brother of Esau. Practical, calculating, adjusts to new people and situations with difficulty; always prefers old friends; very respectful toward his father and remains attached to his father for life; hard working; talented in business; gets along with people; knows how to soften and resolve conflicts; picks a wife who is capable, intelligent and likes being at home; repulsed by women acting authoritatively; diplomatic and avoids offense to women; will try to convince his wife on important matters, but will not stress each other on the unimportant; stays connected with his friends; always ready to help his friends; friends like to visit his home; spends a lot of time with his children; likes to take his family on vacations; difficult for him to say no to people; may be seduced away by another woman. _Jakob Steiner,_ (1796-1863), Swiss mathematician, geometry. _Jacob Epstein,_ (1880-1959), sculptor. _Jacob S. Coxey,_ (1854-1951), businessman, mayor, pushed federal public works program. Totals: writers 24%, statesman 21%, artist 17%, humanitarian 17%, lawyer 14%, businessman 10%, commander 10%, scientist 7%, clergy 7%, commander 7%, humorist, teacher, explorer, inventor.

Jacques. _French form_ of Jacob and James. _Jacques Lipchitz,_ (1891-1973), Cubism sculptor. _Jacques Marquette,_ (1637-75), Jesuit priest, teacher, missionary, explorer, thoughtful and gentle. _Jacques-Yves Cousteau,_ (born 1910), French ocean explorer and pioneer in underwater research, invented scuba. _Jacques Cartier,_ (1491-1557), French explorer, discovered the St. Lawrence River. _Jacques Turgot,_ (1727-81), French economist, shy, serious, minister of finance, great statesman, but lacked rsuasiveness. Totals: statesman 21%, explorer 14%, scientist 14%, artist 10%, clergy 10%, writer 10%, soldier 7%, teacher 7%, historian 7%, inventor 7%, composer 7%, also dancer, musician, philosopher, screenwriter, athlete, financier, atheist.

Jaime // Jayme, Jaymie. _Spanish form_ of James.

Jair // Jairo. **Spanish:** "God teaches".

Jake. _Short form of_ Jacob.

Jalen // Jallon. Geographical: mountains in Mali.

Jamal // Jamaal, Jamil, Jammal. **Arabic:** "beauty". Also a form of Gamal.

James // Diego, Giacomo, Hamish, Iago, Jacques, Jaime, Jameson, Jamesy, Jamey, Jamie, Jamison, Jay, Jayme, Jim, Jimmie, Jimmy, Seamus, Seumas, Shamus. Historical: equated with Jacob (i.e. re-translated as James, the leader of the Twelve Apostles) as concession by King James' translators while making first English Bible translation. Hard working, personal goal focused, fun-loving, playful, zany, optimistic, can set goal many years away and plow to its finish, statesman, writer, businessman, technician, doctor, pastor. This has historically been a very popular name. _James Dean,_ (1931-55), celebrated actor. _James K. Polk,_ (1795-1849), 11th U.S. President. _James Monroe,_ (1758-1831) 5th U.S. President, brave soldier. _James Fenimore Cooper,_ (1789-1851), first U.S. novelist to reach worldwide fame. _James Cook,_ (1728-79), English navigator, explorer, ship Captain. Totals: statesman 28%, writer 24%, businessman 15%, soldier 11%, scientist 9%, lawyer 8%, head of state 6%, educator 6%, actor 5%, inventor 5%, artist 5%, civil rights activist 4%, engineer 4%, jurist 4%, humorist 3%, explorer 3%, psychologist 3%, historian 2%, clergy 2%, physician 2%, musician 2%, athlete 2%, theives 2%, also several kings, astronaut/test-pilot, architect, philosopher. Actors: *James Cromwell, James Dean, James Doohan, James Duval, James Earl Jones, James Hong, James Marshall, James Remar.*

Jamie // Jaime, Jaimie, Jayme. *Familiar form of* James. Actor: *Jamie Kennedy, Jamie Luner.*

Jamil // Jamill. *Arabic:* "handsome".

Jan // Janek, Janos. *Dutch and German form* of John. *Jan Vermeer,* (1632-75), great 17th-century Dutch painter. *Jan Hus,* (1369?-1415), Bohemian Christian martyr, founded the Moravian church. *Jan van Eyck,* (1390?-1441), Flemish painter. *Jan Smuts,* (1870-1950), British statesman, prime minister of South Africa. Totals: painter 23%, statesman 18%, scientist 18%, singer 9%, musician 9%, writer 9%, also clergy, soldier, actor, inventor, athlete, businessman. Actor: *Jan-Michael Vincent.*

Jared // Jarad, Jarid, Jarrad, Jarred, Jarrett, Jarrid, Jarrod, Jerad. *Hebrew:* "descent, one who rules". *Jared Sparks,* (1789-1866), U.S. educator, clergyman (Unitarian), and historian. *Jared Eliot,* (1685-1763), U.S. clergyman and physician, wrote first U.S. work on agriculture. *Jared Ingersoll,* (1749-1822), U.S. jurist and public official, signed United States Constitution for Pennsylvania. *Jared Ingersoll,* (1722-81), British colonial official of Tory sympathies. Actor: *Jared Leto.*

Jarrett // Jarret. *Form of* Garrett.

Jarvis // Jervis. *Old German:* "keen with a spear".

Jason // Jase, Jasen, Jasun, Jay, Jayson. *Greek:* "healer". Greek legend: Jason and his band of Argonauts sailed to find the Golden Fleece. Leader or one of leaders, respected by peers, alternatively sedate/serene and energized/determined. *Jason Robards, Jr.* (born 1922), U.S. actor. *Jason Lee,* (1803-45), U.S. Methodist missionary and Oregon pioneer. *Jason Mizell,* deejay (Jam Master Jay) of rap group RUN-D.M.C. Actors: *Jason Brooks, Jason Marsden, Jason Patric, Jason Weaver.*

Jasper. *English form* of Casper. *Jasper Johns,* (born 1930), U.S. painter.

Javier // Xavier. *Spanish:* "new house owner". *Javier Perez de Cuellar,* (born 1920), Peruvian diplomat to the UN.

Jay // Jae, Jaye, Jayson. *Old French:* "blue jay". *Familiar form of* Jacob, James and Jason. Serene, contemplative, focused, determined, "easy-going", better position goal directed. *Jay Gould,* (1836-92), a most shrewd and successful "robber baron" capitalists. *Jay Leno,* (James Douglas Muir Leno) (born 1950), U.S. comic. *Jay Cooke,* (1821-1905), U.S. investment banker and financier. *Jay Hanna (Dizzy) Dean,* (1911-74), U.S. baseball pitcher. *Jay Norwood Darling,* (pseudonym Ding) (1876-1962), U.S. political cartoonist. *Jay Macpherson,* (born 1931), Canadian poet. Actor: *Jay Mohr.*

Jaylen // Jaylenn. Combination of Jay + Len.

Jean. *French form* of John. Artistic, creative, writer. *Jean de La Fontaine,* (1621-95), one of the world's favorite storytellers. *Jean Lafitte,* (1780?-1826?), pirate and patriot.

Jean Racine, (1639-99), perhaps Frence's greatest dramatic poet. _Jean Jaures_, (1859-1914), French socialist movement leader, great scholar, brilliant orator, and adept political organizer. Totals: artist 30%, writer especially novels and plays 24%, statesman 17%, clergy 10%, scientist 10%, historian 5%, composer 4%, singer 4%, lawyer 4%, pioneer 2%, businessman 2%, explorer 2%, philosopher 2%, inventor 2%, architect 2%, soldier 2%, navigator 2%, also pirate, socialist, movie director, jurist, banker. Actor: _Jean Reno, Jean-Hugues Anglade._

Jed // Jedd, Jeddy. _Short form of_ Jedediah.

Jedediah // Jed, Jedd, Jeddy, Jedidiah. _Hebrew:_ "beloved of the Lord." _Jedediah Smith_, (1798-1831), U.S. trader, explorer. _Jedediah Strutt_, (1726-97), English cotton spinner, invented a machine that revolutionized knitting.

Jeffrey // Geoff, Geoffrey, Jeff, Jefferey, Jeffery, Jeffie, Jeffy, Jeffry. _Old French:_ "heavenly peace." _Form of_ Geoffrey. Bold attitude, confident toward others, full of energy, excitement, game player, relational, fun seeking. _Geoffrey De Havilland_, (1882-1965), British airplane designer and manufacturer. _Geoffrey Palmer,_ (born 1942), New Zealand prime minister, professor of law. _Geoffrey Chaucer,_ called the Father of the English Language, one of the three or four greatest English poets, wrote "Canterbury Tales." Totals: writer 33%, designer 25%, scientist 17%, clergy 17%, also soldier, actor, dancer, director, artist, historian, businessman, politician. Actors: _Jeff Bridges, Jeff Goldblum, Jeffrey Hunter._

Jehoiakim // Akim, Jehoiachim, Jehoiachin, Joachim, Joaquim, Yehoyakem. _Hebrew:_ "God will establish".

Jehoiakim, son of King Josiah and king of Judah (reigned 609?-598 BC), died during revolt, replaced by his son Jehoiachin who was forced to surrender and taken prisoner to Babylon. _Joachim von Ribbentrop_, (1893-1946), German foreign minister hanged for war crimes. _Joachim Murat_, (1767-1815), French Revolutionary cavalry leader and marshal of the empire, declared war on Austria but was defeated, court-martialed and shot. _Joaquin Murieta_, (1830?-53?), Mexican immigrant, outlaw and bandit in California, shot and beheaded. _Joaquin Turina_, (1882-1949), Spanish composer.

Jelani, Jelany. _Swahili:_ "mighty".

Jeremiah // Jeramey, Jeramie, Jere, Jereme, Jeremias, Jeremie, Jeremy, Jeromy, Jerry. _Hebrew:_ "appointed by God, God exalts". Biblical: _Jeremiah_, a great Hebrew prophet. Thinker, free-thinker, creative, philosopher, clergy, economist, linguist, traveler, folklorist, statesman, soldier, scientist, surveyor, silversmith, engraver. _Jeremy Bentham_, (1748-1832), explaining his ideas of the useful and the good, became the first "utilitarian." _Jeremy Collier,_ (1650-1726), English clergyman and pamphleteer. _Jeremiah Jenks_, (1856-1929), U.S. economist and educator. _Jeremiah Black_, (1810-83), U.S. public official. _Jeremiah Curtin_, (1840?-1906), U.S. linguist and world-traveling folklorist. Actors: _Jeremy, Irons, Jeremy London, Jeremy Northam, Jeremy Piven._

Jermaine // Germane, Jermain, Jerman, Jermanie. _Form of_ Germain. _Middle French:_ "having the same parent".

Jerome // Gerome, Gerrie, Gerry, Jere, Jereme, Jerrome, Jerry. _Greek:_ "bearing a holy name". _Jerome Kern_, (1885-

1945), U.S. composer, wrote the musical comedy 'Show Boat'. *Jerome Klapka*, (1859-1927), British humorist and dramatist. Scientists 37%, also humorist, dramatist, engineer, dancer, artist, clergy, singer, composer.

Jerry // Jere, Jerri. *Short form of* Gerald or Jeremiah or Jeremy or Jerome. Helpful, friendly, energetic, hard working, studious, recreational reader, often athletic. *Jerry Voorhis*, (1901-84), U.S. representative. *Jerry L. Falwell*, (born 1933), U.S. clergyman and political lobbyist. *Jerry Lucas*, (born 1940), U.S. basketball player. *Jerry Herman*, (born 1933), U.S. composer-lyricist, 'Mame'. Actors: *Jerry Doyle, Jerry Orbach, Jerry Seinfeld.*

Jesse // Jess, Jessee, Jessey, Jessi, Jessie, Jessy. **Hebrew:** "God exists". Biblical: *Jesse*, the father of King David. Marries young. *Jesse Jackson*, (born 1941), best-known living U.S. black American leader. *Jesse James*, (1847-82), U.S. wild West outlaw. *Jesse Owens*, (1913-80), black American who won four gold medals at the 1936 Olympic Games in Nazi Germany. Totals: athlete 20%, politician 13%, physician 13%, public official 13%, also outlaw, businessman, writer, scientist, director, clergy, soldier.

Jesus // Eesus, Iesus, Isuse. *Greek form of Hebrew* name, Yeshua, or the English name Joshua. Means "God saves." Biblical: *Jesus of Nazareth*, founder of Christianity, son of Mary and Joseph, also called The Son of God, Christ, Messiah and Savior.

Jethro // Jeth. **Hebrew:** "pre-eminence". Biblical: the father-in-law of Moses. *Jethro Tull*, (1674-1741), English farmer and writer. *Jethro Wood*, (1774-1834), U.S. inventor, invented a cast iron plow.

Jim // Jimmie, Jimmy. *Short form of* James. *Jim Henson*, (1936-90), created puppets called the Muppets for TV and movies, Sesame Street and The Muppet Show. *Jim Thorpe*, (1886-1953), unprecedented win of gold medals in both the pentathlon and the decathlon in 1912 Olympics, among U.S. histories greatest athletes, especially in football and baseball, predominantly American Indian. *Jimmy Carter*, (born 1924), 39th U.S. President, labeled as incompetent. *Diamond Jim Brady*, (1856-1917), great railroad businessman, flashy dresser, and lavish entertainer. *Jim Bridger*, (1804-81), U.S. frontiersman, fur trader, businessman, guide. Totals: athlete 38%, businessman 19%, statesman 13%, also puppeteer, frontiersman, aviator, commander, comedian, evangelist, broadcaster, race-car driver, musician. Actors: *Jim Byrnes, Jim Carrey, Jimmy Smits, Jimmy Stewart.*

Jin. *Arabic:* "Genie".

Joaquin. *Spanish form* of Jehoiakim.

Job. **Hebrew:** "the afflicted". Biblical: a righteous man who is tested and endures all afflictions. Physical, strong, friendly, athletic, sensitive to others. *Job Charnock*, (died 1693), English traveler, went to India, founded Calcutta.

Jock // Jocko. *Familiar form of* Jacob and John. *John Hay (Jock) Whitney*, (1904-82), U.S. financier, diplomat, and sportsman. *John Bertrand (Jocko) Conlan*, (1899-1989), U.S. baseball umpire.

Jody // Jodi, Jodie. *Familiar form of* Joseph.

Joe // Joey. *Short form of* Joseph. Humorous, humor is his hobby, perceptive, fun-loving, friendly, out-going, very relational, sport fan. Joeys seem less confident. *Joe Louis*, (1914-81), long-time world heavyweight boxing champion, the "Brown Bomber." *Joe Clark*, (born 1939), Canada's youngest prime minister. *Joe Namath*, (born 1943), best passing football quarterback. Totals: athlete 64%, politician 27%, pilot/astronaut. Actors: *Joe Bob Briggs, Joe Lando, Joe Lara, Joe Pesci, Joey Lawrence.*

Joel. *Hebrew:* "Jehovah is the Lord". Biblical: *Joel* (5th century BC), Hebrew minor prophet. Friendly, easy-going, quiet, handsome, follower, writer, negotiator, politician, cares about people. *Joel Chandler Harris*, (1848-1908), folklore writer of Uncle Remus stories about Brer Rabbit. *Joel Palmer*, (1810-81), U.S. pioneer, politician and author. *Joel Barlow*, (1754-1812), U.S. poet, political leader, chaplain. *Joel Poinsett*, (1779-1851), U.S. statesman, amateur botanist, poinsetta plant.

Joey. *Familiar form of* Joe and Joseph.

John // Evan, Ewan, Ewen, Gian, Giavani, Giovanni, Hanan, Hans, Iain, Ian, Jack, Jackie, Jacky, Jan, Janos, Jean, Jens, Jock, Jocko, Johan, Johann, Johannes, Johnnie, Johnny, Johny, Jon, Jone, Juan, Owen, Sean, Shaughn, Shaun, Shawn, Zane, Yon, Yonne, Yonni. *Hebrew:* "God is gracious". Biblical: name honors *John the Baptist* and *Saint John the Disciple/Evangelist*. Historically a very popular name. Charismatic, open nature, not suspicious toward people, likable, easy to get to know, doesn't have high expectation of others; logical mind; able to set goals far in advance; slightly extreme, stubborn, fervent beliefs, takes failures with optimism, hard working, leader of movements or teams, strong opinion of right and wrong, sees things in black and white, religious in beliefs,

interested in people, but more interested in ideal, egotist, orator, "mouth," critic, straight forward, direct; often marries more than once; reformer, activist, novelist, ideological writer. Possibly marries: Dawn, etc. *King John of England*, (1167-1216), vicious, shameless, and ungrateful, worst king of England. *John Milton*, (1608-74), the second greatest English poet, powerful arguments on divorce and freedom of the press, puritan. *John Locke*, (1632-1704), great English philosopher. *John F. Kennedy*, (1917-63), 35th U.S. President. *John Philip Sousa*, (1854-1932), best-known name in U.S. band music, stirring marches. *John Calvin*, (1509-64), the second of the great 16th-century reformers. *John Bunyan*, (1628-88), great English literary genius, puritan. *John Brown*, (1800-59), staunch abolitionist, martyr, regarded himself as an instrument of God, convinced slavery was a sin against Christianity. Totals: writer 30%, politician 25%, noted as religious 10%, scientist 9%, reformer 8%, businessman 8%, commander 8%, clergy 7%, adventurer 6%, painter 6%, explorer 6%, lawyer 6%, musician 2%, cartoonist 2%, naturalist 2%, philosopher 2%, economist 2%, engineer 2%, educator 2%, inventor 2%, patriot 2%, heroes, doctors, actors, athletes, public official, sportsman, test-pilot/astronaut, coach, singer. Also several popes and kings. Actors: *John Aniston, John Barrymore, John Belushi, John Candy, John Cusack, John de Lancie, John Denver, John Eldredge, John Gegenhuber, John Goodman, John Leguizamo, John Lithgow, John Malkovich, John Phillip Law, John Schneider, John Travolta, John Wayne, John Wesley Shipp, Johnny Crawford, Johnny Carson, Johnny Depp, Johnny Yong Bosch.*

Jon. *Form of* John and short for Jonathan. Actors: *Jon Bon Jovi, Jon Lovitz, Jon Tenney, Jon-Erik Hexum.*

Jonah. *Hebrew:* "dove." Biblical: the prophet who was swallowed by a great fish.

Jonas. *Hebrew:* "doer." *Jonas Salk*, (born 1914), developed poliomyelitis vaccine. *Jonas Lie*, (1833-1908), Norwegian novelist. *Jonas Chickering*, (1797-1853), U.S. piano manufacturer.

Jonathan // John, Johnathan, Johnathon, Jon, Jonathon, Yanaton. *Hebrew:* "God has given". Biblical: the friend of David. Also see John. Handsome, pushes his ideas with speaking and writing with his generally gentle but determined manner, can be a little dogmatic but not know as such, easy-going sometimes to a fault, modest, likable, friendly, relational, not intimidating, annoyed by pompous - grandiose types which he avoids, likewise he doesn't practice pompous or grandiose behavior, may be thought of as an "every-man". *Jonathan Swift*, (1667-1745), author, satirist, wrote 'Gulliver's Travels'. *Jonathan Edwards*, (1703-58), able and eloquent spokesman for conservative Christians, articulate defender, brilliant theological mind. Totals: author 33%, politician 25%, commander 17%, criminal 17%, clergy, jurist, explorer, ornithologist. Actors: *Jonathan Brandis, Jonathan Del Arco, Jonathan Silverman, Jonthan Angel, Jonathan Winters* (comedian).

Jordan // Giordano, Jordon, Jory, Jourdain. *Hebrew:* "descending". Geographical: refers to the river in the Middle East. *Giordano Bruno*, (1548-1600), Italian philosopher, astronomer, and mathematician.

José // Joseito, Pepe, Pepillo, Pepito. *Spanish form of*

Joseph. *Jose Rizal*, (1861-96), Filipino hero and a foremost Philippine author, devoted to freeing Philippines from Spanish colonial rule. *Jose Clemente Orozco*, (1883-1949), most eminent Mexican painter. *Jose Andrada e Silva*, (1763-1838), father of Brazilian independence, statesman, geologist and natural scientist of international repute. *Jose Gervasio Artigas*, (1764-1850), father of Uruguayan independence from Spain. Totals: writer 35%, statesman 29%, revolutionary patriot 24%, commander 15%, artist 9%, scientist 9%, musician 6%, clergy 6%, dancer 6%, philosopher, educator, chess champion, architect.

Joseph // Iosef, Iosif, Iosep, Jo, Joe, Joey, José, Jozef, Yosef. *Hebrew:* "he shall add". Biblical: *Joseph*, Hebrew patriarch, son of Jacob and Rachel, father of Ephraim and Manasseh, Egyptian ruler. Also the step-father of Jesus. Also see Joe. Often an opportunist, strong orator, writer, charismatic, politician, scientist, often liberal as a religious leader or politician, people person, good looking, amiable, compliant, kind, warm hearted, responsive to the needs of others, good husband, good father, several children whom he takes care of for life, many have poor first marriage, first wife often has poor character, second marriage is usually successful, often artistic, salesman. *Joseph Smith*, (1805-44), founder the Mormon church. *Joseph Haydn*, (1732-1809), father of the symphony and string quartet, founded the Viennese classical school with his friend Mozart, and his pupil Beethoven. *Joseph Pulitzer*, (1847-1911), publisher, used every tactic, including sensational yellow journalism to sell newspapers. *Joseph Stalin*, (1879-1953), Soviet Union dictator, among the most ruthless dictators of modern times. *Joseph Swan*, (1828-1914), English physicist and chemist, produced an early electric light bulb and invented the dry photographic plate. Totals: writer 26% often novelist, politician 24%, scientist 23%, religious leader 10% often liberal and political, commander 7%, musician (composer) 5%, businessman 5% probably higher, jurist 5%, lawyer 5%, explorer 5%, artist 5%, physicain 5%, athlete 4%, despot 4%, philosopher 2%, also producer, publisher, social worker, clown, engineer, actor, inventor, test pilot, astronaut. Actors: *Joseph Cotton, Joseph Mascolo, Joseph Perrino.*

Josh. *Short form of* Joshua. Also see Joshua. Athletic, strong, handsome, easy-going, respected, confident. *Josh Gibson*, (1911-47), U.S. baseball catcher. Actor: *Josh Brolin.*

Joshua // Josh, Joshia, Joshuah, Josue. *Hebrew:* "God saves". Biblical: *Joshua*, a confident warrior who led the Israelites campaign entering the Promised Land. Also see Josh. *Joshua Reynolds*, (1723-92), England most successful portrait painter of his day and a distinguished member of London's intellectual society. *Joshua Nkomo*, (born 1917), prominent revolutionary in overthrow of Rhodesia's white government, became Zimbabwe. Totals: politician 33%, also painter, singer, actor, producer, director, architect, clergy, writer, scientist, lawyer, judge. Actor: *Joshua Jackson.*

Josiah // Josias. *Hebrew:* "Jehovah supports". It is interesting that 3 of 13 famous worked with clays. *Josiah Wedgwood*, (1730-95), English ceramics maker, businessman. *Josiah Spode*, (1754-1827), English potter. *Josiah Whitney,* (1819-96), U.S. geologist. Totals: scientist 23%, potter 15%, politician 15%, commander 15%, clergy 15%, educator 15%, author 15%, philosopher.

Jovan // Jovani, Jovanni, Jovanny, Jovany, Jove, Jovial. *Latin:* "like the god Jove (also called Jupiter and Zeus)"; English: "marked by good humor". *Jovan Jovanovic*, (1833-1904), Serbian poet and journalist.

Joyce. *Latin:* "joyous". *Joyce C. Hall,* (1891-1982), U.S. businessman, cofounder and CEO of Hallmark Cards, Inc.

Juan. *Spanish form* of John. Adventurer, leader, emotional. *Juan Jimenez*, (1881-1958), Spanish-language poet. *Juan Ponce de Leon,* (1460-1521), Spanish soldier and explorer, searched for the fabled Fountain of Youth. *Juan Peron*, (1895-1974), charismatic Argentina politician, married 'Evita' (Eva Duarte). *Juan de Onate*, (1550?-1624?), Spanish explorer, founded the colony of New Mexico, convicted of brutality. Totals: explorer 41%, politician 22%, poet 7%, writer 7%, artist 7%, architect 7%, missionary 7%, clergy 7%, brutal 7%, inventor, auto racer.

Judah // Jud, Judas, Judd, Jude. *Hebrew:* "praised". Biblical: *Judah*, patriarch, 4th son of Jacob, lion hearted. *Judah Benjamin*, (1811-84), U.S. lawyer, politician. *Judah Gordon*, (1830-92), Russian writer. *Judd Gregg*, (born 1947), U.S. politician.

Jules // Jule. *French form* of Julius. Artistic, creative, orator. *Jules Verne*, (1828-1905), renoun early science-fiction science-adventure writer. *Jules Michelet*, (1798-1874), writer, historian. *Jules Mazarin*, (1602-61), brilliant diplomat, Catholic cardinal. *Jules Feiffer,* (born 1929), satirical cartoonist and writer. Totals: artist 30%, writer 30%, politician 22%, composer, architect, explorer, scientist.

Julian. *Latin:* "sprung from or belonging to Julius". Handsome. *Julian Pauncefote*, (1828-1902), British diplomat, *Baron. Julian Bond*, (born 1940), U.S. civil rights leader and politician. *Julian H.G. Byng*, (1862-1935), British soldier and public official. *Julian Dixon,* (born 1934), U.S. politician. Totals: politician 44%, author 33%, scientist 22%, soldier, engineer, artist.

Julius // Giulio, Jule, Jules, Julie, Julio. *Greek:* "youthful and downy-bearded". Strategic thinker, charismatic, humanitarian. Historical: *Julius Caesar* was a great general and Roman emperor. *Julius Nyerere*, (born 1922), first president of Tanzania. *Julius Erving,* (born 1950), Basketball great, known as Dr. J. Totals: politician 27%, scientist 27%, commander 14%, businessman 14%, writer 14%, singer 9%, musician 9%, physician 9%, artist 9%, philanthropist, clergy, educator.

Junior // Jr, Junnius. *Latin:* "young".

Justin // Giustino, Giusto, Justen, Justinian, Justino, Justis, Justus. *Latin:* "upright, just". *Justinian I*, (483-565), most famous Byzantine emperor, powerful ruler and law reformer, codified the law. *Justin McCarthy*, (1830-1912), Irish historian, author, and nationalist leader. *Justin Huntly McCarthy*, (1860-1936), poet and dramatist. *Saint Justin Martyr,* (100-165?), Church Father, a foremost Christian apologists. *Justin Combes*, (1835-1921), French statesman. *Justin Winsor,* (1831-97), U.S. historian and librarian. *Justin Morrill*, (1810-98), U.S. legislator.

Many males with first names starting with the letter/sound "k" seem to be in touch with their sensitive side.

Kai. *Hawaiian:* "sea"; *Form of* Kay. *Kai Siegbahn*, (born 1918), award winning Swedish physicist.

Karl. *German and Scandinavian form* of Charles. See Carl.

Kameron. *Form of* Cameron.

Kareem, Karim. *Arabic:* "noble, distinguished". *Kareem Abdul-Jabbar,* (born Lew Alcindor, 1947), extraordinary height and skill enabled him to be a record breaking basketball player.

Kasey. *Form of* Casey.

Keanu. Actor: *Keanu Reeves*.

Keegan // Keagan, Kegan, Keghen. *Gaelic:* "little and fiery".

Keene // Keenan, Keenen. *English:* "descerning"; German: "sharp, bold".

Keith. *Welsh:* "forest"; *Gaelic:* "battle ground". Curious, in touch with sensitive side. *Keith Henderson*, (1883-1982), Scottish painter, illustrator, author. *Keith Haring*, (1958-90), American populist painter, graffiti artist. Actor: *Keith Szarabajka*.

Kelly // Kele, Kellen, Kelley. *Gaelic:* "warrior". Determined, stubborn, friendly, relational.

Kelvin. *Scotch English:* "narrow river".

Ken // Kenn, Kennie, Kenny. *Welsh:* "clear". *Short form of* names containing "ken." Leads but not dominating, bit laissez-faire, business magager or owner type, handsome, bit shy toward relationship with female, thinker, planner, looks to others to co-lead which inevitably leads to problem, optimist, salesman, arbitrator, quick thoughtful talker, calming influence for extremist, pacifies extremists. *Ken Houston*, (born 1944), U.S. football player. *Ken Norton,* (born 1945), U.S. boxer, movie actor.

Kendall // Ken, Kendal, Kendall, Kendel, Kendell, Kenn, Kennie, Kenny. *Old English:* "bright valley". Actor: *Kendall Cunningham.*

Kendrick. *Scotch:* "royal commander".

Kenneth // Ken, Kenn, Kennet, Kennett, Kennie, Kennith, Kenny. *Gaelic:* "handsome". Also see Ken. Good looking, friendly, laissez faire, easy going, likable, gentle, in touch with feminine side, writer, artistic, educator, sires daughters, bit of a moral activist, trustable, fair. *Kenneth Grahame*, (1859-1932), children's writer, 'The Wind in the Willows'. *Kenneth Kaunda*, (born 1924), elected Zambia's first president, mediating influence. *Kenneth Roberts*, (1885-1957), historical novelist, journalist. Totals: writer 38% especially stories, politician 19%, economist 13%, educator 13%, commander 13%, artist 13%, actor, director, producer, scientist, athlete, lawyer, public servant. Actor: *Kenneth Branagh.*

Kent. *Welsh:* "white, bright". *Short form of* Kenton.

Bright, quick mind, relational, energetic, adventurous.

Kenton // Ken, Kenn, Kennie, Kenny, Kent. *Old English:* "king's town". Also see Kent and Ken.

Kenyon // Ken, Kenn, Kennie, Kenny. *Gaelic:* "blond". *Kenyon Cox,* (1856-1919), U.S. painter, art author.

Kermit // Ker, Kermie, Kermy, Kerr. *Gaelic:* "free man". *Kermit Gordon*, (1916-76), U.S. government official. *Kermit Roosevelt,* (1889-1943), U.S. explorer and writer, son of President Theodore Roosevelt.

Kerry // Keary. *Gaelic:* "dark-haired"; *French:* "from Ireland county". See Carey.

Kevin // Kev, Kevan, Keven, Kevon, Kevyn. *Gaelic:* "gentle, lovable". Kevens are typically more friendly, helpful, outgoing and likely to enjoy social chatting than most males, relational, handsome, not dominating, likes to co-lead, in touch with sensitive side. *Kevin Major*, (born 1949), Canadian children's author and educator. Actors: *Kevin Alexander Stea, Kevin Anderson, Kevin Bacon, Kevin Costner, Kevin Kline, Kevin Sorbo, Kevin Spacey, Kevin Stapleton.*

Khalil. *Arabic:* "friend". *Khalil Gibran*, (1883-1931), Lebanese essayist, novelist, and mystic poet, wrote 'The Prophet' a volume of prose poems on religion, death, love, work.

Kiefer. Actor: *Kiefer Sutherland.*

King. *English:* "king". *Short form of* names beginning with "king." *King Vidor*, (1895-1982), U.S. film director.

Kirk // Kerk. *Scandinavian:* "church". Energetic, busy, friendly, relational. *Kirk Munroe*, (1850-1930), U.S. author of boy's adventure books. *Kirk Fordice*, (born 1934), U.S. public official, owned construction company. Actor: *Kirk Douglas* (not his given name).

Kit. *Familiar form of* Christian or Christopher. *Kit (Christopher) Carson*, (1809-68), a great old West hero, fur trapper, guide, Indian agent, soldier, fearless wilderness man, leader of white men, protector and friend of several indian tribes.

Kody. *Form of* Cody.

Kristian. See Christian.

Kristopher // Kris, Kristofer, Kristoffer, Kristofor. *Form of* Christopher. See Christopher.

Kurt. *German form* of Conrad. Also see Curt. Determined, physical, buddy. Actor: *Kurt Russell.*

Kyle // Kiel, Kile, Kiley, Ky, Kyler, Kylie. *Gaelic:* "handsome". Relational, handsome. Actors: *Kyle Chandler, Kyle Howard, Kyle Hudgens.*

Lamar // Lemar. *Old German:* "famous through the land". *Lamar Alexander,* (born 1940), U.S. public official, lawyer, governor of Tennessee. *Lamar Hunt*, (born 1933), U.S. football executive.

Lamont // Lammond, Lamond, Lemont, Monty. *Scandina-vian:* "lawyer"; *Latin:* "the mountain". Actor: *Lamont Bentley.*

Lance // Lancelot, Launce. *Old German:* "land"; English: "spear carried by mounted soldiers". Relational, athletic, mild mannered, bit mischievous, stable. *Lancelot Hogben*, (1895-1975), British zoologist and writer. *Lance Alworth*, (born 1940), U.S. football player, flanker. Actor: *Lance Henriksen.*

Landon // Landan. *English:* "grassy meadow".

Lane // Laney, Lanie. *English:* "narrow passage". *Lane Kirkland,* (born 1922), U.S. labor leader, president AFL-CIO.

Langston // Langsdon. *Old English:* "long town". *Langston Hughes*, (1902-67), "the poet laureate of Harlem," journalist, dramatist, and children's author.

Lanny // Lannie. *Short form of* Orland and Roland.

Larry. Common *Familiar form of* Lawrence. Energetic, mischievous, quick witted, friendly to all, gentle, tend toward expert, researches, perceived as nerd or geek as child but scholarly, succeeds through study, investor, teacher. *Larry Wu-tai Chin*, U.S. collaborator with China in espionage against the U.S. *Larry Holmes*, (born 1949), U.S. boxer, heavyweight boxing champion. *Larry Csonka*, (born 1946), U.S. football player, running back. Actor: *Larry Blyden.*

Lars. *Scandinavian form* of Lawrence. *Lars Onsager,* (1903-76), U.S. chemist, educator. *Lars Nilson*, (1840-99), Swedish chemist, discovered element scandium.

Lawrence // Larry, Lars, Lauren, Laurence, Laurens, Laurent, Laurie, Lauritz, Lawry, Lenci, Lon, Lonnie, Lonny, Lorant, Loren, Lorens, Lorenzo, Lorin, Lorrie, Lorry, Lowrance, Rance. *Latin:* "laurel-crowned, from Laurentum, Italy". Also see Larry. Bit of a nerd, variety jobs, hobbiest, writer. *Lawrence Welk*, (1903-92), U.S. accordionist and orchestra leader, star of ABC-TV program The Lawrence Welk Show. *Lawrence* (or Laurentius, or Lorenzo, called the Deacon) (died 258?), Christian saint and martyr, friend of the poor. *Lawrence Tibbett*, (1896-1960), U.S. baritone, actor. Totals: author 28%, clergy 17%, politician 11%, musician, athlete, civil servant, singer, actor, inventor, explorer, commander, economist, businessman, librarian, scientist, philosopher. Actor: *Laurence Olivier.*

Lawton // Laughton, Law. *Old English:* "hill town". Lawton Chiles, (born 1930), U.S. public official, governor of Florida.

Lazarus // Lazar, Lazare, Lazaro. *Hebrew:* "God will help". Biblical: Jesus restored *Lazarus* from the dead. Friendly, usually hard working, resembles mother, diligent, responsible, usually a good student, engineer, doctor, teacher, hairdresser, electrician, lawyer, computer programmer, reach high professionalism in work, marry late, good father and husband, choose a wife with a complicated personality. *Lazar Moiseevich Kaganovich*, (1893-1991), Soviet government official, top adviser to Joseph Stalin. *Lazare Nicolas Marguerite Carnot*, (1753-1823), French statesman, general, and mathematician. *Lazaro Cardenas*, (1895-1970), Mexican general and political leader.

Lee // Leigh. *Old English:* "meadow". *Short form of* names containing the sound "lee." Thin, strong, handsome, athletic, composed, leader, popular. *Lee De Forest*, (1873-1961), invented radio sound broadcasting. *Lee Trevino*, (born 1939), U.S. golfer. *Lee Stack*, (1868-1924), British statesman. *Lee Atwater*, (1951-91), U.S. political strategist, accomplished rhythm and blues guitarist. Totals: educator 20%, scientist 20%, inventor, athlete, statesman, politician, musician, designer, actor, director, assassin, artist, writer.

Leif // Lief. *Scandinavian:* "beloved". Also look at Leo. *Leif Ericson*, Viking seaman, explorer, first European to reach North American. Actor: *Leif Garrett*.

Leigh. *Form of* Lee.

Leighton // Lay, Layton. *Old English:* "meadow town".

Leland // Lee, Leeland, Leigh. *Old English:* "meadow land". *Leland Stanford (Larry) MacPhail*, (1890-1975), U.S. baseball executive and manager. *Leland Howard*, (1857-1950), U.S. entomologist.

Lemuel // Lem, Lemmie, Lemmy. *Hebrew:* "devoted to the Lord". Determined, focused. *Lemuel Shepherd, Jr.* (born 1896), U.S. Marine Corps officer. *Lem Barney*, (born 1945), U.S. football player. *Lemuel Wilmot,* (1809-78), Canadian political leader. *Lemuel Shaw,* (1781-1861), U.S. jurist, lawyer.

Lenny // Lennie. *Form of* Leonard. *Lenny Bruce*, (1925-66), hipster comedian. *Leonard (Lenny) Moore*, (born 1933), U.S. football player, flanker and running back.

Leo // Lee, Leon, Lev, Lion, Lyon. *Latin:* "lion". *Short form of* Leonard and Leopold. Calm phlegmatic boy, not a whiner or trouble-maker, able to stand-up for himself or his friends, persevering in reaching goal, consciences, successful in society, has very few enemies or persons who don't like him, he radiates warmness and kindness, always ready to help, very friendly to the old and sick so often become doctors, patient, flexible, ability to deny himself; as a leader his patients is not endless, after multiple diplomatic warnings he can become angry; values faithfulness and kindness most in his wife, usually pick an impulsive wife, likes to play noisily with children. *Leo Tolstoi*, (1828-1910), Russia's greatest writer, novelist, wrote 'War and Peace'. *Leo Baeck*, (1873-1956), a leading liberal Jewish theologian, philosopher. *Leo Sowerby*, (1895-1968), U.S. composer. *Leo Szilard*, (1898-1964), U.S. physicist. Totals: writer 23%, composer 23%, scientist 23%, artist 15%, theologian, athlete, manager, announcer, inventor, lawyer, politician.

Leon. *French:* "lion". *Form of* Leo. *Short form of* Leonard and Napoleon. High percentage of non-traditional attitudes - humanist - socialist - anarchist. *Leon Battista Alberti,* (1404-72), Italian humanist, architect, and principal initiator of Renaissance art theory. *Leon Trotsky*, (1879-1940), Russian socialist politician and writer. *Leon Spinks*, (born 1953), U.S. boxer, Olympic gold medalist, heavyweight champion. Totals: writer 27%, physicist 18%, athlete 18%, artistic 18%, humanist, socialist, anarchist, clergy, civil rights activist. Actor: *Leon Lai.*

Leonard // Lee, Len, Lenard, Lennard, Lennie, Lenny, Leo, Leon, Leonardo, Leonerd, Leonhard, Leonid, Leonidas, Lonnard, Lonnie, Lony. *Old German:* "strong or brave as a lion". Friendly, not dominating, easy-going, not pushy, energetic, hobbyist, scientific and artistic explorations,

likes to read, plays sports, resembles mother, personality from father, lazy, not attentive, likes to sleep late, leader in marriage, jurist, doctor, musician, ballet teacher, driver, good relationship with friends and bosses, flexible personality, ability to adapt to people and circumstances, ability to resolve conflicts, can be firm principled when needed, impromptu, likes camping, woman's way to earn his love is through his stomach, very sensitive to remarks made by wife in front of others, jealous. However Leonardo is more augmentative: may provoke fights at school, argue with teacher, stubborn. *Leonid Brezhnev*, (1906-82), general secretary of the Soviet Union, leadership marked by stagnation. *Leonard Bernstein*, (1918-90), American musical genius, popular conductor, composer, pianist, commentator, entertainer and teacher. *Leonhard Euler,* (1707-83), Swiss mathematician and physicist. *Leonard Bloomfield*, (1887-1949), linguistic scientist. *Leonardo da Vinci*, (1452-1519), genious artist, scientist, inventor. Totals: writer 19%, artist 16%, scientist 13%, politicain 13%, musician 13%, commander 13%, athlete 6%, economist 6%, lawyer 6%, explorer 6%, linguist, inventor, actor, director, archaeologist, philosopher, clergy. Actor: *Leonard Nimoy, Leonardo DiCaprio.*

Leonel. *Form of* Lionel.

Leopold // Leo, Leopoldo, Leupold, Lippold. *Old German:* "bold for the people". *Leopold Senghor*, (born 1906), Senegalese statesman, writer, political philosopher. *Leopold Stokowski,* (1882-1977), conductor famous for his flamboyant showmanship. *Leopold von Ranke*, (1795-1886), the leading 19th-century German historian. Totals: musician 40%, historian 20%, scientist 20%, artistic glass worker, politician, writer.

Leroy // Elroy, Lee, Leigh, Leroi, LeRoy, Roy. *Old French:* " the royal, king". Lee + Roy, see both. Friendly, outgoing, confident, bold, tough, strong. *Leroy Walker,* (1817-84), U.S. lawyer and political leader. *Leroy Gordon Cooper, Jr.* (Gordo) (born 1927), U.S. astronaut, U.S. Air Force officer, retired into private business.

Les. *Short form of* Leslie and Lester. Business like, quiet, manager, determined, hobbiest.

Leslie // Lee, Leigh, Les, Lesley, Lezlie. *Gaelic:* "gray fortress". Also See Les. *Leslie Howard,* (1893-1943), British actor, playwright, producer. *Leslie Stephen,* (1832-1904), English biographer and essayist. *Leslie Charles Bowyer Yin,* (born 1907), U.S. writer. *Leslie Groves,* (1896-1970), U.S. Army officer. *Leslie Frost,* (1895-1973), Canadian lawyer and political leader. *Lesley McNair,* (1883-1944), U.S. Army officer. *Leslie E. Keeley,* (1832-1900), U.S. physician. *Leslie Peltier,* (born 1900), U.S. astronomer, draftsman, farmer.

Lester // Leicester, Les. *Latin:* "chosen camp"; *Old English:* "Leicester". Also see Les. *Lester Young,* (1909-59), father of improvisational tenor saxophonists. *Lester B. Pearson,* (1897-1972), Canadian prime minister, statesman. *Lester Fisher,* (born 1921), U.S. zoo director. *Lester B. Patrick,* (1883-1960), Canadian hockey player, established and expanded professional hockey. *Lester Ward,* (1841-1913), U.S. geologist, philosopher, and distinguished sociologist. *Lester Maitland,* (born 1898), U.S. Army Air Force officer, aeronautics research, ordained Episcopal priest.

Lev. *Russian form* of Leo. *Lev Davidovich Landau,* (1908-68), brilliant Soviet theoretical physicist.

Levi // Levey, Levin, Levon, Levy. *Hebrew:* "joined in harmony". Biblical: son of Jacob, name of the priestly tribe of Israel. "Harmony", not pushy, gets along with everyone. *Levi Eshkol,* (1895-1969), Israeli political leader, active in Zionist movement, prime minister of Israel. *Levi Woodbury,* (1789-1851), U.S. jurist and public official. *Levi Coffin,* (1789-1877), U.S. abolitionist, teacher. *Levi Lincoln,* (1749-1820), U.S. statesman. *Levi Morton,* (1824-1920), U.S. banker, statesman, governor of New York. *Levi Strauss,* (1829-1902), American manufacturer of denim blue jeans. Actor: *Liev Schreiber.*

Lewis // Lew, Lewes, Lewie. *Form of* Louis. See Louis.

Liam. *Irish form* of William. *Liam O'Flaherty,* (1897-1984), Irish writer. Actor: *Liam Neeson.*

Lincoln // Linc, Link. *Old English:* "settlement by the pool". Historical: the name honors *Abraham Lincoln,* 16th U.S. president. *Lincoln Colcord,* (1883-1947), U.S. author, spent boyhood on voyages with father, wrote sea stories. *Lincoln Ellsworth,* (1880-1951), U.S. explorer, of Arctic and Antarctic.

Linus. *Greek:* "flaxen-haired". *Linus Pauling,* (born 1901), chemist, anti-nuclear activist, first awarded two unshared Nobel prizes. *Linus Yale,* (1821-68), U.S. inventor, improved locks.

Lionel // Lionello. *Old French:* "young lion, lion cub". *Lionel Gendron,* (born 1924), Canadian physician and author, books on adolescence, marriage, and sex. *Lionel Trilling,* (1905-75), U.S. writer, critic, and English professor.

Lionel Groulx, (1878-1967), Canadian historian, Roman Catholic priest.

Lloyd // Floyd, Loy, Loydie. **Welsh:** "gray-haired". *Lloyd M. Bentsen, Jr.* (born 1921), U.S. public official, attorney. *Lloyd Osbourne*, (1868-1947), U.S. author. *Lloyd Alexander,* (born 1924), U.S. children's author. *Lloyd Waner,* (Little Poison) (1906-82), U.S. baseball outfielder. *Lloyd Douglas*, (1877-1951), U.S. author and clergyman.

Logan // Logen. **Gaelic:** "meadow".

Lon // Lonnie, Lonny. *Short forms of* Alonzo and Lawrence. *Lon Chaney*, (1883-1930), silent film's finest character actor.

London. **Middle English:** "moon fortress."

Loren // Lorenzo, Lorin. *Form of* Lawrence. *Lorin Maazel*, (born 1930), U.S. conductor. *Loren Eiseley*, (1907-77), U.S. anthropologist, educator, author. *Lorenzo Delmonico*, (1813-81), operated the foremost and largest restaurant in the United States. *Lorenzo Ghiberti*, (1378-1455), Sculptor, painter, and metalworker. *Lorenzo Perosi*, (1872-1956), Italian priest and composer. *Lorenzo Valla*, (1407-57), Italian humanist, literary critic, and philosopher. *Lorenzo da Ponte,* (1749-1838), U.S. poet and rhetoric teacher. *Lorenzo de' Medici* (the Magnificent)(1449-92), Florentine statesman and patron of arts.

Lorne // Lorn. *Familiar form of* Lawrence. Actor: *Lorne Green.*

Louis // Aloysius, Lew, Lewes, Lewie, Lewis, Lou, Louie, Lucho, Ludvig, Ludwig, Luigi, Luis, Luiz. **Old German:** "famous warrior". Friendly, handsome, planning. *Lou Gehrig,* (1903-41), baseball player. *Lou Brock*, (born 1939), U.S. baseball outfielder. *Louis Agassiz*, (1807-73), celebrated Swiss-American naturalist, zoology, geology, outstanding teacher. *Louis L'Amour*, (1908-88), best-selling author of Westerns. *Lewis Carroll*, (1832-98), author of 'Alice's Adventures in Wonderland', loved children, hobbies of mathematical puzzles and photography. *Louis Armstrong*, (1900-71), genius improvisational jazz trumpeter, pop singer. *Louis Pasteur,* (1822-95), celebrated French chemist, discovered pasteurization and prevention of several diseases. Total: writer 26%, politician or public servent 23%, scientist 10%, lawyer 10%, commander 10%, artist 8%, athlete 5%, producer 5%, musician 5%, jurist 5%, explorer 5%, publisher 3%, architect 3%, inventor 3%, revolutionary 3%, teacher 3%, clergy 3%, philosopher, historian, sociologist, critic, businessman, actor, engineer, farmer, forest ranger. Actors: *Lou Ferrigno, Lou Gossitt Jr.*

Lowell // Lovell, Lowe. **Old French:** "little wolf". Planning, hard working, steady. *Lowell Mason*, (1792-1872), U.S. musician, composer of hymns. *Lowell P. Weicker, Jr.* (born 1931), U.S. public official, governor (Independent) of Connecticut. *Lowell Thomas*, (1892-1981), U.S. author, lecturer, traveler, radio commentator, historian.

Lucas // Luca, Lucais, Lukas. *Form of* Lucius and Luke. Artistic. *Lucas Cranach*, (1472-1553), important and influential 16th-century Germany artist, vast output of paintings, woodcuts and decorative works. *Lukas Foss*, (born 1922), U.S. composer and pianist. Actor: *Lukas Haas.*

Lucian // Luce, Luciano, Lucias, Lucien, Lucio. *Latin:* "brightly shining". Artistic, performance arts. *Luciano Pavarotti,* (born 1935), Italian opera singer. *Lucien Guitry,* (1860-1925), French actor. *Lucian K. Truscott,* (1895-1965), U.S. general. *Lucio Costa,* (born 1902?), Brazilian architect, preserves historic and artistic monuments.

Ludwig // Ludvig. *German form* of Louis. Fearless, stubborn, likes soccer and wrestling, like to read or view adventures, very emotional; close family, likes to host guests, likes to be a guest, like groups, massage, engineer, artist, architect, computer programmer, detective, actor, economist. *Ludwig van Beethoven,* (1770-1827), most influential composer ever. *Ludwig Erhard,* (1897-1977), West German chancellor, called the "father of the economic miracle." *Ludwig Mies van der Rohe,* (1886-1969), influential architect. *Ludwig Wittgenstein,* (1889-1951), mathematician, engineer, architect, musician, zealous philosopher, never at ease. Totals: writer 25%, economist 17%, architect 17%, philosopher 17%, composer, mathematician, engineer, musician, physicist, philologist, commander, historian.

Luis. *Spanish form* of Louis.

Luke // Lucais, Lucas, Lukas. *Greek:* "from Lucania". Biblical: *Dr. Luke,* writer of the 'Gospel of Luke' and 'Acts of the Apostles'. Gentle, sensitive. *Luke Fildes,* (1844-1927), English painter, best known for 'The Doctor'. *Luke Wright,* (1846-1922), U.S. public official, lawyer. *Luke Appling,* (1907-91), U.S. baseball shortstop. *Luke Howard,* (1772-1864), British scientist. Actor: *Luke Perry.*

Luther // Lothaire, Lothario, Lutero. *Old German:* "famous warrior". Historical: the name honors Christian church reformer Martin Luther. *Luther Burbank,* (1849-1926), developed 220 new varieties of plants. *Luther Terry,* (1911-85), U.S. physician. *Luther Martin,* (1748?-1826), U.S. lawyer and political leader. *Luther Gulick,* (1865-1918), U.S. educator and writer, promoted physical education, founded Camp Fire Girls. *Luther Hodges,* (1898-1974), U.S. business executive and public official. *Luther Holt,* (1855-1924), U.S. physician, child care authority. *Luther Rice,* (1783-1836), U.S. missionary to India.

Lyle // Lisle, Ly, Lyell. *French:* "the island". Friendly, helpful, devoted family-man, quintessential name for bass guitarist.

Lyman. *Old English:* "man from the meadow". *Lyman Duff,* (1865-1955), Canadian jurist. *Lyman Blake,* (1835-83), U.S. inventor. *Lyman Trumbull,* (1813-96), U.S. jurist and legislator. *Lyman Gage,* (1836-1927), U.S. financier. *Lyman Spitzer, Jr.* (born 1914), U.S. astronomer and astrophysicist. *Lyman Lemnitzer,* (1899-1988), U.S. Army commander. *Lyman Hall,* (1724-90), American Revolutionary War leader.

Lynn // Lin, Linn, Lyn. *Old English:* "waterfall and its pool". Unisex name. Energetic, friendly, intelligent, not pushy but suggests, devoted family-man. *Lynn Margulis,* (born 1938), American cell biologist and evolutionist. *Lynn Russell Chadwick,* (born 1914), British sculptor and designer. *Lynn Martin,* (born 1939), U.S. public official. *Lynn Riggs,* (1899-1954), U.S. playwright and poet.

Mac // Mack. *Gaelic:* "son". *Short form of* names beginning with mac or max or mc. *Mack Sennett*, (1880-1960), father of motion picture slapstick comedy, great pioneer Hollywood filmmaker.

Mackenzie // Mac, Mack. *Gaelic:* "son of the wise". *Mackenzie King*, (1874-1950), long-time Canadian prime minister. *Mackenzie Bowell,* (1823-1917), Canadian prime minister, newspaper editor and publisher.

Malcolm // Mal. *Gaelic:* "follower of St. Columba". Adventurer, spokesman, enthusiast, traveler, businessman. *Malcolm X (Little)*, (1925-65), black militant, championed black people's rights and unity. *Malcolm Fraser*, (born 1930), politician, Australian prime minister. *Malcolm MacDonald*, (1901-81), statesman. *Malcolm Forbes*, (1919-90), U.S. millionaire publisher and motorcycling, ballooning, yachting, and travel enthusiast. *Malcolm Campbell,* (1885-1948), British auto, boat, and airplane racer, Lloyd's of London broker, WW II commander, military designer. *Malcolm Cameron*, (1808-76), Canadian statesman. *Malcolm Carpenter*, (born 1925), U.S. astronaut and aquanaut. *Malcolm Ross*, (born 1919), U.S. Naval Reserve officer and atmospheric physicist. *Malcolm Cowley*, (1898-1989), U.S. editor, writer, and translator. *Malcolm Lowry*, (1909-57), British writer. Actor: *Malcolm McDowell.*

Malik. *Form of* Malachi.

Mandel // Mannie, Manny. *German:* "almond". *Mandell Creighton*, (1843-1901), British clergyman and historian, bishop of London.

Manfred // Fred, Freddie, Freddy, Mannie, Manny. *Old German:* "peace among men, man of peace". *Baron Manfred von Richthofen*, (1892-1918), German fighter pilot ace, known as the Red Baron. *Manfred Eigen*, (born 1927), German chemist, professor and administrator.

Manuel // Mano, Manolo. *Short form of* Emmanuel. Politician, leader. *Manuel Quezon*, (1878-1944), Philippino politician, lawyer, shrewd, charming, and gifted orator. *Manuel Noriega*, (born 1938), Panamanian military and political leader, corruption and drug trafficking. *Manuel Gonzalez,* (1833-93), Mexican general and president. *Manuel Lujan, Jr.* (born 1928), U.S. elected official. Totals: politician 58%, commander 33%, teacher 17%, singer 17%, lawyer, explorer, trader, composer, anthropologist, sociologist.

Marc. *French form* of Mark.

Marcel // Marcello, Marcellus, Marcelo. *Latin:* "little and warlike". Creative, innovative, artistic expression. *Marcello Malpighi,* (1628-94), pioneer Italian physician and biologist. *Marcel Proust*, (1871-1922), deep French novelist. *Marcel Duchamp*, (1887-1968), innovative French artist. *Marcel Breuer,* (1902-81), pioneering architect and designer. *Marcel Marceau*, (born 1923), world famous French pantomimist. Totals: story writer 30%, artist 20%, mime, architect, musician, biologist, politician. Actor: *Marcello Mastroianni.*

Marcus // Marco, Marcos. *Form of* Mark. Little fear, adventurer, gung-ho, doer. *Marcus Whitman*, (1802-47), American pioneer and medical missionary to the Indians. *Marcus Claudius Marcellus*, (268?-208 BC), Roman general, conqueror of Syracuse. *Marcus Atilius Regulus*, (died 250? BC), Roman general. *Marcus Albert Reno*, (1835?-89), U.S. military leader, distinguished for bravery. Totals: commander 73%, politician 45%, missionary, historian. Actor: *Marco Sanchez*.

Mario. *Italian form* of Mark. *Mario M. Cuomo*, (born 1932), U.S. public official, governor of New York. *Mario Andretti,* (born 1940), U.S. race car driver. *Mario Llosa*, (born 1936), Peruvian author, "specialist in fantasies," widely traveled lecturer and teacher, broadcast journalist. *Mario Del Monaco*, (1915-82), Italian operatic tenor. *Mario Castelnuovo-Tedesco,* (1895-1968), U.S. composer. Actor: *Mario Lopez.*

Marion. *French form* of Mary usually reserved for boys. *Marion S. Barry, Jr.* (born 1936), U.S. politician, first black militant mayor, Mayor Washington, D.C., corruption, drug scandals, opportunistic, convicted on cocaine possession and perjury charges. *Marion Folsom*, (1893-1976), U.S. business executive and government official. *J. Marion Sims*, (1813-83), U.S. surgeon, gynecological science, president AMA. *Marion Motley*, (born 1920), U.S. football fullback.

Mark // Marc, Marco, Marcos, Marcus, Mario, Marius, Markos, Markus, Marquis, Marquise. **Latin:** "warlike". Biblical: writer of the Gospel of Mark, associate of Paul and Barnabus. Also see Marcus. Bold speaker, leader but not out of felt need, actor, writer, tend to be free spirit,

practical joker, light hearted adventurer, fun loving, likes to find his own life path, loves people, usually determined to do better and achieve more, jokester, somewhat outside of establishment, likes to draw outside the lines and adventure outside of safety and conservative values, sometimes fool hardy, deep inside conservative but maybe frivolous behavior, takes responsibility to lead when asked, difficulty keeping him focused on task given by another, leads others naturally into adventure, doer, joys not in administration, detail man only in his passion, would rather be creative, people person, often marries more serious and detail minded person, nice smile, a little ego-centric, doesn't like others controlling him but hides this pretty well, career oriented, marries very carefully, looks for woman who would be a good friend and unquestioning helper who would sacrifice her interests for his plans; she will need to acknowledge his intellectual superiority even if there is none, a highly talented distinguished wife will rather irritate and depress him, pragmatic, not open and shares little of what he is thinking through, good manager of his household, may seldom do dishes etcetera, rather strict at raising his children, may like to argue his point. *Marcus Antonius (Mark Antony)*, (83?-30 BC), brilliant Roman soldier, statesman, orator, known for his devoted love with Egyptian queen Cleopatra which eventually destroyed his career and he took his own life. *Mark Rothko*, (1903-70), U.S. painter pioneered abstract expressionism. *Mark Hanna*, (1837-1904), industrialist, political activist. Totals: writer 42%, artist 17%, businessman 17%, commander 17%, editor, activist, statesman, orator, lover, athlete, educator, archaeologist. Actors: *Marc Alaimo, Marc Singer, Mark Frankel, Mark Lenard,*

Mark Metcalf, Mark Mortimer, Mark Pinter, Mark Valley.

Marlon // Marlin. *Old French:* "little falcon". *English:* "Marlin, several saltwater fish related to sailfish and spearfish". *Familiar form of* Merlin. *Marlin Perkins,* (1905-86), U.S. reptile expert. *Marlon Brando,* (born 1924), U.S. actor.

Marshall // Marsh, Marshal. *Old French:* "masters of horse". *Marshall Field,* (1834-1906), businessman, merchandiser. *Marshall Field III* (1893-1956), U.S. businessman, publisher as well as *Marshall Field IV* and *Marshall Field V. Marshall Warren Nirenberg,* (born 1927), U.S. biochemist. *Marshall McLuhan,* (1911-80), Canadian communications sociologist and author.

Martin // Maarten, Mart, Martain, Marten, Martie, Martino, Marton, Marty, Martyn. *Latin:* "warlike, of Mars". Likes to explore both the natural and abstract, delving into exploration using scientific logic and philosophic abstractness, often off-beat, philosopher, artistic, inventive, energetic, quick mind, friendly, responsible - everything he starts -he finishes, many are shy and lacking confidence; likes to be home doing project such as repairs, modifications and yard work; likes fishing, playful, likes to play sports, choosy at picking his friends, unassuming, pragmatic, reasoning, peace loving, explorer/scientist. *Martin Heidegger,* (1889-1976), philosopher, author. *Martin Luther,* (1483-1546), father of the Protestant Reformation in Germany, Catholic priest, theologian, writer. *Martin Luther King, Jr.,* (1929-68), black minister protesting racial discrimination, poverty, and war, through loving, peaceful, nonviolent resistance. *Martin Tromp,* (1597-1653), Dutch admiral. Totals: writer 30%, theologian 19%,

clergy 15%, commander 15%, politician 11%, reformer 11%, philosopher 7%, inventor 7%, poet 7%, artist 7%, astronomer 7%, director 7%, explorer 7%, chemist, educator, linguist, producer, actor, geographer, athlete, physician, lawyer.

Marty. *Short form of* Martin.

Marvin // Marv, Marve, Marven, Marwin, Merv, Merven, Mervin, Mervyn, Merwin, Merwyn, Murvyn, Myrvyn, Myrwyn. *Old English:* "sea lover". *Mervyn Dymally,* (born 1926), U.S. politician, teacher, lecturer. *Marvin Hart,* boxer. *Marvin Trachtenberg,* architectural author. *Merv Griffin,* TV producer and talk show host. *Marvin Minsky,* computer artificial intelligence researcher and proponant. *Marvin Gaye,* popular musician. *Marvin Young,* (born 1968), U.S. rap musician Young MC.

Mason // Mace, Maison, Sonnie, Sonny. *Old French:* "stoneworker".

Matt // Mats, Mattie, Matty. *Short form of* Matthew. Also see Matthew. *Martin "Mat" Van Buren,* 8th U.S. president, politician, lawyer, careful thinking and persuasion, warm friendliness. *Matt Biondi,* (born 1966), U.S. swimmer, Olympic gold medalist. *Matt Cetlinski,* U.S. swimmer, Olympic gold medalist. *Mats Wilander,* (born 1964), Swedish tennis world champion. *Matt Groening,* (born 1954), U.S. cartoonist, creator of The Simpsons. Actors: *Matt Damon, Matt Dillon.*

Matthew // Mata, Mateo, Mathe, Mathew, Mathian, Mathias, Matias, Mats, Matt, Matteo, Matthaeus, Matthäus, Mattheus, Matthias, Matthieu, Matthiew, Mattias, Mattie, Matty. *Hebrew:* "gift of God". Biblical:

Matthew-Levi, apostle, tax-collector and author of the First Gospel. Also see Matt. Sportsman, athletic, handsome, relational, amiable, strong, adventurer, explorer, scientist. *Matthew Prior,* (1664-1721), British poet and diplomat. *Matthew Josephson*, (1899-1978), U.S. author, biographies, economic and political studies. *Matthew Maury,* (1806-73), U.S. naval officer and hydrographer. *Matthew Flinders*, (1774-1814), English navigator, charted much of the Australian coast. Totals: politician 24%, writer 24%, geographer 18%, commander 12%, businessman 12%, poet 12%, photographer, chronicler, judge, clergy, engineer, philanthropist, teacher, explorer. Actors: *Matthew Ashford, Matthew Broderick, Matthew Ferguson, Matthew Lillard, Matthew McConaughey, Matthew Mendoza.*

Maurice // Mauricio, Maurie, Maurise, Maurits, Maurizio, Maury, Morey, Morie, Moritz, Morris. *Latin:* "dark-skinned, Moorish". Artistic and relational, persues artistry, creatively artistic writer, smooth diplomatic politician, able capable leader, intelligent. *Maurice Sendak*, (born 1928), illustrator, children's fantasy writer. *Maurice Maeterlinck,* (1862-1949), symbolist poet and playwright. *Maurice Ravel,* (1875-1937), French composer with precision and musical craftsmanship. *Maurice Utrillo*, (1883-1955), self-taught French painter. Totals: writer 27%, artist 20%, politician 17%, commander 10%, composer 7%, actor 7%, civil servant 7%, scientist 7%, poet, singer, financier, philanthropist, economist, dancer, choreographer, clergy, climber, engineer, architect. Actors: *Maurice Benard, Maurice Chevalier.*

Max // Maxie, Maxy. *Short form of* Maximilian or Maxwell.

Relational, buddy, writer, activist, arts, science, actor, sports, music, architect. *Max Beerbohm*, (1872-1956), writer-caricaturist, called "the incomparable Max". *Max Planck,* (1858-1947), German physicist, originator of the quantum theory. *Max Reinhardt*, (1873-1943), Austrian theatrical director, creative artist. *Max Weber,* (1864-1920), political economist, professor, wrote 'The Protestant Ethic and the Spirit of Capitalism'. *Max Ernst*, (1891-1976), a leading surrealist artist, art protested the tragedy of war. Totals: scientist 28%, artist 17%, artistic writer 17%, composer 7%, architect 7%, athlete 7%, theater director, actor, musician, economist, educator, inventor, philosopher, orientalist, civil rights. Actor: *Max von Sydow*.

Maximilian // Mac, Mack, Massimiliano, Massimo, Max, Maxie, Maxim,Maxime, Maximiliano, Maximilianus, Maximilien, Maximo, Maxy. *Latin:* "most excellent". Also see Max. Thinker, persevering, hard working, good student, has many friends, gentle and kind but stubborn, often religious, bit shy but doesn't turn from his principles and beliefs, often not successful in marriage, very patient, children attach to him more than to mother, likes nature, likes animals, works around the house; engineer, artist, coach, computer programmer, hair-dresser, electrician, plumber, wood-worker. Maxime: rich imagination, knowledgeable, not persevering enough, lacks self confidence, doubts his success, beneficial for him to have an encourager, friendly, compassionate toward people, always ready to help, not career oriented, responsible, starts dating early, very patient in marriage, likes children and spends time with them, falls in love easily, remains faithful to his wife, marries strong woman; photographer, journalist, politician. Several emperors and nobility of this name. *Maximilien Robespierre*, (1758-94), cruel and intolerant leader of the French Revolution during its Reign of Terror, juxtaposed to his early years as an able and honest lawyer and judge who opposed the death penalty. *Maxime Weygand,* (1867-1965), French general. *Maximo Gomez y Baez*, (1826?-1905), Cuban patriot general. Totals: statesman 44%, commander 44%, lawyer, judge, financier, writer, editor.

Maxwell // Mac, Mack, Max, Maxie, Maxy. *Old English:* "ruler's well". Also see Max. *Maxwell Anderson*, (1888-1959), U.S. playwright, pro-democracy. *Maxwell Taylor,* (1901-87), U.S. army officer, chairman Joint Chiefs of Staff, author. *Maxwell Bodenheim*, (1893-1954), U.S. poet, novelist, and playwright.

Maynard // Mayne, Menard. *Old German:* "bold in strength, powerful, brave". Adventurous, story writer, lawyer. *Maynard Jackson*, (born 1938), U.S. liberal Democratic government official, lawyer, became politician on spur of the moment. *Mayne Reid*, (Thomas Mayne Reid) (1818-83), Irish writer of adventure tales and hunting romances, traded with American Indians, fought in Mexican War.

Mead // Meade. *Old English:* "meadow". *Meade Lux Lewis*, (1905-64), U.S. jazz pianist, popularized boogie-woogie.

Melvin // Mal, Malvin, Mel, Melvyn, Milvian, Vin, Vinnie, Vinny. *Gaelic:* "polished chief". Athletic, scientific mind, energetic, intellegent, quick mind. *Mel Blanc*, (1908-89), U.S. cartoon voice creator, Looney Tunes, called "man of 1,000 voices". *Melvin Ott,* (1909-58), U.S. baseball player. *Melvin Tolson*, (1898-1966), U.S. poet. *Mel Blount*, (born 1948), U.S. football player. *Melvin Simon*, (born 1926), U.S. real estate developer and pro basketball executive. *Melvin Hein*, (1909-92), U.S. football player. *Melvin Schwartz,* (born 1932), U.S. physicist. *Melvin Calvin*, (born 1911), U.S. organic chemist and educator. *Melvin Laird*, (born 1922), U.S. public official. Totals: athlete 33%, scientist 22%, poet, public official, businessman, educator, voice creator. Actor: *Mel Gibson*.

Merlin // Marlin, Marlon, Merle. *Middle English:* "falcon"; *French:* "blackbird". Literary: a famous wizard in the King Arthur legend.

Merrill // Merill, Merle, Merrel, Merrell, Meryl. *Old French:* "famous, blackbird". *Merle Tuve*, (1901-82), U.S. physicist.

Mervin // Merv, Merwin, Merwyn. *Form of* Marvin.

Meyer // Meier, Meir, Myer. *Hebrew:* "light barer"; *German:* "farmer". *Meyer Guggenheim*, (1828-1905), Swiss capitalist. *Meyer Levin*, (1905-81), U.S. novelist.

Micah // Mic, Mick, Mike, Mikey, Myca, Mycah. *Hebrew form* of Michael. Biblical: *Micah* (about 757-700 BC), one of Hebrew minor prophets.

Michael // Mic, Micah, Michail, Michal, Michale, Micheal, Micheil, Michel, Michele, Mick, Mickey, Mickie, Micky, Miguel, Mikael, Mike, Mikel, Mikey, Mikhail, Mikkel, Mikol, Mischa, Mitch, Mitchel, Mitchell, Mychal. *Hebrew:* "who is like God?". Biblical: the archangel, leader of celestial armies. Very social, serious about life but fun loving, bit insecure but sometimes hides behind pride, athletic, good looking, leader who expects followers, expect to lead, tend to be charismatic, flexible, not an idealist, pragmatist, good ear, may be in children choir, tries to do everything right, logical reasoning mind, teacher, lawyer, commander, quick to orientated in an unfamiliar environment, stable, not too emotional, can control his emotions well, sensitive to criticism, likes animals, often has a pet, children sense his kindness, he likes to play with children and will "spoil" them, enjoys yard work, loneliness is hard for him, patiently cares for his aged parents and not irritated by their capricious behavior, easy to communicate and relate with him, easily forgives, generous, can be sentimental; at parties he is easy-going, joking, singing songs and its soul, likes to show-off a bit, values kindness most in women, tries to avoid rude and gruff women, jealous, can not hide his jealousy. *Mick Jagger,* lead singer of the Rolling Stones. *Mick Taylor,* guitarist in the 1970s for the Rolling Stones. *Michael Jeffery Jordan*, (born 1963), U.S. Basketball superstar, called "Air Jordan", Olympic gold medal. *Michael Faraday*, (1791-1867), English physicist and chemist. *Michael Jackson*, (born 1958), U.S. pop singer. *Michael Bolton*, (born 1954), U.S. singer and songwriter. *Michael Landon*, (1936-91), American actor, producer, and director. *Michael Eisner,* (born 1942), U.S. motion picture company executive, CEO Walt Disney and CEO Paramount Pictures. *Michael Chang,* (born 1972), U.S. tennis pro. Michael Totals: athlete 15%, musician 12%, politician 9%, actor 9%, director 9%, scientist 6%, astronaut 6%, artist 6%, producer 6%, businessman 6%, poet 6%, clergy, financier, inventor, physician, heritic, lawyer, writer, dancer, choreographer, educator, architect, commander. Miguel

Totals: writer 30%, politician 30%, commander 30%, clergy, revolutionary, lawyer, artist, athlete. French Michel Totals: essayist 25%, commander 25%, explorer 25%, philosopher, architect. Actors: *Michael Baldwin, Michael Biehn, Michael Des Barres, Michael Dietz, Michael Dorn, Michael Douglas, Michael Easton, Michael Ironside, Michael J. Fox, Michael Jordan, Michael Landon, Michael Moriarty, Michael Nesmith, Michael O'Leary, Michael Park, Michael Rapaport, Michael Richards, Michael Sutton, Michel Serrault, Micky Dolenz.*

Miguel. *Form of* Michael.

Mike // Mikey. *Short form of* Michael. Also see Michael. Historically large percentage of fighters. *Mike Nichols*, (Michael Igor Peschkowsky) (born 1931), U.S. film and stage director. *Mike Ditka,* (born 1939), U.S. professional football coach and player. *Mike Weaver,* (born 1952), U.S. boxer, heavyweight champion. *Mike Tyson*, (born 1966), U.S. boxer, heavyweight champion. *Mike Mansfield*, (Michael Joseph Mansfield) (born 1903), U.S. statesman and educator. *Mike Fink*, (1770?-1823), U.S. frontier fighter. Actor: *Mike Vitar.*

Miles // Milo, Myles. **Latin:** "soldier". *Miles Coverdale*, (1488?-1569), Augustinian friar, bishop, translated Bible into English. *Miles Goodyear,* (1817-49), U.S. pioneer settler in Utah, famed mountain man. *Miles Franklin*, (1879-1954), Australian writer. *Miles Standish*, (1584?-1656), English soldier, leader of Pilgrims. *Miles Davis*, (1926-91), important jazz bandleader, outstanding trumpet soloist.

Milton // Milt, Miltie, Milty. **Old English:** "mill town".

Creator of something new. *Milton Berle,* (born 1908), U.S. slapstick comedian. *Milton Obote,* (born 1924), first president of the Republic of Uganda. *Milton Hershey,* (1857-1945), U.S. confectioner and philanthropist. *Milton McRae,* (1858-1930), U.S. newspaper publisher. *Milton Caniff,* (1907-88), U.S. cartoonist. *Milton Friedman,* (born 1912), U.S. economist. *Milton Rosenau,* (1869-1946), U.S. physician.

Misha // Mesha, Meshka, Misael, Mischa, Mishcha. Slavic *Familiar form of* Michael. *Mischa Elman,* (1891-1967), U.S. violinist prodigy.

Mitch. *Short form of* Mitchell. Also see Michael. Actor: *Mitch Pileggi.*

Mitchell // Mitch, Mitchel. An *English form* of Michael. *A. Mitchell Palmer,* (1872-1936), U.S. public official, lawyer, created the "red scare" of 1919-20.

Mohammed. *Form of* Muhammad.

Moises. *Form of* Moses.

Monroe // Monro, Munro, Munroe. *Gaelic:* "mouth of the Roe River". Munro Leaf, (1905-76), U.S. author of children's books.

Montague // Monte, Monty. *French:* "pointed mountain". See Monte. *Montague Glass,* (1877-1934), U.S. humorous author.

Monte // Monti, Montl, Monty. *Latin:* "mountain". *Short form of* Montague and Montgomery. Energetic, stays a focused course, persistent, re-plans as necessary, seldom excitable, takes life as it comes, stable, steady.

Montgomery // Monte, Monty. *Old English:* "rich man's mountain". Also see Monte. *Montgomery Blair,* (1813-83), U.S. judge and lawyer. Actor: *Montgomery Cliff.*

Monty. *Short form of* names beginning with "mont". See Monte.

Mordecai // Mord, Mordy, Mort, Mortie, Morty. *Hebrew:* "belonging to Marduk," the Babylonian creation god. *Mordecai Richler,* (born 1931), Canadian author of adult and children's books. *Mordecai Johnson,* (1890-1976), U.S. educator.

Morey // Morie, Morrie, Morry. *Familiar forms of* Maurice, Morris, Morse and Seymour.

Morgan // Morgen, Morgun. *Gaelic:* "dweller on the sea, sea edge". *Morgan G. Bulkeley,* (1837-1922), U.S. baseball organizer. Actors: *Morgan Freeman, Morgan Weisser.*

Morley // Morlee, Morly. *Old English:* "moor". *Morley Callaghan,* (born 1903), Canadian writer, realism and treatment of moral problems.

Morris // Morey, Morie, Morrie, Morry, Morse. *English form* of Maurice. *Morris West,* (born 1916), Australian author and temporary monastic. *Morris Hillquit,* (1869-1933), U.S. lawyer and Socialist leader. *Morris Graves,* (born 1910), U.S. painter, fanciful and mysterious works. *Morris Gest,* (1881-1942), U.S. theatrical producer. *Morris Travers,* (1872-1961), English chemist. *Morris Dees,* (born 1937), U.S. civil rights lawyer.

Mort // Mortie, Morty. *Short form of* Mordecai and Mortimer.

Mortimer // Mort, Mortie, Morty. *Old French:* "still water". *Mortimer Adler,* (born 1902), author, teacher, philosopher, educator, editor, and encyclopaedist.

Morton // Morten. *Old English:* "town near the moor". *Morton F. Plant*, (1852-1918), U.S. railroad business man. *Morton Feldman*, (1926-87), U.S. composer. *Morton Downey, Jr.* (born 1933), U.S. originator of rude-and-crude school of late-night television. *Morton Gould*, (born 1913), U.S. pianist and composer.

Moses // Moe, Moise, Moisés, Mose, Moshe, Moss, Mozes. *Hebrew:* "saved". Biblical: greatest of the Israelite prophets, founder of Israel as a nation, its lawgiver, priest, and intermediary with God. Calm child, no trouble for parents and teachers, surrounded with friends, good grades, involved with music, likes to read a lot, helps mother around the house, resembles mother; writer, accountant, artist, doctor, jurist, priest; curious, finds even petty things of interest, good craftsman, don't like moving or business trips. *Moses Mendelssohn*, (1729-86), greatest of 18th-century Jewish philosophers. *Moshe Dayan*, (1915-81), soldier and statesman. Totals: politician 45%, commander 27%, philosopher, businessman, philanthropist, pioneer, lawyer, historian, educator, inventor, electrician, architect.

Muhammad // Hamid, Hammad, Mahmoud, Mahmud, Mohammed. *Arabic:* "praised". Historical: the founder of the Islamic religion, soldier. Several Turkish sultans. *Muhammad Iqbal*, (1877?-1938), poet, philosopher, lawyer, father of modern Pakistan. *Muhammad ibn Tughluq*, (1290?-1351), ruled the Delhi sultanate, controlled a large part of India, sometimes ruthlessly cruel. *Mohammed Naguib*, (1901-84), Egyptian army officer and statesman.

Totals: politician 90%, soldier 55%, reformer 36%, brutal 27%, lawyer 27%, poet, philosopher.

Murray // Murry. *Gaelic:* "sailor". *Murray Gell-Mann*, (born 1929), physicist, organizer.

Myles // Mylo. *Form of* Miles.

Mynor. *Form of* minor.

Myron // Meron, Miron, My, Ron, Ronnie, Ronny. *Greek:* "fragrant ointment". Also see Ron. Very kind, compliant, hard working, resembles mother and treats her warmly, his honesty and faithfulness to his promise attract friends, a leader among co-workers, very charming, talented, appears soft mannered, persevering in his work, will finish what he started, likes to be at home, attached to his family and home, doesn't like long lasting trips, very faithful to his children, however often unlucky in marriage, he is not one to divorce and will bear it for the children. *Myron Timothy Herrick*, (1854-1929), U.S. capitalist and diplomat. *Myron* (5th century BC), Greek sculptor.

Napoleon // Leon, Nap, Napoléon, Nappie, Nappy. *Greek:* "woodland valley lion"; *Italian:* "from Naples". Historical: the French Emperor *Napoleon Bonaparte*. *Napoleon (Larry) Lajoie*, (1875-1959), U.S. baseball second baseman.

Nate // Nat. *Short form ofms of* Nathan and Nathaniel. Nat Turner, (1800-31), a young black man who led the most effective U.S. slave revolt. Nat King Cole, (originally Nathaniel Adams Coles) (1919-65), U.S. singer and jazz pianist. Nate Holden, U.S. politician.

Nathan // Nat, Nate. *Hebrew:* "given, gift". *Short form ofm of* Nathaniel. Biblical: Hebrew prophet, counselor to King David, adviser to Solomon. Typically quiet but as young man may sharply rebel from his submissive ways, artistic, cerebral, not a trouble maker as a child, calm, obedient, good grades, doesn't conflict with peers, reasoning, likes music, likes drawing, plays chess, resembles mother's appearance and character, involved, kind, tender, often appears lacking in confidence, craftsman, good at working with his hands, responsible, finishes what he starts, compliant husband and father, not leaders in the family, rely on wife to manage the household, usually marry late, not picky about foods - but squeamish, very hospitable, not boastful and dislikes other's boasting, responsive to help people, helpful, volunteer, may volunteer to do work in community in any way in which he can help, always willing to volunteer and be faithful to tasks which might be considered unglamorous and unrewarding to others such as school-crossing guard or care toward elderly, persevering, may be stubborn. *Nathan Hale*, (1755-76), U.S. patriot, soldier, spy, admired for his learning and athletic prowess and the way he maintained discipline without severity. *Nathan Soderblom*, (1866-1931), Archbishop of Sweden, chief architect of the ecumenical movement. *Nathan Straus*, (1848-1931), U.S. merchant and philanthropist. Totals: author 23%, lawyer 23%, commander 23%, judge 15%, clergy, merchant, philanthropist, journalist, reformer,

editor, translator, musician, inventor, politician, farmer. Actor: *Nathan Lane*.

Nathaniel // Nat, Nataniel, Nate, Nathan, Nathanael, Nathanial, Natty. *Hebrew:* "gift of God". Biblical: one of the Twelve Apostles also called Bartholomew. Also see Nathan. *Nathaniel Hawthorne*, (1804-64), writer, "the Scarlet Letter". *Nathanael Greene*, (1742-86), American Revolutionary War general, brilliant wartime strategy. *Nathaniel Bacon*, (1647-76), North American colonial leader of Bacon's Rebellion. Totals: commander 27%, writer 20%, businessman 20%, politician 13%, scientist 13%, explorer 13%, publisher, pioneer, architect, clergy.

Neal // Nealy. *Irish form of* Neil. See Neil.

Ned // Neddie, Neddy. *Familiar form of* names beginning with "ed". *Ned Kelly*, (1855-80), most notorious Australian outlaw, "bushrangers". *Ned Ray McWherter*, (born 1930), U.S. public official, governor of Tennessee.

Nehemiah. *Hebrew:* "compassion of God". Biblical: *Nehemiah* (5th century BC), governor of Judea. *Nehemiah Grew*, (1641-1712), English botanist.

Neil // Neal, Neale, Neall, Nealon, Neel, Neill, Neils, Nels, Nial, Niall, Niel, Niels, Nil, Niles, Nils. *Gaelic:* "champion". Historical: *Niall of the Nine Hostages*, famous Irish ruler. "Champion", energetic, strong leader, charismatic, athletic, sportsman, dynamic, organizer, loved, respected, discounts conflicting ideas, genuinely concerned. *Neil Diamond*, (born 1941), U.S. singer, composer, and musician. *Neil Simon*, (born 1927), U.S. playwright and television and motion picture writer. *Neil Armstrong*, (born 1930), U.S. astronaut, the first man on the moon. *Nils*

Nordenskjold, (1869-1928), Swedish explorer. *Niels Bohr,* (1885-1962), a foremost 20th century scientist, Nobel prizewinning physicist. Totals: scientist 50%, politician 21%, activist 14%, engineer, inventor, playwright, musician, astronaut, composer, lawyer, businessman. Actors: *Neal McDonough, Neil Patrick Harris.*

Nels // Nils. *Scandinavian form of* Neil or Nelson.

Nelson // Nealson, Neils, Neilson, Nels, Nielsen, Nielson, Niles, Nils, Nilson, Nilsson. *English:* "son of Neil". Also see Neil. *Nelson Mandela,* (born 1918), South African president and anti-apartheid political and human rights activist. *Nelson Algren,* (1909-81), U.S. novelist and short-story writer. *Nelson Eddy,* (1901-67), U.S. baritone. *Nelson Aldrich,* (1841-1915), U.S. politician. *Nelson Dingley, Jr.* (1832-99), U.S. statesman and journalist. *Nelson Miles,* (1839-1925), U.S. soldier. Actor: *Nelson Eddy.*

Nestor // Nester. *Greek:* "traveler, wise".

Neville // Nev, Nevil, Nevile. *Old French:* "new town". *Neville Chamberlain,* (1869-1940), British politician, prime minister and businessman. *Nevil Shute,* (1899-1960), British author and aeronautical engineer. *Nevil Maskelyne,* (1732-1811), English astronomer royal. *Nevill Mott,* (born 1905), British physicist.

Newton. *Old English:* "new town". Honors: *Sir Isaac Newton,* chief figure of the 17th century scientific revolution. *Newton Minow,* (born 1926), U.S. lawyer and government official. *Newton Baker,* (1871-1937), U.S. lawyer and political leader.

Nicholas // Claus, Colas, Cole, Colet, Colin, Klaus, Niccolo, Nichole, Nichols, Nick, Nickey, Nickie, Nickolas, Nickolaus, Nicky, Nicol, Nicolai, Nicolas, Nicolis, Niki, Nikita, Nikki, Nikolai, Nikolas, Nikolaus, Nikolos, Nikos. *Greek:* "victorious among the people, victory of the people". Historical: *Saint Nicholas,* (4th century), bishop of Myra of which great modern legend has evolved. Humorous, fun-loving, very relational, center of attention, energetic, adventurous, artistic, creative, quick mind, athletic, strong, active, smart, good grades, independently handles difficulties, compliant, hard working, bit money motivated, friendly, easy-going, as leader may behave a bit sovereign, poorly controls himself when angry or jealous, falls in love easily and passionately, quick to ask for marriage, diligent at improving the house, does many of his own repairs, loving toward children, personality switches around children, lenient and spoiling toward children, self-loving; not only does woman's beauty matter, but so does her character and intelligence. *Niccolo Machiavelli,* (1469-1527), thoughtful Italian Renaissance writer of powerful prose, politician. *Niccolo Paganini,* (1782-1840), Italian violinist and composer, flamboyant showman. *Nicholas Biddle,* (1786-1844), U.S. statesman, financier, and author. *Nicholas Butler,* (1862-1947), U.S. educator, publicist and writer. Also several Popes and Russian czars by this name. Totals: politician 33%, writer 19%, clergy 15%, composer 11%, businessman 11%, scientist 11%, architect 11%, educator 7%, artist 7%, commander 7%, inventor 7%, philosopher, publicist, pioneer, lawyer. Actors: *Nicholas Brendon, Nicholas Lea, Nicolas Cage.*

Nick // Nickie, Nicky. *Short form ofm of* Nicholas. Also see Nicholas. *Nick Faldo,* (born 1959), English golfer.

Niels // Niles, Nils. *Danish form of* Neil and Nelson.

Nigel // Nye. *Latin:* "black". Actor: *Nigel Bennett.*

Nikko // Niko. *Form of* Nicholas.

Noah // Noach, Noak, Noe. *Hebrew:* "wandering, rest". Biblical: the patriarch who built the Ark. *Noah Webster,* (1758-1843), wrote Webster's Dictionary, teacher, lawyer, judge, politician. *Noah Swayne,* (1804-84), U.S. jurist, lawyer and politician. *Noah Porter,* (1811-92), U.S. educator, editor. *Noah Beery,* (1884-1945), U.S. film actor. Actors: *Noah Hathaway, Noah Taylor, Noah Wyle.*

Noe. Possibly *form of* Noel.

Noel // Nowell. *French from Latin:* "the Nativity, Christmas". *Noel Coward,* (1899-1973), actor, singer, and composer. *Noel Chabanel,* (1613-49), Canadian Jesuit missionary.

Nolan // Noland. *Gaelic:* "famous, noble". Peace-loving, industrious, helpful, "noble", good. *Nolan Ryan,* (Lynn Nolan Ryan, Jr.) (born 1947), U.S. baseball pitcher.

Norbert // Bert, Bertie, Berty, Norberto, Norbie, Norby. *Scandinavian:* "brilliant hero". *Norbert Rillieux,* (1806-94), U.S. scientist. *Norbert,* (died 1134), German saint, archbishop of Magdeburg, founded Premonstratensian monastic order. *Norbert Wiener,* (1894-1964), scientist, professor of mathematics, cybernetics.

Norman // Norm, Normand, Normie, Normy. *Old French:* "Norseman, Norman, North-man". Peaceful, not pushy, able. *Norman Rockwell,* (1894-1978), celebrated Americana painter of The Saturday Evening Post. *Norman Thomas,* (1884-1968), clergyman, social reformer, editor, political candidate, Socialist. *Norman Mailer,* (born 1923), author, engineer. *Norman Lear,* (born 1922), U.S. TV producer, writer, director. *Norman Vincent Peale,* (1898-1988), U.S. clergyman and writer. *H. Norman Schwarzkopf,* (born 1934), U.S. Army general. Totals: writer 42%, editor 13%, scientist 13%, artist/designer 13%, doctor 8%, agriculturist 8%, clergy 8%, businessman, athlete, politician, composer, educator, commander, producer, director, reformer.

Norris // Norrie, Norry. *Old French:* "man from the north". *Norris Ray Crump,* (born 1904), Canadian business executive.

Northrop // North Northrup. *Old English:* "north farm". *Northrop Frye,* (1912-91), Canadian educator and literary critic.

Obadiah // Obadias, Obed, Obediah, Obi, Obie, Oby. *Hebrew:* "servant of God". Biblical: *Obadiah,* (6th century BC), Hebrew minor prophet. *Obed Hussey,* (1792-1860), U.S. inventor, invented corn grinder.

Octavio // Octavius. *Latin:* "eighth". *Octavio Paz,* (born 1914), Mexican poet and diplomat.

Ogden // Ogdan, Ogdon. *Old English:* "oaked terrain". *Ogden Nash,* (1902-71), American humorist. *Ogden Reid,*

(1882-1947), U.S. newspaperman, editor. *Ogden Mills*, (1884-1937), U.S. lawyer and political leader.

Olaf // Olav, Ole, Olen, Olin. *Scandinavian:* "ancestral talisman". Historical: five Norwegian kings bore this name. Also see Oleg. *Ole Bull*, (1810-80), Norwegian violinist and composer. *Olav Duun*, (1876-1939), Norwegian novelist. *Ole Roemer,* (or Olaus Romer) (1644-1710), Danish astronomer.

Oleg. *Scandinavian:* "sacred". *Oleg* (died 912?), Viking leader who became founder of Kievan Rus' state. *Oleg D. Baklanov*, (born 1932), hard-line Soviet politician, armaments specialist, first deputy chairman of Defense Council, was one of the "gang of 8" leaders of Aug. 1991 coup. *Oleg Konstantinovich Popov*, (born 1930), Russian, famed as world's greatest living clown. Easily influenced child, parents should be aware of his friends, learns bad habits quickly, talented in exact sciences, analytical mind, tendency to analyze everything; principled adult, fighting for his opinion even if incorrect, pursues and reaches his goals, his ability to concentrate gives good results in science, attached to his parents - especially mother, polite but cold relation with in-laws, doesn't hide his belief that his mother is the ideal woman, tries to make his wife similar to his mother, helps without ulterior motives, his capabilities and stubbornness make relating difficult; he is not always able to suppress his feelings of superiority, faithful husband but a bit cold.

Olin. *English form of* Olaf. *Olin Warner,* (1844-96), U.S. sculptor.

Oliver // Oliveira, Olivero, Olivier, Oliviero, Ollie, Olly,

Olvan. *Latin:* "olive tree". *Scandinavian:* "kind, affectionate". Family man, friendly, peaceable, scheming. *Oliver Wendell Holmes*, (1809-94), famous U.S. writer, surgeon, teacher, and lecturer. *Oliver Wendell Holmes, Jr.* (1841-1935), one of the most famous U.S. Supreme Court justices. *Oliver Cromwell*, (1599-1658), Lord Protector of Great Britain, soldier, statesman, chief leader of the Puritan Revolution. *Oliver Perry* (1785-1819), U.S. navel commander and hero. Totals: politician 33%, commander 24%, writer 24%, scientist 19%, judge 10%, lawyer 10%, composer, artist, humorist, actor, director, inventor, farmer. Actors: *Oliver Platt, Olivier Tuinier.*

Omar. *Arabic:* "first son, highest". *Omar* (581?-644), 2nd Muslim caliph, organizer of Muslim power from warring sect to empire. *Omar Bradley*, (1893-1981), U.S. Army 5-star General, chairman of the Joint Chiefs of Staff. *Omar Khayyam,* (1048-1122), brilliant scholar and poet, mastered mathematics, philosophy, astronomy, law, medicine, and history. Actor: *Omri Katz.*

Orion. *Greek:* "son of fire". Greek Mythology: a mighty hunter who became the constellation of Orion.

Orland // Land, Lannie, Lanny, Orlan, Orlando, Orlon. *Old English:* "pointed land". Also see Roland. *Orlando di Lasso,* (1532?-94), celebrated composer. *Orlando Gibbons*, (1583-1625), English composer.

Orson // Orsen, Orssen, Sonnie, Sonny, Urson. *Latin:* "bearlike". *Orson Welles,* (George Orson Welles) (1915-85), U.S. actor, writer, and producer for radio, stage, and screen.

Orville // Orv. *Old French:* "golden estate". *Orville Wright,* (1871-1948), co-inventor and pilot of first successful powered airplane. *Orville Freeman,* (born 1918), U.S. public official. *Orville Browning,* (1806-81), U.S. politician and lawyer. *Orville Platt,* (1827-1905), U.S. politician.

Osborn // Osborne, Osbourn, Osbourne, Ozzie, Ozzy. *Old English:* "warrior of God". *Scandinavian:* "divine bear". *Osborne Reynolds,* (1842-1912), British physicist.

Oscar // Oskar, Ossie, Ossy, Ozzie, Ozzy. *Scandinavian:* "spear of a deity, divine spearman". High percentage (39%) famous for some aspect of the performing arts of music or theater. Can't sit still as child, provoking behavior, likes learning, persistent, many friends at school; fascinated with music chess and tennis; lack patients in everything, calmer as adult, well educated, offended easily, hospitable, prefers to host over being a guest, doctor, musician, computer programmer, journalist, teacher, coach, artist, architect, jeweler. *Oscar Wilde,* (1854-1900), Irish poet and comedy dramatist. *Oscar Hammerstein,* (1847-1919), U.S. opera and theater director. *Oscar Hammerstein,* II (1895-1960), U.S. lyric writer and librettist, 'The Sound of Music'. *Oscar Straus,* (1870-1954), Austrian composer and musical conductor. Totals: politician 17%, composer 11%, musician 11%, athlete 11%, writer 11%, dramatist, actor, conductor, lyricist, director, musicologist, architect, artist, lawyer, public servant, inventor, physiologist, librarian.

Osmar. *Germanic:* "god of the sea".

Oswald // Osbaldo, Ossie, Ossy, Osvaldo, Oswaldo, Oswell, Ozzie, Ozzy, Wald, Waldo. *Old English:* "having power from God". *Oswald Spengler,* (1880-1936), German

historical political philosopher. *Oswald Mosley*, (1896-1980), British politician. *Oswald Avery,* (1877-1955), U.S. bacteriologist. *Oswald Villard*, (1872-1949), U.S. journalist. *Oswald Jacoby*, (1902-84), U.S. bridge card game expert.

Otis // Oates, Otes. *Old English:* "son of Otto". *Greek:* "keen of hearing". *Otis Barton*, (born 1899?), U.S. oceanic explorer. *Otis Skinner,* (1858-1942), U.S. actor.

Otto // Odo, Othello, Otho. *Old German:* "rich". *Otto von Bismarck*, (1815-98), Germany's "iron chancellor" who created a powerful empire. *Otto Klemperer*, (1885-1973), last of the "Austro-German" conductors. *Otto Jespersen*, (1860-1943), linguist and a foremost authority on English grammar. *Otto I* (912-73), a strong Holy Roman emperor from 962 to 973. *Otto Hahn*, (1879-1968), German chemist and co-discoverer of nuclear fission. Totals: scientist 39%, commander 17%, conductor, linguist, explorer, athlete-manager-coach, dramatist-novelist, inventor, composer, psychoanalyst, banker, lyricist.

Owen // Ewen. *Form of* Even. *Owen Tudor*, (1400?-61), handsome Welsh border lord, who gave name to House of Tudor. *Owen Chamberlain*, (born 1920), U.S. physicist, discovered the antiproton. *Owen Lattimore*, (1900-89), U.S. author and educator, international relations adviser. Totals: author-novelist-playwright 33%, scientist 25%, lawyer 17%, commander 17%, labor leader, judge, astronaut.

Ozzie // Ozzy. *Short form ofm of* names beginning with "os".

Pablo. *Spanish form of* Paul. *Pablo Neruda*, (1904-73), Latin American poet, committed to politics and social reform. *Pablo Picasso*, (1881-1973), primarily a painter, also a fine sculptor, engraver, and ceramist. *Pablo Casals*, (1876-1973), Spanish violoncellist, pianist, conductor, and composer. *Pablo de Sarasate*, (1844-1908), Spanish violinist. *Pablo Morales*, (born 1965), U.S. swimmer.

Paddy. *Irish familiar form of* Patrick.

Park // Parke. *Short form ofm of* Parker.

Parker // Park, Parke. *Middle English:* "guardian of the park". Parker Fillmore, (1878-1944), U.S. author, folktales and fairy tales for children.

Parry. *Form of* Perry.

Pasha. *Turkish:* former title of nobility.

Pat // Pattie, Patty. *Short form ofm of* names containing "pat". *Pat Riley*, (born 1945), winningest 1980s National Basketball Association coach. *Pat Robertson*, (Marion Gordon Robertson) (born 1930), U.S. religious broadcaster.

Patrick // Paddie, Paddy, Padraic, Padraig, Padriac, Pat, Paton, Patric, Patrice, Patricio, Patrizio, Patrizius, Patsy, Patten, Pattie, Patty. *Latin:* "nobleman, patrician". Historical: *St. Patrick* (5th century) - Missionary to Ireland. converting the people of Ireland to Christianity. Adventurous, belongs to a group, helper, accepting of others until shown disrespect. *Patrice Lumumba*, (1925-61), first prime minister of the Congo, now Zaire, folk hero. *Patrick Henry*, (1736-99), Fearless and eloquent American Revolutionary War orator and leader. *Patrick White*, (1912-90), Australian author of plays, novels, and short stories. *Patrick Swayze*, (born 1952), U.S. actor, star athlete in high school and college. Totals: politician 21%, clergy 16%, lawyer 16%, writer 11%, commander 11%, actor, physician, editorial cartoonist, scientist, artist, band master, sheriff, judge. Actors: *Patrick McGoohan, Patrick Muldoon, Patrick Stewart.*

Paul // Pablo, Pall, Paolo, Paulie, Pauly, Pavel, Poul. *Latin:* "small, little". Biblical: *Saul of Tarsus*, (AD 10?-67?), renamed Paul at his conversion was the great missionary apostle of Christianity to the non-Jews. Very friendly, kind, responsive, as child playing with peers he is responsible and tries to keep his peers from over-running other's boundaries and getting into trouble, calm, compassionate, these qualities attract others to him who confide in him, not gruff or rough personality; love to be excited and happy especially working with others, affectionate, joke around to build relationships, confident/optimistic, energetic, quick mind, thinker, usually picks an occupation which fits his personality, tend to be a philosopher; although not silent - he doesn't talk very much; in his calm personality everything seems in harmony and nothing stands out as distinctive; loves his wife with warmth and stability, not passionately or stormily; would take extra work if they need the money and it doesn't change his stable life; colleges like his unassuming attitude, hard work, reliability and readiness to assist; writer, artistic expression usually through words or two dimensional art, explorer of thoughts and ideas. Many significant Pauls. Many Popes assumed this name. *Paul Ehrlich*, (1854-1915), microbiologist physiological scientist. *Paul Tillich*, (1886-1965), influential and creative Protestant theologians. *Paul Revere*, (1735-1818), American revolutionary patriot, metal smith, minuteman, inventor. *Paul Cezanne*, (1839-1906), artist, "the father of modern painting". *Paul Gauguin,* (1848-1903), leading French painter. Totals: author (novelist, poet, dramatist, etc.) 29%, scientist 17%, politician 16%, artist 13%, historian 5%, clergy 5%, businessman 5%, song writer 4%, economist 4%, educator 4%, actor 4%, noted scholar 2%, commander 2%, patriot 2%, composer 2%, athlete 2%, explorer 2%, civil servant 2%, director 2%, photographer, theologian, singer, architect, inventor, librarian, astronaut, coach. Actors: *Paul Gross, Paul Michael Valley, Paul Newman, Paul Nicholls, Paul Petersen.*

Paxton // Packston, Paxon. *Latin:* "peaceful town". *Paxton Hibben,* (1880-1928), U.S. journalist.

Pedro. *Spanish form of* Peter. *Pedro Calderon de la Barca*, (1600-81), great Spanish playwright, themes were love, honor, patriotism, religion, and philosophy, studied law, cavalryman, priest, chaplain to the king. *Pedro Menendez de Aviles,* (1519-74), Spanish explorer, founded forts, massacred a nearby colony of French Protestants. *Pedro Alvares Cabral,* (1467?-1520), Portuguese explorer, discovered Brazil. Totals: soldier 56%, writer 33%, explorer 33%, brutal, director, educator, politician, priest.

Percival // Parsifal, Perceval, Percy, Purcell. *Old French:* "pierce the valley". Literary: the hero in Chretien de Troyes grail search epic. *Percy Shelley*, (1792-1822), English lyric poet. *Percy Ellis Sutton*, (born 1920), U.S. legislator and public official. *Percy Grainger,* (1882-1961), U.S. pianist and composer. *Percy Bridgman*, (1882-1961), U.S. physicist. *Percival Wren*, (1885-1941), British novelist. *Percy MacKaye*, (1875-1956), U.S. dramatist and poet. *Percy Pilcher,* (1866-99), British aviation pioneer. *Percy Julian*, (1899-1975), U.S. chemist.

Perry // Parry. *Middle English:* "pear tree". *Old French:* "little Peter". *Familiar form of* Peter. *Perry Como*, (originally Pierino Como) (born 1913), U.S. singer, radio, movies, television. *Perry Ellis*, (1940-86), U.S. sportswear fashion designer.

Peter // Farris, Ferris, Parry, Peadar, Pearce, Peder, Pedro, Peirce, Perkin, Perren, Perry, Pete, Peterus, Petey, Petr, Pierce, Pierre, Pierson, Pieter, Pietrek, Pietro, Piotr. *Greek:* "stone, pebble". Biblical: *Simon (called Peter)* was a leader of the Twelve Apostles. Confident, athletic, intelligent, stable, not imprudent, enjoys adventure but not fool hardy, fairly wise, respected and trusted leader, noble demeanor, broad interests and abilities; curious boy who wants to know everything; often talented in music and has good voice; seldom has problem with studies; pursues higher education; takes his profession seriously - tries to be one of the best; ability to analyze; systematical; detective, writer, scientist; looks for a long time to find a girl who matches his ideal, then moves in quickly with determination; mainly values faithfulness in a wife, other qualities are not so important for him; caring, likes to care for children and old people; very attached to mother; wife will have to bear with the importance he places on his mother's opinion; jealous; can be unfaithful only when in conflict with his wife as a way to gain self-affirmation. *Peter the Great*, (1672-1725), founder of the Russian Empire. *Peter Fabergé,* (1846-1920), among the greatest goldsmiths, jewelers, and designers in Western decorative arts. *Peter Ilich Tchaikovsky,* (1840-93), composer of 'Swan Lake', shy man, expressed his emotions in music. Totals: author-novelist-playwright-folklorist-editor-etc 19%, politician 14%, businessman 14%, artist 10%, scientist 9%, clergy 9%, inventor 7%, actor 7%, educator 5%, zoologist 3%, director 3%, hero 3%, sailer, logition-teacher-theologean, composer, "anarchist-communism", jewler, musician, clockmaker, producer, architect, printer, explorer, philanthropist, jurist, doctor, conductor, lawyer, athlete, engineer. Actors: *Pete Postlethwaite, Peter Berg, Peter MacNicol, Peter O'Toole, Peter Reckell, Peter Sellers, Peter Tork, Peter Wingfield.*

Peyton // Pate, Payton. *Old English:* "warrior estate". *Peyton Randolph,* (1721?-75), North American statesman and patriot. *Peyton March,* (1864-1955), U.S. Army general and chief of Army General Staff.

Phil. *Short form ofm of* Filbert, Filmore and Philip. *Phil Hill,* (born 1927), U.S. auto racing driver. *Phil Collins,* (born 1951), British rock musician, drummer, lead singer, songwriter. *Phil Donahue*, (born 1935), long-reigning white-maned daytime talk-show host, ardent feminist, interview style is aggressive. *Phil Esposito*, (Philip Anthony Esposito) (born 1942), Canadian ice-hockey player.

Philip // Felipe, Filip, Filippo, Phil, Philipp, Phillip, Phillipe, Phillipp, Pippo. *Greek:* "lover of horses". Biblical: one of the Twelve Apostles. Fun-loving, thinker, relational, able, humanitarian, courteous, genteel, often writer, often political, creative mind; capricious and stubborn child; resembles mother; squeamish; a bit scatter brained; jealous; many are self-loving; often don't like big groups; talented but these may lay undiscovered; marriage is often a bit difficult due to his stubbornness; doctor, jurist, electrician, singer, engineer, aviator. *Philip Sheridan*, (1831-88), U.S. army general, one of the three great Union commanders of the American Civil War. *Philip John Schuyler,* (1733-1804), American Revolutionary War general, statesman, and wealthy landowner. *Philip Glass*, (born 1937), modern composer, also degrees in mathematics and philosophy. *Filippo Brunelleschi,* (1377-1446), "a man of great genius," architect, goldsmith, sculptor, invented machines, studied mathematics, hydraulics, time and motion. Totals: writer 23%, politician 19%, commander 13%, clergy 10%, artist 10%, physician 8%, architect 4%, labor leader 4%, businessman 4%, scientist 4%, theater manager 4%, actor-director, hero, composer-musician, bacteriologist-serologist, philanthropist, historian, equestrian, lawyer, corrupt.

Phineas. *Hebrew:* "oracle". *Phineas Fletcher,* (1582-1650), English poet. *Phineas Quimby*, (1802-66), U.S. spiritualist and healer. *P.T. (Phineas Taylor) Barnum*, (1810-91), U.S. entertainer, hoaxes, said the "public loves to be fooled".

Pierce // Pearce, Peirce. *English form of* Peter. *Pierce Butler,* (1866-1939), U.S. jurist, lawyer. Actor: *Pierce Brosnan.*

Pierre. *French form of* Peter. Politician, artistic type. *Pierre Trudeau,* (born 1919), Canada's 15th prime minister.

Pierre Laval, (1883-1945), twice elected premier of France. *Pierre Cardin*, (born 1922), French dress designer. Totals: politician 26%, writer-poet-novelist-playwright 18%, explorer-fur trader 10%, clergy 10%, artist 8%, scientist 6%, mathematician 4%, conductor 4%, engraver 4%, architect 4%, philosopher 4%, lawyer 4%, engineer 4%, dancer, commander, dress designer, educator-sportsman, businessman, archaeologist, zoologist.

Preston. *English:* "priest's estate".

Prince // Prinz. *Latin:* "prince". *Prince Hall,* (1748-1807), U.S. champion of black peoples' rights.

Quentin // Quent, Quincy, Quinn, Quint, Quintin, Quinton, Quintus. *Latin:* "fifth". *Quentin Matsys*, (1466-1530), Flemish realistic artist. *Quentin Reynolds*, (1902-65), U.S. journalist and writer. *Quintus Roscius*, (died 62 BC), great Roman comic actor actor. *Quintus Ennius*, (239-169 BC), Latin epic poet, called father of Roman poetry. Actor: *Quentin Tarantino*.

Quinn. *Gaelic:* "wise". *Short form ofm of* Quentin, Quincy and Quinlan.

Rad // Raddie, Raddy. *Short form ofm of* names beginning with "rad".

Rafael // Rafe, Raffaello. *Spanish form of* Raphael.

Rafe. *Short form ofm of* Rafferty, Ralph and Raphael.

Rainer. *German form of* Raynor.

Ralph // Rafe, Raff, Ralf, Raoul, Raul, Rolf, Rolph. *Germanic:* "wolf in counsel, wolf-counselor". Determined, constant, quite sociable, writer, not usually a scientist (except for "soft" sciences), often salesman or buyer, bit artistic. Totals: writer 40%, politician 10%, potter 10%, philosopher 10%, educator 10%, artist 10%, athlete 10%, composer, consumer advocate, clergy-civil rights leader, actor, architect, lawyer, publisher, anthropologist. Actors: *Ralph Fiennes, Ralph Macchio*.

Ramiro. *Latin:* "highest judge".

Ramon. *Spanish form of* Raymond. Also see Raymond. *Ramon Magsaysay*, (1907-57), Philippine political leader, army guerrilla. *Ramon Llull*, (1235?-1315), Spanish scientist and missionary, authority on Arabic.

Ramsay // Ram, Ramsey. *Old English:* "ram's island". *Ramsay MacDonald*, (1866-1937), first Labour party prime minister of Great Britain. *Ramsey Clark*, (William Ramsey Clark) (born 1927), U.S. lawyer and public official.

Rand. *Old English:* "warrior, shield". *Short form ofm of* Randall and Randolph.

Randall // Rand, Randal, Randell, Randy. *Modern form of* Randolph. Also see Randy. *Randall Thomas Davidson*, first baron of Lambeth (1848-1930), British clergy, archbishop of Canterbury. *Randall Jarrell*, (1914-65), U.S. children's poet and university professor. *Randall Terry*, founder of U.S. antiabortion group Operation Rescue.

Randolph // Rand, Randal, Randall, Randell, Randolf, Randy. *Germanic:* "shield-wolf". Also see Randy. *Randolph Caldecott*, (1846-86), English artist of everything countryside, loved horses, dogs, and countryside. *Randolph Churchill*, (1849-95), British statesman and Lord. *Randolph Rogers*, (1825-92), U.S. sculptor. *Randolph Pate*, (1898-1961), U.S. Marine Corps 4-star general.

Randy // Randi, Randie. *Short form ofm of* Randall and Randolph. Athletic, group activities. *Randy Travis*, (born 1959), country music singer and songwriter.

Ransom. *English:* "ransom"; *Old English:* "shield's son". *Ransom Eli Olds*, (1864-1950), U.S. pioneer automobile builder.

Raoul // Raul. *French form of* Ralph and Rudolph. *Raoul Wallenberg*, (1912-47?), Swedish businessman-diplomat, civilian WW II hero, helped 100,000 Hungarian Jews escape deportation to Nazi death camps. *Raul H. Castro*, (born 1916), U.S. governor of Arizona. *Raoul Dufy*, (1877-1953), French artist. *Raoul Lufbery*, (1884-1918), U.S. aviator ace. *Raul Alfonsin*, (born 1926), Argentine lawyer and middle-of-the-road politician. *Raul Castro*, (born

1930), Cuban revolutionist. Actor: *Raul Julia*.

Raphael // Falito, Rafael, Rafaelle, Rafaello, Rafe, Rafi, Ray. *Hebrew:* "God has healed". Literary: from Apocryphal book 'Tobit' - the angel Gabriel's brother. Artistic type. *Raphael*, (1483-1520), Italian master painter and architect. *Rafael Trujillo Molina*, (1891-1961), tyrannical dictator of the Dominican Republic, general. Totals: writer 27%, politician 18%, commander 18%, composer 18%, conductor, pianist, illustrator, geologist-traveler, engraver, painter-architect.

Rashad. *Arabic:* "wise counselor".

Raul. *Form of* Ralph. *Raul H. Castro*, (born 1916), U.S. public official, first Mexican-American governor of Arizona. *Raul Castro*, (born 1930), Cuban revolutionist, brother of Fidel Castro. *Raul Alfonsin*, (born 1926), Argentine lawyer and middle-of-the-road politician.

Ray. *Old French:* "kingly". *Short form ofm of* names beginning with "ray". Also see Raymond. Inner strength. *Sugar Ray Leonard*, (popular name of Ray Charles Leonard) (born 1956), U.S. boxing champion. *Ray Charles*, (Ray Charles Robinson) (born 1932), U.S. singer and recording star. *Ray Kroc*, (1902-84), U.S. founder of the fast-food industry with his worldwide McDonald's enterprise. *Ray Bradbury*, (born 1920), U.S. author, science fiction and fantasy short stories. Totals: athlete 42%, politician 25%, musician, businessman, writer, educator, clergy.

Raymond // Raimondo, Raimund, Raimundo, Ramón, Ray, Raymund, Reamonn. *Germanic:* "mighty or wise protector". Good natured, inner strength, easy going. *Raymond*

Massey. (1896-1983), Canadian-American actor. *Raymond Poincare*, (1860-1934), French statesmen and premier. *Raymond Spruance*, (1886-1969), U.S. naval officer, commanded Fifth Fleet during World War II. Totals: public official 21%, architect 14%, athlete 14%, actor, politician, zoologist, sculptor, lawyer, businessman, industrial designer, economist, biologist-statistician, restaurateur, commander.

Raynor // Ragnar, Rainer, Ray, Rayner, Reiner. *Scandinavian:* "mighty army". *Rainer Rilke*, (1875-1926), German author and poet. *Ragnar Frisch*, (1895-1973), Norwegian economist. *Ragnar Granit,* (born 1900), Swedish neurophysiologist.

Reece // Rees, Reese, Rice. *Celtic:* "hero". *Old Welsh:* "stream". *Reece (Goose) Tatum*, (1921-67), U.S. basketball player, Harlem Globetrotters, later had own team, Harlem Road Kings.

Reed // Read, Reade, Reid. *Old English:* "red-haired". *Reed Smoot*, (1862-1941), U.S. political figure and Mormon leader.

Reginald // Reg, Reggie, Reggis, Reginauld, Reinald, Reinaldo, Reinaldos, Reinhold, Reinwald, Renault, Rene, Reynold, Reynolds, Rinaldo. *Germanic:* "wise ruler"; *Old English:* "powerful and mighty". There seems to be a strong artistic side here, especially musical. *Reginald Marsh,* (1898-1954), American painter. *Reginald De Koven,* (1859-1920), U.S. composer, founded and conducted Washington Symphony Orchestra. *Reginald Stewart,* (born 1900), Canadian pianist and conductor. Totals: politician 25%, clergy 25%, conductor 25%, composer,

pianist, painter, physicist-engineer, banker, lawyer.

Reid. *Form of* Reed.

René. *French from Latin:* "reborn". *French short form ofm of* Reginald. *Rene Descartes*, (1596-1650), began both modern philosophy and modern mathematics. *Rene Laennec*, (1781-1826), French physician who invented the stethoscope. *Rene Dubos*, (1901-82), bacteriologist. Totals: politician 29%, scientist 18%, missionary 12%, philosopher, actor-director, museum director, physician, lawyer, jewler, jurist, poet, economist, aviator ace, artist, explorer. Actor: *Rene Auberjonois*.

Reuben // Reuven, Rouvin, Rube, Ruben, Rubin, Ruby. *Hebrew:* "behold, a son". Biblical: the eldest son of Jacob and patriarch of the tribe of Reuben. Somewhat nervous; hard working; loves children, not just his own; good intuition; discerning about people; scatter-brained, not ordinary in his thinking; hospitable; likes to be a guest; likes to give gifts. *Ruben Dario*, (1867-1916), great poet. *Rubin Goldmark*, (1872-1936), U.S. composer and teacher of music. *Rube (Reuben) Goldberg* (1883-1970), cartoonist, satirist, poked fun at unnecessary complications of modern technology.

Rex. *Latin:* "king". *Rex Harrison*, (1908-90), British actor, Professor Henry Higgins movie 'My Fair Lady'.

Rey // Reyes. *Form of* Ray and names which start with Rey.

Reynard // Ray, Raynard, Reinhard, Renard, Renaud, Rey. *Old French:* "fox"; *Old German:* "mighty". Literary: Reynard the Fox (in German, Reineke Fuchs), popular character depicted in medieval Beast Epic and in later fables and stories. *Reinhard Scheer,* (1863-1928), German WW I admiral. *Reinhard Heydrich,* (1904-42), German political leader, director of Gestapo.

Reynold // Renado, Renaldo, Renato, Reynaldo, Reynolds. *English form of* Reginald. *Reynaldo Bignone,* (born 1928), Argentine general, president of Argentina.

Rhett. *Welsh form of* Reece. Literary: Rhett Butler, hero of Margaret Mitchell's saga 'Gone with the Wind'.

Ricardo. *Form of* Richard. Actor: *Ricardo Montalban.*

Rich // Richie, Richy, Ritchie. *Short form ofm of* Richard.

Richard // Dick, Dickie, Dicky, Ric, Ricard, Ricardo, Riccardo, Rich, Richardo, Richart, Richie, Richy, Rick, Rickard, Rickert, Rickey, Ricki, Rickie, Ricky, Rico, Riki, Riocard, Ritchie. *Germanic:* "strong ruler". Very relational, relational leader, fun-loving, humorous, focused, determined, enough confidence even when feeling lacking, what he lacks in knowledge or intelligence he makes up in relational ability, he finds most everything interesting and can do most anything, typical politician type, usually a faithful and caring spouce. Several kings of England bore this name. *Richard M. Nixon,* first U.S. president to resign. *Richard Rodgers,* (1902-79), composer of musical comedy theater classics including 'The Sound of Music'. *Richard Wagner,* (1813-83), among the great theater composers. *Richard E. Byrd,* (1888-1957), pioneer aviator and polar explorer. Totals: politician 30%, writer 27%, lawyer 10%, commander 8%, scientist 6%, explorer-adventurer 4%, actor 4%, composer 4%, inventor 4%, businessman 4%, educator 4%, clergy 3%, athlete 3%, architect 3%, comedian 2%, artist 2%, classical scholar 2%, reformer 2%,

geographer, historian, pioneer aviator, publisher, musician, cartoonist, engineer, naturalist, jurist, philosopher, economist, conductor, astronaut, librarian. Actors: *Richard Biggs, Richard Burgi, Richard Burton, Richard Dean Anderson, Richard Dreyfuss, Richard Gere, Richard Lee Jackson, Richard Lynch.*

Richmond // Richmound. *Old German:* "powerful protector". *Richmond Hobson,* (1870-1937), U.S. Navy hero and politician.

Rick // Ric, Rickie, Ricky, Rik. *Short form ofm of* Richard and names containing the sound "rik". *Rick Mears,* (born 1951) U.S. race car driver. *Ricky Skaggs,* country music performer. *Ricky Henderson,* professional baseball player, held the stolen-base record. Actors: *Rick Schroder, Ricky Martin.*

Riley. *Gaelic:* "valiant".

Rip. *Dutch:* "ripe, full-grown". *Short form ofm of* Ripley and *familiar form of* Robert and Rupert. Actor: *Rip Torn.*

River. *English:* "river". Actor: *River Phoenix.*

Roarke // Rorke, Rourke. *Gaelic:* "famous ruler". *Roark Bradford,* (1896-1948), U.S. novelist and short-story writer. Actor: *Roark Critchlow.*

Rob // Robb, Robbie, Robby. *Short form ofm of* Robert. Actor: *Rob Schneider.*

Robert // Bob, Bobbie, Bobby, Rab, Riobard, Rip, Rob, Robb, Robbie, Robby, Robers, Roberto, Robin, Rupert, Ruperto, Ruprecht. *Germanic:* "bright fame". Warm, determined, responsible, serious, leader, manager, blue collar or professional, talker, relational, self confident, able, orator, strangley small number of clergy, seem to be more relational than religious, not likely to be a comedian or cartoonist, not the funny type, problem solver. *Robert Frost,* (1874-1963), great U.S. poet, tells of simple things, deep feeling for life's fundamentals love, loyalty, awareness of nature and of God. *Robert Fulton*, (1765-1815), successful inventor pioneer of steamboats. *Robert E. Lee*, (1807-70), general, the American Confederacy's greatest soldier. *Robert Louis Stevenson*, (1850-1894), gifted English storyteller, poet, and essayist, 'Treasure Island'. *J. Robert Oppenheimer,* (1904-67), theoretical physicist, director of the scientists who developed the atomic bomb. Totals: politician 30%, writer 24%, scientist 14%, commander 12%, lawyer 12%, businessman 8%, artist 8%, explorer-adventurer 4%, actor 4%, judge 4%, athlete 4%, educator 4%, reformer 3%, inventor 3%, engineer 3%, editor 2%, publisher 2%, director 2%, composer, photojournalist, singer, conductor, conspirator, clergy, theatrical designer, dancer, test pilot, agnostic, sociologist. Actors: *Robert Beltran, Robert Davi, Robert De Niro, Robert Duncan McNeill, Robert O'Reilly, Robert Picardo, Robert Redford, Robert Rodriguez, Robert Sean Leonard, Robert Shayne, Robert Trebor, Robert Vaughn, Robert Wagner.*

Robin. *English:* "robin, a type of bird". *Familiar form of* Robert and a *short form ofm of* Robinson. Legend: Robin Hood of England. Relational, fairly athletic, a bit distinctive character. *Robin Williams*, (born 1952), U.S. actor and comedian. *Robin Collingwood*, (1889-1943), British historian and philosopher of history. *Robin Roberts*, (born 1926), U.S. baseball player. Actors: *Robin Shou, Robin Williams.*

Robinson // Robin, Robinet. *English:* "son of Robert". *Robinson Jeffers*, (1887-1962), U.S. poet, work shows rugged strength, tragic, often violent intensity of passion.

Rockwell. *Old English:* "rock well". *Rockwell Kent*, (1882-1971), artist, talented author, adventurous traveler.

Rock // Rockie, Rocky. *Short form ofm of* Rochester and Rockwell.

Rocky // Rockey, Rockie. *Modern familiar form of* Rochester, Rock and Rockwell. *Rocky Marciano*, (originally Rocco Marchegiano) (1923-69), U.S. boxer. *Rocky Graziano,* (1918?-90) (originally Thomas Rocco Barbella), U.S. boxer, known for brawling style and brutal fights, became popular as actor.

Rod // Rodd, Roddie, Roddy. *Short form ofm of* names beginning with "rod". *Rod Serling*, (1924-75), U.S. playwright, TV series: Twilight Zone. *Rod Stewart*, (born 1945), British musician, 'Hot Legs'. *Rod McKuen*, (born 1933), U.S. singer, composer, and poet. *Rod Laver,* (born 1938), Australian tennis champion.

Roderick // Rod, Rodd, Roddie, Roddy, Roderic, Roderich, Roderigo, Rodrick, Rodrigo, Rodriguez, Rodrique, Rory, Rurik, Ruy. *Germanic:* "famous ruler". *Roderick* (or Roderic), last king of the Visigoths reigning in Spain 710-11. *Rurik*, (died 879), Norse chieftain, founder of first Russian dynasty. *Roderick Finlayson*, (1818-92), Canadian fur trader, commanded Fort Victoria, B.C. *Roderick McKenzie*, (1761?-1844), Canadian fur trader, built Fort Chipewyan. *Roderick John (Bobby) Wallace*, (1874-1960), U.S. baseball player, chiefly a shortstop. *Roderick*

Murchison, (1792-1871), British geologist. *Roderick Haig-Brown,* (1908-76), Canadian writer, naturalist, and magistrate, books for children.

Rodger. *Form of* Roger.

Rodney // Rod, Rodd, Roddie, Roddy. *Old English:* "island clearing". Possibly: (Strong, muscular, solid build, buddy, athlete, sportsman, adventurer.) *Rodney Porter,* (1917-85), British biochemist and educator.

Rodolfo. *Form of* Rudolph.

Rodrigo. *Form of* Roderick.

Rogelio. *Spanish:* "famous warrior".

Roger // Rodge, Rodger, Rog, Rogerio, Rogers, Rudiger, Ruggiero, Rutger, Ruttger. *Germanic:* "famous spear or spearman". Relational, reader, learner, writer, often sportsman, original thinker. *Roger Bannister,* (born 1929), first athlete to run the mile in less than four minutes. *Roger Bacon,* (1214?-1294?), English friar, one of the earliest and most farseeing of scientists. *Roger Staubach,* (born 1942), U.S. football player, all-Ohio high school athlete in football, baseball, basketball, outstanding quarterback, 5 Super Bowls. Totals: writer 30%, scientist 19%, politician 19%, athlete 15%, clergy 11%, doctor 7%, educator 7%, lawyer-judge, media consultant-political imagemaker, classical scholar, commander, artist, composer, photographer. Actor: *Roger Howarth*.

Roland // Lannie, Lanny, Rolando, Roldan, Roley, Rolland, Rollie, Rollin, Rollins, Rollo, Rowland. *Germanic:* "famous land". Historical: hero of Charlemagne's army, favorite French hero of medieval legend. *Roland Ritchie,* (1910-88),

Canadian jurist. *Rowland Hill,* (1795-1879), British administrator, postal innovator. *Roland Garros,* (1888-1918), French aviator. *Roland Hayes,* (1887-1976), U.S. tenor, noted for singing of Negro spirituals. *Rowland Emett,* (born 1906), British cartoonist.

Rolf // Rolfe, Rollo, Rolph. *Old German:* "famous wolf". *German form of* Ralph and *short form of* Rudolph. *Rolf Hochhuth,* (born 1931) German playwright, movement known as Theater of Fact.

Roman // Roma, Romain. *Latin:* "from Rome". Can't stand a monotonous life; determined; athletic; he can move on to another task even when close to reaching a goal; falls in love easily; can change girl friends often, until he finds the one who will be fully devoted to him, this doesn't mean that he will be an ideal husband; his love of excitement can complicate his family life when first married; when his children are born he usually settles down and becomes a good father; usually a fun marriage partner; leader of the family, but not dictatorial or stubborn; helpful around the house; not frugal. *Roman Polanski,* film director.

Romeo. *Italian:* "pilgrim to Rome". Literary: the hero of Shakespeare's 'Romeo and Juliet'.

Ron // Ronnie, Ronny. *Short form ofm of* Aaron and Ronald. Stubborn, tenacious, tend to be physical, liking to work with hands, be carpenter or in construction, when not in these industries they tend to be physical through sports such as racket-ball or running. Marries: often marries Cindy. *Ron Howard,* (born 1954), U.S. actor and director. *Ron Mix,* (born 1938), U.S. football player, offensive tackle.

Ronald // Ron, Ronn, Ronnie, Ronny. *Scottish form of* Reginald. *Ronald Reagan*, (born 1911), extreamly popular 40th U.S. president, won the 'Cold War' against the Soviet Union. *Ronald Ross*, (1857-1932), British physician, proved role of mosquito in malaria transmission. *Ronald L. Ziegler*, (born 1939), U.S. advertising executive, chief press aide to *Richard M. Nixon*. Totals: politician 27%, scientist 27%, writer 18%, astronaut 18%, actor, advertising, lawyer, economist, world traveler, physician, judge.

Rory. *Gaelic:* "red king". *Irish familiar form of* Roderick. Quick mind, energetic.

Roscoe // Rosco, Ross, Rossie, Rossy. *Scandinavian:* "deer forest". *Roscoe Robinson, Jr.* (born 1928), U.S. Army four-star general. *Roscoe Conkling*, (1829-88), U.S. lawyer and political leader. *Roscoe Pound*, (1870-1964), U.S. lawyer and educator. Actor: *Roscoe Arbuckle*.

Ross // Rosse, Rossie, Rossy. *Old French:* "red"; *Gaelic:* "headland". *Short form ofm of* Roscoe. Overjoyed by praise, athletic, individualistic, short-sighted.

Roy // Roi, Ruy. *Gaelic:* "red"; *Old French:* "king". A *short form ofm of* Royal and Royce. Easy going, relational, friendly, helpful. *Roy Acuff*, (1903-92), U.S. country singer, songwriter, and fiddler, 'The Wabash Cannonball'. *Roy Orbison*, (1936-88), U.S. singer, songwriter, guitarist, 'Oh, Pretty Woman'. *Roy Lichtenstein*, (born 1923), painter pioneer in the so-called pop art movement. Totals: politician 33%, businessman 22%, musician 17%, athlete 11%, civil-rights leader 11%, lawyer, labor union criminal, explorer-naturalist-writer, historian, artist. Actors: *Roy Dupuis, Roy Rogers.*

Royal // Roy, Royall. *Old French:* "royal". *Royal Earl House*, (1814-95), American inventor, invented printing telegraph. *Royal Eason Ingersoll,* (1883-1976), U.S. Navy officer, deputy chief naval operations.

Ruben. *Form of* Reuben.

Rudd // Ruddie, Ruddy, Rudy. *Old English:* "ruddy-complection". *Short form ofm of* Rudyard. Also see Rudy.

Rudolph // Raoul, Raul, Rodolfo, Rodolph, Rodolphe, Rolf, Rolfe, Rolio, Rolph, Rudie, Rudof, Rudolfo, Rudy. *Germanic:* "famous wolf". Very talented; hard working; stubborn; filled with ideas; analytical mind; good in science; many inventors; when he lights up with a new idea, he can't do anything else, which irritates people; argumentative, likes to prove his point; one woman man, faithful; lets his wife make the lesser decisions, but makes the bigger decisions himself; jealous; talented sportsman; trust worthy; he discovers his talent after age thirty. *Rudolph*, (in French, Raoul) (died 936), duke of Burgundy and king of the Franks. *Rudolf Diesel*, (1858-1913), German engineer, invented diesel engine. *Rudolf Ludwig Mossbauer*, (born 1929), German-born physicist, discoveries helped prove Einstein's general theory of relativity. *Rudolph Valentino*, (Rodolfo d'Antonguolla) (1895-1926), U.S. silent motion-picture actor, very popular romantic actor. Totals: scientist 32%, musician 18%, philosopher 18%, dancer 9%, actor, engineer-inventor, auto racer, occultist, artist, commander. Actor: *Rudolph Valentino*.

Rudy // Rudie. *Short form ofm of* names beginning with "rud". *Rudy Perpich*, (born 1928), U.S. public official, governor of Minnesota. *Rudi Gernreich*, (1922-85), U.S. dress designer noted for off-beat fashions. *Rudy Vallee*, (called the Vagabond Lover) (1901-86), U.S. bandleader, saxophonist, and singer.

Rudyard // Rudd, Ruddie, Ruddy, Rudy. *Old English:* "red enclosure". *Rudyard Kipling*, (1865-1936), British writer, author of 'The Jungle Book'.

Rufus // Rufe *Latin:* "red (haired)". Lawyer, political leader, author, editor. *Rufus Putnam*, (1738-1824), U.S. general and businessman. *Rufus Peckham*, (1838-1909), U.S. jurist, lawyer. *Rufus Choate*, (1799-1859), U.S. lawyer, famous orator. *Rufus King*, (1755-1827), U.S. statesman. *Rufus Isaacs*, (1860-1935), British jurist and political leader. *Rufus Jones*, (1863-1948), U.S. educator, author, humanitarian, leading Quaker theologian. *Rufus Griswold*, (1815-57), U.S. editor and author, editor for Edgar Allan Poe. Actor: *Rufus Sewell.*

Rupert. *Italian form of* Robert. Rupert Brooke, (1887-1915), English poet, wrote vividly and sensitively. *Rupert Hughes,* (1872-1956), U.S. editor and writer. Actors: *Rupert Everett, Rupert Graves.*

Russ. *Short form ofm of* Cyrus, Ruskin and Russell.

Russell // Russ, Rustie, Rusty. *French:* "red-haired, fox-colored". Relational, concentration on goal. *Russell Sage*, (1816-1906), U.S. capitalist, politician, railway speculator. *Russell Schweickart*, (born 1935), U.S. astronaut, government official. *Russell Cone*, (1896-1961), U.S. civil engineer chief. *Russell Carter,* (1892-1957), U.S. author, historical and adventure stories. *Russell Alger,* (1836-1905), U.S. public official, lawyer, major general, businessman, governor of Michigan. *Russell Conwell*, (1843-1925), U.S. Baptist clergyman, author, educator, lecturer, founder and president Temple University. *Russell Long*, (born 1918), U.S. political leader.

Rusty // Rustin. *French:* "redhead". *Short form ofm of* Russell.

Rutger. *Form of* Roger. Actor: *Rutger Hauer.*

Rutherford. *Old English:* "cattle ford". *Rutherford B. Hayes*, (1822-1893), 19th U.S. president, lawyer, politician, religious, conservative.

Ryan // Ryon, Ryun. *Gaelic:* "little king". Strong, stable, confident, hard worker. Actors: *Ryan Phillippe, Ryan Stiles*.

The letter "Z" is used in some cultures instead of the letter "S". Parents desiring a name which starts with the letter "S" may give the name a unique twist while retaining personality characteristics by substituting the letter "Z".

Salaam // Salam, Saleem, Salem, Salim, Salom. *Arabic:* "peace, safe". *Salem Poor,* African American soldier and Revolutionary War hero. Actor: *Salman Khan.*

Salvatore // Salvador, Salvidor, Sauveur. *Italian:* "savior". Soldier, hero and social reform themes. *Salvador Dali* (1904-89), Spanish surrealist artist. *Salvador Gossens*, (1908-73), Chilean physician and political leader. *Salvatore Quasimodo*, (1901-68), Italian poet. *Salvatore Vigano*, (1769-1821), Italian dancer, choreographer and composer.

Salvador Luria, (1912-91), U.S. biologist. *Salvator Rosa*, (1615-73), Italian painter and poet. *Salvador de Madariaga*, (1886-1978), Spanish writer and statesman.

Sam // Sammie, Sammy, Shem. *Hebrew:* "to hear". *Short form ofm of* Samson and Samuel. Relational, very social. *Sammy Kaye*, (1910-87), American bandleader. *Sammy Davis, Jr.* (1925-90), U.S. singer, actor, and dancer. *Sam Walton,* (1918-92), U.S. executive, founder and director of Wal-Mart Stores and Sam's Wholesale Clubs. *Sam Shepard,* (Samuel Shepard Rogers) (born 1943), U.S. playwright and film actor. *Sam Houston*, (1793-1863), commander that won Texas' independence, twice elected president of the Republic of Texas, U.S. congressman and governor. Totals: politician 22%, writer 22%, commander, athlete, businessman, actor, musician, spy-hero, film director. Actors: *Sam Neill, Sam Waterston.*

Samir. *Arabic:* "entertaining companion".

Samson // Sam, Sammie, Sammy, Sampson, Sanson, Sansone, Shem. *Hebrew:* "like the sun". Biblical: the hero betrayed by Delilah, see Sam.

Samuel // Sam, Sammie, Sammy, Samuele, Shem. *Hebrew:* "name of God, heard or asked of God". Biblical: a famous prophet and judge. Fairly high percentage of writers, clergy, and inventors. *Samuel Colt*, (1814-62), American manufacturer of firearms, invented the Colt revolver. *Samuel Morse*, (1791-1872), invented the electric telegraph. *Samuel de Champlain*, (1567-1635), founded Quebec in Canada, ship captain and explorer. *Samuel Wilberforce*, (1805-73), British clergyman, bishop of Oxford. Totals: writer 29%, politician 21%, clergy 13%,

inventor 11%, lawyer 8%, commander 7%, businessman 7%, artist 6%, scientist 5%, jurist 5%, educator 4%, historian 4%, doctor 4%, athlete 3%, explorer 3%, musician 3%, art patron 2%, reformer 2%, film producer, photographer, scholar, semantics expert, labor union founder, editor-publisher. Actor: *Samuel L. Jackson.*

Sandy. *English:* "the hair color of sand". *Familiar form of* Alexander and a *short form ofm of* names beginning with "san". *Sandy Koufax*, (born 1935), U.S. left-handed baseball pitcher, TV sportscaster.

Sanford // Sandy. *Old English:* "sandy river crossing". *Sanford Ballard Dole*, (1844-1926), Supreme Court judge of the former Kingdom of Hawaii, its only president and its first state governor.

Santos // Santiago, Santo. *Spanish:* "saint, holy".

Santiago. *Spanish:* "Saint Jocob" through San Jacobo and San Yago. *Santiago Ramon y Cajal*, (1852-1934), award winning Spanish histologist.

Sarkis // Sarkes, Sercq. Geographical: an English channel island.

Saul // Sol, Sollie, Solly, Zollie, Zolly. *Hebrew:* "asked for". Biblical: the King of Israel and father of Jonathan; also *Saul of Tarsus* became St. Paul. Determined leader, calculating, shrewd, brave. *Saul Steinberg*, (Saul Jacobson) (born 1914), cartoonist and illustrator. *Saul Alinksy,* (1909-72), U.S. social reformer. *Saul Bellow*, (born 1915), Jewish writer, concerned with basic human dilemmas.

Schuyler // Sky, Skye, Skylar, Skyler. *Dutch:* "sheltering".

Schuyler Wheeler, (1860-1923), U.S. electrical engineer, inventor, and motor manufacturer. *Schuyler Colfax,* (1823-85), U.S. journalist and political leader.

Scott // Scot, Scotti, Scottie, Scotty. *Old English:* "Scotsman". Relational, not pushy, firm opinion, energetic, marries: often marries Sherry. *Scott O'Dell,* (1898-1989), U.S. author. *Scott Joplin,* (1868-1917), black U.S. composer and pianist. *F. Scott Fitzgerald* (1896-1940), novelist and short story writer. Actors: *Scott Baio, Scott Bairstow, Scott Bakula, Scott Glenn, Scott MacDonald, Scott Wentworth, Scott Wolf.*

Sean // Shane, Shaughn, Shaun, Shawn. *Irish form of* John. Bold, handsome, determined, stubborn, impetuous, relational, behaviour not confined by other peoples' expectations, determined to enjoy life. *Sean O'Faolain,* (1900-91), Irish author. *Sean O'Kelly,* (1882-1966), Irish newspaper publisher and statesman, a founder of Sinn Fein, president of Ireland. *Sean MacBride,* (1904-88), Irish diplomat, trial lawyer, founder of Republican party, member Dail Eireann, chairman of Amnesty International. *Sean O'Casey,* (originally John Casey) (1880-1964), Irish playwright, self-taught, theatrical skill, keen humor, and merciless realism of his plays. Actors: *Sean Astin, Sean Bean, Sean Connery, Sean Penn, Sean Pertwee.*

Sebastian // Bastian, Bastien, Sebastiano, Sebastien. *Latin:* "venerated, majestic". Sebastian Vizcaino, 16th-century Spanish merchant-explorer. *Sebastian de Benalcazar,* (1495?-1551), Spanish conqueror of Nicaragua, Ecuador, and southwestern Colombia. Totals: businessman 40%, commander 30%, explorer 20%, politician, engineer, artist, philanthropist, theologian,

geographer, mathematician, clergy.

Serge // Sergei, Sergey, Sergio. *Latin:* "attendant". Reserved mannered; prefers actions to emotions; keeps his promises; responsible; not talkative; keeps his opinion to himself; actor, musician, composer, artist; compliant to his parents and loved ones; tries to not offend others; gets offended easily; good self control, doesn't show that he is offended; tries not to complicate the relationship with destructive emotions; prefers calm home-body women; helps wife around the home; not picky about foods; likes to tell anecdotes in groups; jealous; often marries twice. *Serge Koussevitzky,* (1874-1951), first major Russian conductor. *Sergei Prokofiev,* (1891-1953), one of the Soviet Union's greatest composers. *Sergio Leone,* (1929-89), Italian film director of called spaghetti Westerns, 'The Good, the Bad, and the Ugly'.

Seth. *Hebrew:* "substitute, appointed". Biblical: the third son of Adam. Calm mind, strong, energetic, problem solver. *Seth Thomas,* (1785-1859), U.S. pioneer clock manufacturer, his son, *Seth Thomas* (1816-88) enlarged the factory and developed a world business. *Seth Boyden,* (1788-1870), U.S. inventor, named one of America's greatest inventors by Thomas Jefferson. *Seth Warner,* (1743-84), American Revolutionary War soldier, leader of Green Mountain Boys. *Seth Low,* (1850-1916), U.S. merchant, educator, administrator, and politician.

Seymour // Morey, Morie, Morrie, Morry, See. *Old French:* "St. Maur". *Seymour Parker Gilbert,* (1892-1938), U.S. lawyer and financial expert.

Shamus. *Irish form of* James through Seamus.

Shane // Shaine, Shayn, Shayne. *Irish form of* John through Sean.

Shantae // Chante, Shant, Shantelle, Shanti, Shanty. *Latin:* "sing". *Form of* Chante.

Shaquille. Athlete/actor: *Shaquille O'Neal.*

Shaun // Shawn. *Irish form of* John through Sean.

Sheb. Actor: *Sheb Wooley.*

Shelby // Shell, Shelley, Shelly. *Old English:* "ledge estate". *Shelby Cullom*, (1829-1914), U.S. political leader. *Shelby Foote*, (born 1916), U.S. novelist and historian specializing in studies of the American Civil War.

Sheldon // Shelden, Shell, Shelley, Shelly, Shelton. *Old English:* "farm on the ledge". *Sheldon Glashow*, (born 1932), U.S. physicist. *Sheldon Jackson*, (1834-1909), U.S. Presbyterian missionary.

Sherman // Man, Mannie, Manny, Sherm, Shermie, Shermy. *Old English:* "shearer". *Sherman Greene*, (born 1886), U.S. religious leader. *Sherman Minton*, (1890-1965), U.S. jurist, politician. *Sherman Fairchild*, (1896-1971), U.S. inventor and manufacturer, inventor of cameras, builder of airplanes.

Sherwood // Shurwood, Wood, Woodie, Woody. *Old English:* "bright forest". *Sherwood Anderson*, (1876-1941), U.S. writer of short stories and novels.

Sid // Syd. *Short form ofm of* Sidney. *Sid Luckman*, (born 1916), U.S. football quarterback.

Sidney // Sid, Sidnee, Syd, Sydney. *Old French:* "St. Denis". Famous: *Sidney Poitier* - US actor; Confident, steady. *Sidney Webb*, (1859-1947), socialist economists. *Sydney Smith*, (1771-1845), English clergyman and author. *Sidney Kingsley*, (born 1906), U.S. playwright. Totals: author 38%, musician 15%, artist 15%, actor 15%, socialist economist, clergy, scientist, politician educator.

Siegfried // Siffre, Sig, Sigfrid, Sigfried, Sigvard. *German:* "victorious peace". Literary: Siegfried, Scandinavian epic folk hero. *Siegfried Marcus*, (1831-99), Austrian mechanic and inventor, pioneer automobile builder. *Siegfried Sassoon*, (1886-1967), British poet. *Siegfried Wagner*, (1869-1930), German composer and conductor.

Sigmund // Sig, Sigismondo, Sigismund, Sigismundo, Sigsmond. *German:* "victorious protector". Emotional, emotion driven. *Sigmund Freud*, (1856-1939), noted founder of disproved psychoanalysis. *Sigismund* (1368-1437), Holy Roman emperor. *Sigmund Spaeth*, (1885-1965), U.S. writer and lecturer on music. *Sigismund Stojowski*, (1870-1946), Polish pianist, teacher, and composer. *Sigmund Romberg*, (1887-1951), U.S. composer.

Silas // Silvain, Silvan, Silvano, Silvanus, Silvio, Sylas, Sylvan. Latin Mythology: "Silvanus, the god of field and forest". *Silas Deane*, (1737-89), U.S. statesman and diplomat. *Silas Mitchell,* (1829-1914), U.S. neurologist and novelist.

Silvester // Silvestre. *Form of* Sylvester.

Simon // Si, Sim, Simeon, Simmonds, Simone, Syman, Symon. *Hebrew:* "he who hears". Biblical: two of the Twelve Apostles: *Simon called Peter* and *Simon the Zealot*. Resembles mother; gentle, kind; not evil by nature; very faithful friend who will help when needed; musician, doctor, teacher, writer; generally capable and talented; goal directed; often successful; doesn't pay much mind or attention to remembering small things like birth dates and doctor appointments; wife often considers herself fortunate to have married him; helpful, good household manager; loves his children; spends a lot of time with his family. Low percentage of writers and fairly high percentage for politicians and commanders. *Simon Bolivar,*(1783-1830), liberator of Venezuela, Colombia, Panama, Ecuador, Peru, and Bolivia from Spanish rule, great statesman, writer, and revolutionary general. *Simon Wiesenthal,* (born 1908), famed "Nazi hunter" who attempted to find them and bring them to trial. *Simon de Montfort,* (1208?-65), assembled England's first Parliament, efforts to reform the misrule of Henry III. Totals: politician 33%, commander 29%, scientist 13%, explorer 13%, businessman 13%, writer 8%, engineer 8%, hunter of Nazis, economist, musician, inventor, lawyer, philosopher, traitor, artist.

Sinclair // Clair, Clare, Sinclare. *Old French:* "St. Clare". *Sinclair Lewis*, (1885-1951), celebrated novelist, wrote 'Arrowsmith' and 'Elmer Gantry'.

Skip // Skipp, Skipper, Skippie, Skippy, Skipton. *Scandinavian:* "shipmaster". Optimistic, positive attitude.

Skyler // Sky, Skye, Skylar. *Form of* Schuyler.

Smith // Smitty. *Old English:* "blacksmith". *Smith Jelliffe*, (1866-1945), U.S. neurologist, managing editor, pioneer in psychoanalysis in U.S. *Smith Thompson*, (1768-1843), U.S. jurist and public official. *B. Smith Hopkins*, (1873-1952), U.S. chemist.

Solomon // Salmon, Salomo, Salomon, Salomone, Sol, Sollie, Solly, Zollie, Zolly. *Hebrew:* "peaceful". Biblical: a king of Israel famous for his wisdom. *Solomon Juneau*, (1793-1856), U.S. pioneer, first mayor of Milwaukee, Wis. *Salomon Andree*, (1854-97), Swedish scientist and aeronaut. *Solomon Spiegelman*, (1914-83), U.S. geneticist. *Salmon Levinson*, (1865-1941), U.S. lawyer, leader of movement to outlaw war. *Solomon R. Guggenheim*, (1861-1949), U.S. philanthropist.

Sonny // Sonnie. *English:* "son, boy". *Familiar form of* names ending in "son".

Spencer // Spence, Spense, Spenser. *Middle English:* "dispenser of provisions". *Spencer Cavendish*, (1833-1908), British statesman, leader of Liberal Unionists. *Spencer Tracy*, (1900-67), U.S. actor, 'Boys' Town'. *Spencer Baird,* (1823-87), U.S. naturalist and vertebrate zoologist. *Spencer Williams*, (1889-1965), U.S. jazz composer.

Stafford // Staffard, Staford. *Old English:* "riverbank landing". *Stafford Cripps,* (1889-1952), British lawyer and statesman.

Stan. *Short form ofm of* names containing "stan". *Stan Brakhage*, (born 1933), U.S. underground filmmaker. *Stan Laurel*, (1890-1965), film actor, producer, and director, comedy team 'Laurel and Hardy'. *Stan Jones*, (born 1931), U.S. football player. *Stan Kenton*, (1912-79), U.S. bandleader. Actor: *Stan Kirsch*.

Stanford // Ford, Stan, Standford, Stanfield. *Old English:* "rocky ford". *Stanford Ovshinsky*, (born 1922), U.S. inventor, devised semiconductor switches. *Stanford Moore*, (1913-82), U.S. biochemist, helped invent the automatic amino acid analyzer. *Stanford White*, (1853-1906), U.S. architect, designed Madison Square Garden.

Stanley // Stan, Stanleigh, Stanly. *Old English:* "rocky meadow". *Stanley Kubrick*, (born 1928), U.S. motion picture director, '2001: A Space Odyssey'. *Stanley Baldwin* (1867-1947), three times British prime minister. *Stanley Matthews*, (1824-89), U.S. judge, journalist, lawyer and newspaper editor. Totals: politician 31%, lawyer 23%, judge 15%, athlete 15%, writer 15%, journalist, scientist, artist, educator, editor, film director.

Stephen // Esteban, Estevan, Etienne, Stefan, Stefano, Steffen, Stephan, Stephanus, Steve, Steven, Stevie, Stevy. *Greek:* "crown". Confident bearing, leader, able, focused, respected, reaches goals, professional; very energetic child, not patient enough to study long, but learns well because of his good memory; quick tongued; many are artistically talented: painters, actor, designer; many friends and acquaintances; always wants to be around people because he wants spectators; enjoys the company of women more than men; always finds a complement for each woman; marriage is more often not happy, manly because he is unfaithful and falls in love easily; not jealous; loves his children but doesn't spend enough time with them because it is not natural for him; kind; doesn't hold grudges. *Stephen King,* (born 1947), U.S. novelist. *Steven Spielberg*, (born 1947), U.S. motion-picture producer, director, and writer. *Steve Martin*, (born 1945), U.S. actor and comedian. *Stephen Austin*, (1793-1836), U.S. founder of principal settlements of English-speaking people in Texas. Totals: writer 26%, politician 20%, scientist 13%, commander 7%, lawyer 7%, educator 6%, athlete 6%, clergy 6%, inventor 6%, artist 6%, business-man 6%, musician 4%, comic 4%, engineer 4%, jurist 4%, architect, pioneer printer, actor, linguist, explorer, philanthropist, film producer-director. Actors: *Stephen Baldwin, Stephen Chow, Stephen Collins, Stephen Dorff, Stephen Nichols, Steve Burton, Steve Cardenas, Steve Martin, Steven Seagal, Steven Weber, Steven Williams.*

Sterling // Stirling. *Old English:* "valuable". *Sterling Price*, (1809-67), U.S. political leader and Confederate general, governor of Missouri. *Stirling Moss*, (born 1929), British auto-racing driver. *Sterling Hendricks*, (1902-81), U.S. plant physiologist.

Steve // Stevie, Stevy. *Short form ofm of* Stephen. See Stephen.

Steven. *Form of* Stephen.

Stewart // Steward. *Form of* Stuart.

Stuart // Steward, Stewart, Stu. *Old English:* "caretaker, steward". Historical: the name of many British kings. Athletic, studious, strong. *Stewart White*, (1873-1946), U.S. novelist. *Stewart Udall,* (born 1920), U.S. public official and lawyer. *Stuart Symington*, (1901-88), U.S. public official and industrialist. *Stuart Chase*, (1888-1985), U.S. economist and writer. *Stuart A. Roosa*, (born 1933), U.S. astronaut and U.S. Air Force experimental test pilot. *Stuart Cloete*, (1897-1976), South African writer. *Stuart Davis*, (1894-1964), U.S. painter, lithographer, and writer on art.

Sumner. *Middle English:* "church officer, summoner". *Sumner Welles*, (1892-1961), U.S. diplomat.

Sven // Svend, Swen. ***Scandinavian:*** "youth". *Sven Hedin,* (1865-1952), Swedish explorer, lead expeditions through Central Asia.

Syed. ***Arabic:*** "happy".

Sylvester // Silvester, Sly. ***Latin:*** "woodsy, of the woods". *Silvestre Velez de Escalante,* (fl. 1768-79), Spanish Franciscan missionary and explorer. *Sylvester Graham,* (1794-1851), U.S. reformer, advocated temperance, vegetarianism, use of whole wheat (graham) bread. *Silvestre Revueltas,* (1899-1940), Mexican violinist and composer. Actor: *Sylvester Stallone.*

Tad. *Familiar form of* Thaddeus.

Tanner. ***English:*** "tanner".

Taylor // Tailor, Tayler. ***English:*** "tailor".

Ted // Tedd, Teddie, Teddy, Tedman, Tedmund. *Familiar form of* names beginning with "ted". Also see Theodore. Seem to have a mental focus which may be called fanaticism in some. *Teddy Kollek,* (born 1911), Israeli public administrator. *Teddy Wilson,* (Theodore Wilson) (1912-86), U.S. jazz pianist and arranger. Actors: *Ted Marcoux, Ted Raimi.*

Terence // Tarrance, Terencio, Terrance, Terrence, Terry. ***Latin:*** "smooth". Literary: the name honors the Roman

dramatist (185?-159? BC). Word-smith, stubborn. *Terence Sawchuck,* (1929-70), U.S. ice-hockey player. *Terence Powderly,* (1849-1924), U.S. labor leader. *Terence White,* (1906-64), English author, social historian and satirist. *Terence James Cooke,* (1921-83), U.S. Roman Catholic prelate. *Terence MacSwiney,* (1879-1920), Irish leader. *Terence Rattigan,* (1911-77), British playwright.

Terrill // Taral, Terrel, Terrell, Tirrell. ***Old German:*** "martial, belonging to Thor. Actor: *Taral Hicks.*

Terry // Terri. *Familiar form of* Terence. *Terry Waite,* (Terence Hardy Waite) (born 1939), British religious official, taken hostage in Beirut. *Terry Anderson,* (born 1947), Associated Press in Beirut, held hostage for six years. *Terry Bradshaw,* (born 1948), U.S. football superstar, quarterback. *Terry Fox,* (1958-81), Canadian student and national hero, afflicted with cancer and right leg amputated, attempted to run across North America to raise money for cancer research. *Terry Branstad,* (born 1946), U.S. public official, governor of Iowa.

Tevin. Unknown meaning and origin. See Kevin.

Thaddeus // Tad Tadd, Taddeo, Taddeusz, Tadeo, Tadeusz, Tadio, Thad, Thaddäus. ***Greek:*** "courageous"; ***Latin:*** "praiser". Biblical: one of the Twelve Apostles. *Thaddeus Stevens,* (1792-1868), U.S. politician, fought to end slavery. *Thaddeus Fairbanks,* (1796-1886), U.S. manufacturer, patented portable platform scale. *Thaddeus Kosciusko,* (1746-1817), Polish general fought for freedom on two continents, American Revolutionary war commander. *Tadeusz Mazowiecki,* (born 1927), Polish public official.

Thane // Thain, Thaine, Thayne, Thegn. ***Anglo-Saxon:***

"servant or soldier, attendant warrior".

Theo. *Short form of* names beginning with "theo".

Theodore // Feodor, Teador, Ted, Tedd, Teddie, Teddy, Teodoor, Teodor, Teodoro, Theo, Theodor, Théodore, Tudor. *Greek:* "gift of God". Also see Ted and Theodoric. Deep but narrow thinker, usually relational and well liked, highly intelligent, eccentric, a bit quirky, man of action, hidden side, high percentage of educators and reformers. Seemingly high number of serial killers, quirky and mentally unstable. *Theodore Roosevelt*, U.S. president, tremendous energy and high spirits, statesman, cowboy, soldier, hunter, naturalist, and explorer. *Theodore von Karman*, (1881-1963), scientist, teacher, research organizer, and promoter of international scientific cooperation. *Theodore Parker*, (1810-60), U.S. Unitarian clergyman and social reformer, a leading abolitionist, held liberal religious views. *Theodore Weld*, (1803-95), U.S. abolitionist. *Theodore Dwight*, (1822-92), U.S. jurist and educator, famous law teacher and founder of law school at Columbia University, writer on law subjects, active in political and social (chiefly prison) reform. *Theodore Beza*, (1519-1605), French theologian and Protestant Reformer. *Theodore (Ted) Kaczynski*, Unabomber serial killer, mathematician, educator, technology reformer. *Ted (Edward) Kennedy*, U.S. politician, known for juvenile drunken adulterous behavior. *Ted Bundy*, convicted serial murderer, law student. Totals: writer 24%, scientist 22%, politician 16%, educator 14%, reformer 11%, businessman 8%, lawyer 8%, musician 5%, commander 5%, adventurer, clergy, theologian, inventor, economist, engineer, historian, scholar, athlete.

Theodoric // Derek, Dieter, Dietrich, Dirk, Ted, Tedd, Teddie, Teddy, Teodorico, Thedric, Thedrick, Theo. Note: this name may not be related to Theodore. Also see Ted and Theodore.

Thomas // Tam, Tamas, Tammie, Tammy, Thom, Thoma, Tom, Tomás, Tomaso, Tome, Tomkin, Tomlin, Tommie, Tommy. *Aramaic:* "twin". Biblical: one of the Twelve Apostles. Intelligent, scholarly, quick learner, shows wisdom, problem solver, mischievous, relational, one-of-the-boys, wide range of interests, often reader, high percentage of writers; often engineer, teacher, historian. *Thomas Aquinas*, (1225?-74), regarded by the Roman Catholic church as its greatest theologian and philosopher. *Thomas More*, (1478-1535), among the most respected figures in English history, statesman, scholar, author, noted for wit and devotion to his religion. *Thomas Cromwell*, (1485?-1540), virtually the ruler of England, established the English Reformation. *Thomas Jefferson*, 3rd U.S. president, author of the Declaration of Independence and Virginia Statute for Religious Freedom, human rights. Totals: writer 37%, politician 24%, clergy 10%, businessman 9%, commander 8%, artist 7%, lawyer 7%, judge 6%, humorist 5%, scientist 4%, historian 4%, orator 3%, scholar 3%, explorer 3%, philosopher 2%, educator 2%, inventor 2%, athlete 2%, film director 2%, doctor 2%, architect 2%, humanist 1%, social reformer 1%. Actor: *Thomas Mitchell.*

Thor // Thorin, Thorvald, Tore, Torin, Torre, Tyrus. *Scandinavian:* "thunder". Mythological: the god of thunder. *Thor Heyerdahl*, (born 1914), anthropologist, made several expeditions on primitive ocean-going vessels to prove the possibility of transoceanic contact between ancient, widely separated civilizations, 'Kon-Tiki'.

Thornton // Thorn, Thornie, Thorny. *Old English:* "thorny town". *Thornton Wilder,* (1897-1975), U.S. novelist and playwright.

Thurston // Thorstein, Thorsten, Thurstan. *Scandinavian:* "Thor's stone". *Thorstein Veblen,* (1857-1929), U.S. economist and social critic. Actor: *Thorsten Kaye.*

Tim // Timmie, Timmy. *Short form of* Timothy. *Tim Keefe,* (1856-1933), U.S. baseball pitcher. *Tim (Timothy) Mara,* (1887-1959), founder of New York Giants football team. Actors: *Tim Allen, Tim Curry, Tim Roth.*

Timothy // Tim, Timmie, Timmy, Timofei, Timon, Timoteo, Timothee, Timotheus, Tymon, Tymothy. *Greek:* "revering God, honoring God". Biblical: *Timothy* (or Timotheus), disciple and assistant of St. Paul. Fun and games, light-hearted, sensitive to others, somewhat reserved, generally not appear bold, rather timid, generally a follower, nice guy, usually avoids making waves, hard worker, marries: someone a bit more serious, leader. *Timothy Manning,* (1909-89), U.S. Roman Catholic prelate. *Timothy Dwight,* (1752-1817), U.S. clergyman and educator, able teacher and writer on religion and politics. *Timothy Healy,* (1855-1931), Irish leader, self-educated, eloquent. *Timothy McVey,* Oklahoma city bomber. *Tim McVey,* dismissed from Navy as homosexual. *Timothy Leary,* (1920-1996), recreational drug use advocate, educator. Totals: clergy 33%, educator 22%, writer 22%, politician 22%, scientist, speculator-businessman, artist, lawyer, judge. Actor: *Timothy Dalton.*

Titus // Tito, Titos. *Greek:* "of giants". Biblical: St. Paul's disciple to whom a book of the Bible was written. *Tito,* (1892-1980), leader of Yugoslav Partisans successful fight against Nazis, Yugoslav socialist state leader. *Tito Gobbi,* (1915-84), Italian baritone. *Tito Schipa,* (1889-1965), Italian dramatic tenor. *Titus Quintius Flamininus,* (228?-174 BC), Roman general. *Titus* (Titus Flavius Sabinus Vespasianus) (AD 40?-81), Roman emperor, humane and able ruler. *Titus Maccius Plautus,* (254?-184 BC), Roman comic poet and dramatist. Actor: *Titus Welliver.*

Tobias // Tobe, Tobey, Tobiah, Tobie, Tobin, Tobit, Toby. *Hebrew:* "the Lord is good". Good natured, strong. *Tobias Asser,* (1838-1913), Dutch statesman, professor of law, author of works on international law. *Tobias Matthay,* (1858-1945), British pianist and teacher. *Tobias Smollett,* (1721-71), English novelist called "founder of the satirical novel".

Todd // Toddie, Toddy. *Middle English:* "fox". Sly, clever, silver tongued, knowledgeable. Actor: *Todd Karns.*

Tom // Thom, Tommie, Tommy. *Short form of* Thomas. Also see Thomas. Use of Tommy often reflects "free spirit" attitude or "one of the boys". Use of Tom often reflects an attitude with a bit determination, goal orientation and sticks to business or play when appropriate. *Tommy Dorsey,* (1905-56), trombonist and bandleader. *Tommy G. Thompson,* (born 1941), U.S. public official. Actor: *Tom Baker, Tom Berenger, Tom Cruise, Tom Eplin, Tom Hanks, Tommy Lee Jones.*

Tony // Toni, Tonnie. *Familiar form of* Anthony or of names ending in "ton". Also see Anthony. *Tony Sarg,* (Anthony Frederick Sarg) (1882-1942), U.S. artist. *Toni*

Morrison, (born 1931), U.S. author. *Tony Lazzeri*, (1903-46), U.S. baseball player. *Tony Esposito*, (Anthony James Esposito) (born 1943), Canadian ice-hockey player. *Tony Robert-Fleury*, (1837-1911), French painter.

Torrance // Tore, Torey, Torin, Torr, Torrence, Torrey, Torrin, Torry. *Gaelic:* "knolls".

Townsend // Town, Towney, Townie, Towny. *Old English:* "town's end". *Townsend Harris*, (1804-78), U.S. merchant, political leader, diplomat.

Tracy // Trace, Tracey, Tracie. *Gaelic:* "battler". *Latin:* "courageous". "Courageous", determined, befriending, helpful.

Travis // Travell, Traveon, Traver, Travers, Travion, Travois, Travon, Travus. *Old French:* "crossroads"; *English:* "travel".

Trent // Trenton. *Latin:* "torrent".

Trevor // Trevon. *Gaelic:* "prudent".

Tristan // Tris, Tristam, Tristram, Tristran. *Welsh:* "sorrow-ful". Literary: Tristram of Lyonesse - hero of Celtic legend.

Troy. *Gaelic:* "foot soldier".

Truman // Trueman, Trumaine, Trumann. *Old English:* "faithful man". Historical: Harry S Truman, 33rd U.S. president. *Truman Capote*, (1924-84), U.S. writer noted for eccentric characters and bizarre situations, 'Breakfast at Tiffany's'. *Truman Newberry*, (1864-1945), U.S. public official, businessman and banker.

Tucker. *English:* refering to cloth.

Ty. *Short form of* names beginning with "ty". *Ty (Tyrus)*

Cobb, (1886-1961), baseball's greatest and fiercest player in its history. Actor: *Ty O'Neal*.

Tyler // Tiler, Ty, Tye, Tylor. *Old English:* "tile maker, tile installer".

Tyree. *Scotch:* "island dweller". Refers to the island refuge during siege of the ancient city of Tyre.

Tyrell. *Form of* Terell.

Tyrone // Ty, Tye, Tyron. *Greek:* "sovereign". *Gaelic:* "land of Owen". Daring, entrepreneurial, friendly. *Tyrone Guthrie*, (1900-71), theatrical director.

Ulysses // Ulick, Ulises. *Latin:* "wrathful". Literary: the hero of Homer's 'Odyssey'. *Ulysses Kay*, (born 1917), U.S. composer. *Ulysses S. Grant*, (1822-85), 18th U.S. president, general, Civil War commander of all the Federal armies.

Uriel // Uri, Yuri. *Hebrew:* "God is my flame". Also see Yuri.

Vahe. Unknown origin and meaning.

Valentine // Val Valentijn, Valentin, Valentino. *Latin:*

"strong, healthy". Strong, muscular; as a child he likes to befriend and protect the girls; as teenager he's interested in philosophy and psychology; later may become a psychiatrist or psychologist; talented, strong willed, usually a good friend who can keep secrets, likes nature outings, doesn't enjoy yard work, enjoys chess and scrabble, not picky about cooking, values a quiet spirit in women, friendly and helpful to relatives and neighbors, doesn't fall in love easily, faithful to his wife. *Saint Valentine*, Christian martyr of the 3rd century. *Valentin Hauy*, (1745-1822), French professor, established a school for blind children. *Valentin Kataev*, (1897-1986), Soviet novelist, short-story writer, and playwright. *Val L. Fitch*, (born 1923), U.S. physicist. *Valentin Varennikov*, (born 1923), Soviet politician, commander of Soviet ground forces. *Valentin S. Pavlov*, (born 1938), Soviet politician, former finance minister, prime minister, charged with high treason. Actor: *Val Kilmer*.

Van. *Dutch:* "noble descent". *Short form of* many Dutch surnames. *Van Wyck Brooks*, (1886-1963), U.S. literary critic.

Vance. *Middle English:* "thresher". *Vance D. Brand*, (born 1931), U.S. astronaut, test pilot.

Vern. *Short form of* Vernon.

Vernon // Vern, Verne, Verney. *Latin:* "springlike, youthful". Humorous, jokester, friendly, helpful, quick wit, quick learner. *Vernon Parrington*, (1871-1929), U.S. educator and writer. *Vernon Castle*, (1887-1918), British dancer and aviator. *Vernon Gomez*, (1909-89), U.S. baseball pitcher. *Vernon E Jordan, Jr.* (born 1935), U.S. lawyer and adminis-

trator. *Vernon Kellogg*, (1867-1937), U.S. zoologist.

Victor // Vic, Vick, Victoir, Vittorio. *Latin:* "conqueror". Often concrete thinker, trusting, doesn't hold a grudge, forgives easily, even trusts those who previously wronged him, often more comfortable in career which requires concrete thinking; sportsman, coach, electrician, may have artistic talent, desires justice, many qualities to make a successful marriage: stable, calm, likes work that requires patients, may stay in marriage out of responsibility, may blame himself for divorce; strict father, formal uninspiring teacher of his children may cause them to leave home early; addicts easily to alcohol. *Victor Hugo*, (1802-85), great French novelist and poet, 'The Hunchback of Notre Dame'. *Victor Fleming*, (died 1949), U.S. motion-picture director, 'Gone with the Wind', 'The Wizard of Oz'. *Victor Berger*, (1860-1929), U.S. Socialist party political leader first Socialist ever elected to Congress. The three Savoy rulers of Italy were each named *Victor Emmanuel*. Totals: politician 41%, writer 29%, scientist 12%, artist 12%, businessman 12%, communist 12%, composer, philosopher, lawyer, film director, educator-historian. Actor: *Victor Alfieri*.

Vidal. *Latin:* "clearly see".

Vincent // Vin, Vince, Vincente, Vincents, Vincenty, Vincenz, Vincenzo, Vinnie, Vinny, Vinson. *Latin:* "conquering". *Saint Vincent de Paul*, (1576-1660), benevolent priest. *Vincent van Gogh*, (1853-90), 2nd greatest Dutch painter. *Vincent Massey*, (1887-1967), 1st Canadian-born citizen governor-general of Canada. Totals: politician 18%, clergy 18%, composer 18%, scientist 18%, coach, educator, artist, inventor, businessman, socialist, theatrical producer. Actors: *Vincent Larusso, Vincent Perez, Vincent Price.*

Vinny // Vin, Vinnie. *Familiar form of* Vincent.

Virgil // Verge, Vergil, Virge, Virgie, Virgilio. **Latin:** "rod or staff bearer". *Virgil,* (70-19 BC), the greatest of the Roman poets. *Virgil Partch II* (born 1916), U.S. cartoonist. *Virgil Ivan (Gus) Grissom,* (1926-67), U.S. astronaut. *Virgil Thomson,* (1896-1989), U.S. composer and critic.

Vladimir // Vladamir, Vladimar, Vlady. **Slavic:** "possessor of the world, powerful prince". Distinguished as curious and intelligent, tends toward risk, adventurous, leader, tries to avoid conflicts with people, likes comfort, likes expensive beautiful furniture, neat, active, diplomatic, quick reacting, self loving, likes to be praised or honored, enterprising, knows how to reach the goal, good communicator, often reach high success, finds it difficult to forgive, falls in love easily, tends to idealize the woman he loves; if faithful in marriage it is because he is too busy or doesn't want to complicate life; doesn't like to disciple his children, but enjoys teaching them. *Vladimir I* (or Saint Vladimir) (956?-1015), first Christian sovereign of Russia. *Vladimir Zworykin,* (1889-1982), Russian-born inventor and electronics engineer is called the father of modern television. *Vladimir Nabokov,* (1899-1977), Russian-born American writer. *Vladimir Horowitz,* (1903-89), Russian-born concert pianist. Totals: writer 36%, musician 21%, scientist 14%, cosmonaut 14%, philosopher, politician, producer, inventor.

Wade // Wadsworth. **Old English:** "advancer, river crossing". *Wade Hampton,* (1818-1902), U.S. statesman and Confederate general.

Waite. **Middle English:** "guard". *Waite Charles (Schoolboy) Hoyt,* (1899-1984), U.S. baseball pitcher.

Waldo // Wald, Wallie, Wally. **Old German:** "ruler". *Familiar form of* Oswald or Waldemar. *Waldo Peirce,* (1884-1970), U.S. artist. *Waldo Frank,* (1889-1967), U.S. novelist and critic.

Walker // Wallie, Wally. **Old English:** "thickener of cloth, fuller". *Walker Hancock,* (born 1901), U.S. sculptor. *Walker Percy,* (1916-90), U.S. writer.

Wallace // Wallache, Wallas, Wallie, Wallis, Wally, Walsh, Welch, Welsh. **Old English:** "Welshman". *Wallace Fard,* (1877-1934?), founder of the Nation of Islam (Black Muslim) movement in the U.S. *Wallace Wilkinson,* (born 1941), U.S. public official, millionaire businessman. *Wallace Carothers,* (1896-1937), U.S. chemist. *Wallace Stegner,* (born 1909), U.S. writer, professor of English. *Wallace Greene, Jr.* (born 1907), U.S. Marine Corps officer, 4-star general. *Wallace Stevens,* (1879-1955), U.S. poet and insurance executive. *Wallace Harrison,* (1895-1981), U.S. architect.

Wally // Wallie. *Familiar form of* names beginning with "wal".

Walt. Often a *Short form of* Walter and Walton. Writer, artist, humorist. *Walt Disney*, (1901-66), U.S. cartoonist. *Walt Whitman*, (1819-92), U.S. poet. *Walt Kelly*, (1913-73), U.S. cartoonist. *Walt Mason*, (1862-1939), U.S. writer of humorous verse. *Walt Kuhn*, (1877-1949), U.S. modernist painter. *Walt Whitman Rostow*, (born 1916), U.S. economist.

Walter // Wallie, Wally, Walt, Walther, Wat. *Germanic:* "ruling army, powerful warrior". Also see Walt. Often writers, strong opinions, good nature, adventurer; as child: enjoys to be around adults more than peers, fearless, energetic, fair grades, likes to play sports, feisty, argumentative, kind, leader among peers, friends can rely on them, social, liked by girls; engineer, animal trainer, acrobatic, mechanic, teacher, actor, dentist, construction, wood working; doesn't fear work, usually marry late, may marry twice, likes nature outings, may write poetry. *Walter Winchell*, (1897-1972), radio personality of newspaper columnist, irreverent, opinionated, controversial, and audacious. *Walter Raleigh*, (1554?-1618), politician, poet, soldier, sailor, explorer, historian. *Walter Payton*, (born 1954), football star, Chicago Bear running back. *Sir Walter Scott*, (1771-1832), English poet, novelist and lawyer. *Walter Reed*, (1851-1902), doctor, scientist, leader in conquering the dreaded disease yellow fever. Totals: writer 38%, politician 20%, scientist 13%, businessman 9%, educator 8%, athlete 8%, artist architect craftsman 6%, commander 6%, lawyer 6%, doctor 4%, musician 4%, actor 3%, engineer 3%, astronaut 3%, inventor 3%, explorer, historian, communist, economist, philosopher, jurist, philologist, clergy, philanthropist, psychologist, labor leader, social idealist, conservationist, civil rights, radio pesonality. Actors: *Walter Koenig, Walter Pidgeon.*

Ward // Warde, Warden, Worden. *Old English:* "guardian". *Ward Hunt*, (1810-86), U.S. jurist, lawyer, politician. *Ward Hill Lamon*, (1828-93), U.S. law partner, secretary, and biographer of Abraham Lincoln.

Warner // Werner, Wernher. *Germanic:* "army of the Varini tribe, armed defender". *Werner Janssen*, (born 1900), U.S. conductor and composer. *Werner Forssmann*, (1904-79), German physician, researcher. *Werner von Siemens*, (1816-92), German inventor. *Werner Arber*, (born 1929), Swiss microbiologist. *Wernher von Braun*, (1912-77), German-born engineer in rocketry and space exploration. *Werner Heisenberg*, (1901-76), German physicist.

Warren // Ware, Waring. *Old German:* "defender". Orderly, adventurous, athletic, gentleman, ladies man. *Warren G. Harding*, 29th U.S. president. *Warren Spahn*, (born 1921), left-handed U.S. baseball pitcher. *Warren Burger*, (born 1907), chief justice of the U.S. Supreme Court. *Warren Austin*, (1877-1962), U.S. political leader. *Warren Cole*, (born 1898), U.S. surgeon. *Warren Hastings*, (1732-1818), British official, first governor-general of India. *Warren Giles*, (1896-1979), U.S. baseball executive. Actor: *Warren Beatty.*

Washington // Wash. *Old English:* "perceiver's town". The name honors George Washington, 1st U.S. president. *Washington Irving*, (1783-1859), essayist, historian, and story writer. *Washington DePauw*, (1822-87), U.S. manufacturer and philanthropist. *Washington Allston*, (1779-1843), U.S. painter. *Washington Gladden*, (1836-1918), U.S.

clergyman, social reformer, and author.

Wayland // Land, Way, Waylan, Waylen, Waylin, Waylon, Weylin. *Old English:* "land near the road". *Waylon Jennings,* country singer.

Wayne. *Old English:* "wagon maker". *Short form of* Wainwright. Buddy, strong, crafty, athletic. *Wayne Gretzky,* (Great Gretzky) (born 1961), Canadian professional hockey player. *Wayne Morse,* (1900-74), U.S. lawyer and political leader. *Wayne Millner,* (1913-76), U.S. football end, professional coach. *Wayne King,* (Waltz King) (born 1901), U.S. saxophonist and orchestra leader. Actor/singer: *Wayne Newton.*

Webster // Webb, Weber. *Old English:* "weaver".

Wendell // Wendall, Wendel. *Old German:* "wanderer". *Wendell Phillips,* (1811-84), U.S. lawyer, foremost abolitionist, reformer, and orator. *Wendell Stanley,* (1904-71), U.S. biochemist. *Wendell Willkie,* (1892-1944), U.S. lawyer and public utility executive.

Werner // Wernher. *German form* of Warner.

Wes. *Short form of* names beginning with "wes". Actor: *Wes Studi.*

Wesley // Lee, Leigh, Wes, Westleigh, Westley. *Old English:* "Western meadow". Quick-learner, understands detail. *Wesley Mitchell,* (1874-1948), U.S. economist. *Wesley Merritt,* (1834-1910), U.S. Army general. *Wesley Dennis,* (1903-66), U.S. artist and author of children's books.

Westbrook // Brook, Brooke, Wes, West, Westbrooke. *Old English:* "Western brook". *Westbrook Pegler,* (1894-1969),

U.S. journalist.

Weston // Wes, West. *Old English:* "Western estate". *Weston Fulton,* (1871-1946), U.S. inventor, 125 patents include depth bomb and thermostat.

Whit. *Old English:* "white". *Short form of* Whitman, Whitney, Whittaker and Whitby. *Whit Burnett,* (1899-1973), U.S. editor and writer.

Whittaker // Whit, Whitaker. *Old English:* "white field". *Whittaker Chambers,* (1901-61), U.S. journalist, former Communist agent.

Wilbur // Wilbert, Wilburt. *German form* of Gilbert. Athletic, speed-adventurer. *Wilbur Wright,* (1867-1912), U.S. pioneer aviator and inventor. *Wilbur Cross,* (1862-1948), U.S. editor, author, public official, educator. *Wilbur Shaw,* (1902-54), U.S. auto-racing driver. Totals: politician 27%, athlete-manager-coach 27%, writer 18%, educator 18%, aviator-inventor, auto-racer, clergy-reformer, historian.

Wiley // Willey, Wylie. *Old English:* "water meadow". *Wiley Post,* (1899-1935), U.S. aviator. *Wiley Rutledge, Jr.* (1894-1949), professor of law, associate justice U.S. Supreme Court.

Wilfred // Wilfrid, Will, Willie, Willy. *Germanic:* "desired peace, resolute and peaceful". *Wilfred Grenfell,* (1865-1940), English medical missionary. *Wilfrid Laurier,* (1841-1919), 1st French Canadian prime minister of Canada. *Wilfred Judson,* (born 1902), Canadian jurist, justice of Supreme Court of Canada.

Will // Willie, Willy. *Short form of* names beginning with "wil". Also see William. Resembles mother, good grades, many friends, may be serious about music, choleric, feisty, hot temper, easily provoked anger, likes to argue, become successful, kind, likable, respected, trusted; singer, engineer, doctor, coach, teacher, jurist, artistic, producer; first marriage is often not successful, not very adaptable, likes traveling, likes animals, very devoted to his work. Actors: *Wil Wheaton, Will Friedle, Will Patton, Will Smith.*

William // Bill, Billie, Billy, Guillaume, Guillermo, Liam, Vilhelm, Wilek, Wilhelm, Will, Willem, Willi, Willie, Willis, Willy, Wilmar, Wilmer. *Old German:* "desired helmet, determined guardian". Also see Will. Tend to lead, strong leaders, tend to have charisma, strong character, pragmatist, dogged toward goal/obsessive, gung-ho, don't ask too much of others, asks in balance from each person, idealistic, view goals as reachable therefore succeed, daring, hard worker, very focused about their interest, fun-loving, like to help people, friendly toward others and easy to build initial relationship with, many friendships, not balanced, humorous, tend to be very physical especially in athletics, very competitive especially in sports, often sports fan, direct, not very subtle, average speed of learning but very stick-to-it attitude makes them valuable, rather insensitive to others emotions, stubborn, not necessarily religious but identifies with the religious, protector of the down-trodden. Marries: likes to be dominant, but marries able female with strong opinions, but willing to follow his lead. *William Penn*, (1644-1718), wealthy Englishman, founder of the Pennsylvania colony. *William Tell*, (14th century), archer, forced to shoot an apple off his son's head. *William Shakespeare*, the world's

most popular playwright for 350 years. *William H. Taft*, 27th U.S. president, chief justice of the U.S. Supreme Court. Also 2 emperors of Germany and 4 kings of England. Totals: politician 30%, writer 24%, commander 15%, scientist 12%, lawyer 12%, businessman 10%, protector of the down-trodden 8%, physician 8%, jurist 8%, clergy 4%, artist 4%, musician 3%, philosopher 3%, educator 3%, zoologist 2%, historian 2%, engineer 2%, psychologist, explorer, singer, librarian, astronaut, philologist, architect. Actors: *Willem Dafoe, William H. Macy, William Hurt, William McNamara, William Shatner.*

Willie // Will, Willy. *Short form of* names beginning with "wil". Large percentage of competitors and athletes. Name popular among black Americans. *Willie Nelson*, (born 1933), king of Austin's outlaw country music movement. *Willie Mays, Jr.* (born 1931), U.S. baseball player. *Willie Wood*, (born 1936), U.S. football player. Totals: athlete 38%, writer 23%, billiards player 15%, politician 15%, bank robber, artist, musician. Actor: *Willie Aames*.

Willis. *Form of* William. *Willis Gorman*, (1816-76), U.S. lawyer, 2nd territorial governor of Minnesota, brigadier general. *Willis Carrier*, (1876-1950), U.S. mechanical engineer. *Willis Lamb, Jr.* (born 1913), U.S. physicist. *Willis Whitney*, (1868-1958), U.S. chemical engineer. *Willis Van Devanter*, (1859-1941), U.S. jurist, associate justice of U.S. Supreme Court. *Willis Potts*, (1895-1968), U.S. physician, medical researcher.

Wilmer // Wilmar. *German:* "determined".

Wilson. *English:* "Will's son".

Wilton // Will, Willie, Willy, Wilt. *Old English:* "estate by the spring". *Wilt (Wilton) Chamberlain*, (born 1936), first outstanding 7-footer in basketball, nicknamed Wilt the Stilt.

Winfield // Field, Win, Winifield, Winn, Winnie, Winny, Wyn. *Old English:* "friendly field". *Winfield Scott*, (1786-1866), U.S. general, demanded formality in military dress and behavior. *Winfield Hancock*, (1824-86), U.S. general, one of the best Union officers of the Civil War. *Winfield Schley,* (1839-1909), U.S. Navy officer.

Winslow // Win, Winn, Winnie, Winny, Wyn. *Old English:* "friend's hill". *Winslow Homer,* (1836-1910), One of the greatest of American painters.

Winston // Win, Winn, Winnie, Winny, Winstonn, Wyn. *Old English:* "friendly town". *Winston Churchill*, (1874-1965), one of Britain's greatest prime ministers. *Winston Churchill,* (1871-1947), U.S. historical novelist.

Winthrop // Win, Winn, Winnie, Winny, Wyn. *Old English:* "wine village". *Winthrop Rockefeller,* (1912-73), U.S. business executive and political leader. *Winthrop Crane,* (1853-1920), U.S. manufacturer and politician.

Wolfgang // Wolf, Wolfe, Wolfie, Wolfy. *Old German:* "advancing wolf". *Wolfgang Amadeus Mozart*, (1756-91), often considered the greatest musical genius of all time. *Wolfgang Pauli,* (1900-58), considered the most brilliant theoretical physicists of the 20th century. *Wolfgang von Kapp,* (1858-1922), German monarchist, leader of revolt. *Wolfgang Sawallisch,* (born 1923), German conductor and pianist. *Wolfgang Capito*, (1478-1541), German theologian and Protestant Reformer. *Wolfgang Kohler,* (1887-1967), U.S. psychologist. *Wolfgang Paul*, (born 1913), German physicist.

Woodrow // Wood, Woodie, Woodman, Woody. *Old English:* "passage in the woods". *Woodrow Wilson (Woody) Herman,* (1913-87), U.S. composer, clarinetist, saxophone player, and bandleader. *Woodrow Wilson,* (1856-1924), 28th U.S. President, educator, politician.

Woody // Wood, Woodie. *Familiar form of* names containing "wood". See Woodrow. *Woody Guthrie,* (1912-67), U.S. folksinger, 'This Land Is Your Land'. *Woody Hayes,* (1913-87), U.S. football coach. Actors: *Woody Allen* (Allen Stewart Konigsberg), *Woody Harrelson*.

Worth // Worthington, Worthy. *Old English:* "farmstead". *Short form of* names ending in "worth".

Wright. *Old English:* "carpenter". *Short form of* Wainwright. *Wright Morris*, (born 1910), U.S. novelist.

Wyatt // Wiatt, Wye. *Old French:* "little warrior". *Wyatt Earp*, (1848-1929), one of many frontier lawmen, transformed into heroic legend by TV and film.

Wylie // Lee, Leigh, Wiley, Wye. *Old English:* "charming". See Wiley.

Wyndham // Windham. *Gaelic:* "village near the winding road". *Wyndham Lewis*, (1884-1957), British author and artist.

Xavier // Javier, Xaver, Xever. *Arabic:* "bright". *Javier Perez de Cuellar*, (born 1920), Peruvian diplomat. *Xavier Suarez,* (born 1949), U.S. public official.

Ximenes // Xymenes, Ximenez. *Spanish form* of Simon. Often the letter Y is used instead of the letter J in many languages as the English letter J did not exist before the middle ages and is currently not used in many languages. Following this tradition, some parents, especially imagrants, choose to use the letter Y in the spelling of many names which Americans and English usually start with the letter J. Yasmin-Jasmine is a prime example of this practice, but most any letter J in a name may be found with a Y substituting for it.

Yancy // Yance, Yancey, Yank, Yankee. *American Indian:* "Englishman".

Yehudi // Yehuda, Yehudit. *Hebrew:* "praise of the Lord". *Hebrew form* of Judah. *Yehudi Menuhin*, (born 1916), U.S. violinist and conductor.

Yuri // Uri. Abriviated form of Slovic Yeorgie from Greek name George: "farmer"; *Familiar form of* Hebrew Uriel: "God is my flame". Calm, somewhat withdrawn into himself; reserved manners, philosophical mind; gesticulating, facially expressive and mime-like; artistic speaker; women are immediately favorable toward him; somewhat passive in attracting women; women actively pursue him; takes care of his family's finances; helps with domestic chores; very honoring toward his mother. *Yuri Gagarin*, (1934-68), world's first astronaut, Soviet aviator. *Yuri Andropov,* (1914-84), politician, leader of the Soviet Union. *Uri Shulevitz*, (born 1935), author and illustrator of books for children.

Yves // Ives. *French form* of Ivar. *Yves Tanguy*, (1900-55), U.S. painter. *Yves Montand*, (1921-91), Italian-born French actor and singer, Gallic sophistication, charm, and nonchalance.

The letter "Z" is used in some cultures instead of the letter "S". Parents desiring a name which starts with the letter "S" may give the name a unique twist while retaining personality characteristics by substituting the letter "Z".

Zachariah // Zacarias, Zaccaria, Zach, Zacharia, Zacharias, Zacharie, Zachary, Zacherie, Zachery, Zack, Zackariah,

Zak, Zakarias, Zechariah, Zeke. **Hebrew:** "God's remembrance, God hath remembered". Biblical: _Zechariah_ - Prophet and book. Focused achiever, athletic, sportsman, attentive and caring toward others, hobbies in high tech; likes nature: forest, river, wild fields are his weakness; kind, generous, out-going, hospitable, good relations with neighbors; like to clean his house with his children; considers work to be the best training for children; responsible toward parents; somewhat sacrificial when helping others; doesn't take advantage of others; not calculating his own gain; marries woman who comes out of an unhappy relationship or a single mother, soft and kind personality, allows his wife to take leadership, wife's tactful leadership works fine, usually faithful, trusts his wife, he likes to be home. _Zachary Taylor_, , U.S. president, general and popular hero of the Mexican War, 12th U.S. president. _Zachary Macaulay_, (1768-1838), English philanthropist, governor Sierra Leone. _Zachariah Chandler_, (1813-79), U.S. political leader. _Zacharias Janssen_, (fl. 16th century), Dutch spectacle maker, inventor of compound microscope. _Zacharias Topelius_, (1818-98), Finnish author, father of the Finnish historical novel. _Zacharias Werner_, (1768-1832), German romantic dramatist, Catholic priest with impassioned preaching. _Zachariah Wheat_, (1888-1972), U.S. baseball outfielder.

Zane. _English form_ of John. _Zane Grey_, (1875-1939), U.S. novelist.

Zebadiah // Zeb, Zebedee. **Hebrew:** "the Lord's gift". Biblical: _Zebedee_, father of Apostles James and John.

Zebulun // Zabulon, Zeb, Zebulen. **Hebrew:** "dwelling place". Biblical: son of Jacob and patriarch of the tribe of Zebulun. _Zebulon M. Pike_, (1779-1813), American explorer and U.S. Army general. _Zebulon Vance_, (1830-94), U.S. statesman.

Zedekiah // Zed. **Hebrew:** "God is mighty and just". Biblical: _Zedekiah_, (6th century BC), last king of Judah.

Zeke. _Short form of_ Ezekiel and Zachary.

Zollie // Zolly. Familiar forms of Saul and Solomon.

WARNING: It is very important to read the first chapters of this book. Failure to heed the first chapters may cause serious detrimental consequences in your hopes and dreams for the person who's name you intend to choose!